Machine Learning and Big Data

Scrivener Publishing
100 Cummings Center, Suite 541J
Beverly, MA 01915-6106

Publishers at Scrivener
Martin Scrivener (martin@scrivenerpublishing.com)
Phillip Carmical (pcarmical@scrivenerpublishing.com)

Machine Learning and Big Data

Concepts, Algorithms, Tools and Applications

Edited by
Uma N. Dulhare, Khaleel Ahmad and Khairol Amali Bin Ahmad

Scrivener
Publishing

WILEY

This edition first published 2020 by John Wiley & Sons, Inc., 111 River Street, Hoboken, NJ 07030, USA and Scrivener Publishing LLC, 100 Cummings Center, Suite 541J, Beverly, MA 01915, USA
© 2020 Scrivener Publishing LLC
For more information about Scrivener publications please visit www.scrivenerpublishing.com.

Wiley Global Headquarters
111 River Street, Hoboken, NJ 07030, USA

For details of our global editorial offices, customer services, and more information about Wiley products visit us at www.wiley.com.

Library of Congress Cataloging-in-Publication Data

ISBN 9781119654742

Cover image: Pixabay.Com
Cover design by Russell Richardson

Set in size of 11pt and Minion Pro by Manila Typesetting Company, Makati, Philippines

10 9 8 7 6 5 4 3 2 1

Contents

Section 2: Big Data and Pattern Recognition   71

4 Data Preprocess   73
Md. Sharif Hossen

Preface

Nowadays, increasing use of social sites, search engines, and various multimedia sharing, stock exchange, online gaming, online survey and news sites among others has caused the amount and variety of data to grow very rapidly to terabytes or even zettabytes. As a consequence, extracting useful information from these big data has become a major challenge.

Machine Learning is a subset of Artificial Intelligence that provides systems with the ability to automatically learn and improve from experience without being explicitly programmed. By using machine learning, computers are taught to perform complex tasks which humans are not able to accomplish. In this latest approach to digital transformation, computing processes are used to make intelligent decisions that are more efficient, cost-effective and reliable. Therefore, there are huge applications for machine learning algorithms for management of species, crops, field conditions and livestock in the agriculture domain; medical imaging and diagnostics, drug discovery and development, treatment and prediction of disease in the healthcare domain; social media monitoring, chatbot, sentiment analysis and image recognition in the social media domain; and fraud detection, customer data management, financial risk modeling, personalized marketing, lifetime value prediction, recommendation engine and customer segmentation in the banking and insurance services domain.

This field is so vast and popular these days that there are a lot of machine learning activities occurring in our daily lives that have become an integral part of our daily routines through applications like Siri, Cortana, Facebook, Twitter, Google Search, Gmail, Skype, LinkedIn, Viber, WhatsApp, Pinterest, PayPal, Netflix, Uber, Lyst, Spotify, Instagram and so forth.

The intent of this book is to provide awareness of algorithms used for machine learning and big data in the academic and professional community. While it dwells on the foundations of machine learning and big data as a part of analytics, it also focuses on contemporary topics for research and development. In this regard, the book covers machine learning algorithms and their modern applications in developing automated systems.

The topics in this book are categorized into five sections including a total of seventeen chapters. The first section provides an insight into mathematical foundation, probability theory, correlation and regression techniques. The second section covers data pre-processing and the concept of big data and pattern recognition. The third section discusses machine learning algorithms, including supervised learning algorithm (Naïve-Bayes, KNN, HMM, Bayesian), semi-supervised learning algorithms (S3VM, Graph-Based, Multiview), unsupervised learning algorithms (GMM, K-mean clustering, Dirichlet process mixture model, X-means), and reinforcement learning algorithm (Q-learning, R learning, TD learning, SARSA Learning). The section also dwells on applications of machine learning for video surveillance, social media services, email spam and malware filtering, online fraud detection, financial services, healthcare, industry, manufacturing, transportation, etc.

While section four presents the theoretical principle, functionalities, methodologies and applications of transfer learning as well as its relationship with deep learning paradigms, the final section explores the hands-on machine learning open source tool. A case study is also discussed in detail. At the end of this section, various open challenges are discussed, such as the implication of electronic governance activities which can be solved by machine learning technique in order to help guide leadership to create well-versed decisions, appropriate economic planning and policy formulation that can solve the major issues of all developing countries like a weak economy, unemployment, corruption and many more.

It is a great pleasure for us to acknowledge the contributions and assistance of many individuals. We would like to thank all the authors who submitted chapters for their contributions and fruitful discussions that made this book a great success. We are also thankful to the team from Scrivener Publishing for providing the meticulous service for timely publication of this book. Also, we would like to express our gratitude for the encouragement offered by our college/university. Last but not least, we gratefully acknowledge the support, encouragement and patience of our families.

Uma N. Dulhare
Khaleel Ahmad
Khairol Amali Bin Ahmad
June 2020

Section 1
THEORETICAL FUNDAMENTALS

1

Mathematical Foundation

Afroz* and Basharat Hussain

*Department of Mathematics, Maulana Azad National Urdu University,
Hyderabad, India*

Abstract

The aim of this chapter is to provide the reader an overview of basics of linear algebra and introductory lecture on calculus. We will discuss concept of real vector spaces, basis, span, and subspaces. The idea of solving the system of equations using matrix approach will be discuss. Linear transformation by means of which we can pass from one vector space to another, inverse linear transformation, and transformation matrix will be explain with detail examples. Definition of eigenvectors, eigenvalues, and eigendecomposition along with thorough examples will be provided. Moreover, definition of function, limit, continuity, and differentiability of function with illustrative examples will be included.

Keywords: Vector spaces, basis, linear transformation, transformation matrix, eigenvalue, eigenvector, eigen decomposition, continuous functions, differentiation

1.1 Concept of Linear Algebra

1.1.1 Introduction

Basics problem of linear algebra is to solve n linear equations in n unknowns. For example,

$$2x - y = 0$$

$$-x + 2y = 3$$

*Corresponding author: afroz.ahmad@manuu.edu.in

Uma N. Dulhare, Khaleel Ahmad and Khairol Amali Bin Ahmad (eds.) Machine Learning and Big Data: Concepts, Algorithms, Tools and Applications, (3–30) © 2020 Scrivener Publishing LLC

The above system is two dimensional (n = 2), i.e., two equations with two unknowns. The solution of the above system is the values of unknowns x, y, satisfying the above linear system. One can easily verify that x = 1, y = 2 satisfy the above linear system.

Geometrically, each of the above equation represents a line in R2-plane. We have two lines in same plane and if they do intersect (it is possible that they may not intersect as parallel line don't intersect) on same plane their point of intersection will be the solution of system as illustrated in Figure 1.1.

The matrix (2D-array) representation of above system will be

$$\begin{bmatrix} 2 & -1 \\ -1 & 2 \end{bmatrix} \begin{bmatrix} x \\ y \end{bmatrix} = \begin{bmatrix} 0 \\ 3 \end{bmatrix}.$$

The matrix $A = \begin{bmatrix} 2 & -1 \\ -1 & 2 \end{bmatrix}$ is coefficient matrix, and vector $\mathbf{x} = \begin{bmatrix} x \\ y \end{bmatrix}$ is the column vector of unknowns. The values on the right-hand side of the equations form the column vector **b**.

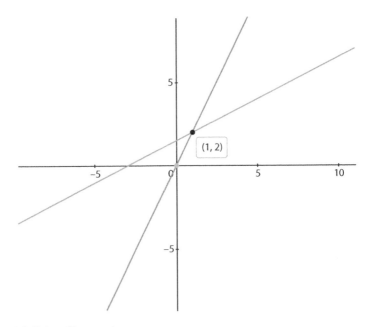

Figure 1.1 Point of intersection.

Matrix A has two vectors in its column (2, −1) and (−1, 2). The product:

$$Ax = \begin{bmatrix} 2 & -1 \\ -1 & 2 \end{bmatrix} \begin{bmatrix} x \\ y \end{bmatrix} = \begin{bmatrix} 2x - y \\ -x + 2y \end{bmatrix}$$

For any input vector **x** the output of the operation "multiplication by A" is some vector **b**. A deeper question is to start with a vector **b** and ask "for what vectors **x** does Ax = b?" [1]. In our example, this means solving two equations in two unknowns. Solving:

$$Ax = \mathbf{b}$$

is equivalent to solving:

$$2x - y = 0$$

$$-x + 2y = 3$$

$$x = A^{-1}b$$

$$= \begin{bmatrix} 2/3 & 1/3 \\ 1/3 & 2/3 \end{bmatrix} \begin{bmatrix} 0 \\ 3 \end{bmatrix} = \begin{bmatrix} 1 \\ 2 \end{bmatrix}.$$

The only difference between the three-dimensional matrix picture and two-dimensional one is change in size of the vectors and matrices.

In general, a system of linear equations can easily be transformed into the matrix equation Ax = b. The solution of which, if it exists, can easily be find using computer software. Like method of elimination can be used provided that matrix A is non-singular (det (A)≠ 0), i.e., A is invertible [2, 3].

1.1.2   Vector Spaces

Definition. [4, 5] "A vector space (or linear space) consists of following:

1. A field **F** of scalars;
2. A set of vectors **V**;

3. Two rules (or operations) are defined:
   a. Vector addition, i.e., vectors can be added together, and the resulting vector belongs to **V**.
   b. Scalar multiplication, i.e., a vector from **V** can be multiplied by an element of **F**, and resulting element will be a vector belongs to **V**.
4. Under these two operation **V** must satisfy
   (i) There exists an additive identity (symbol 0) in **V** such that $x + 0 = x$ for all **x** belongs to **V**.
   (ii) For each $x \in V$, there exists an additive inverse (written $-x$) such that $x + (-x) = 0$.
   (iii) There exists a multiplicative identity (written 1) in **F** such that $1x = x$ for all $x \in V$.
   (iv) Commutativity: $x + y = y + x$ for all $x, y \in V$
   (v) Associativity: $(x + y) + z = x + (y + z)$ and $\alpha(\beta x) = (\alpha\beta)x$ for all $x, y, z \in V$ and $\alpha, \beta \in F$
   (vi) Distributivity: $\alpha(x + y) = \alpha x + \alpha y$ and $(\alpha + \beta)x = ax + \beta y$ for all $x, y \in V$ and $\alpha, \beta \in F$."

When there is no chance of confusion, we may simply refer to the vector space as V, or when it is desirable to specify the field, we shall say **V** is a vector space over the field **F**, denoted by **V(F)**. One can take field **F** = ℝ (set of real number) to avoid the unnecessary diversion into abstract algebra. We will take field of real number throughout the book, unless otherwise stated.

Example 1. "ℝ (ℝ), $ℝ^2$ (ℝ), $ℝ^3$ (ℝ) are vector spaces over the field of real numbers ℝ"

Example 2. $M_{m,n}$ (ℝ) is a vector space of matrices of order $m \times n$ over the field of real numbers ℝ where $M_{m,n}$ (ℝ)=$\{[a_{ij}]\}_{m \times n}, a_{ij} \in ℝ\}$=set of all $m \times n$ matrices whose entries are from field ℝ"

Example 3. P_n(ℝ) is a vector space of polynomials of degree at most n over the fields of real numbers ℝ.

Where, P_n (ℝ) = $\{a_0 + a_1 x + ... + a_n x^n : a_i \in ℝ$ and n is any non–negative integer$\}$ = set of all polynomials whose cofficients from ℝ."

1.1.3   Linear Combination

Definition. [4] "A vector **y** in **V** is said to be a linear combination of the vectors $x_1, x_2, ... x_n$ in **V** provided there exist scalars $\alpha_1, \alpha_2, ..., \alpha_n$ in **F** such that

$$y = \alpha_1 \mathbf{x}_1 + \alpha_2 \mathbf{x}_2 \ldots \alpha_n \mathbf{x}_n$$

$$= \sum_{k=1}^{n} \alpha_k \mathbf{x}_k.$$

1.1.4 Linearly Dependent and Independent Vectors

Two (or n) vectors are said to be linearly dependent if they lie on same straight line, and if they lie on different straight line, they are linearly independent.

Clearly, vectors v_1, v_2 are linearly dependent and u_1, u_2 are linearly independent as shown in Figure 1.2 and Figure 1.3.

Definition. "A non-empty set S of **V** containing n vectors $\mathbf{x}_1$, $\mathbf{x}_2$,..., $\mathbf{x}_n$ are linearly dependent if and only if there exists scalars (belongs to $\mathbb{R}$) α_1, α_2,..., α_n, not all zero, such that

$$\sum_{i=1}^{n} \alpha_i x_i = 0.$$

If no such scalars exist, then the vectors are said to be linearly independent [4]."

Example 4. Consider $\{(1, 0), (-5, 0)\}$ subset of $\mathbb{R}^2$ these two vectors are linearly dependent because there exist 5, 1 ($\neq 0$) in R such that $5(1, 0) + 1(-5, 0) = 0$.

Figure 1.2 Linearly dependent.

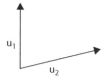

Figure 1.3 Linearly Independent.

Before moving further, let's take a simple case of two linearly independent vectors say $u_1 = (1, 0)$ and $u_2 = (0, 1)$ belongs to $\mathbb{R}^2$ and take all possible linear combinations of these two vectors. What will happen? These linear combinations fill up the whole plane or space $\mathbb{R}^2$. Mathematically, we say these vectors u_1, u_2 span $\mathbb{R}^2$. So, basically these vectors u_1, u_2 work as a basis for the plane $\mathbb{R}^2$.

1.1.5   Linear Span, Basis and Subspace

Definition. [4] "If S is nonempty subset of the vector space V, then $L(S)$, the linear span of S, is the set of all linear combinations of finite sets of elements of S. Consider $\mathbf{v}_1, \mathbf{v}_2, \ldots, \mathbf{v}_n$ n vectors $\in S \subset \mathbf{V}$, then span $\{\mathbf{v}_1, \mathbf{v}_2, \ldots, \mathbf{v}_n\}$ is $L(S) = \{\mathbf{v} \in \mathbf{V} : \exists \alpha_1, \alpha_2, \ldots, \alpha_n$ such that $\alpha_1 \mathbf{v}_1 + \alpha_2 \mathbf{v}_2 + \ldots + \alpha_n \mathbf{v}_n = \mathbf{v}\}$."

Definition. [4] "A non-empty set B of n vectors act as a basis for a space $\mathbf{V}$ if

  i.   Set B is linearly independent.
  ii. $L(B) = \mathbf{V}$, i.e., linear span of B is $\mathbf{V}$ (i.e., all possible linear combinations of vectors in B generate whole space $\mathbf{V}$)."

Example 5. (i). $\{(1, 0), (0, 1)\}$ is the standard basis for vector space $\mathbb{R}^2$. (ii). $\{(1, 0, 0), (0, 1, 0), (0, 0, 1)\}$ is the standard basis for vector space $\mathbb{R}^3$.

Number of vectors in B gives the dimension of the space $\mathbf{V}$. Both finite- and infinite-dimensional spaces exists. Our scope of study is limited to finite dimensional space. $\mathbb{R}^2$, $\mathbb{R}^3$ are conceivable examples of finite dimensional spaces of dimension 2 (two vectors in basis) and 3 (three vectors in basis set), respectively. Can we remove any single vector from basis set? Absolutely not! If we drop any vector from basis set the span will be different. Think of simple case of $\mathbb{R}^2$, what will happen if we remove one vector from the basis set?

Note: The vector space $\mathbf{V}$ is said to *finite-dimensional* (over $\mathbf{F}$) if there is a *finite* subset S in $\mathbf{V}$ such that $\mathbf{V} = L(S)$. Our focus of study will be *n-dimensional Euclidean space*, i.e., $\mathbb{R}^n$.

Definition. [4, 6] "A subset $\mathbf{W}(\neq \Phi)$ is said to be a subspace of $\mathbf{V}$ if $\mathbf{W}$ is a vector space under the same operations (or rules) of vector addition and scalar multiplication as in $\mathbf{V}$."

Example 6. (i). Vector space $\mathbb{R}^2$ over the field $\mathbb{R}^2$(written as $\mathbb{R}^2$ ($\mathbb{R}$) is subspace of $\mathbb{R}^3$ ($\mathbb{R}$).

(ii). A line passing through origin in XY-plane is subspace of vector space XY-plane.

(iii). A plane through the origin is subspace of $\mathbb{R}^3$.

1.1.6 Linear Transformation (or Linear Map)

Definition and Examples

Let U and V be real vector spaces. A linear transformation from U into V is a function T from U into V such that

(i). $T(u_1 + u_2) = T(u_1) + T(u_2)$ for all $u_1, u_2 \in U$

(ii). $T(\alpha u) = \alpha\, T(u)$ for all $u \in U, \alpha \in \mathbb{R}$

"A linear transformation $T:U \to U$ is also called a linear transformation (or map) on Whenever we say $T:U \to U$ is a linear transformation, then U and V shall be taken as vector spaces over the same field, which is $\mathbb{R}$ in our case as we are dealing with real vector spaces [7]. In algebraic terms, a linear transformation is called a homomorphism of vector spaces. An invertible homomorphism (where the inverse is also a homomorphism) is called an isomorphism" [8].

"If there exist an isomorphism from U to V, then U and V are said to be isomorphic written as $U \cong V$. Isomorphic vector spaces are essentially 'the same' in terms of their algebraic structure. Finite-dimensional vector spaces of same dimension are always isomorphic" [2, 8].

Example 7. "The transformation $T:U \to V$ defined by $T(u) = Tu = 0$ for all $u \epsilon\ U$ is a linear transformation."

Example 8. "The transformation $I:U \to V$ defined by $I(u) = Iu = u$ for all $u \epsilon U$ is a linear map and is called identity map."

Example 9. "The function $f:\mathbb{R} \to \mathbb{R}$. Defined by $f(x) = x + a_0 (a_0$ is fixed) linear function but not linear transformation as it does not follow the definition."

Example 10. "Consider $U = \mathbb{R}^m$ and $V = \mathbb{R}^n$ where $m \geq n$. Define a transformation $T:U \to V$ by $T(x_1, x_2, ..., x_m) = (x_1, x_2, ..., x_n)$. Here, we drop the last (m-n) coordinates of the vectors from $\mathbb{R}^m$. This is called natural projection of $\mathbb{R}^m$ onto $\mathbb{R}^n$ and is a linear transformation."

Example 11. "Define $T:\mathbb{R}^2 \to \mathbb{R}^2$ by the rule

$$T(x_1, x_2) = (x_1, -x_2)$$

Then, this is a linear map and is called the reflection in the x-axis."

Example 12. "Let $T{:}\mathbb{R}{\rightarrow}\mathbb{R}$ defined by $T(x) = x^2$. Then, T is not linear transformation."

1.1.7 Matrix Representation of Linear Transformation

The concept of vector spaces is quite abstract in nature. In order to implement vectors and linear transformation in computer, we use rectangle arrays of number called as matrices.

Definition. "A matrix is an ordered rectangular array of numbers or functions. The numbers or function are called the elements or the entries of matrix" [9].

Example 13.

$$A = \begin{bmatrix} 1\ 5\ 6 \\ 2\ 4\ 8 \\ 5\ 6\ 9 \end{bmatrix}, B = \begin{bmatrix} x^2 & cosx & logx \\ x & 1-x^3 & 2 \end{bmatrix}$$

A matrix having m rows and n columns is called a matrix of order $m \times n$ When $m = n$ the matrix is called square matrix. In above example, matrix A is square matrix of order 3×3 and matrix B is of order 2×3. Generally, matrix M of order $m \times n$ is denoted by $M_{m \times n}$. Sometimes, it is necessary to visualize vectors of $\mathbb{R}^n$ as column vectors, i.e., a vector $(x_1, x_2,..., x_n)$ of n-dimensional vector space $\mathbb{R}^n$ can be treated as column vector $(x_1, x_2,..., x_n)^T$.

Transpose of matrix is nothing but interchange of rows and column. If A is any $m \times n$ matrix, then A^T is n × m matrix whose rows are the columns of the matrix A and columns are rows of the matrix A.

Some algebraic properties on transpose of a matrix:

(i) $(A^T)^T = A$
(ii) $(A + B)^T = A^T + B^T$
(iii) $(\alpha A)^T = \alpha A^T$.
(iv) $(AB)^T = B^T A^T$

1.1.7.1 Transformation Matrix

"Let U and V be finite-dimensional vector spaces of dimension m and n, respectively. Let $\{e_1, e_2,..., e_m\}$ and $\{e'_1, e'_2 ..., e\acute{n}\}$ be the bases of U and V, respectively.

Consider $T:U{\to}V$ is a linear transformation. Then, $T(e_i) \in V$. Therefore,

$$T(e_i) = \sum_{j=1}^{n} \alpha_{ij} ej', 1 \le i \le m.$$

We write this in an expanded form

$$Te_1 = \alpha_{11}e_1' + \ldots + \alpha_{1n}e_n'$$
$$Te_2 = \alpha_{21}e_1' + \ldots + \alpha_{2n}e_n'$$
$$\vdots$$
$$Te_m = \alpha_{m1}e_j' + \cdots + \alpha_{mn}e_n'.$$

Now, define a matrix $M_U^V(T)$ of T which is the transpose of the coefficient matrix of the above equation, i.e.,

$$M_U^V(T) = \begin{pmatrix} \alpha_{11} & \cdots & \alpha_{m1} \\ \vdots & \ddots & \vdots \\ \alpha_{1n} & \cdots & \alpha_{mn} \end{pmatrix}$$

The matrix $M_U^V(T)$ is called the matrix associated with T with respect to the basis $\{e_i\}$ and $\{e_i'\}$. Also, $M_U^V(T)$ is called the matrix representation or transformation matrix of T with respect to these bases. Conversely, every matrix $A \in \mathbb{R}^{m \times n}$ induces a linear map, say, $T: \mathbb{R}^n {\to} \mathbb{R}^m$ given by

$$T\mathbf{x} = A\mathbf{x}.$$

And the matrix of this map with respect to standard bases of $\mathbb{R}^n$ and $\mathbb{R}^m$ is of course simply A [7, 10]."

Note: The matrix $M_U^V(T)$ is the $n \times m$ matrix whose ith column is the coefficient of Tv_i when expressed as a linear combination of $\{e_j'\}, 1 \le i \le m$.

Example 14. "Consider the linear transformation $T: \mathbb{R}^3 {\to} \mathbb{R}^4$ defined by

$$T(x,y,z) = (x + y + z, 2x + z, 2y - z, 6y).$$

We use the standard bases $B_1 = \{e_1 = (1,0,0), e_2 = (0,1,0), e_3 = (0,0,1)\}$ and $B_2 = \{e_1' = (1,0,0,0), e_2' = (0,1,0,0), e_3' = (0,0,1,0), e_4' = (0,0,0,1)\}$ on both $\mathbb{R}^3$ and $\mathbb{R}^4$. We want the matrix associated to T with respect to these bases. Therefore,

$$Te_1 = (1,2,0,0) = 1.e_1' + 2.e_2' + 0.e_3' + 0.e_4'$$
$$Te_2 = (1,0,2,6) = 1.e_1' + 0.e_2' + 2.e_3' + 6.e_4'$$
$$Te_3 = (1,1,-1,0) = 1.e_1' + 1.e_2' + -1.e_3' + 0.e_4'$$

Thus, the matrix associated with T with respect to basis B_1 and B_2 is

$$M_{\mathbb{R}^3}^{\mathbb{R}^4}(T) = \begin{bmatrix} 1 & 1 & 1 \\ 2 & 0 & 1 \\ 0 & 2 & -1 \\ 0 & 6 & 0 \end{bmatrix}$$

$M_{\mathbb{R}^3}^{\mathbb{R}^4}(T)$ is called the matrix representation of T with respect to these bases and sometimes denoted by [T]."

Example 15. Consider the linear transformation $T: P_3(\mathbb{R}) \to P_2(\mathbb{R})$ defined by

$$T(\alpha_0 + \alpha_1 x + \alpha_2 x^2 + \alpha_3 x^3) = \alpha_3 + (\alpha_2 + \alpha_3)x + (\alpha_0 + \alpha_1)x^2.$$

In order to find transformation matrix of T with respect to the standard bases,

$B_1 = \{b_1 = 1, b_2 = x, b_3 = x^2, b_4 = x^3\}$ and $B_2 = \{b_1' = 1, b_2' = x, b_3' = x^2\}$.

We write,

$$T(b_i) = \sum_{j=1}^{3} \alpha_{ij} b_j', \quad 1 \le i \le 4$$

That is,

$$Tb_1 = \alpha_{11}b_1' + \alpha_{12}b_2' + \alpha_{13}b_3'$$
$$Tb_2 = \alpha_{21}b_1' + \alpha_{22}b_2' + \alpha_{23}b_3'$$
$$Tb_3 = \alpha_{31}b_1' + \alpha_{32}b_2' + \alpha_{33}b_3',$$

which is

$$T(1) = 0.1 + 0.x + 1.x^2$$

$$T(x) = 0.1 + 0.x + 1.x^2$$

$$T(x^2) = 0.1 + 0.x + 1.x^2$$

$$T(x^3) = 1.1 + 1.x + 0.x^2$$

Thus, required transformation matrix [T] is

$$[T] = \begin{bmatrix} 0 & 0 & 0 & 1 \\ 0 & 0 & 1 & 1 \\ 1 & 1 & 0 & 0 \end{bmatrix}$$

Note: The associated transformation matrix depends on the choice of bases.

1.1.8   Range and Null Space of Linear Transformation

Definition. "Let U *and* V be vector spaces over the field F and let T be a linear transformation from U *into* V. Then, null space (kernel) of T is denoted by $N(T)$ and is a set containing all those vectors u in U such that $T(u) = 0$, i.e, $N(T) = \{u \in U: Tu = 0\}$. It is also denoted as kerT [7].

Note: Null space is a subspace of U and its dimension is called nullity of T.

Definition. "Let U *and* V be real vector spaces and let $T:U \rightarrow V$ be a linear transformation, then the range of T or image of T is denoted by $R(T)$or $T(U)$ and is defined by

$$R(T) = \{v \in V \mid \text{there exist } u \in U \text{ such that } T(u) = v\}$$

In other words, range of T is the set of all those vectors of V which are images of vectors of U under the transformation T [7]."

Example 16. "Find the range and kernel of $T: \mathbb{R}^3 \rightarrow \mathbb{R}^3$ defined by

$$T\,(x, y, z) = (x + z, x + y + 2z, 2x + y + 3z),$$

$$\ker(T) = \{(x, y, z) \in \mathbb{R}^3 \,|\, T\,(x, y, z) = (0,0,0)\}.$$

Now, $T\,(x, y, z) = (0,0,0)$ implies

$$x + z = 0$$

$$x + y + 2z = 0,$$

$$2x + y + 3z = 0.$$

From above, we have $z = -x$, $y = x$.
Therefore,

$$\ker(T) = \{(\alpha, \alpha, -\alpha) \,|\, \alpha \in \mathbb{R}\}$$

$$= \{\alpha\,(1,1,-1) \,|\, \alpha \in \mathbb{R}\}.$$

Let $(x, y, z) \in \mathbb{R}^3$, if $(x, y, z) \in$ range of T, then $\exists\,(x', y', z') \in \mathbb{R}^3$ such that $T\,(x', y', z') = (x, y, z)$, i.e.,

$$R\,(T) = \{(x, y, z) \,|\, \text{there exist } (x', y', z') \in \mathbb{R}^3$$
$$\text{such that } T\,(x', y', z') = (x, y, z)\}$$

Or

$$(x' + y', x' + y' + 2z', 2x' + y' + 3z' = (x, y, z)$$

This implies

$$x' + y' = x$$

$$x' + y' + 2z' = y$$

$$2x' + y' + 3z' = z.$$

Hence,

$$R\,(T) = \{(x, y, x + y) \,|\, x, y \in \mathbb{R}\}$$

$$= \{x\,(1,0,1) + y\,(0,1,1)\,|\, x, y \in \mathbb{R}.\text{''}$$

1.1.9   Invertible Linear Transformation

Definition. [1] "Let U and V be two real vector spaces. Let $T:U{\to}V$ be a linear transformation, then inverse of T is denoted by T^{-1} and is a mapping from V to U.

Let $T:U{\to}V$ be a linear transformation, then T is said to **one-one** if

$$\mathbf{u}_1, \mathbf{u}_2 \in U \text{ and } \mathbf{u}_1 \neq \mathbf{u}_2 {\Rightarrow} T\mathbf{u}_1 \neq T\mathbf{u}_2.$$

In other words, T is said to be one-one if

$$\mathbf{u}_1, \mathbf{u}_2 \in U \text{ and } T\mathbf{u}_1 = T\mathbf{u}_2 {\Rightarrow} \mathbf{u}_1 = \mathbf{u}_2$$

Further, T is said to be onto if

$$\text{for every } \mathbf{v} \in \mathbf{V} {\Rightarrow} \exists\, \mathbf{u} \in U \text{ such that } T(\mathbf{u}) = \mathbf{v}.$$

If $T: U{\to}V$ is one-one and onto, then the inverse of T is the function

$$T^{-1}:V{\to}U$$

Defined by

$$T^{-1}(\mathbf{v}) = \text{that unique } \mathbf{u} \in U \text{ for which } T(\mathbf{u}) = \mathbf{v}."$$

1.2   Eigenvalues, Eigenvectors, and Eigendecomposition of a Matrix

Consider a linear operator $A: \mathbb{R}^n{\to}\mathbb{R}^n$ where A is associated matrix of linear transformation (say, T). A real number λ is an eigenvalue of A if there exist a nonzero vector $\mathbf{x} \in \mathbb{R}^n$ such that $A\mathbf{x} = \lambda\mathbf{x}$ and the nonzero vector $\mathbf{x} \in \mathbb{R}^n$ is called eigenvector of A corresponding to eigenvalue λ.

Note: If $T: \mathbb{R}^n{\to}\mathbb{R}^m$ is a linear transformation and A_{mn} be the corresponding matrix of T relative to some bases, then

$$Tx \cong A_{mn}\, x. \text{ Where } x = (x_1, x_2, \ldots x_n) \in \mathbb{R}^n$$

1.2.1   Characteristics Polynomial

Definition. "If A is a square matrix of order n, then the matrix $A - \lambda I$ is called the characteristics matrix of A, where I is the identity matrix of order n and $\lambda \in \mathbb{R}$. The determinant of matrix $A - \lambda I$ is a polynomial in λ and is called the characteristics polynomial of the matrix A. Note that the polynomial det $(A - \lambda I)$ is of degree n and hence, there can be at most n distinct roots" [4].

If $T: \mathbb{R}^n \to \mathbb{R}^n$ is a linear transformation and A_n (n square matrix) is associated matrix of T. Let $\mathbf{x} \neq 0 \in \mathbb{R}^n$ be an eigenvector. Therefore,

$$A_n \mathbf{x} = \lambda \mathbf{x}$$

$$\text{or } A_n \mathbf{x} - \lambda \mathbf{x} = 0$$

$$\text{or } (A_n - \lambda I_n)\mathbf{x} = 0. \tag{i}$$

System (i) has nonzero solution $\mathbf{x} \in \mathbb{R}^n$, this implies that det $(A_n - \lambda I_n) = 0$, which is the characteristics equation of the matrix An and roots of this equation are eigenvalues corresponding to eigenvector $\mathbf{x}$.

1.2.1.1   Some Results on Eigenvalue

If λ is an eigenvalue of matrix A, then

(i) λ^n is an eigenvalue of A^n.
(ii) $\alpha \lambda$ is an eigenvalue of αA, where α is scalar.
(iii)   If A is invertible and α is eigenvalue of A then α^{-1} is eigenvalue of A^{-1}.
(iv) $g(\lambda)$ is an eigenvalue of $g(A)$, where g is a polynomial.

Example 17.
"Consider

$$A = \begin{bmatrix} 3 & 1 \\ 6 & 2 \end{bmatrix}$$

For eigenvalues of A, we solve

$$\det (A - \lambda I) = 0.$$

$$\begin{vmatrix} 3-\lambda & 1 \\ 6 & 2-\lambda \end{vmatrix} = 0.$$

This gives

$$(3 - \lambda)(2 - \lambda) - 6 = 0.$$

$$6 - 5\lambda + \lambda^2 - 6 = 0.$$

$$\lambda^2 - 5\lambda = 0.$$

$$\lambda(\lambda - 5) = 0.$$

That is

$$\lambda = 0, \lambda = 5.$$

So, the eigenvalues of A are

$$\lambda_1 = 0, \lambda_2$$

For eigenvector corresponding to $\lambda_1 = 0$ we have

$$\begin{bmatrix} 3 & 1 \\ 6 & 2 \end{bmatrix} \begin{bmatrix} x_1 \\ x_2 \end{bmatrix} - \lambda_1 \begin{bmatrix} 1 & 0 \\ 0 & 1 \end{bmatrix} \begin{bmatrix} x_1 \\ x_2 \end{bmatrix} = \begin{bmatrix} 0 \\ 0 \end{bmatrix}$$

i.e.,

$$\begin{bmatrix} 3 & 1 \\ 6 & 2 \end{bmatrix} \begin{bmatrix} x_1 \\ x_2 \end{bmatrix} = \begin{bmatrix} 0 \\ 0 \end{bmatrix}.$$

This implies $\quad 3x_1 + x_2 = 0, 6x_1 + 2x_2 = 0.$

This gives $x_1 = -\dfrac{x_2}{3}$. Thus, the eigenvector corresponding to $\lambda_1 = 0$ is of

the form $\left(-\dfrac{x_2}{3}, x_2 \right)$ where $x_2 \neq 0.$

For eigenvector corresponding to $\lambda_1 = 5$, we have

$$\begin{bmatrix} 3 & 1 \\ 6 & 2 \end{bmatrix}\begin{bmatrix} x_1 \\ x_2 \end{bmatrix} - \lambda_2 \begin{bmatrix} 1 & 0 \\ 0 & 1 \end{bmatrix}\begin{bmatrix} x_1 \\ x_2 \end{bmatrix} = \begin{bmatrix} 0 \\ 0 \end{bmatrix}$$

i.e.,
$$\begin{bmatrix} -2 & 1 \\ 6 & -3 \end{bmatrix}\begin{bmatrix} x_1 \\ x_2 \end{bmatrix} = \begin{bmatrix} 0 \\ 0 \end{bmatrix}.$$

This implies $-2x_1 + x_2 = 0, 6x_1 - 3x_2 = 0.$

This gives $x_1 = \dfrac{x_2}{2}$. Thus, the eigenvector corresponding to $\lambda_1 = 5$ is of the form $\left(\dfrac{x_2}{2}, x_2 \right)$, where $x_2 \neq 0$."

1.2.2   Eigendecomposition [11]

"Eigendecomposition of a matrix involves decomposing a square matrix into a set of eigenvalues and eigenvectors. Suppose A is square matrix of order n, let $\mathbf{q}_1, \mathbf{q}_2 ..., \mathbf{q}_n$ be eigenvectors and $\lambda_1, \lambda_2,...,\lambda n$ be eigenvalues. Let Q be matrix whose columns are eigenvectors $\mathbf{q}_i's$ and Λ is diagonal matrix whose diagonal entries are eigenvalues $\lambda_i's$ of A. Then, Eigendecomposition of A is given by

$$A = Q\Lambda Q^{-1}$$

Note: If the matrix A is symmetric, then Q will be orthogonal matrix and its decomposition is given by

$$A = Q\Lambda Q^{-T}."$$

Example 18. "Consider

$$A = \begin{bmatrix} 1 & 3 \\ 2 & 2 \end{bmatrix}$$

For eigenvalues, we have

$$\det (A - \lambda I) = 0,$$

$$\text{i.e., } (1-\lambda)(2-\lambda) - 6 = 0$$

$$\lambda^2 - 3\lambda - 4 = 0$$

$$\text{or } (\lambda + 1)(\lambda - 4) = 0$$

That is $$\lambda = -1, \lambda = 4,$$

So, the eigenvalues of A are $\lambda_1 = -1, \lambda_2 = 4$.

For eigenvector corresponding to $\lambda_1 = -1$, we have

$$\begin{bmatrix} 1 & 3 \\ 2 & 2 \end{bmatrix} \begin{bmatrix} x_1 \\ x_2 \end{bmatrix} - \lambda_1 \begin{bmatrix} 1 & 0 \\ 0 & 1 \end{bmatrix} \begin{bmatrix} x_1 \\ x_2 \end{bmatrix} = \begin{bmatrix} 0 \\ 0 \end{bmatrix}$$

$$\begin{bmatrix} 2 & 3 \\ 2 & 3 \end{bmatrix} \begin{bmatrix} x_1 \\ x_2 \end{bmatrix} = \begin{bmatrix} 0 \\ 0 \end{bmatrix}$$

This implies $$2x_1 + 3x_2 = 0, \, 2x_1 + 3x_2 = 0.$$

This gives $x_1 = \dfrac{-3x_2}{2}$. Thus, the eigenvector corresponding to $\lambda_1 = -1$ is of the form $\left(\dfrac{-3x_2}{2}, x_2 \right)$ where $x_2 \neq 0$. In particular, $(-3, 2)$, is an eigenvector.

For eigenvector corresponding to $\lambda_1 = 4$, we have

$$\begin{bmatrix} 1 & 3 \\ 2 & 2 \end{bmatrix} \begin{bmatrix} x_1 \\ x_2 \end{bmatrix} - \lambda_1 \begin{bmatrix} 1 & 0 \\ 0 & 1 \end{bmatrix} \begin{bmatrix} x_1 \\ x_2 \end{bmatrix} = \begin{bmatrix} 0 \\ 0 \end{bmatrix}$$

$$\begin{bmatrix} -3 & 3 \\ 2 & -2 \end{bmatrix} \begin{bmatrix} x_1 \\ x_2 \end{bmatrix} = \begin{bmatrix} 0 \\ 0 \end{bmatrix}.$$

This implies $\qquad -3x_1 + 3x_2 = 0, 2x_1 - 2x_2 = 0.$

This gives $x_1 = x_2$. Thus, the eigenvector corresponding to $\lambda_1 = 4$ is of the form (x_1, x_2) where $x_2 \neq 0$. In particular, $(1,1)$ is an eigenvector.

So, $\qquad Q = \begin{bmatrix} -3 & 1 \\ 2 & 1 \end{bmatrix}$ and $\Lambda = \begin{bmatrix} -1 & 0 \\ 0 & 4 \end{bmatrix}$.

Hence, we have the decomposition $A = Q\Lambda Q^{-1}$.

$$= \begin{bmatrix} -3 & 1 \\ 2 & 1 \end{bmatrix} \begin{bmatrix} -1 & 0 \\ 0 & 4 \end{bmatrix} \begin{bmatrix} -\dfrac{1}{5} & \dfrac{1}{5} \\ \dfrac{2}{5} & \dfrac{3}{5} \end{bmatrix}$$

1.3   Introduction to Calculus

1.3.1   Function

"Functions are the objects which helps us to describe the real world into mathematical term. A function f from a set X to a set Y is a rule which associates each element $x \in X$ to a unique element of in Y denoted by $f(x)$. $f(x)$ is called the image of x under f and x is the pre-image of $f(x)$. The set X is called the domain of f, set Y is called co-domain of f. It is not necessary that each element of Y has pre-image, thus the set of all those elements of co-domain holding pre-images is called the range of f, i.e., the set $\{f(x): x \in X\}$ is range of f. We shall use the standard notation $f: X \rightarrow Y$ to denote the function f from X to Y. If domain and co-domain are subset of $\mathbb{R}$, then it is called *real valued function* of a real variable. Note that f is function and $f(x)$ is image of x" [12].

Example 19. "Let $A, B, \subset \mathbb{R}$. A function $f: A \rightarrow B$ defined by

$$f(x) = K, \forall x \in A,$$

where K is a constant belongs to $\mathbb{R}$ is called constant function."

Example 20. "A function $f: \mathbb{R} \rightarrow \mathbb{R}$ *defined by*

$$f(x) = x, \forall x \in \mathbb{R}$$

is called identity function and is denoted by *I*."

Example 21. "A function *f*: $\mathbb{R} \to \mathbb{R}$ *defined by*

$$f(x) = x^n, \forall \ x \in \mathbb{R} \text{ and } n \in \{0\} \cup \mathbb{N}$$

is called power function."

Example 22. "A function *f*: $\mathbb{R} \to \mathbb{R}$ satisfying

$$f(-x) = f(x), \forall \ x \in \mathbb{R}$$

is called an even function."

Example 23. "A function *f*: $\mathbb{R} \to \mathbb{R}$ satisfying

$$f(-x) = -f(x), \forall \ x \in \mathbb{R}$$

is called an odd function."

Example 24. "A function *f*: $\mathbb{R} \to \mathbb{R}$ *defined by*

$$f(x) = \begin{cases} -x, x < 0 \\ x, x \geq 0 \end{cases}, \forall \ x \in \mathbb{R}$$

is called absolute function."

Example 25. "A function *f*: $\mathbb{R} \to \mathbb{R}$ *defined by*

$$f(x) = \begin{cases} 1, & x > 0 \\ 0 & x = 0 \\ -1, & x < 0 \end{cases}, \forall \ x \in \mathbb{R}$$

is called signum function. Range is $\{1, 0, -1\}$."

1.3.2   Limits of Functions

"Let *f* be a real valued function defined in an interval I except possibly at $x_0 \in I$. Then,

(a) $l \in \mathbb{R}$ is called the left-hand limit of *f* if for each $\epsilon > 0$, $\exists$ a $\delta > 0$ such that

$$|f(x) - l| < \epsilon \text{ whenever } x_0 - \delta < x < x_0 \text{ and } x \in I,$$

i.e., $f(x)$ tends to a limit $l \in \mathbb{R}$ as x tends to x_0 from left [12].

It is denoted by $\lim\limits_{n \to x_0 - 0} f(x) = l$ or $f(x_0 - 0) = l$ or $\lim\limits_{x \to x_0-} f(x) = l$.

(b)$l \in \mathbb{R}$ is called the right-hand limit of f if for each $\epsilon > 0$, $\exists$ a $\delta > 0$ such that

$$|f(x) - l| < \epsilon \text{ whenever } x_0 < x < x_0 - \delta \text{ and } x \in I,$$

i.e., $f(x)$ tends to the limit $l \in \mathbb{R}$ as x tends to x_0 from right [12].

It is denoted by $\lim\limits_{n \to x_0 - 0} f(x) = l$ or $f(x_0 - 0) = l$ or $\lim\limits_{x \to x_0-} f(x) = l$.

(c) $l \in \mathbb{R}$ is called the limit of f if for each $\epsilon > 0$, a $\delta > 0$ such that

$$|f(x) - l| < \epsilon \text{ whenever } 0 < x - x_0 < \delta \text{ and } x \in I.$$

That is, the value of $f(x)$ is close to the number $l \in \mathbb{R}$ whenever x is close to x_0 (on either side of x_0). It is denoted by $\lim\limits_{n \to x_0} f(x) = l$."

Note: "When there is no number l satisfying (c), we say that limit of $f(x)$ as x approaches x_0 does not exist. Clearly, the limit of a function f exists at x_0 if both left-hand limit and right-hand limit exist and are equal,

i.e., $\lim\limits_{n \to \infty} f(x) = l$ if

$$\lim\limits_{x \to x_0-} f(x) = \lim\limits_{x \to x_0+} f(x) = l.$$

However, if $\lim\limits_{x \to x_0-} f(x) \neq \lim\limits_{x \to x_0+} f(x)$, we say that $\lim\limits_{n \to x_0} f(x)$ does not exist."

1.3.2.1   Some Properties of Limits

"If l, l', x_0, and k are real numbers and $\lim\limits_{x \to x_0} f(x) = l$, and $\lim\limits_{x \to x_0} g(x) = l'$, then:

(1) The limit of the sum (difference) of two functions is the sum (difference) of their limits.

$$\lim\limits_{x \to x_0} \left(f(x) \pm g(x) \right) = l \pm l'.$$

(2) The limit of the product of two functions is the product of their limits.

$$\lim_{x \to x_0} \left(f(x) * g(x) \right) = l * l'.$$

(3) The limit of a constant times a function is the constant times the limit of the function.

$$\lim_{x \to x_0} \left(kf(x) \right) = k.l.$$

(4) The limit of the quotient of two functions is the quotient of their limits, provided the limit of the denominator is non-zero

$$\lim_{x \to x_0} \left(\frac{f(x)}{g(x)} \right) = \frac{l}{l'}, \, l' \neq 0.$$

(5) If m and n are integers with no common factor and $n \neq 0$, then the limit of a rational power of a function that power of the limit of the function, provided that limit is a real number, i.e.,

$$\lim_{x \to x_0} \left(f(x) \right)^{\frac{m}{n}} = l^{\frac{m}{n}}.$$

Provided that $l^{\frac{m}{n}}$ is real number (assume that $l > 0$)."

Example 26. Evaluate the limit of the function f at $x = 1$ defined by

$$f(x) = \frac{(x+2)^2 - 4x - 5}{x - 1}$$

Solution. "Given $f(x) = \dfrac{(x+2)^2 - 4x - 5}{x - 1}$. Then, left-hand limit is given by

$$\lim_{x\to1-} f\left(x\right) = \lim_{x\to1-} \frac{\left(x+2\right)^2 - 4x - 5}{x-1}$$

$$= \lim_{x\to1-} \frac{x^2 + 4 + 4x - 4x - 5}{x-1}$$

$$= \lim_{x\to1-} \frac{x^2 + 4 + 4x - 4x - 5}{x-1}$$

$$= \lim_{x\to1-} \frac{x^2 - 1}{x-1}$$

$$= \lim_{x\to1-} \frac{\left(x-1\right)\left(x+1\right)}{x-1}$$

$$= \lim_{x\to1-} \left(x+1\right)$$

$$= 2.$$

The right-hand limit is given by

$$\lim_{x\to1+} f\left(x\right) = \lim_{x\to1+} \frac{\left(x+2\right)^2 - 4x - 5}{x-1}$$

$$= \lim_{x\to1+} \frac{x^2 + 4 + 4x - 4x - 5}{x-1}$$

$$= \lim_{x\to1+} \frac{x^2 + 4 + 4x - 4x - 5}{x-1}$$

$$= \lim_{x\to1+} \frac{x^2 - 1}{x-1}$$

$$= \lim_{x\to1+} \frac{\left(x-1\right)\left(x+1\right)}{x-1}$$

$$= \lim_{x\to1+} \left(x+1\right)$$

$$= 2.$$

This gives
$$\lim_{x\to1-} f\left(x\right) = \lim_{x\to1+} f\left(x\right) = 2$$

Hence, $\lim\limits_{x \to 1} f(x)$ exists and equals 2."

Example 27. Evaluate the limit of the function $e^{\frac{1}{x}}$ as $x \to 0$.

Solution. "Let $f(x) = e^{\frac{1}{x}}$. Then, the left-hand limit is given by

$$\lim_{x \to 0-} f\left(x\right) = \lim_{x \to 0-} e^{\frac{1}{x}} = 0$$

The right-hand limit is given by

$$\lim_{x \to 0+} f\left(x\right) = \lim_{x \to 0+} e^{\frac{1}{x}} = \infty$$

This gives

$$\lim_{x \to 0-} f\left(x\right) \neq \lim_{x \to 0+} f\left(x\right).$$

Hence, $\lim\limits_{x \to 0} f\left(x\right)$ does not exist."

1.3.2.2   Infinite Limits

"Let f be a real valued function defined in an interval I except possibly at $x_0 \in I$. Then,

   (a) We say that $f(x)$ approaches infinity as x approaches x_0 and write

$$\lim_{x \to x_0} f\left(x\right) = \infty.$$

If for every real number $k > 0$, $\exists$ a $\delta > 0$ such that $f(x) > -k$ whenever $0 < |x - x_0| < \delta$ and $x \in I$ [12].

   (b) We say that $f(x)$ approaches minus infinity as x approaches x_0 and write

$$\lim_{x \to x_0} f\left(x\right) = -\infty$$

If for every real number $-k < 0$, $\exists$ a $\delta > 0$ such that $f(x) < -k$ whenever $0 < |x - x_0| < \delta$ and $x \in I$ [12]."

1.3.2.3   Limits at Infinity

(a) "We say that $f(x)$ approaches limit l as x approaches *infinity*, and write

$$\lim_{x \to \infty} f(x) = l.$$

If for each $\epsilon > 0$, $\exists$ a real number $\gamma > 0$ such that

$$|f(x) - l| < \epsilon \text{ whenever } x > \gamma."$$

(b) "We say that $f(x)$ approaches limit l as x approaches minus infinity, and write

$$\lim_{x \to -\infty} f(x) = l.$$

If for each $\epsilon > 0$, $\exists$ a real number $\gamma > 0$ such that

$$|f(x) - l| < \epsilon \text{ whenever } x < \gamma."$$

1.3.3   Continuous Functions and Discontinuous Functions

"A function $f(x)$ is said to be continuous at a point x_0 of its domain if for each $\epsilon > 0$, $\exists$ a $\delta > 0$ such that $|f(x) - f(x_0)| < \epsilon$ whenever $|x - x_0| < \delta$ and x belongs to its domain. If f is continuous at each point of domain, then f is said to be continuous on whole domain [13, 14]."

It is clear from definition of continuity of a function at a point x_0 of its domain that

$$\lim_{x \to x_0} f(x) = f(x_0).$$

Therefore, a function f is said to be continuous at x_0 belongs to its domain if

$$\lim_{x \to x_0+} f(x) = \lim_{x \to x_0-} f(x) = f(x_0).$$

Note that domain is an interval of real line of type [a, b] (a, b) [a, b), [a, b) where a < b.

If [a, b] be the domain of f and α is the left endpoint of its domain, then we say f is continuous at α if $\lim\limits_{x \to a+} f(x) = f(a)$, i.e., f must be right continuous at α. Also, b is the right endpoint of its domain, then we say f is continuous at b if $\lim\limits_{x \to b-} f(x) = f(a)$, i.e., f must be left continuous at b.

1.3.3.1   Discontinuous Functions

A function f is said to be discontinuous at a point x_0 of its domain, if it is not continuous at x_0 [13].

1.3.3.2   Properties of Continuous Function

"Let f and g be continuous functions at some point x_0 of domain I and let k ∈ R. Then,

(a) The functions f + g, f − g, kf and fg are continuous at x_0.

(b) The function $\dfrac{f}{g}$ is continuous at x_0, provided g (x_0) ≠ 0."

Example 28. sin (x) and cos (x) are continuous function on any real interval.

Example 29. Examine the continuity of the function

$$h(x) = \begin{cases} 1, & x \in \left[0, \dfrac{1}{2}\right) \\[2ex] -1, & x \in \left[\dfrac{1}{2}, 1\right) \end{cases} \qquad x = \dfrac{1}{2}$$

Solution. "We have

$$\lim\limits_{x \to \frac{1}{2}-} h(x) = 1$$

$$\lim\limits_{x \to \frac{1}{2}+} h(x) = -1$$

and
$$h\left(\frac{1}{2}\right)=-1\,.$$

This gives

$$\lim_{x\to\frac{1}{2}^-} h\left(x\right)\neq \lim_{x\to\frac{1}{2}^+} h\left(x\right)=h\left(\frac{1}{2}\right)$$

Hence, the function h is not continuous at $x=\frac{1}{2}$."

1.3.4   Differentiation

Definition. [13, 15] "Let f be a function defined on domain D. The function f is said to be differentiable at an interior point $x_0 \in D$ if the following limit exist:

$$\lim_{x\to x_0} \frac{f\left(x\right)-f\left(x_0\right)}{x-x_0}$$

We call this limit, the derivative of f at x_0 is denoted by $f'(x_0)$ [12].

If f is differentiable at evy point of its domain, then we say f is differentiable on domain.

Alternatively, the derivative of f with respect to independent variable x is the function whose value at x is

$$f'\left(x\right)= \lim_{h\to 0} \frac{f\left(x+h\right)-f\left(x\right)}{h}\,."$$

Example 30. Prove that the function

$$f=\left|x\right|= f\left(x\right) = \begin{cases} -x, & x<0 \\ x, & x\geq 0 \end{cases}$$

is not differentiable at $x = 0$.

Solution. "We have

$$\lim_{x \to 0-} \frac{f(x)-f(0)}{x-0} = \lim_{x \to 0-} \frac{x}{x} = -1$$

$$\lim_{x \to 0+} \frac{f(x)-f(0)}{x-0} = \lim_{x \to 0+} \frac{x}{x} = 1$$

Since both the limits are not ual, this implies that limit does not exists; hence, f is not differentiable at $x = 0$."

Example 31. "Polynomial of degree n is continuous as well as differentiable on $\mathbb{R}$."

Note: Any differentiable function is always continuous but the converse is not always true.

Example 32. "Function $f(x) = \begin{cases} -x, & x<0 \\ x, & x \geq 0 \end{cases}$ is continuous on $\mathbb{R}$ but not differentiable on $\mathbb{R}$."

Note: One nice application of derivative is that it helps us to find the extreme points of the function.

References

1. Strang, G., *Introduction to Linear Algebra*, 4th ed., Wellesley-Cambridge Press, Wellesley, MA, 2009.
2. Kumaresan, S., *Linear Algebra: A Geometric Approach*, PHI Learning Private Limited, New Delhi, 2011.
3. Noble, B., *Applied linear algebra, vol. III*, Prentice-Hall, New Jersey, 1988.
4. K. Hoffman, R.K., *Linear Algebra*, 2nd ed., Prentice Hall Inc., New Jersey, 1971.
5. Howard Anton, C.R., *Elementary Linear Algebra*, 11th ed., John Wiley & Sons, 2013.
6. Leon, S.J. and Hohn, T., *Linear algebra with applications*, Macmillan, New York, 1980.
7. Krishnamurthy, V.V., *An Introduction to Linear Algebra*, Ist ed., East-west Press Pvt. Ltd., New Delhi, 1938.
8. Axler, S., *Linear Algebra Done Right*, 3rd ed., Springer International Publishing, 2015.

9. NCERT, *Mathematics Text Book for Class XII*, first ed., National Council of Education Research and Training, New Delhi, 2012.

10. Cooperstein, B., *Advanced Linear Algebra*, Chapman and Hall/CRC, 2015.

11. Weisstein, E.W., *Eigen Decomposition*, MathWorld–A Wolfram Web Resource. Retrieved from http://mathworld.wolfram.com/EigenDecomposition.html.

12. Ahmad, K., *Textbook of Differential Calculus*, Anamaya Publishers, New Delhi, 2004.

13. George B. Thomas, J., *Thomas' Calculus*, 13, illustrated ed., Pearson Higher Education & Professional Group, 2016.

14. Lang, S., *A first course in calculus*, Springer Science & Business Media, 2012.

15. Apostol, T.M., *Calculus: One-variable Calculus, with an Introduction to Linear Algebra*, 2nd ed., vol. I, John Wiley & Sons, 2007.

## 2

Theory of Probability

Parvaze Ahmad Dar and Afroz*

*Department of Mathematics, Maulana Azad National Urdu University,
Hyderabad, India*

Abstract

This chapter is dealing with the theory of probability and its basic and higher concepts like probability, sample space, trial, event, null event, exhaustive events, mutually exclusive events, equally likely events, sure event permutation, and combination, etc. Later on, the Concept of Independence in Probability and Conditional in Probability are discussed. By conditional probability, the occurrence of first event is to expect the probability of second event, this process of reversing such probabilities is known as Baye's theorem. Finally, we conclude this chapter with the concept of Multivariate Gaussian Function.

Keywords: Event, mutually exclusive events, sample space, independent even, conditional probability, cumulative distribution, Baye's theorem, multivariate gaussian function

2.1 Introduction

In simple words, "Probability or Chance" state indirectly that its ambiguity about the occurrence of any event. For example, after tossing unbiased coin, the outcome may be head or tail, i.e., there is equal chance or probability of each. The origin of the probability theory is in the games of chance, which is connected to betting like drawing of cards and throwing of a die [1–4].

2.1.1 Definition

2.1.1.1 Statistical Definition of Probability

"Among n trails, an occurrence of the event E happened m times; thus, the probability of happening of an event E is shown below [3]

Corresponding author: afroz.ahmad@manuu.edu.in

Uma N. Dulhare, Khaleel Ahmad and Khairol Amali Bin Ahmad (eds.) Machine Learning and Big Data: Concepts, Algorithms, Tools and Applications, (31–52) © 2020 Scrivener Publishing LLC

$$P\ (E) = \underset{n \to \infty}{Lt}\ \frac{m}{n}.\text{''}$$

2.1.1.2   Mathematical Definition of Probability

The experiment results in n "exhaustive, mutually exclusive and equally likely cases and m of them are favorable to occurrence of the event E" [5].
  "Thus, the probability of happening of event E is shown as

$$P(E) = \frac{\text{Favourable number of cases}}{\text{Exhaustive number of cases}} = \frac{m}{n}.$$

Here, the cases unfavorable to the happening of event E is n-m. The chance of event E will not occur is shown as

$$q \text{ or } P(\bar{E}) = \frac{\text{Unfavourable number of cases}}{\text{Exhaustive number of cases}} = \frac{n-m}{n}$$

$$= 1 - \frac{m}{n} = 1 - p$$

$$= p + q = 1$$

$$\text{i.e., } P(E) + P(\bar{E}) = 1$$

here, p and q are non-negative, not exceeds unity,

$$0 \leq p \leq 1,\ 0 \leq q \leq 1.\text{''}$$

2.1.2   Some Basic Terms of Probability

2.1.2.1   Trial and Event

"When a trial (real or conceptual) is repeated beneath some essential conditions and let it result in any one of the several possible outcomes. This type of experiment is called Trial, and the possible outcomes of an experiment are called event [2, 3, 5, 6]."
  Example: If we toss an unbiased coin, it's called trail, and outcome head or tail is called an event.

2.1.2.2   Exhaustive Events (Exhaustive Cases)

"The all total outcomes of the experiment are called exhaustive events. For example, we toss a coin once there are two exhaustive events, head or tail. Similarly, if we draw a die, the total possible exhaustive events are 1, 2, 3, 4, 5, and 6."

2.1.2.3   Mutually Exclusive Events

"We say that two events are mutually exclusive when the happening of one makes impossible to the happening of rest one. For example, when we have two mutually events A and B such that if A happens, then B not happen and vice versa [5]."

Example: "If we toss of a coin, the events head and tail are mutually exclusive, because both cannot appear at the same time".

2.1.2.4   Equally Likely Events

We say that two events are "equally likely", when there haven't any reason to expect anyone in preference to others.

Example: "If we toss a coin, the events head and tail are equally likely. Similarly, if we throw a die, all six faces (1, 2, 3, 4, 5, and 6) are equally likely [6]."

2.1.2.5   Certain Event or Sure Event

The certain event is another name of sample space S which is a subset U (Universal Set), it is produced after every trial.

Example: Lets toss a coin, getting of Head or Tail is a certain event. It is denoted by S, i.e., S = {H, T}.

2.1.2.6   Impossible Event or Null Event (ϕ)

In the experiment, the event which has zero possibility of occurrence is known as impossible event.

Example: Getting of both head and tail in s single toss of coin is impossible event.

2.1.2.7   Sample Space

"In the fair experiment, all possible outcomes are collectively known as sample space, shown by symbol **S**. Sample space is always subset of the universal set U, i.e., S $S \subseteq U$ [6]."

2.1.2.8   Permutation and Combination

"In simple words, we can say permutation is selection and arrangement of factors, it is denoted by a symbol $^n P_r$ or $P(n, r)$ [3, 7]."

"Here, we say that $^n P_r$ is equal to number of paths of falling 'r' places with 'n' elements,

$$^n P_r = \frac{n!}{(n-r)!}$$

$$^7 P_4 = \frac{7!}{(7-4)!} = \frac{7 \times 6 \times 5 \times 4 \times 3 \times 2 \times 1 \times 0!}{4 \times 3 \times 2 \times 1 \times 0!}$$

$$= 210$$

Another side combination means selections which will be taken through by taking a few or all the factors collectively known as combination, symbolically written as [3, 5];"

$$^n C_{r \text{ or }} c(n, r) \text{ or } \binom{n}{r}.$$

So,

$$^n C_r = \frac{n!}{(n-r)!r!}$$

$$^7 C_4 = \frac{7!}{(7-4)!4!} = \frac{7!}{3! \times 4!} = \frac{7 \times 6 \times 5 \times 4!}{3 \times 2 \times 1 \times 4!}$$

$$= 35$$

Example: We have two elements say A and B, here is only one way to select both A and B, so we select both of them.

Note: a). $^n C_n = {^n C_0} = 1$, b). $^n C_r = {^n C_{n-1}}$, and c). $^n C_x = {^n C_y}$.

2.1.2.9   Examples

1. After tossing an unbiased coin, find the probability of obtain
   a) Head
   b) Tail

Solution: If we toss a unbiased coin, we get "sample space, S = {H, T}"

a) Probability of getting head,

b) $P = \dfrac{n(E)}{n(S)}$, here

   n(E) = Number of Favorable Events = {H} = 1, and
   n(S) = Number of Exhaustive Events = {H,T} = 2

$$p = \dfrac{1}{2}$$

c) For getting tail, $p = \dfrac{n(E)}{n(S)} = \dfrac{1}{2}$; here, n (E)= {T} =1 and n (S) = {H,T}= 2.

2. When we throw an ordinary die, what is the probability

   a)   Getting face 3
   b)   Getting face 5
   c)   Getting the even number
   d)   Getting the odd number
   e)   Getting the number divisible by 2
   f)   Getting number divisible by 3

Solution: The sample space is given as if die is rolled once, S= {1, 2, 3, 4, 5, 6}

a) Probability of getting three,

$$P = \dfrac{Number\ of\ favourable\ Events}{Number\ of\ exhaustive\ Events}.$$

Here, Number of Favorable Events n (E) = {3} or n(E) = 1 and Number of Exhaustive Events n(S) = {1, 2, 3, 4, 5, 6} or n(S) = 6

So,

$$P = \dfrac{1}{6}.$$

b) Probability of getting five, $p = \dfrac{n(E)}{n(S)} = \dfrac{1}{6}$, here n $(E) = \{5\} = 1$ and $n(S) = \{1, 2, 3, 4, 5, 6\} = 6$

c) Probabivlity of getting even number, $P = \dfrac{n(E)}{n(S)}$; here, $n(E) = \{2, 4, 6\} = 3$ and $n(S) = \{1, 2, 3, 4, 5, 6\} = 6$.

So

$$P = \frac{3}{6} = \frac{1}{2}$$

d) Probability of getting odd number,

$$P = \frac{Number\ of\ favourable\ Events}{Number\ of\ exhaustive\ Events}.$$

Here, $n(E) = \{1, 3, 5\}$ or $n(E) = 3$ and $n(S) = \{1, 2, 3, 4, 5, 6\}$ or $n(S) = 6$

So,

$$P = \frac{3}{6} = \frac{1}{3}$$

e) Probability of numbers divisible by 2,

$$P = \frac{n(E)}{n(S)}.$$

Here, n $(E) = \{2, 4, 6\} = 3$, and $n(S) = \{1, 2, 3, 4, 5, 6\} = 6$

So,

$$P = \frac{3}{6} = \frac{1}{2}.$$

f) Probability of number divisible by 3,

$$P = \frac{n(E)}{n(S)}$$

here, n (E) = {3, 6} = 2 and n(S) = {1, 2, 3, 4, 5, 6} or n(S) = 6

So,

$$P = \frac{2}{6} = \frac{1}{3}.$$

3. What is the probability throwing 10, when two dice experiment is done.

Solution: When two dices are thrown, the total possible ways are $6 \times 6 = 36$

Here, the possible ways of getting 10 are $(4, 6), (5, 5), (6, 4) = 3$

$$Probability = \frac{Number\ of\ favourable\ Events}{Number\ of\ exhaustive\ Events} = \frac{3}{36} = \frac{1}{12}.$$

4. In a 52 pack of cards, one card is picked out randomly. What is the probability that the picked out card is king?

Solution: We know there are four kings in a pack of cards, and the way of selecting one card is = 52,

$$\text{i.e., } Probability = \frac{Number\ of\ favourable\ Events}{Number\ of\ exhaustive\ Events} = \frac{4}{52} = \frac{1}{13}$$

5. What is the probability of the card is heart, when a single card is drawn from the well-shuffled pack.

Solution: We know that there are 52 ways of getting one card from well-shuffled pack of cards. Also, one heart is can be drawn = 13 ways because there are a total of 13 heart cards in the whole pack.

$$Probability = \frac{Number\ of\ favorable\ Events}{Number\ of\ exhaustive\ Events} = \frac{13}{52} = \frac{1}{4}.$$

6. A bag contains 7 white balls and 11 red balls. What is the probability that drawing "ball is white".

Solution: One ball can be drawn among 7 white balls as

$$C(n,r) = \frac{n!}{(n-r)!r!} = \frac{7!}{(7-1)!1!} = \frac{7!}{6!} = \frac{7 \times 6!}{6!} = 7$$

∵ Number Favorable of cases = 7

∵ Exhaustive number of cases = 7 + 11 = 18

∵ Probability $= \dfrac{7}{18}$

    7. What is the probability that the "leap year selected at random will contain 53 Sundays".

Solution: The leap year contains total of 366 days. Among these 366 days, there are 52 weeks and 2 extra days. Therefore, these 2 days may be

  a. "Sunday, Monday"
  b. "Monday, Tuesday"
  c. "Tuesday, Wednesday"
  d. "Wednesday, Thursday"
  e. "Thursday, Friday"
  f. "Friday, Saturday"
  g. "Saturday, Sunday"

Among the above seven cases, Sunday is contained in two favorable cases in a. and g.

$$\therefore \text{Probability} = \frac{Number\ of\ favorable\ Events}{Number\ of\ exhaustive\ Events} = \frac{2}{7}$$

2.2 Independence in Probability

2.2.1 Independent Events

"In a trial, two events A and B are said to be independent if the happening of event A does not affect (influence) in any way the happening of event B or vice versa, i.e., if we roll a dice, the event happening in one face is independent to what is happening in the remaining faces, twice, thrice, etc. [2–4, 6, 8]."

2.2.2 Examples: Solve the Following Problems

  a. A man **A** is identified to strike the target two out of five shots, while another man **B** is identified as to strike the targets three out of four shots. What is the probability when the target being strike at all when they both try.

Solution: Probability that the first man hits target

$$P = \frac{n(B)}{n(S)}$$

$$P(A) = \frac{2}{5}$$

The probability that the second man hits the target

$$P = \frac{n(E)}{n(S)}$$

$$P(B) = \frac{n(B)}{n(S)} = \frac{3}{4}$$

Here, P(A) and P(B) are not mutually exclusive because as both can hit the target, P (AB) = P (A)P(B) as "A and B are independent events."

Required probability is $= \left(\frac{2}{5} + \frac{3}{4}\right) - \left(\frac{2}{5} \times \frac{3}{4}\right)$.

$$P = \frac{23}{20} - \frac{6}{20} = \frac{17}{20}$$

b. If there is are 15 students in 4th class, among these 5 are boys and remaining students were girls. What is the probability that the selected student may be a girl?

Solution: Total students in a class = 15
Number of boys = 5
Number of girls = 15−5 = 10
"Favorable Number of Cases" = 10
"Exhaustive number of Cases" = 15
Probability that the student selected is girl

$$= \frac{\text{Favorable number of cases}}{\text{Exhaustive number of cases}} = \frac{10}{15} = \frac{2}{3}$$

c. A card is picked out from 52 pack of cards. What is the probability that it is one of the court cards.

Solution: We know that there are 4 × 3 = 12 court cards (kings, jacks, queens) in a pack (52 cards).

∵ Number favorable of cases = 12

∵ Exhaustive number of cases = 52

∵ Probability $= \dfrac{12}{52} = \dfrac{3}{13}$

d. Find out probability that the "picking card is black or red", when a single card is drawn.

Solution: Probability of (black or red) = P (black) + P (red).

We know there are 26 black and 26 red cards in a pack of cards.

Therefore, the required probability is given as

$$\frac{26}{52} + \frac{26}{52} = 1$$

e. Find the probability when a card is picked was heart or spade.

Solution: Probability of (heart or spade) = P (heart) + P (spade).

We know that there are 13 heart and 13 spade cards in a pack of cards.

Therefore, the required probability is given as

$$\frac{13}{52} + \frac{13}{52} = \frac{1}{2}$$

f. A box hold "5 blue, 4 white, and 7 black" balls. What is the probability of given ball is "blue, white, and black, when 3 balls are drawn at random".

Solution: Total balls are = 5 + 4 + 7 = 16.

Here, exhaustive cases are $^nC_r = \dfrac{n!}{(n-r)!r!} = {}^{16}C_3 = 560$.

Favorable cases $= {}^5C_1 \times {}^4C_1 \times {}^7C_1 = 140$

$$\text{Probability} = \frac{140}{560} = \frac{1}{4}$$

g. A number is chosen from each set.

Set $S_1 = \{1, 2, 3, 4, 5, 6, 7, 8, 9\}$ and Set $S_2 = \{1, 2, 3, 4, 5, 6, 7, 8, 9\}$. If P_1 denotes the probability that the sum of the two numbers be 8 and P_2 denotes the probability that the sum of the two numbers be 9. Find probability of $F_1 + F_2$.

Solution: There are two sets with the same elements, thus the ways of choosing one number from each one are

$$^9C_1 \times {}^9C_1 = 81.$$

Hence, the exhaustive number of cases = 81.
Now, the sum of 8 can be obtained in these ways
(1,7), (7,1), (2,6), (6,2), (3,5), (5,3), (4,4)
Which are 7 in all; therefore, the favorable number of cases are = 7

$$P = \frac{7}{81}$$

Also, the sum of 9 can be obtained from the following ways:
(1,8), (8,1), (2,7), (7,2), (3,6), (6,3), (4,5), (5,4), which are 8 in all.
Therefore, the favorable number of cases are = 8

$$P_2 = \frac{8}{81}.$$

Therefore,

$$P_1 + P_2 = \frac{7}{81} + \frac{8}{81} = \frac{15}{81} = \frac{5}{27}.$$

2.3 Conditional Probability

2.3.1 Definition

"The happening of the probability of event T_1 if it is confirmed that the event T_2 is earlier happened is known as Conditional Probability and it's written as [2–4, 6, 8],

$$P(T_1/T_2) = P\left(\frac{T_1 \cap T_2}{T_2}\right) = \frac{P(T_1 \cap T_2)}{P(T_2)}, \ P(T_2) \neq 0 \ \text{ or}$$

$$P(A \cap B) = P(A/B)P(B)."$$

Note: 1). "When T_1, T_2 are two mutually exclusive events, we know $P(T_1/T_2) = 0$

$$P(T_2/T_1) = \frac{P(T_1 \cap T_2)}{P(T_1)} = \frac{P(\phi)}{P(T_1)} \quad \therefore \text{Events a and b disjoint, i.e., } T_1 \cap T_2 = 0$$

2). $P(T_1/T_1) = 1$ and $P(T_2/T_2) = 1$

3). $P(T_2 / T_1) = \dfrac{P(T_1 \cap T_2)}{P(T_1)}$, $P(T_1) \neq 0$

4). $P(T_1/T_2)$ is not defined if $P(T_2) = 0$"

2.3.2 Mutually Independent Events

If T_1 and T_2 are two events, therefore event T_1 is known as independent on the event A_2 if $P(T_1/T_2) = P(T_1)$, i.e., "If the probability of happening of an event T_1 is independent of happening to an event T_2."

2.3.3 Examples

a). What is the probability when picking "a king and a jack" from a well-shuffled pack of cards in two consecutive draws, without replaced cards which are drawn.

Solution: $P(king\ drawn\ from\ well\ shafled\ pack) = \dfrac{4}{52}$

$P(A) = \dfrac{5}{52}$ = P (drawn a jack after a king has been drawn) $= \dfrac{4}{51}$

$$P\left(\frac{B}{A}\right) = \frac{5}{51}$$

$$P(AB) = P(A)P(B/A)$$

$$\therefore \frac{4}{52} \times \frac{4}{51} = \frac{4}{663}$$

b). Find the probability when 3 cards were drawn from a pack of cards, i.e., a jack, a king, and an ace with three consecutive draws, without replaced cards which are drawn.

Solution: Probability of picking out a jack $= \dfrac{4}{52}$

Probability of picking out a king after jack has been drawn $= \dfrac{4}{51}$

Probability of picking out of an ace after a jack and a king has been drawn $= \dfrac{4}{50}$

Therefore, these all events are dependent.
So, the required compound probability is given as

$$P = \frac{4}{52} \times \frac{4}{51} \times \frac{4}{50} = \frac{64}{132600} = \frac{8}{16575}.$$

c). If a mathematical problem is given to four students, T_1, T_2, T_3, and T_4. With chances of solving it is $\frac{1}{3}, \frac{1}{4}, \frac{1}{5}$, and $\frac{1}{6}$, respectively. Find probability of solving problem.

Solution: P (T_1) = P $(T_1$ will not solve the problem) $= 1 - \frac{1}{3} = \frac{2}{3}$

P (T_2) = P $(T_2$ will not solve the problem) $= 1 - \frac{1}{4} = \frac{3}{4}$

P (T_3) = P $(T_3$ will not solve the problem) $1 - \frac{1}{5} = \frac{4}{5}$

P (T_4) = P $(T_4$ will not solve the problem) $= 1 - \frac{1}{6} = \frac{5}{6}$

Now, P (all of four not solve the problem) $= \frac{2}{3} \times \frac{3}{4} \times \frac{4}{5} \times \frac{5}{6} = \frac{1}{3}$

Hence, P(all of four will solve the given problem) $= 1 - \frac{1}{3} = \frac{2}{3}$

d). A bag contains six red ball and four blue balls. Three balls picked out, one after another by means of no replacement. What is the probability that all drawn balls are blue.

Solution: $P(T_1)$ = P (drawn a blue ball in the first draw) $= \frac{4}{10} = \frac{2}{5}$

$P\left(\frac{T_2}{T_1}\right)$ = P(drawn a second ball, and it is sure that the first ball drawn is blue) $= \frac{3}{9} = \frac{1}{3}$

Hence, P(AB) = P (both balls drawn are blue)

$$P(T_1/T_2) = P(T_1) \times P(T_2/T_1)$$

$$\frac{2}{5} \times \frac{1}{3} = \frac{2}{15}$$

2.4 Cumulative Distribution Function

"The CDF of a continuous random variable z with density f is given as" [4],

2.4.1 Properties

$$F(z) = F_z(z) = P(Z \leq z) = \int_{-\infty}^{z} f(t)dt, -\infty < z < \infty$$

Note: The "probability density function" of variable x can be obtained by differentiating a cumulative distributing function

$$\frac{d}{dz} \int_{-\infty}^{z} f(t)dt = f(z)$$

$f(z) = \dfrac{d}{dz} F(z)$, how long derivative exists.

a). $0 \leq P(z) \leq 1 - \infty \leq z \leq \infty$
b). $F(-\infty) = 0, F(\infty) = 1$
c). If $z_1 < z_2$ then $F(z_1) < F(z_2)$
d). $P(z_1 < Z \leq z_2) = F(z_2) - F(z_1)$
Note: $P(Z > z_1) = P(z_1 < Z < \infty)$

$$P(\infty) - F(z_1) = 1 - F(z_1)$$

2.4.2 Example

1. Find out CDF, when an unbiased coin is tossed two times and if X be the number of observed heads.

Solution: The range of X = {0, 1, 2}, i.e., {HH, HT, TH}

$$P_Z(z) = P(Z = 0) = \frac{1}{4}$$

$$P_Z(1) = P(Z = 1) = \frac{1}{2}$$

$$P_Z(2) = P(Z = 2) = \frac{1}{4}$$

Now, we find CDF, so if z < 0, then
$F_Z(z) = P(Z = z)\ 0, for\ z < 0$
Now if $z \geq 2$
$F_Z(x) = P(Z \geq z) = 1, for\ z \geq 2$
$if\ 0 \leq z < 1$

$$F(z) = P(Z = Z) = P(Z = 0) = \frac{1}{4}$$

At last, $0 \leq z < 2$

$$F_Z(z) = P(Z = z) = P(Z = 0) + P(Z = 1)$$

$$\frac{1}{4} + \frac{1}{2} = \frac{3}{4} \qquad ,0 \leq x < 2$$

Thus, CDF is given as below

$$F_Z(z) = \begin{cases} 0 & for\ z < 0 \\ \dfrac{1}{4} & for\ 0 \leq z < 1 \\ \dfrac{3}{4} & for\ 1 \leq z < 2 \\ 1 & for\ z \geq 2 \end{cases}$$

2. If the continuous random variable functions X has the probability function,

$$f(z) = \begin{cases} \dfrac{z^3}{3} & ,-1 < z < 2 \\ 0 & ,\ elsewhere \end{cases}$$

Find the CDF or F(Z)

Solution:

$$F_Z(z) = \int_{-\infty}^{z} f(t)\,dt$$

$$\int_{-\infty}^{-1} f(t)\,dt + \int_{-1}^{z} f(t)\,dt = 0 + \int_{-1}^{z}\left(\frac{t^3}{3}\right)dt$$

$$= \frac{1}{3}\left[\frac{t^4}{4}\right]_{-1}^{z} = \frac{1}{3}\left[\frac{z^4}{4} + \frac{1}{4}\right] = \frac{z^4+1}{12}$$

$$F(z) = \begin{cases} 0, & x \le -1 \\ \dfrac{z^4+1}{12}, & -1 < z < 2 \\ 1, & z \ge 2 \end{cases}$$

2.5   Baye's Theorem

"The name of 'Baye's Theorem' was framed on the name of British mathematician Thomas Baye's in (1701–1761 and later in 1763 was published the first time in the simple paper. 'According to the concept of conditional probability, it is mentioned that the information regarding the happening of one event to guess the probability of another event. This fact can be extended by **reverse** the probabilities based on new information'. The way of reversing such probabilities is known as Baye's theorem [1, 3, 4, 7]."

2.5.1   Theorem

"Let $T_1, T_2, T_3, \ldots, T_n$ be "**n** mutually exclusive and exhaustive events" with P $(P(T_i) \ne 0)$ for i = 1,2,…,n [7].
Also, let M be an event such that $M \subset \bigcup_{i=1}^{n} T_i$, $P(M) \ne 0$. Then,

$$P(T_i/M) = \frac{P(T_i) \odot P(M/T_i)}{\displaystyle\sum_{i=1}^{n} P(Ti) \odot P(M/T_i)} .$$ "

Proof: "It's given that $M \subset \bigcup\limits_{i=1}^{n} T_i$.

So, $M = M \cap \left(\bigcup\limits_{i=1}^{n} T_i \right) = \bigcup\limits_{i=1}^{n} (M \cap T_i)$ ($\because$ Distributive law)

we can be represented $P(B \cap A_i)$ in two ways (by conditional probability)

i). $P(M \cap T_i) = P(M) \, P(T_i/M)$

ii). $P(M \cap T_i) = P(T_i) \, P(M/T_i)$

$$P(M) = P \left[\bigcup\limits_{i=1}^{n} (M \cap T_i) \right] = \sum\limits_{i=1}^{n} P(M \cap T_i)$$

$\because \, M \cap T_i \, (i=1,2,3,.....,n)$ are mutually disjoint events

Therefore, $P(M) = \sum\limits_{i=1}^{n} P(T_i) P(M/T_i)$ .... [by (ii)]

So, we have

$$P(M \cap T_i) = P(M) \, P(T_i/M) \, ... \text{ [by (i)]}$$

$$P(T_i/M) = \frac{P(M \cap T_i)}{P(M)}$$

$$P(T_i/M) = \frac{P(T_i) \cdot (M \cap T_i)}{\sum\limits_{i=1}^{n} P(T_i) \cdot P(M/T_i)} \, ... \text{ [by (ii)]."}$$

2.5.1.1   Examples

a). If there are four unbiased (true) coins and one biased (false) coin with 'head' on both sides. A coin is chosen randomly and tossed five times. If the head occurs all five times, find probability that the unfair coin has been chosen.

Solution:

P (M$_1$) = P (The coin is unbiased)

$$= \frac{Number\ of\ unbiased\ coins}{Total\ number\ of\ biased} = \frac{4}{5}$$

P (M$_2$) = P (The coin is biased)

$$= \frac{Number\ of\ biased\ coins}{Total\ number\ of\ biased} = \frac{1}{5}$$

Let us suppose, that A is the event of getting all heads in 5 tosses.

$$P(T/M_1) = \frac{1}{2} \times \frac{1}{2} \times \frac{1}{2} \times \frac{1}{2} \times \frac{1}{2} = \frac{1}{32}$$

$$P(T/M_2) = 1$$

Hence, by Baye's theorem, the unbiased coin being chosen

$$P(T/M_2) = \frac{P(M_2) \times P(T/M_2)}{P(M_2) \times P(T/M_2) + P(M_1)P(T/M_1)}$$

$$\frac{\frac{1}{5} \times 1}{\left(\frac{1}{5} \times 1\right) + \frac{4}{5} \times \frac{1}{32}} = \frac{\frac{1}{5}}{\frac{1}{5} + \frac{1}{40}} = \frac{\frac{1}{5}}{\frac{9}{40}} = \frac{1}{5} \times \frac{40}{9}$$

$$= \frac{8}{9}$$

b). A bag contains seven balls. Among these, it's unknown how many balls are black inside the bag. Four balls are drawn randomly and are all black. Find the probability that all balls being black.

Solution: Here, we see four balls which are drawn are black, so it must contain four, five, six seven, and eight black balls.

B$_1$ = Event of the bag containing four black balls.

B_2 = Event of the bag containing five black balls.
B_3 = Event of the bag containing six black balls.
B_4 = Event of the bag containing seven black balls.
B_5 = Event of the bag containing eight black balls.
Here, A is the event drawing four black balls.

$$P\left(\frac{A}{B_1}\right) = \frac{4_{C_4}}{8_{C_4}} = \frac{4 \times 3 \times 2 \times 1}{8 \times 7 \times 6 \times 5} = \frac{1}{70}$$

$$P\left(\frac{A}{B_2}\right) = \frac{5_{C_4}}{8_{C_4}} = \frac{5 \times 4 \times 3 \times 2}{8 \times 7 \times 6 \times 5} = \frac{1}{14}$$

$$P\left(\frac{A}{B_3}\right) = \frac{6_{C_4}}{8_{C_4}} = \frac{6 \times 5 \times 4 \times 3}{8 \times 7 \times 6 \times 5} = \frac{3}{14}$$

$$P\left(\frac{A}{B_4}\right) = \frac{7_{C_4}}{8_{C_4}} = \frac{7 \times 6 \times 5 \times 4}{8 \times 7 \times 6 \times 5} = \frac{1}{2}$$

$$P\left(\frac{A}{B_5}\right) = \frac{7_{C_4}}{8_{C_4}} = \frac{8 \times 7 \times 6 \times 5}{8 \times 7 \times 6 \times 5} = 1$$

Here, blackballs inside the bag are not known, i.e, B_i's are equally likely

$$\therefore \; P(B_1) = P(B_2) = P(B_3) = P(B_5) = \frac{1}{5}$$

So, by Baye's theorem

$$P\left(\frac{B_5}{A}\right) = \frac{P(B_5)P\left(\frac{A}{B_5}\right)}{\sum_{i=1}^{5} P(B_i)P\left(\frac{A}{B_i}\right)}$$

$$= \frac{\frac{1}{5} \times 1}{\frac{1}{5}\left(\frac{1}{70} + \frac{1}{14} + \frac{3}{14} + \frac{1}{2} + 1\right)} = \frac{1}{57}$$

c). The probabilities of T_1, T_2, and T_3 becoming teachers are 5/9, 3/8, and 4/7. The probabilities of the bonus scheme will be introduced if T_1, T_2, and T_3 become teachers that are 7/9, 2/7, and 5/8, respectively.

    I. "What is the probability that the bonus scheme will be introduced"?

    II. "If the bonus scheme has been introduced, what is the probability that the teacher appoints was T_1."

Solution: The probabilities of T_1, T_2, and T_3 for becoming teacher are:

P (T_1) = Probability that T_1 become a teacher
P (T_2) = Probability that T_2 become a teacher
P (T_3) = Probability that T_3 become a teacher.

Let P(B/T_1) = Probability that the bonus scheme is introduced when T_1 becomes teacher. Similarly, we can define P(B/T_2) and P(B/T_3).

So, we have P (T_1) $= \dfrac{5}{9}$, P (T_2) $= \dfrac{3}{8}$, and P (T_3) $= \dfrac{4}{7}$.

P (B/T_1) $= \dfrac{7}{9}$, P (B/T_2) $= \dfrac{2}{7}$, and P (B/T_3) $= \dfrac{5}{8}$.

We have P (B) = P(B T_1) + P(B T_2) + P(B T_3)

$$\frac{5}{9} \times \frac{7}{9} + \frac{3}{8} \times \frac{2}{7} + \frac{4}{7} \times \frac{5}{8} = \frac{2033}{2268} = 0.896.$$

2.6   Multivariate Gaussian Function

Multivariate Gaussian Function (MGF), "Multivariate Normal Distribution (MND), or Joint Normal Distribution (JND) is a generalization of the one-dimensional (univariate) normal distribution to high dimensions" [4, 9, 10].

2.6.1   Definition

2.6.1.1   Univariate Gaussian (i.e., One Variable Gaussian)

"If the random variable $X \sim N (\mu, \sigma^2)$, $\mu \in R$, $\sigma^2 > 0$.
    Then, X has density function, i.e.,

$$f(x) = \frac{1}{\sqrt{2\pi\sigma^2}} \exp\left(-\frac{1}{2\sigma^2}(x-\mu)^2\right)."$$

2.6.1.2   Degenerate Univariate Gaussian

"To generate univariate Gaussian, we have to put

$$X \sim N(\mu, 0) \text{ if } X \equiv \mu,$$

i.e., $X(\omega) = \mu, \forall \omega \in \Omega$ (sample space)."

2.6.1.3   Multivariate Gaussian

"A random variable $X \in R^n$ is multivariate Gaussian over multivariate normal if any linear combination is unvariate Gaussian, i.e.,

$$a^T X = \sum_{i=1}^{n} a_i X_i \text{ is Gaussian such that } \forall a \in R^{n}"$$

References

1. Gupta, S.P., Statistical Methods, in: *Sultan Chand Sons Educ. Publ. 23, Daryagangj*, Sultan Chnad and Sons, pp. 751–765, 2008.
2. Devore, J.L., *Probability and Statistics for Engineering and the Sciences*, Richard Stratton, Cengage Learning, 2010.
3. Ross, S.M., *Introduction to probability and statistics for engineers and scientists*, Academic Press, vol. 9, 2018.
4. Forbes, C., Evans, M., Hastings, N., Peacock, B., *Statistical Distributions, Fourth Edition*, Publisher Wiley, 2010.
5. Bali, N.P., *Golden Statistics*, Laximi Publications (P) Ltd, 113, Golden House, Daryaganj New Delhi 110002, 2016.
6. Walpole, R.E., Myers, R.H., Myers, S.L. Ye, K.Y., Probability & Statistics for Engineers and Scientists. 9th Edition, Pearson, London, 2016.
7. Krishna, P.R.G., Pradeep, N., Gaud, K., Yarramalla, R., *Probability & Statistic*, Professional Publications, Frist Floor, Telegraph Office Building, Beside Swathe Tiffin Centre, Medhipatnam, Hyderabad-500028 A.P India, 2015.
8. Soong, T.T., *Fundamentals of probability and statistics for engineers*, John Wiley & Sons, 2004.
9. Ribeiro, M.I., Gaussian probability density functions: Properties and error characterization. *Inst. Super. Tcnico, Lisboa, Port. Tech. Rep*, 1049–001, 2004.
10. Ahrendt, P., The Multivariate Gaussian Distribution. *A Found. Digit. Commun.*, 454–493, 2005 January.

3

Correlation and Regression

Mohd. Abdul Haleem Rizwan

Department of Mathematics, Muffakham Jah College of Engineering and Technology, Hyderabad, India

Abstract

The focus of this chapter is to show the relationship between correlation and regression analysis. Correlation may be considered first than regression analysis and simple correlation coefficient concept which provides the idea of linear relationship between two variables. The existence of any linear relationship between two variables can be shown by drawing a scatter diagram. There are invalidations and genuine changes of sources of both variables in the correlation coefficient and the value always lies amidst minus one (−1) and plus one (+1) if there is a movement of dispersed points close to the straight line depending on whether the relation is negative or positive. The straight line relation between the two variables can be found by least squares (LS) method. The simple correlation coefficient measures the linear regression by multiple linear regression model, we have more than two independent variables. The goodness of fit in this case is measured by coefficient of determination which is the square of the multiple correlation coefficient.

Keywords: Regression analysis, correlation coefficient, simple and multilinear regression models

3.1 Introduction

Correlation can be seen in daily life to represent some method of relationship. Correlation is observed in the foggy climate and outbreaks of breathlessness. The relationship between two quantitative variables can be denoted by using correlation in statistical expressions. With the increase or decrease of a particular quantity for a unit of one variable, there will be increase or decrease in the relationship which is assumed to be linear. Regression is another

Email: haleemrizwan@mjcollege.ac.in

Uma N. Dulhare, Khaleel Ahmad and Khairol Amali Bin Ahmad (eds.) *Machine Learning and Big Data: Concepts, Algorithms, Tools and Applications,* (53–70) © 2020 Scrivener Publishing LLC

method used in these conditions which encompasses by approximating the finest straight line to recapitulate the relationship. The step of association can be found by the correlation technique between two or more variables.

3.2   Correlation

It is defined as the association between two variables in such a way that a variation in one variable effects on the other variable either positively or negatively. It is also defined as higher variation in one variable causing higher or lower variation in another variable. There are three types of correlation, mainly:

    i.   Positive correlation and Negative correlation
   ii.   Simple correlation and Multiple correlation
  iii.   Partial correlation and Total correlation

3.2.1   Positive Correlation and Negative Correlation

- Positive correlation is defined when two variables incline towards together in the similar way.
- If two variables have a tendency to move in a reverse way, then it is called a negative correlation.
- For instance, elevation and mass, income and expenditure, and claim and resource.

3.2.2   Simple Correlation and Multiple Correlation

- An association between two variables such as X and Y is known as simple correlation.
- A simultaneous study of more than two variables then the correlation is said to be multiple correlation.
- Such as analysis of demand and value and quantity of a product.

3.2.3   Partial Correlation and Total Correlation

- Partial correlation is defined as the variables that eliminate approximately the other variables.
- Total correlation is defined as when all the data is taken into consideration.

- For instance, analyzing the price and demand and rejecting the supply of product.

3.2.4   Correlation Coefficient

The unit of relationship is restrained by a correlation coefficient which is represented by "r". Moreover, it is at times termed as Pearson's correlation coefficient. Conditionally, a curved line is required to definite the association. Furthermore, complex procedures of the correlation have to be used.

The measurement of correlation coefficient on a gauge differs from plus one over zero to minus one. In addition to this, plus one or minus one is said to be completed when there is a correlation between both variables. When there is an increase in one variable with the increase of other variable, the result of the correlation will be positive. On the other hand, if one variable decreases with the increase of the other then the correlation will be negative. Zero represents the complete absence of correlation. One such graphical representation of correlation is given in the following figure.

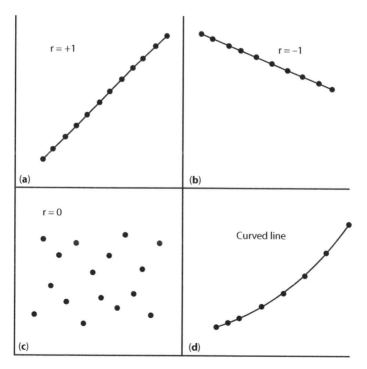

Figure: Correlation illustrated.

Calculation of the Correlation Coefficient
The range or point of association between both variables restrained in relations of a different factor is known as coefficient correlation. It is represented by the letter "r".

$$r = \frac{\sum dxdy}{\sqrt{\sum dx^2 \sum dy^2}}$$

$$\text{where} \quad dx = x - \bar{x}$$

$$dy = y - \bar{y}$$

$$dx^2 = \left(x - \bar{x}\right)^2$$

$$dy^2 = \left(y - \bar{y}\right)^2$$

$$\bar{x} = \frac{\sum x}{n}$$

$$\bar{y} = \frac{\sum y}{n}.$$

The classification of correlation mentioned below gives the value of "r":

1. If r is equal to one, then the value of X and Y variables rise
   or reduce in the same proportion. This is actually known as
   Perfect Positive Correlation.
2. If r is equal to minus one, then the values of X and Y variables are inversely proportional to each other. This is given
   by the Perfect Negative Correlation.

3. If r is equal to zero, then the correlation does not exist amid the variables X and Y.
4. Partial positive correlation between X and Y exist if zero is less than "r" and "r" is less than one.
5. There is said to a partial negative correlation amidst the variables X and Y if minus one is less than "r" and "r" is less than zero.

3.3 Regression

In regression, we can estimate the answer of a variable with the significance of the other variable which is known. The statistical method is helpful to evaluate the new value of one variable from the acknowledged value of the associated variable is termed as regression. After establishing the fact of correlation between two variables, it is natural curiosity to know the extent to which one variable varies in response to a given variation in the other variable that is, one is interested to know the nature of association between the two given variables.

Regression Analysis

An assessment of independent variable of a variable that remains constant can be estimated by regression analysis. Logistic regression is used if the variable is dependent and bifurcated. Logistic and linear regression gives same outcome if the dependent variable ends up with 50–50. Continuity or dichotomy is the main feature of the independent variables used in regression. In regression analysis, more than two levels of independent variables but have to be converted into two levels of variables. Generally, the use of regression analysis is with the naturally occurring variables. On the other hand, casual association between the variables cannot be taken into consideration with regression analysis. According to the explanation, it is clear that X "calculates" Y and it cannot be said that X "causes" Y.

Regression Equation

The regression line x on y passing through $(\bar{x}, \bar{y})$ is

$$(x - \bar{x}) = b_{xy}(y - \bar{y})$$

$$\text{where } b_{xy} = \frac{\sum (x-\bar{x})(y-\bar{y})}{\sum (y-\bar{y})^2}$$

The regression line y on x passing through $(\bar{x}, \bar{y})$ is

$$(y-\bar{y}) = b_{yx}(x-\bar{x})$$

$$\text{where } b_{yx} = \frac{\sum (x-\bar{x})(y-\bar{y})}{\sum (x-\bar{x})^2}$$

Q1. Find the coefficient of correlation for the following data.

x	1	2	3	4	5	6	7	8	9
y	10	11	12	14	13	15	16	17	18

Sol: Calculate $\quad \bar{x} = \dfrac{\sum x}{n} = 5 \text{ and } \bar{y} = \dfrac{\sum y}{n} = 14$

Computation Table

x	$dx = x - \bar{x}$	$dx^2 = (x-\bar{x})^2$	y	$dy = y - \bar{y}$	$dy^2 = (y-\bar{y})^2$	$dxdy = (x-\bar{x})(y-\bar{y})$
1	-4	16	10	-4	16	16
2	-3	9	11	-3	9	9
3	-2	4	12	-2	4	4
4	-1	1	14	0	0	0
5	0	0	13	1	1	0
6	1	1	15	1	1	1
7	2	4	16	2	4	4
8	3	9	17	3	9	9
9	4	16	18	4	16	16
$\sum x = 45$	$\sum dx = 0$	$\sum dx^2 = 60$	$\sum y = 126$	$\sum dy = 0$	$\sum dy^2 = 60$	$\sum dxdy = 59$

$$r = \frac{\sum dxdy}{\sqrt{\sum dx^2 \sum dy^2}}$$

$$r = \frac{59}{\sqrt{60 X 60}} = 0.9833$$

Q2. Solve the given data to find the coefficient of correlation and also the regression lines.

X	1	2	3	4	5	6	7
Y	2	4	7	6	5	6	5

Sol: Calculate

$$\bar{x} = \frac{\sum x}{n} = 4$$

$$\bar{y} = \frac{\sum y}{n} = 5$$

$$r = \frac{\sum dxdy}{\sqrt{\sum dx^2 \sum dy^2}}$$

Computation Table

x	$dx = x - \bar{x}$	$dx^2 = (x - \bar{x})^2$	y	$dy = y - \bar{y}$	$dy^2 = (y - \bar{y})^2$	$dxdy = (x - \bar{x})(y - \bar{y})$
1	$1-4 = -3$	9	2	$2-5 = -3$	9	9
2	$2-4 = -2$	4	4	$4-5 = -1$	1	2
3	$3-4 = -1$	1	7	$7-5 = 2$	4	-2
4	$4-4 = 0$	0	6	$6-5 = 1$	1	0
5	$5-4 = 1$	1	5	$5-5 = 0$	0	0
6	$6-4 = 2$	4	6	$6-5 = 1$	1	2
7	$7-4 = 3$	9	5	$5-5 = 0$	0	0
$\sum x = 28$	$\sum dx = 0$	$\sum dx^2 = 28$	$\sum y = 35$	$\sum dy = 0$	$\sum dy^2 = 16$	$\sum dxdy = 11$

$$r = \frac{11}{\sqrt{28 \times 16}} = 0.5197$$

The regression line x on y passing through $\left(\bar{x}, \bar{y}\right)$ is

$$\left(x - \bar{x}\right) = b_{xy}\left(y - \bar{y}\right)$$

where $b_{xy} = \dfrac{\sum\left(x - \bar{x}\right)\left(y - \bar{y}\right)}{\sum\left(y - \bar{y}\right)^2}$

$$b_{xy} = \frac{11}{16} = 0.6875$$

$$(x - 4) = 0.6875(y - 5)$$

$$x - 4 = 0.6875y - 3.4375$$

$$x = 0.6875y + 0.5625$$

The regression line y on x passing through $\left(\bar{x}, \bar{y}\right)$ is

$$\left(y - \bar{y}\right) = b_{yx}\left(x - \bar{x}\right)$$

$$\text{where } b_{yx} = \frac{\sum \left(x - \bar{x}\right)\left(y - \bar{y}\right)}{\sum \left(x - \bar{x}\right)^2}$$

$$b_{yx} = \frac{11}{28} = 0.3928$$

$$(y - 5) = 0.3928\,(x-4)$$

$$y - 5 = 0.3928x - 1.5712$$

$$y = 0.3928x + 3.4288$$

****

Reason for the use of regression analysis

It is clearly explained that the analysis of regression is done to evaluate the association between two or among more variables. It can be understood with few more examples.

If the estimation growth of a company's sales is to be analyzed based on present economical situations, then it can be calculated with the data provided as two and a half times approximately the economic growth of the sales of a company. It indicates the growth of the present data of the company is approximately two and a half times. Moreover, based on the present and past data, the value of future sales of the company can be estimated.

Regression analysis provides many profits such as: It shows the substantial associations between dependent and independent variable and also shows strong point of effect of multiple independent variables on a dependent variable.

Comparison of variables on different scales is measured by regression analysis, for instance, the impact of rate change and marketing accomplishments. These profits support market scholars/data and market analysts/data technologists to eradicate and estimate the finest result of variables.

Regression analysis is of many types like linear, logistic, stepwise, ridge, lasso, elastic net, and polynomial.

3.3.1   Linear Regression

This is the well-known technique of modeling and is commonly used by the people to learn analytical modeling. A continuous dependent variable and an independent variable (continuous or discrete) are analyzed with this technique. The feature and characteristic of regression line remains linear.

An association between Y and X which are dependent variables and one or more independent variables respectively with a regression line is established by linear regression.

Y = a + b * X + e is denoted as an equation, where "a" denotes intercept, "b" denotes the line's slope, and "e" represents an error term. The objective variable's value established on assumed analyst variable can be calculated by this equation.

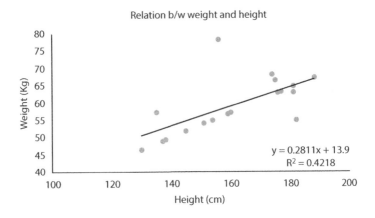

The variance among simple linear regression and multiple linear regression can be shown if simple linear regression has only one independent variable and a multiple linear regression has greater than one independent variable. Here, the question rises that how to get "best fit line".

3.3.2   Logistic Regression

The technique used to solve the probability of result equal to success (result = success) and result equal to failure (result = failure). When the dependent variable is mentioned as binary: True/False, Yes/No, 0/1, logistic regression is used. The value of Y ranges from 0 to 1 and the equation can be represented.

$$\text{Odds} = p/(1\text{-}p)$$

(probability of result occurrence/probability of no occurrence of result)

$$\text{Ln (odds)} = \ln (p/(1\text{-}p))$$

$$\text{Logit(p)} = \ln(p/(1\text{-}p)) = b0 + b1X1 + b2X2 + b3X3 .... + bkXk$$

where "p" is the probability of presence of interest. One can interrogate here that is "what is the use of log in the equation?" Here, a binomial distribution needs a link function which is suitable for the distribution and it is **logit** function. Above equation deals with the factors that are selected to maximize the sample values preferably minimizing squared errors' sum as it is done in ordinary regression.

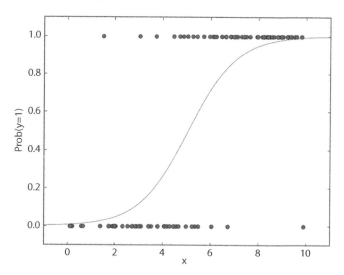

3.3.3 Polynomial Regression

If the command of variable which is independent is more than one, then it is said to be a polynomial regression. The equation is represented as:

$$Y = a + b^*x^2.$$

The best fit line in this technique is a curve that fits into the statistical facts rather than a straight line.

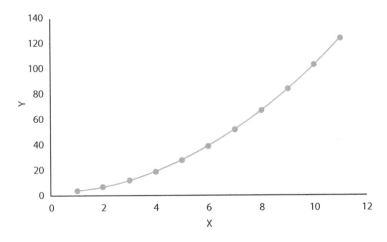

3.3.4   Stepwise Regression

This technique is used if the variables of multiple independent of regression are present. It deals with the help of automatic procedure when there is a choice of independent variables and with no human interference.

This achievement of observed data results like R-square, t-stats, and AIC metric to a determined significant variable. Stepwise regression is the regression of adding/dropping of covariates only one at a time on the specified criterion. Stepwise regression methods are listed below:

- Standard stepwise regression adds and removes interpreters as required for individually.
- Forward selection begins with the most important interpreter in the model and adds variable for every step.
- Backward elimination begins with all interpreters in the model and removes the least important variable for every step.

The purpose of this technique is to maximize the likelihood rule with minimum number of interpreter variables. Higher dimensionality of statistics set is handled by one of the above methods.

3.3.5   Ridge Regression

When independent variables are highly correlated and multicollinearity, then the ridge regression technique is used. The variances are more even when the least squares (LS) is estimated in multicollinearity. A deviation is observed extreme from the value that is true. Ridge regression value decreases the standard errors if a degree of bias is added to the regression.

We know that linear regression equation is represented as:

$$y = a + b^*x.$$

The above equation contains an error term. The actual equation can be written as:

$$Y = a + b^*x + e \text{ (error term)},$$

(Error term can be defined as the value required to rectify an interpreted error between the observed and estimated value)

$$\Rightarrow y = a + y = a + b1x1 + b2x2 + \ldots + e, \text{ for multiple independent}$$
variables.

Prediction errors can be disintegrated into two sub-modules in a linear equation. One is because of **biased** and the other is because of **variance**. This error may happen owing to any one of these two or both modules. The error caused due to variance is shown below:

Ridge regression solves the multicollinearity problem by using shrinkage parameter lambda (λ). The equation below:

$$= \underset{\beta \in \mathbb{R}^p}{\arg\min} \underbrace{\left\| y - X\beta \right\|_2^2}_{\text{Loss}} + \lambda \underbrace{\left\| \beta \right\|_2^2}_{\text{Penalty}}$$

Here, first is LS term and second is lambda of the summation of beta square (where β is the coefficient). In order to shrink the parameter to have a very low variance, this is added to LS term.

3.3.6   Lasso Regression

$$= \underset{\beta \in \mathbb{R}^p}{\arg\min} \underbrace{\left\| y - X\beta \right\|_2^2}_{\text{Loss}} + \lambda \underbrace{\left\| \beta \right\|_1}_{\text{Penalty}}$$

Lasso is least absolute shrinkage and selection operator and is similar to ridge regression. The absolute size of the regression coefficients can be penalized by Lasso. Moreover, it can reduce the variability and can improve the accuracy of linear regression models. Observe the equation below:

Lasso regression when compared to ridge regression uses absolute values rather than squares in the penalty function. This gives the sum of absolute values of the estimates and leads to correcting. And the considerable values give zero exactly. With the increase in penalty, the estimation shrinks to absolute zero.

3.3.7   Elastic Net Regression

The hybrid technique is elastic net regression and is trained with L1 and L2 prior as standardizer. Multiple features when correlated, Elastic net is used. Lasso regression is used randomly to choose any one of these whereas both are picked up in elastic net.

$$\hat{\beta} = \arg\min_{\beta} \left(\left\| y - X\beta \right\|^2 + \lambda_2 \left\| \beta \right\|^2 + \lambda_1 \left\| \beta \right\|_1 \right)$$

Elastic net succeeds to some stability of Ridge below variation which is a concrete benefit of trading-off between Lasso and Ridge.

3.4   Conclusion

The use of correlation and simple linear regression examine the existence of a linear association between two variables. They provide definite norms about the facts which are satisfactory. The correlation coefficient between two variables can be achieved by most of the data, series, and databases. The limit is in between −1 and 1 of the correlation coefficient which results into the linear relationship between two variables. When one of the variables increases, then the other also increases, and if one decreases, then the other also decreases; then, the coefficient is said to be close to 1 and a strong positive relationship between two variables. Similarly, if the association is between two variables is said to have a strong negative relationship and a coefficient close to −1, when there is a higher value in one of the variables consider to have a low value in the other and vice versa. No linear association between the two variables is considered when a coefficient is close to zero. Hence, simple linear regression explains the relationship between Y and X by the representation of the equation

$$Y = a_0 + a_1 X \text{ (useful for prediction).}$$

Karl Pearson product moment formula is actually used to extent the power of relationship between or more variables in correlation coefficient "r".

$$r = \frac{\sum dx dy}{\sqrt{\sum dx^2 \sum dy^2}}$$

References

1. Jain, R.K. and Iyengar, *Advanced Engineering Mathematics*, New Delhi, Narosa Publishing House, 2014.
2. Grewal, B.S., *Higher Engineering Mathematics*, New Delhi, Khanna Publishers, 2017.
3. Sivarama Krishna Das, P. and Vijaya Kumar, C., *Engineering Mathematics*, Pearson India Education Services Pvt. Ltd, 2016.
4. Bali, N.P. and Goyal, M., A text book of Engineering Mathematics, New Delhi, Laxmi Publications, 2010.
5. Gupta, S.C. and Kapoor, V.K., *Fundamentals of Mathematical Statistics*, New Delhi, S. Chand & Son Educational Publishers, 2002.
6. Russell, M.A.H., Cole, P.Y., Idle, M.S., Adams, L., Carbon monoxide yields of cigarettes and their relation to nicotine yield and type of filter. *BMJ*, 3, 713, 1975.

Section 2

BIG DATA AND PATTERN RECOGNITION

4

Data Preprocess

Md. Sharif Hossen

Department of Information and Communication Technology,
Comilla University, Cumilla, Bangladesh

Abstract

A large amount of data is collected every day from different sources. Most of them are unprocessed, which are difficult to analyze and sometimes become useless as the datasets tend to be inconsistent, missing, and noisy. Before using those datasets, the quality must be maintained. Data preprocessing is a step of the knowledge discovery process that ensures the consistency and quality of the data. Data preparation is a compulsory step in data preprocessing, which prepares the useless data in a usable format to analyze in the next step of data mining. There are several techniques in data preparation, e.g., data cleaning, integration, reduction, transformation, normalization, de-noising, and dimensionality reduction, and so on. In this chapter, we will discuss how to measure the quality of data, address missing data, clean the noisy data, and perform transformation on certain variables.

Keywords: Data processing, data mining, knowledge discovery, data transformation

4.1 Introduction

Real-world raw data can be unarranged, inconsistent, incomplete, incorrect, unprocessed, and dirty. Data processing can play an important role to enhance the quality of data by providing the accuracy and efficiency of the data in the succeeding process. Good decisions are made to ensure the data quality by finding anomalies in data, filtering them as soon as possible. It is the preceding step, which is applied before the unprocessed data sent to

---

Email: sharif5613@gmail.com

Uma N. Dulhare, Khaleel Ahmad and Khairol Amali Bin Ahmad (eds.) Machine Learning and Big Data: Concepts, Algorithms, Tools and Applications, (73–104) © 2020 Scrivener Publishing LLC

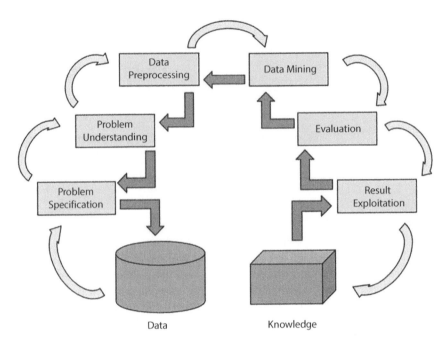

Figure 4.1 Steps of knowledge discovery process.

the data mining phase [1]. Data mining can be viewed as the main phase of the knowledge discovery process as shown in Figure 4.1 [2, 3].

Data refers to the collection of raw materials which is unprocessed most of the time. It consists of objects and their properties. In the real world, everything can be considered as an object. The properties of objects are also called attributes. Examples of objects are cars, people, dog, chair, table, text, image, web, audio or video, etc. [4].

4.1.1   Need of Data Preprocessing

When we collect raw data from the real world, we found it inconsistent, noisy, unprocessed, redundant, unsupportable format, and incomplete. We can ensure our data consistent if we get the quality data. Data quality can be achieved through several factors, namely, consistency, accuracy, timeliness, value-added, believability, interpretability, accessibility, and completeness [2, 4].

Sometimes, the same data exists in different locations with different formats and versions. This situation is called as data inconsistency. This increases the data redundancy because the same information are available in different formats, e.g., containing discrepancies in codes or names. So, data should be consistent.

Data accuracy is difficult if user input disguised missing data, i.e., the default value in the software, which is incorrect. For example, your age is 30 but you use the default value 28, which is wrong. During data collection, we can get incorrect data for equipment malfunctions. Besides, typos can be occurred by human.

Data quality can be degraded if we do not collect our day on a timely basis. In a company, sales representatives should keep the monthly records of how many sales there are. If they do not submit the one or more records of sales, data are incomplete, which impact the quality of data. So, data should be complete and timely.

Believability and interpretability are two factors, which are also related to the quality of data. Users can lose their trust in previous experience of a company's past errors. This trust is referred to as believability. Sometimes, new users cannot understand the product codes of different companies, which arises the problem of interpretability. So, without fulfilling believability and interpretability, it is impossible to keep the product quality in a good manner.

Data accessibility should be maintained. Sometimes, wrong or incorrect addresses are given mistakenly to access a database, which prevents the user to access it. So, addresses should be accurate.

4.1.2   Main Tasks in Data Preprocessing

This section covers the major tasks included in data preprocessing, which are data cleaning, integration, reduction, and transformation [2, 5, 6] as shown in Figure 4.2.

(i)   Data Cleaning

Data cleaning is necessary when the raw data is inconsistent, noisy, and incomplete. Duplicate records are also processed by data cleaning. In the library management system, we need to integrate multiple files, databases, tables, etc. During the integration, we can find the same attribute in different tables and databases as different names, which can cause data inconsistency. For example, the attribute "student id" is found as "stuId" in one table, but as "sId" in another table, which can cause the duplication or redundancy. Besides, the same book can be stored in several names, which causes also the redundancy. For a large management system, this can reduce the efficiency or slow down the knowledge discovery mechanism. Therefore, data redundancy should be reduced. For this reason, data integration and data cleaning are used as a preprocessing phase during the

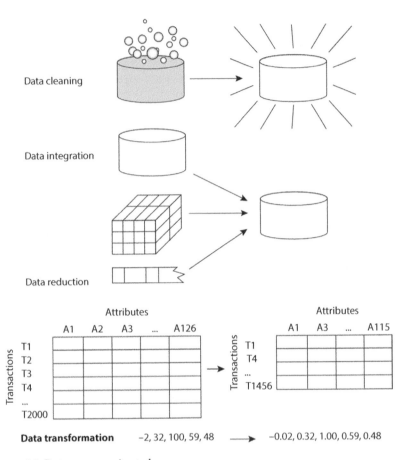

Figure 4.2 Data preprocessing tasks.

preparation of data to store in a data warehouse. Data cleaning is done by filling in lost values, smoothing noisy data, finding or omitting outliers, and ensuring the consistency of the data.

(ii)   Data Integration
During data analysis, we work with multiple files from different sources. These files should be integrated to reduce the inconsistencies and redundancies because these files may exist in different databases. So, data integration plays an important role to minimize the inconsistencies and redundancies.

(iii) Data Reduction
To further reduce the redundancy, we need to use a data reduction technique, which reduces the dimension of data in a much smaller volume. Different data reduction techniques, namely, data cube aggregation, attribute subset selection, numerosity reduction, and dimensionality reduction, are used to minimize the volume of data.

(iv) Data Transformation
Since data are collected from different sources and in different formats, so, it is transformed from a large volume of data into a smaller subset, which is called data transformation. Normalization, attribute selection, discretization, and concept hierarchy generation are the techniques of transformation.

4.2 Data Cleaning

The available data collected from different sites can be missing, noisy and inconsistent. Hence, data cleaning is necessary [2, 4, 6]. It requires the following two ways to clean the data.

4.2.1 Missing Data

Missing data in the dataset can be handled in several ways.

(i) Ignore the Records
In this approach, the rows or records or tuples are removed due to the missing values of several attributes. This approach is not enough good as the tuples that are ignored are not used. So, it can be used only when the number of missing values is not severe.

(ii) Fill the Missing Values (manually, by constant, or by mean or by most probable value)
There are several approaches to get the corrected tuple instead of removing the tuples permanently.

If the missing data is too less, then it can be changed manually and preferred. But, when the number of missing values is too large, then the manual approach is useless and unfeasible as it will take a long time to correct those tuples.

Another approach is to replace the missing values by a fixed value, say, CONST. It can help to continue the task without removing any tuple, but it is also not reasonably good as it does not give the appropriate results.

The use of mean or median values can give the nearest value to replace with the missing one. Besides, data prediction techniques, e.g., decision tree, can be used to determine the probable value to replace the missing values.

4.2.2   Noisy Data

The data, which are collected from different sources, can have unnecessary information, which is called the noisy data. The following three techniques are used to smooth the data.

(i)   Binning Method

Binning [2, 7] is referred to as discretization where continuous features are partitioned into discretized form. It is used to handle noisy data. In this approach, at first, the data is sorted and then values are partitioned by equal frequency bins where values are put into an equal number of bins. Smoothing can be in three ways:

(a) Smoothing by bin means where the mean value is used to replace each value.

(b) Smoothing by bin median where the median value is used to replace the bin value.

(c) Smoothing by bin boundary where closest boundary value is determined from the maximum and minimum values in the bin and then that value is used to replace the bin value.

The following example shows the binning concepts. Sorted data for price (in dollars) are 5, 9, 16, 22, 22, 25, 26, 29, and 35.

Partition into equal depth bins:
Bin 1: 5, 9, 16
Bin 2: 22, 22, 25
Bin 3: 26, 29, 35

Smoothing by bin means:
Bin 1: 10, 10, 10
Bin 2: 23, 23, 23
Bin 3: 30, 30, 30

Smoothing by bin median:
> Bin 1: 9, 9, 9
> Bin 2: 22, 22, 22
> Bin 3: 29, 29, 29

Smoothing by bin boundaries:
> Bin 1: 5, 5, 16
> Bin 2: 22, 22, 25
> Bin 3: 26, 26, 35

(ii) Regression

Another approach to smooth the data is a regression technique, which predicts unknown data from known data and fits it using a function. There are two types of regression techniques, namely, linear and multiple linear [4, 8].

In linear regression, a known value is used to predict the unknown one where the relationship between two values is best fitted with a straight line. The function can be expressed as follows:

$$y = \theta_2 x + \theta_1 + e \tag{4.1}$$

where θ_2 is the angle for straight line and a point as well as θ_1 is the point in which x = 0. Figure 4.3 shows the linear regression with a single predictor.

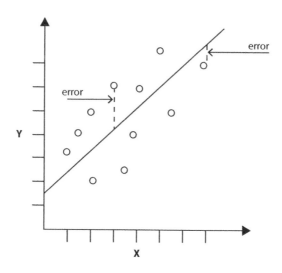

Figure 4.3 Linear regression.

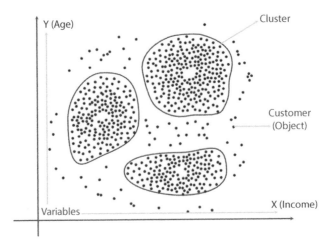

Figure 4.4 Outlier analysis using clustering.

In multivariate linear regression, more than one attribute value is used to fit more noisy data. The expression of the function is as follows:

$$y = \theta_1 + \theta_{2x1} + \theta_{3x2} + \ldots + \theta_n x_{n-1} + e \qquad (4.2)$$

(iii) Clustering to Reduce Outliers

There can be some distinctions of few data from the rest of the data within the dataset. This unusual behavior of data is called an outlier. If you consider the points within a range, then outliers are those points, which are outside this range. In another way, it can be understood as a value, which is very small or large than all the values in the dataset. Say, the values in the scores are 27, 30, 2, 43, 32, 36, and 97. Here, 2 and 97 are outliers [2, 4].

To categorize the outliers, we can create grouping in the dataset with similar properties. So, this set of grouping with the similarity of values is called clusters. We can minimize or reduce outliers in the given dataset using clusters. For example, in Figure 4.4, we saw some points outside the three clusters, which are different from other data in the dataset. Dataset values have been grouped into three groups (i.e., three clusters) and the remaining points outside those three clusters are outliers, which can be easily identified.

4.3   Data Integration

In data mining, data integration is a technique to form a single dataset by integrating data from various sources (e.g., databases, flat files, etc.).

When we collect and integrate data from different sources, we should be careful about the fact that no redundant and inconsistent data exists in the dataset because data redundancy and inconsistency can slow down and reduce the accuracy of data [3]. Data integration combines multiple heterogeneous sources and generates a unified view of processed data as shown in Figure 4.5 [9, 10].

Integrating meta-data from various sources is called schema integration. During this integration, care should be taken that redundancy and inconsistency are minimized. Here, at first, we need to identify the objects or the entities in the dataset by data structure, i.e., their attributes, values, meaning, etc., so that similar objects can be matched, which can help reduce redundancy. Data redundancy can be appeared from the redundant attributes or inconsistencies of attributes from different databases. Attribute redundancy can be identified by correlation analysis. The $\chi 2$ (Chi-squared) test is the appropriate choice for nominal data, while the correlation coefficient and covariance are used for numeric data, which have been discussed in Sections 4.3.1, 4.3.2, and 4.3.3, respectively.

There are several approaches to integrate the data, namely, data warehousing, federated database, and mediation as shown in Figure 4.6 [9, 10].

In data warehousing shown in Figure 4.6a, data from different sources are copied and then stored in the warehouse through the Extract Transform Load (ETL) process.

In the federated database scheme shown in Figure 4.6b, every data source can build mapping and transformation through the wrapper, which maps the queries.

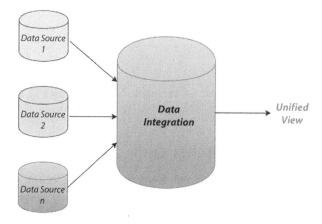

Figure 4.5 Unified view of data.

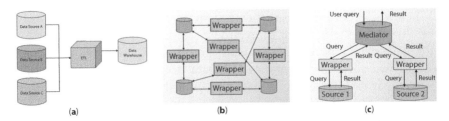

Figure 4.6 Models of data integration: (a) data warehousing, (b) federated databases, and (c) mediation.

In the mediation approach shown in Figure 4.6c, the user query is mapped to all queries, which are forwarded to every source. Every source then checks the query and sends the result to the mediator where all queries are merged. Mediator then sends it to end-users.

4.3.1　χ2 Correlation Test

If A and B are two nominal attributes with respective distinct values c and r, namely, $a_1,...,a_c$ and $b_1,...,b_r$, then for joint event, (Ai, Bj), χ2, can help find the correlation between A and B as follows:

$$\chi^2 = \sum_{i=1}^{c} \sum_{j=1}^{r} \frac{\left(o_{i,j} - e_{i,j}\right)^2}{e_{i,j}} \tag{4.3}$$

where observed frequency of (A_i, B_j) is $o_{i,j}$, and expected frequency, $e_{i,j}$, is as follows:

$$e_{i,j} = \frac{N_{A=a_i} \times N_{B=b_i}}{n} \tag{4.4}$$

where n denotes the number of records, $N_{A=a_i}$ and $N_{B=b_i}$ indicates the number of records with a_i for A and b_i for B, respectively.

4.3.2　Correlation Coefficient Test

The correlation coefficient between two numerical attributes is checked to determine the redundancy by knowing if they are highly correlated or not. It is given by the following equation:

$$r_{A,B} = \frac{\sum_{i=1}^{n}(a_i - \bar{A})(b_i - \bar{B})}{n\,\sigma_A\sigma_B} = \frac{\sum_{i=1}^{n}(a_ib_i) - n\bar{A}\bar{B}}{n\,\sigma_A\sigma_B} \qquad (4.5)$$

where the means, $\bar{A}$, and $\bar{B}$ has been specified in Equation 4.8, and standard deviations, σ_A, and σ_B in Equation 4.9. Here, $-1 \le r_{A,B} \le +1$. Two attributes of A and B are highly correlated if $r_{A,B} > 0$ and hence, one of them can be removed to reduce the redundancy. If $r_{A,B} = 0$, then there is no correlation between the attributes and they do not depend on each other. If $r_{A,B} < 0$, then they are negatively correlated, i.e., if the value of one increases, then other decreases.

4.3.3   Covariance Test

Both correlation and covariance check how much two variables change together. Covariance, $Cov\,(A, B)$, between A and B can be calculated from Equation 4.15 and the relationship between covariance and correlation is determined from Equation 4.16.

$Cov\,(A, B)$ will be positive if $A > \bar{A}$, and $B > \bar{B}$. While it will be negative if $(A > \bar{A}$ and $B < \bar{B})$ or $(A < \bar{A}$, and $B > \bar{B})$. A and B will be independent if $Cov\,(A, B) = 0$.

4.4   Data Transformation

Data transformation is a data preprocessing technique, which is used to transform or convert the data from one format into an appropriate acceptable format [2, 11, 12].

4.4.1   Normalization

It is a data transformation technique [2, 4, 13], which is used to reduce the duplicate data in the dataset. That is, it minimizes the data redundancy and ensures the proper use of data storage. When the attribute values in a table carry various scales, then it is difficult to analyze the data using data mining. Hence, we can normalize the data in the fixed range, e.g., 0.0 to 1.0 or −1.0 to 1.0. There are three ways of data normalization, namely, min-max, z-score, and decimal scaling normalization.

(i)   In min-max normalization, normalized value (x') of an attribute value x is determined by finding the maximum (*max*) and minimum (*min*) value in the dataset within the normalized range (0.0 to 1) as follows:

$$x' = \frac{x - min}{max - min}\left(new_{max} - new_{min}\right) + new_{min} \qquad (4.6)$$

For example, if the *max* and *min* values of attribute age are 80 and 10, respectively, then the normalized value x' for age $x = 30$ with the range [0.0, 1.0] is as follows:

$$x' = \frac{30 - 10}{80 - 10}\left(1.0 - 0.0\right) + 0 = 0.286$$

(ii)   In z-score (zero-mean) normalization, the normalized value is determined using the mean and standard deviation of the attribute as follows:

$$x'_i = \frac{x_i - \bar{x}}{\sigma_x} \qquad (4.7)$$

where $x_1 = x_1, x_2,..., x_n$, $i = 1,2,...,n$ are the attribute values in the dataset, and mean, $\bar{x}$, is as follows:

$$\bar{x} = \frac{x_1 + x_2 + ... + x_n}{n} \qquad (4.8)$$

Standard deviation, σ_x, is as follows:

$$\sigma_x = \sqrt{\frac{\sum\left(x - \bar{x}\right)^2}{n}} \qquad (4.9)$$

For example, if the mean and standard deviation of attribute age are 24 and 5, respectively, then the normalized value x' for age $x = 30$ using z-score normalization is as follows:

$$x' = \frac{30 - 24}{5} = 1.2$$

Min-max normalization cannot handle the outliers properly while z-score handles those but cannot generate the normalized value with the proper scale.

In decimal scaling normalization, the normalized value of an attribute is obtained by dividing the attribute value by the number of decimal points of values of that attribute, which is shown in Equation 4.10.

$$x'_i = \frac{x_i}{10^k} \tag{4.10}$$

where $|x'_i| < 1$ and k is the decimal scaling.

For example, suppose the values of x scale from -580 to 528. The absolute value of x is 580. Here, with $k=3$, the normalized values for 580 and 528 using decimal scaling will be 0.580 and 0.528, respectively.

4.4.2   Attribute Selection

It is another approach to reduce data redundancy in data mining. We sometimes work with a large dataset having lots of attributes. For efficient data processing, we do not need those attributes which have irrelevant information. That means we can remove the unnecessary attributes. The attribute selection approach chooses the necessary attributes without which we cannot process the dataset. That is, this approach helps to omit irrelevant attributes, which does not contribute more in the data analysis [14, 15]. Sometimes, we need to add new attributes in the organized data, called attribute construction, which can ensure the accuracy of data in the large dataset. For example, given the height and width of a rectangle, we can add a new attribute area for better understanding.

There are several approaches of attribute selections, which are (i) stepwise forward selection, (ii) backward elimination, (iii) combination of (i) and (ii), and (iv) decision tree induction. These approaches will be discussed in Section 4.5.2.

The brute force approach uses all combinations of attribute values to determine each subset. For this reason, it is so much expensive. Rather, another way is used to find the best attribute, which is called the greedy approach. In this approach, an ideal value is chosen and methods of attribute selection are applied again and again until the probability value less than or equal to the ideal value [16, 17].

4.4.3   Discretization

Discretizing or dividing the large collection of data or attribute values into intervals is called as data discretization. It transforms quantitative data into qualitative data, i.e., data from one format to another. It is used to easily manipulate and evaluate the data. For example, if the "age" attribute contains the values 12, 15, 16, 18, 20, 33, 37, 43, 47, 60, 71, 74, 78, 80 as the people age, then we can discretize the values as young, mature, and old as follows:

Young: 12, 15, 16, 18, 20
Mature: 33, 37, 43, 47
Old: 71, 74, 78, 80

There are several approaches to discretization. These approaches fall into two classes: supervised, which needs known data to create the intervals, and unsupervised, which does not need any information to create the intervals [2, 18].

4.4.4   Concept Hierarchy Generation

Concept hierarchy [19] forms a group of level of attributes from lower to higher. We can consider an example of a concept hierarchy using the city locations in different countries as shown in Figure 4.7 [2]. That is, a city can be formed into a country. Here, the cities are Urbana, Chicago,

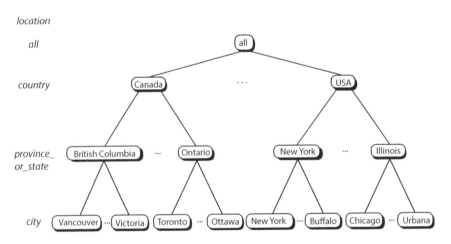

Figure 4.7 Example of concept hierarchy.

Vancouver, Victoria, Toronto, Ottawa, Network, Buffalo, etc. These cities can be grouped under province, e.g., Ottawa is under the state of Ontario. Again, states can be categorized under the country, e.g., Illinois can be under the country USA.

There are four techniques to create concept hierarchies. In the first approach, at the schema level, the concept hierarchy can be defined using a group of attributes. For example, in a given dataset if we consider the attributes of country, street, city, state, etc., the concept hierarchy can be defined as street < city < state < country. This approach can be called as the reordering of given attributes according to the user at the schema level. Another example can be in the case of electronics with attributes electronics, computers, accessory, etc. In this case, the concept hierarchy will be defined as accessory < computers < electronics.

In the second approach, explicit data with intermediate levels are grouped to form the concept hierarchy. For example, we consider a few intermediate data in the first approach like "{Saskatchewan, Alberta, Manitoba} ⊂ Prairies_Canada" and "{British_Columbia, Prairies_Canada} ⊂ Western_Canada."

In the third approach, no partial ordering of attribute is needed, and here, they are automatically generated. That is, concept hierarchy is constructed by automatically generating the ordering of attributes without using any partial ordering. The greatest distinct values are positioned at the bottom of the hierarchy. Figure 4.8 shows the automatically generated

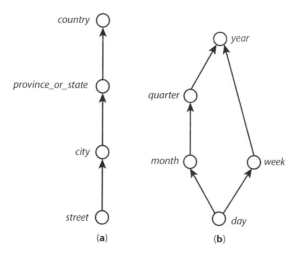

Figure 4.8 Example of automatic concept hierarchy.

concept hierarchy of different office locations in a region. An example of the exceptional case is weekday, month, quarter, and year.

In the last approach, only a few attributes are needed instead of using all attributes. It is called also the use of partial attributes. For example, sometimes, the user can notify only the city and street to indicate his location.

4.5   Data Reduction

We can collect huge amounts of data from different sources, e.g., twitter, facebook, news portals, linkedin, research gate, publon, etc. It is not so much difficult to collect those data but is difficult to analyze those dataset, which will take a lot of time and sometimes makes hardware failure, memory leakage problems, and storage inefficiency. Hence, some unnecessary data with selected attributes will be reduced so that data can be analyzed easily. This process of omitting the data is called data reduction. That is, it is a process by which data can be represented in a reduced set of volumes with exactly a similar analytical outcome. This technique is divided into data cube aggregation, attribute subset selection, numerosity, and dimensionality reduction [2, 20].

The dimensionality reduction uses the encoding techniques to produce a compressed version of the input data. These encoding techniques are principal component analysis and wavelet transforms. On the other hand, numerosity reduction replaces the data by alternative representations using the regression model.

4.5.1   Data Cube Aggregation

Data cube is a multidimensional matrix or array of data or facts. When we do coding to manipulate the data we use matrix. Actually, data are stored in a database, which consists of rows and columns, i.e., a matrix. Consider that we have collected the annual sales quarterly per year, i.e., every four months; we collect the sales from a company. But, we are interested to find the annual sales per year. Hence, we have to sum up the total sales in a year. The summation of sales per year is called as data cube aggregation. Figure 4.9 shows the data cube aggregation for the years 2008 to 2010. On the left side of Figure 4.9, total sales data are shown quarterly from year 2008 to 2010. To calculate the total sales per year, the aggregated data has been shown on the right side. The aggregated data now is smaller in size with no loss of any information [2, 3].

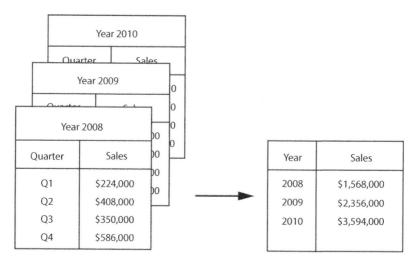

Figure 4.9 Sales data quarterly for years 2008 to 2010 are aggregated.

Data cube consists of cells or blank spaces. The default value is zero for each blank cell. The cube can help get any information within the database. For example, in Figure 4.10, someone is interested to retrieve the item "type", which has been made the greatest sales. Hence, aggregation can easily retrieve the solution [21].

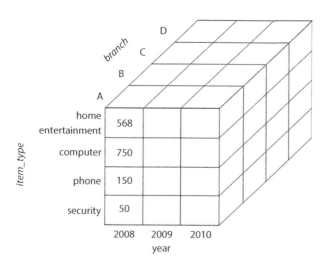

Figure 4.10 Data cube for sales.

4.5.2   Attribute Subset Selection

A huge amount of data is collected without any thinking of relevant or irrelevant data. We certainly analyze only a few features from the dataset. The remaining features are unnecessary. To properly analyze the data, at first, we need to ease the analysis by reducing the data size without any loss of important features. So, we can detect the relevant attributes and then remove the remaining irrelevant or redundant attributes. This is called the attribute subset selection. It is defined as "the process of determining the optimal subset from the given dataset according to the criteria of selecting optimal attribute" [22].

The brute force approach requires 2^n possible combinations for n attributes to generate the subset. It consumes much time to do it. So, a statistical approach, called greedy, is used to find the optimal subset of n attributes where an optimal threshold value is predefined.

Attribute subset selection can be done in various ways as shown in Figure 4.11 [2].

(i)   Stepwise forward selection is a process, which begins with an initially empty set. When an optimal attribute is found after iteration, then it is inserted at the set which was empty. The subset is then formed with the remaining iteration.

(ii)   Stepwise backward selection is a process, which begins with all original attributes. After each iteration, it omits the irrelevant attribute from the reduced set. This process continues until the optimal subset of an attribute is determined.

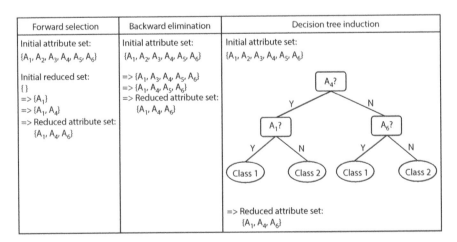

Figure 4.11 Example of attribute subset selection.

(iii)   A combination of forward selection and backward elimination is a process where the selection of appropriate attributes and the elimination of the worst one are determined at each iteration.

(iv)   Decision tree induction consists of a tree with parent and child node. Each attribute is used as a node where an algorithm is applied to check if the attribute is "best" or "worst". If the attribute is best, then it is put in a reduced subset.

4.5.3   Numerosity Reduction

Numerosity reduction is a reduction technique by which a huge amount of data can be reduced or represented within a much smaller subset of attributes. It can reduce the large volume of data by smaller forms of data representation. There are two ways of doing numerosity reduction, one is parametric and the other is nonparametric. In the parametric numerosity reduction technique, data are fitted by some models to reduce the size of data where only model parameters except the actual data parameters are used and stored. Some outliers may be stored within the model parameters. Examples of parametric models are log-linear and regression. While, in the nonparametric numerosity reduction technique, no such models are used, which need the data parameters. Here, the reduced representations of data are used. There are several approaches to nonparametric numerosity reduction techniques, namely, sampling, histograms, clustering, and data cube aggregation [23].

Parametric Numerosity Reduction Techniques

(i)   Regression is a model for estimating or predicting a numeric value using the given dataset. It is used to predict a land's value based on the land size location near to institutions, prices, etc. It is also used to predict the financial forecasting, market planning, and trends analysis. It can be linear and multivariate linear regression. In linear regression, only a single attribute is used to form a linear line by estimating the relationship between two attributes. Least square methods are used to properly fit the straight line. It uses the following equation of straight line

$$y = mx + b \tag{4.11}$$

where the relationship between attributes x and y is represented by a linear line with respect to y and x-axis. m and b are the regression coefficients, which indicate respectively the slope of the straight line and y-intercept. While, in multiple linear regression, two or more attributes as a linear function of y are used to form the regression.

(ii)   The log-linear model is used in such a situation when multidimensional attributes are needed to approximate into a smaller subset of dimensions. It reduces the very high dimensions of data into appropriate lower-dimensional space. For this reason, it is considered for data smoothing and dimensionality reduction.

Both regression and log-linear models can handle disperse data but they work well conditionally. Regression is useful to handle skewed data while log-linear models work well for large dimensions up to 10 or greater. There are several tools to analyze the regression and log-linearity problems, such as SPSS.

Nonparametric Numerosity Reduction Techniques

Here, we will discuss nonparametric numerosity reduction techniques.

(i)   Sampling is a statistical analysis approach, which reduces the size of data in data mining by selecting the subset from the given dataset. Sampling techniques can be categorized in two ways: probability sampling and non-probability sampling [24, 25].

Probability sampling also called random sampling selects or chooses the items or data randomly without any manual selection. There are several approaches to probability sampling as follows.

(a)   Simple Random Sampling
In this approach, each data or item has an equal possibility to be selected as the sample as there is no prior information.

(b)   Stratified Sampling
This approach divides the total data items into some subgroups using homogeneous and heterogeneous properties. In this approach, prior information is needed to identify the homogeneous and heterogeneous properties.

(c) Systematic Sampling

Systematic clustering selects each cluster after fixed interval among the group of clusters without using any random selection of those except the first selection of clusters. That means, first cluster is selected randomly and then an interval is used for selecting another cluster. For example, consider 20 clusters, namely, C_1, C_2, C_3,..., C_{20}. If each cluster consists of four attributes and the second cluster, C_2, is selected randomly, then according to the systematic clustering approach, the next cluster will be $(20/4)+2=5+2=7$, i.e., 7th cluster will be used.

(d) Cluster Sampling

Cluster sampling partitions the dataset into several groups with similar properties. After creating the clusters from the dataset, each cluster is selected randomly. Cluster sampling can be of two types: single-stage and two-stage. In single-stage clustering, a cluster is selected randomly. While, in two-stage clustering, some attributes are selected randomly after finding the randomly selected cluster.

(e) Multi-Stage Sampling

Combination of random, stratified, systematic, and or cluster sampling is called as multi-stage sampling.

Non-probability sampling, also called non-random sampling, does not use random selection to select any item. There are several techniques of non-probability sampling as follows.

i. Convenience Sampling

This approach uses the available dataset as the sample. This is used when the data is not available.

ii. Purposive Sampling

This approach uses those data as the sample, which fits best for specific criteria.

iii. Quota Sampling

It uses those attributes as the sample if there exists sufficient values in various groups.

iv. Referral/Snowball Sampling

It is used in such a situation when the dataset is completely unknown.

(ii)   Histogram is a data reduction technique that shows a visual interpretation of the dataset by partitioning the distribution of dataset into disjoint subsets in terms of frequency of similar data. These subsets are called buckets or bins. Subsets can be formed in terms of the frequency of single attribute value or the ranges of attribute values. If a single attribute is used to form the bins, then it is called as singleton bins or buckets. If the ranges of attribute values are used, then it is known as multiton buckets. Consider the following list of items sold by a company in ascending order as follows:

1, 1, 5, 5, 5, 5, 5, 8, 8, 10, 10, 10, 10, 12, 14, 14, 14, 15, 15, 15, 15, 15, 15, 18, 18, 18, 18, 18, 18, 18, 18, 20, 20, 20, 20, 20, 20, 20, 21, 21, 21, 21, 25, 25, 25, 25, 25, 28, 28, 30, 30, 30.

Figure 4.12 illustrates the concept of singleton buckets. Basically, partitioning of data can be in two ways: equal frequency and equal width. In equal frequency histogram analysis, the frequency of similar data, i.e., how many times a number or value occurs in a dataset is represented visually. For example, from the above list, 5 occur 5 times, 10 occur 4 times, 20 occur 7 times, and so on, which has been implemented in Figure 4.12.

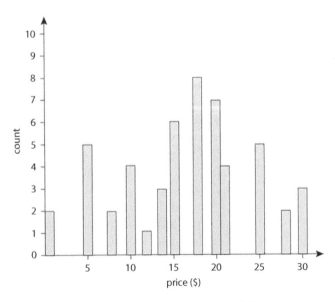

Figure 4.12 Example of histogram using singleton with equal frequency.

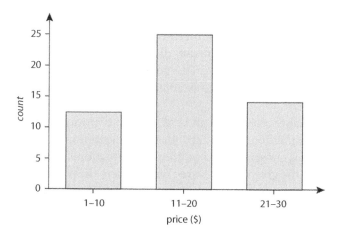

Figure 4.13 Example of histogram using multiton with equal width.

On the other hand, an equal width histogram uses the range of data and counts the total frequency of similar data within that range.

For example, from the above list, we see 1 occurs 2 times, 5 occurs 5 times, 8 occurs 2 times, and 10 occurs 4 times, 20 occurs 7 times, and so on. Now, we consider the ranges for the above list as 1–10, 11–20, and 21–30. For range 1–10, an equal width histogram represents the total frequency as 13 (2 + 5 + 2 + 4 = 13), which has been implemented in Figure 4.13.

- Clustering consists of similar objects or attributes or sets of attributes. Objects in one cluster carry different properties from the objects of another cluster. Thus, data redundancy is minimized and the analysis will be easier because one can find similar objects in a particular cluster. In Section 4.2.2, clustering has been discussed in detail.
- Data Cube Aggregation is an aggregation of certain data in a data cube to represent the reduced data without any loss of information. It has been discussed in Section 4.5.1.

4.5.4   Dimensionality Reduction

Generally, dimensionality reduction is a way of minimizing the dimension of certain features, i.e., minimizing certain attributes or variables. Reduction or minimization is done in such a way that analysis can be done easily without losing major features. Sometimes, when analyzing important features with higher dimensions does not exist with the features with lower dimensions, then the curse of dimensionality occurs. Dimensionality reduction can be applied in several applications, e.g., text mining, face recognition, digit recognition, protein classification, intrusion detection, etc. The goal of dimensionality reduction is to use a low-dimensional representation of data with possibly important information.

Dimensionality reduction can be done into two ways: feature selection and feature extraction techniques. In feature selection, the subset of the given features is chosen under nonlinear combination. In feature reduction or extraction, the given features are chosen where the transformed features are the linear combination.

Linear Dimensionality Reduction

There are several approaches to linear dimensionality reduction by feature extractions. These are principal component analysis (PCA), factor analysis (FA), linear discriminant analysis (LDA).

(i) Principal Component Analysis (PCA) is one of the most popular approaches of linear, orthogonal dimensionality reduction, which is used to bring the higher dimensionality features into lower dimensions by feature extraction [26]. It uses the correlation among the attributes using a set of smaller linear transformations. These transformations are known as components. PCA changes the direction of data with the increase of variance. When new features with maximum variance are created, then they are called principal components (PCs). During the analysis, it is noted: (a) total number of PCs <= Initial features, (b) First PC is a linear combination which carries maximum variance of the given features [27] (c) Second PC is a linear combination, which carries variance of as much not extracted by the first PC. Basically, PCs are weighted summation or linear combinations of the initial variables. Here, the first and second principal components (PC1 and PC2) are expressed by the following equations.

$$PC_1 = \alpha_{11}x_1 + \alpha_{12}x_2 +... \alpha_{1n}x_n = \alpha_1 x \qquad (4.12)$$

$$PC_2 = \alpha_{21}x_1 + \alpha_{22}x_2 +... \alpha_{2n}x_n = \alpha_2 x \qquad (4.13)$$

Principal components do not correlate with each other. Figure 4.14 shows the orthogonal directions of the initial variables. PC_1 and PC_2 show the variations using linear combinations.

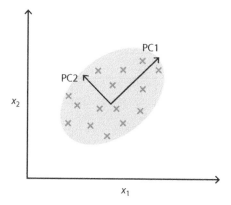

Figure 4.14 Two principal components with sample values.

From Section 4.3.1, we have defined the mean and standard deviation for n given attributes. Here, we need to know the calculation of variance and correlation. Variance of attribute set x is

$$\sigma^2 = \frac{1}{n-1}\left[\left(x_1 - \bar{x}\right)^2 + \left(x_2 - \bar{x}\right)^2 + \ldots + \left(x_n - \bar{x}\right)^2\right] \quad (4.14)$$

Correlation is used to determine the relationship between two features, i.e., how they are related to each other. Considering two vectors $x = x_1$, $x_2, \ldots, x_n$ and $y = y_1, y_2, \ldots, y_n$, the correlation $cor(x, y)$ is determined after calculating covariance $cov(x, y)$ as follows:

$$cov\left(x, y\right) = \frac{1}{n-1}\left[\left(x_1 - \bar{x}\right)\left(y_1 - \bar{y}\right) + \left(x_2 - \bar{x}\right)\left(y_2 - \bar{y}\right) + \ldots + \left(x_n - \bar{x}\right)\left(y_n - \bar{y}\right)\right]$$

$$cor\left(x, y\right) = \frac{cov\left(x, y\right)}{\sigma^x \sigma^y}$$

4.16

where σ^x and σ^y are standard deviations, which can be calculated from Equation 4.9. Consider the dataset for houses in a region shown in Table 4.1. Dataset has been featured using four dimensions. How can you differentiate or characterize one house from another using those features? It is not so easy to visualize the importance of those values. At first, we can

Table 4.1 Dataset for house values in district.

House no.	Value	Area	Floors	Household
1	148	72	4	20
2	156	76	4	22
3	160	86	4	22
4	165	79	4	24
5	169	88	5	30
6	184	90	5	35

determine the variance of each feature and select the maximum variance to get a better analysis [29]. Using Equation 4.14 of variance, we can find the values of variance of respective features as follows:

$$\sigma^2_{value} = 27$$

$$\sigma^2_{Area} = 43$$

$$\sigma^2_{Floor} = 0.2$$

$$\sigma^2_{Household} = 0.28$$

We found the variances of area and value are 43 and 127, respectively. That means if we use those features, i.e., "area" and "value" than "floor" and "household", then they can be very much informative and helpful to represent the data that can help easily distinguish the houses. From Table 4.1, we see that Value is approximately twice of Area and Household is five times of Floors. That means we can deduce the property of one from another without using two at a time. So, this is known as covariance. When the value of covariance for two variables (that can be calculated from Equation 4.15) is high, then those two variables are highly correlated (which can be calculated from Equation 4.16), i.e., there can be some redundant data. So, there is little possibility to differentiate two items as there is redundancy with less information.

(ii) Factor Analysis (FA) is a technique to minimize the variables in a specific number of factors to explore the data for patterns. It is related to PCA, but two are not similar. In PCA, we consider those components if they (a) have maximum variance, (b) are orthogonal to other components, (c) have a linear transformation of the observed features. While, in FA, factors require (a) covariance among items, i.e., items are correlated to each other, (b) not to be orthogonal, (c) linear combination as like as PCA, i.e., factors should be combined linearly with other factors. Figure 4.15 shows an example of FA where unobserved latent variables or factors are noticed. Finding these unobserved variables or factors, researchers can draw a summary of their work. It is used in finance, advertising, market research, psychology, etc. [30–32]. Factor analysis can be classified as Exploratory Factor Analysis (EFA) and Confirmatory Factor Analysis (CFA) [33]. CFA and EFA are used in scale development and adaptation studies. Generally, EFA is used when there is no relationship among the features while if the similarity among items is found, then CFA is preferred.

That means we can use EFA if we have no information about the variable, called as manifest or indicator variables. In EFA, we need to create the variables and here we have no assumption of how many they will be created. On the other hand, in CFA, we have prior knowledge about the indicator variables [34–36].

(iii) Linear Discriminant Analysis (LDA) ensures maximum separation among the classes by projecting the attribute values, unlike PCA where

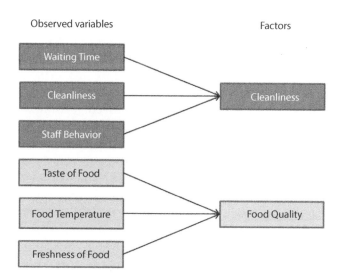

Figure 4.15 Example of factor analysis.

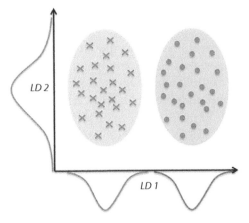

Figure 4.16 Class separation by linear discriminant analysis.

variance among the components is important not the classification. Figure 4.16 shows the class separation by linear discriminant analysis using the projection among attribute values.

Nonlinear Dimensionality Reduction

When data or attribute values are not transformed in a linear way, then we have to do it in a non-linear way. That is, non-linear dimensionality reduction is a way of reducing the dimensions of certain features in non-linear form. Actually, sometimes data are organized in such a form that the linear transformation of the dataset does not work to predict the target values [27, 28].

Non-linear dimension reduction techniques [37] are categorized by kernel-based and manifold-learning based techniques. Kernel-based approaches transform the given features into higher dimensional structures. This approach helps the transformed data to work with the linear techniques. It can be sub-classified as kernel principal component analysis (KPCA) [38] and kernel Fisher discriminant analysis (KFDA) [39] [40]. Unlike kernel approaches, the manifold-learning based approach gives the full concentration of working with the lower-dimensional data without transforming it to higher-dimension. Available approaches of manifold-learning are local linear embedding [41], isometric feature mapping [42], Laplacian Eigen map [43], and graph embedding [44].

4.6   Conclusion

The world is surrounded by a lot of data. Most of these huge amounts of data are inconsistent, disconnected, irrelevant, etc. Data preprocessing is a necessary step in data mining that helps easily analyze the data. It is such a technique, which is used to transform the data in an acceptable format so that the consistency and quality of data are maintained. It includes certain techniques to complete the preparation of data. These are data cleaning, data integration, data transformation, and data reduction. In this chapter, we have discussed how to measure the quality of data, address missing data, clean the noisy data, and perform the transformation on certain variables.

Acknowledgements

The author would like to thank the anonymous reviewers, Editors and Publisher of the book.

References

1. Sarkar, A., Automatic bangla text summarization using term frequency and semantic similarity approach, in: *21st International Conference of Computer and Information Technology (ICCIT)*, pp. 1–6, 2018, December 2018.
2. Han, J. and Kamber, M., *Data Mining: Concepts and Techniques (3 ed.)*, Morgan Kaufmann Publishers Inc., US, 2012.
3. Garcia, S., *Data preprocessing in data mining*, Springer, Cham, 2014.
4. Yin, Y., *Data mining: Concepts, methods and applications in management and engineering design*, Springer, London, 2011.
5. Wang, J., *Data mining: Opportunities and challenges*, Idea Group Pub., Hershey, Pa, 2003.
6. Gorunescu, F., *Data mining: Concepts, models and techniques*, Springer, Berlin; Heidelberg, 2011.
7. Wu, Y., MaxBin: An automated binning method to recover individual genomes from metagenomes using an expectation-maximization algorithm. *Microbiome*, 2, 1, 26, 2014.
8. Fernández-Delgado, M., An extensive experimental survey of regression methods. *Neural Networks*, 111, 11–34, 2019.
9. Doan, A., Reconciling schemas of disparate data sources: A machine-learning approach. *ACM SIGMOD Record*, 30, 2, 509–520, 2001.
10. Doan, A., Learning to match the schemas of data sources: A multistrategy approach. *Mach. Learn.*, 50, 3, 279–301, 2003.

11. Kusiak, A., Feature transformation methods in data mining. *IEEE Trans. Electron. Packag. Manuf.*, 24, 3, 214–221, 2001.

12. Lin, T.Y., Attribute transformations for data mining I: Theoretical explorations. *Int. J. Intell. Syst.*, 17, 2, 213–222, 2002.

13. Bhandare, S.K., Data perturbation method for privacy preserving data mining based on Z-Score normalization. *Int. J. Adv. Res. Comput. Sci.*, 2, 5, 334–339, 2011.

14. Tan, K., A hybrid evolutionary algorithm for attribute selection in data mining. *Expert Syst. Appl.*, 36, 4, 8616–8630, 2009.

15. Sangeetha, R., Preprocessing using attribute selection in data stream mining. *2018 3rd International Conference on Communication and Electronics Systems (ICCES)*, pp. 431–438, 2018, October.

16. Bolón-Canedo, V., *Feature Selection for High-Dimensional Data*, Springer International Publishing: Imprint: Springer, Cham, 2015.

17. Witten, I.H., *Data mining: Practical machine learning tools and techniques*, 3rd ed, Morgan Kaufmann Publishers, Burlington, Mass, 2011.

18. Abraham, R., A comparative analysis of discretization methods for Medical Data mining with Naive Bayesian classifier. *9th International Conference on Information Technology (ICIT'06)*, pp. 235–236, 2006, December.

19. Modak, M., Privacy preserving distributed association rule hiding using concept hierarchy. *Procedia Comput. Sci.*, 79, 993–1000, 2016.

20. Houari, R., Dimensionality reduction in data mining: A Copula approach. *Expert Syst. Appl.*, 64, 247–260, 2016.

21. Riedewald, M., Agrawal, D., El Abbadi, A., Flexible data cubes for online aggregation, in: *Lecture Notes in Computer Science. vol. 1973*, Springer, Berlin, Heidelberg, 2001.

22. Demisse, G.B., Tadesse, T., Bayissa, Y., Data mining attribute selection approach for drought modeling: A case study for Greater Horn of Africa. *Int. J. Data Min. Knowl. Manage. Process*, 7, 4, 1–16, 2017.

23. Kalegele, K., Numerosity reduction for resource con-strained Learning. *J. Inf. Process.*, 21, 2, 329–341, 2013.

24. Ramos Rojas, J.A., Sampling techniques to improve big data exploration. *IEEE 7th Symposium on Large Data Analysis and Visualization (LDAV)*, pp. 26–35, 2017, October.

25. Lutu, P., Database sampling for data mining. Encyclopedia of data warehousing and mining, Second Edition. *IGI Global*, 604–609, 2009.

26. Larose, D.T., *Data Mining and Predictive Analytics (2.)*, John Wiley Sons, Incorporated, New York, 2015.

27. Kazor, K., Comparison of linear and nonlinear dimension reduction techniques for automated process monitoring of a decentralized wastewater treatment facility. *Stochastic Environ. Res. Risk Assess.*, 30, 5, 1527–1544, 2016.

28. Lee, J.A. and Verleysen, M., *Nonlinear Dimensionality Reduction*, Springer Science+Business Media, LLC, New York, NY, 2007.

29. Abdullatif, H. *Dimensionality Reduction For Dummies. Part 1*, 2018. https://towardsdatascience.com.
30. Wang, H.F. and Kuo, C.Y., Factor analysis in data mining. *J. Comput. Math. Appl.*, 48, 1765–1778, 2004.
31. Zhirong, L., Data mining algorithm application in influencing factors analysis of college students' physical health. *RISTI - Revista Iberica de Sistemas e Tecnologias de Informacao*, E12, 189–201, 2016.
32. https://en.wikipedia.org/wiki/Factor_analysis.
33. Bandalos, D.L. and Finney, S.J., Factor analysis: Exploratory and confirmatory, in: *The reviewer's guide to quantitative methods in the social science*, G.R. Hancock, R.O. Mueller (Ed.), pp. 93–114, Routledge, New York, NY, 2010.
34. Souza, W.E., Factor analysis in data mining applied for recogni- tion and classification pattern for smart grid, in: *IEEE PES Conference on Innovative Smart Grid Technologies (ISGT Latin America)*, pp. 1–8, 2013, April.
35. Kline, R.B., *Principles and practice of structural equation modelling (3rd ed)*, Guilford Press, New York, 2011.
36. Orcan, F., Exploratory and confirmatory factor analysis: Which one to use first? *J. Meas. Eval. Educ. Psychol.*, 9, 4, 414–421, 2018.
37. Yang, J., Jin, Z., Yang, J., Non-linear techniques for dimension reduction, in: *Encyclopedia of Biometrics*, Li S.Z., Jain A. (eds.), pp. 1001–1007, Springer, Boston, MA, 2009.
38. Schölkopf, B., Smola, A., Muller, K.R., Nonlinear component analysis as a kernel eigenvalue problem. *J. Neural Comput. IEEE*, 10, 5, 1299–1319, 1998.
39. Mika, S., Rätsch, G., Weston, J., Schölkopf, B., Müller, K.R., Fisher discriminant analysis with kernels, in: *IEEE International Workshop on Neural Networks for Signal Processing IX*, Madison (USA), pp. 41–48, 1999.
40. Baudat, G. and Anouar, F., Generalized discriminant analysis using a kernel approach. *J. Neural Comput. IEEE*, 12, 10, 2385–2404, 2000.
41. Roweis, S.T. and Saul, L.K., Nonlinear dimensionality reduction by locally linear embedding. *Sci. Mag. MIT Press*, 290, 2323–2326, 2000.
42. Tenenbaum, J.B., de Silva, V., Langford, J.C., A global geometric frame- work for nonlinear dimensionality reduction. *Sci. Mag. MIT Press*, 290, 2319–2323, 2000.
43. Belkin, M. and Niyogi, P., Laplacian eigenmaps for dimensionality reduction and data representation. *J. Neural Comput. IEEE*, 15, 6, 1373–1396, 2003.
44. Yan, S., Xu, D., Zhang, B., Zhang, H.J., Yang, Q., Lin, S., Graph embedding and extensions: A general framework for dimensionality reduction. *J. IEEE Trans. Pattern Anal. Mach. Intell.*, 29, 1, 40–51, 2007.

5

Big Data

R. Chinnaiyan

*Department of Information Science and Engineering,
CMR Institute of Technology, Bengaluru, India*

Abstract

Massive amount of data is created, processed, stored, and communicated every moment with the advancement of information and communication technologies. Analytics of these datasets needs plenty of hard work at numerous stages for information extraction and rational decision making. The objective of this entire chapter is to see the insights of big data tools and techniques. Also, this chapter narrates all the use cases of big data in the fields of Machine Learning, Cloud Computing, and Internet of Things. As a result, this entire chapter provides a clear picture about the Big Data concepts, tools, techniques, and use cases. It opens an innovative opportunities for the researchers in the bringing novel solutions for challenging issues and problems of the society.

Keywords: Data, extraction, decision making, big data, machine learning, cloud computing, IoT

5.1 Introduction

Big data is technique which surpasses the handling ability of obsolete database structures. The data is excessively big, changes too speedy, and is not suitable for the configurations of our database designs [1, 2]. To advance value from this data, individual must adopt a substitute technique to process it. Daily 2.5 quintillion bytes of data to a countless range of 90% of the data in the biosphere today have been designed in the past two years only. It is predicted that the development of big data is assessed to touch 25 billion by 2015 [3].

Email: vijayachinns@gmail.com; chinnaiyan.r@cmrit.ac.in

Uma N. Dulhare, Khaleel Ahmad and Khairol Amali Bin Ahmad (eds.) Machine Learning and Big Data: Concepts, Algorithms, Tools and Applications, (105–130) © 2020 Scrivener Publishing LLC

Big data is one of the growing technologies for the next age group of information and communication-based industries [4], which are largely made on the third platform, mostly mentioning to big data, cloud computing, Internet of Things (IoT), and societal trade.

There is a necessity for labeling the data revolt [5]. Considerable investigation was conceded out by many scientists on big data with its inclinations [6–8]. An outline to examine data and information is deliberated through Das and Kumar [12]. Likewise, facet clarification of data investigation for public tweets was also conferred through [13, 19]. Big data analytics handles enormous volume of datasets as listed in Table 5.1. The input data to big data systems could be babbled from

- Social and collaboration networks
- Log files from web server
- Sensor data and data from satellite images
- Audio and video streams
- Transactions in bank
- Web pages content data
- Government documents and files
- Telemetry from automobiles
- Data from financial markets.

This chapter focuses on the basic concepts, issues, challenges, tools and techniques, and big data applications. Furthermore, open research problems are discussed.

Table 5.1 Memory symbolize and size: handled by big data.

S. No.	Memory	Symbolize	Size
1	1 Kilobyte	KB	10^3
2	1 Megabyte	MB	10^6
3	1 Gigabyte	GB	10^9
4	1 Terabyte	TB	10^{12}
5	1 Petabyte	PB	10^{15}
6	1 Exabyte	EB	10^{18}
7	1 Zettabyte	ZB	10^{21}
8	1 Yottabyte	YB	10^{24}

5.2   Big Data Evaluation With Its Tools

The term Big Data was conceived by Roger Mougalas in the year 2005. Big data and the quest to recognize availability data is somewhat that has been in presence in extensive period. Table 5.2 lists the big data analytics evolution and Table 5.3 list the big data analytics tools evolution.

5.3   Architecture of Big Data

Big data is a field that analyzes and systematically extracts the information from other data sets. Figure 5.1 depicts the big data architectural framework.

5.3.1   Big Data Analytics Framework Workflow

- i. Big data sources
- ii. Batch data storage
- iii. Real-time message incorporation
- iv. Batch processing
- v. Stream processing and machine learning
- vi. Analytical big data store
- vii. Big data analytics
- viii. Reporting

Table 5.2 Big data analytics evolution.

S. No.	Year	Technology	Key enablers
1.	1950's	Highly Complex Data (Unstructured)	
2.	1970's	Statistical Techniques	
3.	1980's	Data Mining Techniques	
4.	1990's	Business-Intelligence 1.0 (BI 1.0)	Enterprise wide Information-Systems
5.	2000's	Business-Analytics 2.0 (BI 2.0)	Internet, Web-Based Systems
6.	2010's	Big-Data-Analytics 3.0 (BI 3.0)	RFID, Sensor-Based Devices and Internet of Things

Table 5.3 Big data analytics tools evolution.

Evolution of big data tools			
1.	2003	Google File System	Batch
2.	2004	MapReduce—Simplified Processing of Big Cluster	
3.	2005	Doug Cutting Starts Developing Hadoop	
4.	2006	Yahoo starts working on Hadoop	
5.	2008	Hadoop comes to production	
6.	2009	Yahoo creates pig Facebook creates Hive	
7.	2010	Yahoo creates S4 Cloudera creates Flume	
8.	2011	Nathan Marz creates Strom Spark is Released	
9.	2012	LinkedIn creates kafka Nathan Marz defines lamda architecture	Real Time
10.	2013	LinkedIn creates Samza Start Lambdoop and Summingbird	
11.	2014	Stratosphere evolves Flink Jay kreps defines kappa architecture	Hybrid
12	2015	Kudu is released by Cloudera	
13	2016	Google Creates Beam	

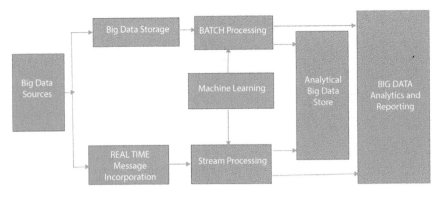

Figure 5.1 Big data architectural framework.

5.4   Issues and Challenges

Pace growth of big data caused new-fangled issues and challenges in data administration and investigation. Three vital issues are volume, variety, velocity. In this section, 10 V's of big data were discussed. Each V characterizes a vital problem of technical research that needs a debate. Table 5.4 lists the 10 V's of big data.

The important 10 V's of big data are depicted in the Figure 5.2, which clearly symbolizes the benefits of big data analytics. The features of big data [47, 48] are categorized into three V's and are explained below.

5.4.1   Volume

The volume of huge data refers to the enormous quantity of data generated every second through some digital universe. All devices are connected to sensors that produce a huge volume of data every second [11, 14]. In case of health care, about 2.5 billion terabytes of data are generated every year oil and refineries also generate huge amount of data through the sensors connected to it.

Table 5.4 10 V's of big data.

S. No.	10 V's	Meaning
1	Volume	Enormous volume of real-time flowing data
2	Variety	Text dataset, images data, music data, videos data, graphical data
3	Velocity	Rapidity movement of data from several bases
4	Veracity	Reliable dataset incoming from several locations
5	Validity	Dataset storing in terms of authenticity and stages of time
6	Value	Value of dataset kept and work out the earnestness
7	Variability	Altering the dataset with dataset flow
8	Venue	Storage and retrieval of dataset
9	Vocabulary	Linguistic compactness and understanding
10	Vague	Dataset unstructured

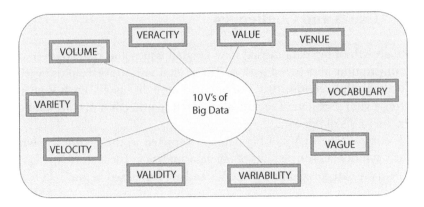

Figure 5.2 10 V's of big data.

5.4.2 Variety of Data

In recent years, the data is generated in a huge way that leads from structured to unstructured data. Varieties of data sources are available such as

- Data through Internet
- Research (primary and secondary)
- Location data (GPS, Google Map)
- Image and data from devices like sensors

5.4.3 Velocity

Velocity denotes to the rapidity at which the data is made and transformed. It also specifies the amount by which the facts are been created, stored, analyzed, and viewed. Nowadays, real time data are generated through various devices connected through internet, sensors, cables etc., through which data are transformed immediately as when it is created.

5.5 Big Data Analytics Tools

Many analytics tools are available to process big data. Here, we talk over some present methods for examining big data with emphasis on fifteen significant evolving tools. Many researchers proposed an excellent list of big data tools and techniques [6, 34]. Table 5.5 lists the big data tools.

Table 5.5 Big data tools.

S. No.	Big data tool name	S. No.	Big data tool name
1	Apache Hadoop	9	Storm
2	CDH (Cloudera Distribution for Hadoop)	10	Apache SAMOA
3	Cassandra	11	Talend

(Continued)

Table 5.5 Big data tools. (*Continued*)

S. No.	Big data tool name	S. No.	Big data tool name
4	Knime	12	Rapidminer
5	Datawrapper	13	Qubole
6	MongoDB	14	Tableau

(*Continued*)

Table 5.5 Big data tools. (*Continued*)

S. No.	Big data tool name	S. No.	Big data tool name
7	Lumify	15	R
8	HPCC		

5.6 Big Data Use Cases

- Banking and finance
- Fraud detection
- Customer division and personalized marketing
- Customer support
- Risk management
- Life time value prediction
- Cyber security analytics
- Insurance industry
- Health care sector
- Internet of Things
- Weather forecasting
- Telecom

5.6.1 Banking and Finance

The bank and finance service industries were changed proportionally after the growth of big data analytics. Improved regularity inspection combined with greater client prospects has posed severer experiments and new research works to those companies. On the way to attain this, both bank and finance service organizations are taking on big data tools to bring improved services and improve the customer satisfaction with the following diver set of solutions.

- Customized solutions
- Fraud detection
- Risk management
- Customer services

5.6.2 Fraud Detection

Community dataset, such as provided data and programmers for health care processes, is combined and handled over the big data. This processed and analyzed data which performed enormous de-normalization to dispense data into numerous tables and fields. Figure 5.3 depicts the fraud detection using big data.

5.6.3 Customer Division and Personalized Marketing

Customer division in any company involves a group of people or organization to manage customer complaints and feedback and responses and

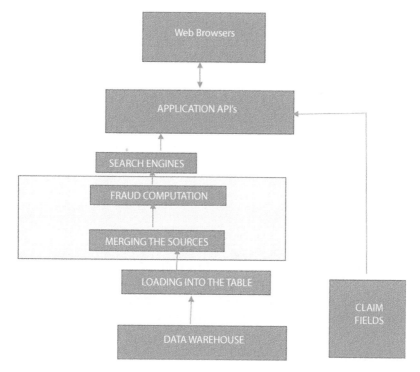

Figure 5.3 Fraud detection using big data.

to gain more information about their needs. Division is more like happening certain responsibilities to a group of people based on their qualifications and capabilities [19]. Figure 5.4 depicts the customer division using big data.

5.6.4   Customer Support

Here are some of the ways that big data is supporting revolutionary customer service.

1. Access to available resources
2. Accessibility to assistance
3. Enhanced response time
4. Responsiveness and sympathy
5. Anticipating the customer requirements
6. Increase the problem solving efficiency
7. Personalized customer support

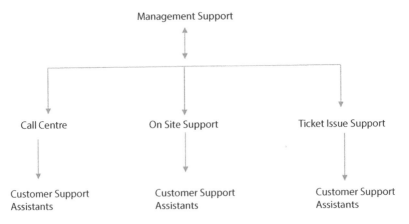

Figure 5.4 Customer division using big data.

Big data for customer support can be done in the following variety of ways, such as analyst, marketing operations, product manager analytical support, sales operations, developers support, operational analyst support, product support, business users support, and data architect support.

5.6.5   Risk Management

Figure 5.5 depicts the risk management using big data. Big data helps the companies in handling the following risks.

- Fraud detection and management
- Credit management
- Money laundering cases detection and management
- Market and commercial loans
- Operational risk management
- Integrated risk management

5.6.6   Life Time Value Prediction

One needs to identify these behavior patterns, segment, and act accordingly. Calculating life time value is very easy. It can be selected for a duration of 12 months and 24 months where it can be used by using opt formula.

Life time value = Total Gross Revenue – Total Cost

- Things to be done for life time value prediction
- Defining appropriate time frame for customer life time value calculation

Figure 5.5 Risk analytics and management using big data.

- Check if useful
- Build and run machine learning models for life time value prediction

5.6.7   Cyber Security Analytics

Numerous security procedures were faced by the use cases of big data such as network scaling, hand held devices, mobile banking, electronic funds transfer, electronic data interchange, security monitoring [24], and absence of intrusion system [25, 26]. In cyber security, big data techniques find an application in the following ways.

- Analyzing large networks for vulnerability
- Helps in the efficient retrieval of information "track files" which are really large files containing billions of leached passwords which can be used to test the security of the system
- Using cloud to better help brute forcing by reducing the time taken
- Using natural network to analyze the system such as network and databases for vulnerabilities

5.6.8   Insurance Industry

Big data analytics is a novel technology that supports insurance industries in handling tough situations and taking rational decisions by providing them with intuitive insights on available big data. Big data use cases in insurance industries represent that what a business can fix, given the precise insights. Figure 5.6 depicts the insurance industry handling using big data.

Role of Big Data in Insurance Industry

- Customer acquisition
- Customer retention
- Risk assessment
- Fraud detection and management
- Cost reductions

5.6.9   Health Care Sector

Health care big data denotes to gathering examining and leveraging the patient's medical diagnosis data that is huge or difficult to be recognize by old-fashioned means of statistics handling [21, 22, 23]. Big data analytics is usually handled by machine learning algorithm and data securities. Numerous research has been made by the researchers for solving the issues of health sector face [9, 50]. Figure 5.7 depicts the health care handling using big data.

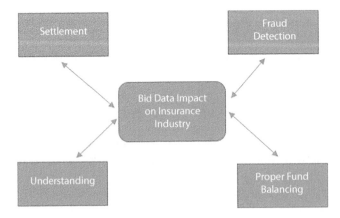

Figure 5.6 Insurance industry handling using big data.

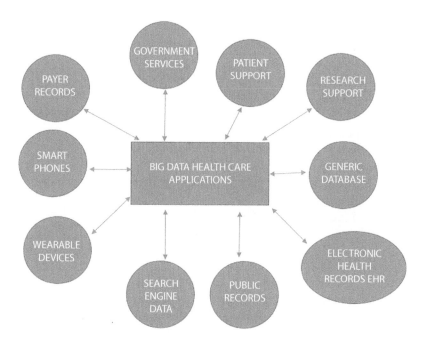

Figure 5.7 Health care handling using big data.

Needs of Big-Data Analytics in Health Care Sector

- Doctors rely on patient's clinical health records [44] which mean a huge amount of data in present and processing this by using old techniques is very tedious and slow and inefficient [33, 35].
- From patient records to billing systems, there is certainly a large variety of data driving the need for big data to tackle this.
- The real challenge is how to process and analyze such huge amount of data to predict outcomes and make decisions. There is a need for development of new infrastructure which can integrate this large variety of data.

Examples of Big Data Analytics in Health Care

1. Predictive analytics in healthcare
2. Electronic health records
3. Real-time monitoring
4. Prevention of prescribing and medication errors

Sources of Big Data
This method is so operative in healthcare societies and is utilized to achieve:

- Health challenges and issues of patients and all diseased people
- Detection of frauds and its effective management
- Medical diagnosis and treatment of patients using clinical support system
- Effective research and development and utilization of medical drugs
- Introduction of novel treatments for disorders like cancer, diabetes, etc.
- Product analytics before it reaches market

5.6.9.1   Big Data Medical Decision Support

The medical decision support system (MDSS) is vital area that is done via big data analytics and the targets are set by experts to rise the patient health care services by improving the outcomes [10]. The main aim of this MDSS system is to propose the valid information to the patients and their relatives on right time [49]. It helps the doctors, pharmaceuticals, and patients to be aware of the information in any specific medical related data [49, 50].

5.6.9.2   Big Data–Based Disorder Management

It helps to analyze various disorders and its origin by using the clinical examination. This helps in find the accurate information by enabling the outcomes of the patient disorders. This involves the data support from several groups, therapeutic depositories, and the persons.

5.6.9.3   Big Data–Based Patient Monitoring and Control

Using prescriptive analytics in big data clarifications, patient-centric medical method is initiated. Information and communication engineering domain helps to find the previous disorder datasets and its management system through which patient's disorder can be cured by knowing the indications of the disorder instead of generic conclusion on disorder.

5.6.9.4   Big Data–Based Human Routine Analytics

This approach is aimed to offer the optimal solutions based on numerous means and also different lifestyle of the human beings. Today, identifying the various causes of health-related issues and disorders and lifestyle of a human being plays a foremost role. This helps in studying the impacts and the causes of human routine.

5.6.10   Internet of Things

Big data analytics provides a wide variety of support for IoT-based applications. Mishra, Lin, and Chang [27] have done much research in the areas of big data and IoT. Also, much researches were done in the novel technologies that are related with IoT [28]. Figure 5.8 depicts the IoT applications using big data, namely, smart phones, smart vehicles, smart home lighting, smart home, smart music player, smart kitchen, smart dust bin, smart washroom management, smart agriculture, smart cattle farming, smart fish farming, smart services, etc. and are depicted in the following Figure 5.8.

5.6.11   Weather Forecasting

With an abundance of satellites and remote sensing devices monitoring weather systems all ones the world, meteorologists now have more data available to them than even before. But more data does not necessarily

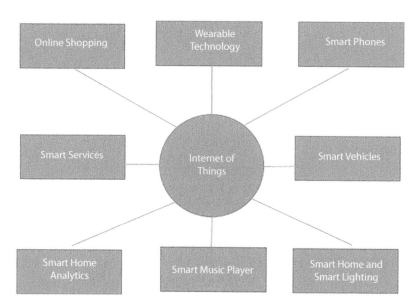

Figure 5.8 Internet of Things applications using big data.

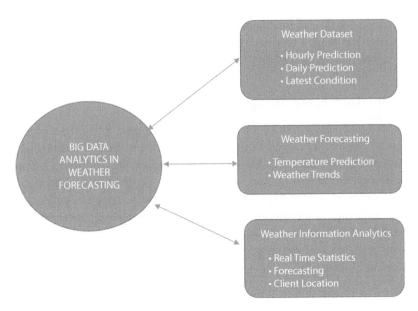

Figure 5.9 Weather forecasting applications using big data.

translate into improved predictions. Cloud computing and big data are key factors for the success of weather decision operations. Figure 5.9 depicts the weather forecasting applications using big data.

5.7   Where IoT Meets Big Data

The data generated from IoT devices or sensors needs a big data platform to collect historical and current data and discover the insights using big data tools and build a machine learning model to predict the devices health or apply the data to any industry specific use cases mentioned in the above section.

5.7.1   IoT Platform

The below diagram depicts the components that are required to setup an IoT platform and the communication between the different components. The role of IoT edge and cloud platform [42, 43, 46] which controls the IoT devices, sensors, and gateway is also explained below. Figure 5.10 depicts the IoT components and topology.

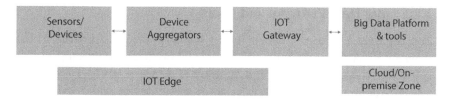

Figure 5.10 IoT components and topology.

5.7.2 Sensors or Devices

The sensors or wearable or tags or actuators emit the data in the form of binary or prescribed format with a supported protocol.

Examples:

- Sensors: temperature, humidity, weight scale, blood pressure, and glucose
- Actuators: latch, alarm, and motor
- Tags: RFID (radio frequency identification), barcode, finger print, biometrics

5.7.3 Device Aggregators

The aggregators play a vital role of collecting the data from multiple sensors and send the summarized data to the gateway or protocol translator component. It is essential for industrial IoT environment where array of wearables, sensors, and devices needs aggregated transactions to visualize or build analytics. The event-based data comes from individual devices that are sending with a detailed timestamp. The aggregators will aggregate milliseconds event data to seconds or hourly data based on the data requirement.

5.7.4 IoT Gateway

It is typically employed between the network of the machine-to-machine (M2M) devices and the remote clients over the internet. It helps to collect data from heterogeneous devices which emit data using different protocols. It acts a single end point to get data from different devices. Cloud platform highly relies in the gateway end point to control the sub devices that are configured in the gateway using device twin model or device control model [40, 41, 45].

5.7.5   Big Data Platform and Tools

The big data platforms are currently available in cloud providers like Amazon S3, Azure Data Lake, and Google File systems which support data collection, data aggregation, and curation at different levels [29, 30]. The raw data comes from the IoT gateway or direct device end points which continuously push or tools like Kafka or message queue tools that synchronize the data using publisher/consumer model with an orchestration tools like Zoo Keeper. The reliable communication between the IoT gateway to the data platform (e.g., Apache Hadoop or Azure Data Lake) is taken care through message broker tools.

The high availability and data replication is essential for IoT data set for legal and regulatory needs which is supported by the big data platforms (e.g., Azure Data Lake or Azure Blob Store) The streaming of data from IoT edge to Big data platform is seamless through message brokers and stream analytics tools like Spark and Azure Stream Analytics. It clearly shows the IoT meets big data when the volume of data is growing up and it needs a platform to collect and perform analysis or analytics in either real-time or batch mode.

5.8   Role of Machine Learning For Big Data and IoT

Machine learning is a method of data analysis that automates model building in a platform using algorithms and mathematical procedures [15–18]. Based on the type of data (e.g., streaming data sets like audio, video, event-based data sets like temperature, humidity, meters, etc.), the analytical model needs to be built and train the model with either pre-built attributes (e.g., classification models like naïve Bayes, decision tree, etc.) or unknown attributes to be the discovered [20] (e.g., clustering techniques—K means clustering, DBScan, etc.). The dataset available in either IoT edge or big data platform has to undergo the following steps before we build a machine learning model.

a. Definition a business problem or case study to be solved
b. Identify the data sources (e.g., IoT Edge or Data Lake) where we need to get the data to build the model
c. Select the right data from the collected dataset and cleanse the data to remove errors or anomalies
d. Transform the data [aggregate (SUM, AVG, MIN, MAX, etc.)] based on the level of granularity that we are looking

to build the model and discover the data patterns. Analyze the data using tools like scatter plot, bar graph, and interpret the data pattern and build the rules [37, 38] (e.g., association analysis, dependency matrix, etc.)

e. Build the model using based on the interpreted patterns

f. Validate and train the model and test it with trained dataset and automate the model learning

5.8.1 Typical Machine Learning Use Cases

a. Prediction of Temperature of city and recommend the right transport route, e.g., city of Canada needs data from the temperature sensors installed on the road to recommend the citizen to plan their trip ahead of a day. It might help them to avoid driving on heavy snow during the winter season.

   a.1 Role of IoT: temperature sensor, gateway at the zone or traffic control collects the data from IoT sensors.

   a.2 Role of Big Data: continuously ingests the data in the platform where it needs constant learning of the model that we built to predict and recommend the right route map for the citizen.

   a.3 Role of Machine Learning: model building to predict the temperature of next 5 days and build a recommendation engine based on the road side values and incidents data and suggest the right route map. The model needs to be constantly trained and learnt with current data values gathered from the IoT devices.

b. Public Safety Protection:

   Major cities need a constant monitoring of public safety in a crime zone area or low safety zones. The data comes from CCTV cameras and public WiFi devices installed by the city needs to be analyzed and build a video analytics model to find intruders or offenders who are wandering on that area. It will help the public safety department to send the alerts to city police officers who are on patrol or send the alerts with footages to the control room that monitors that particular zone or area.

   b.1 Role of IoT: CCTV cameras and public WiFi are the two IoT data sources which continuously stream the data to IoT gateway. Public WiFi helps to get the people details who all are on the street and registered the WiFi to access through their mobile devices [39].

b.2 Role of Big Data: the big data platforms like Hadoop needs to store large unstructured data files of CCTV (video files) and WiFi logs.

The processing engine like Spark or MapReduce framework needs to process these large files into small chunks (e.g., images or frames from the video dataset) and tag the image with a right time stamp and geo location details. The WiFi logs need a compressed storage like Parquet or Avro to store the data for quick retrieval using Hadoop Hive or MapReduce. Big data platform supports the machine or deep learning framework (either Mahout or Pytorch or Keras or Theano or Tensorflow) to build a model which needs continuous learning to discover the data sanity and eliminate anomalous records.

b.3 Role of Machine Learning: Machine learning frameworks or deep learning frameworks need to be evaluated for object detection and object recognition. The image metadata is very essential to mash it with the collected data set of CCTV and detects the intruders or offender with right precision. The log analytics also needs to build to identify the anomalies and extract the people's information and relate it with the CCTV footage for better tagging and build the alerts based on that log information.

5.9 Conclusion

Big data is a comprehensive, quickly developing subject. While it is not like-minded for all sorts of computing, several establishments are revolving to big data for convinced categories of assignments and utilizing it to add-on their current investigation and corporate implements. Big data systems are exclusively well-matched for developing difficult-to-detect designs and provided that insight into manners that are intolerable to discovery over orthodox means. By properly implementing systems that agreement with big data, IoT and machine learning establishments can take advantage of incredible worth from data that is previously offered. It will be evident that big data will reap the benefits based on the business cases which we identified for a specific domain.

References

1. Kakhani, M.K., Kakhani, S., Biradar, S.R., Research issues in big data analytics. *Int. J. Appl. Innovation Eng. Manage.*, 2, 8, 228–232, 2015.
2. Gandomi, A. and Haider, M., Beyond the hype: Big data concepts, methods, and analytics. *Int. J. Inf. Manage.*, 35, 2, 137–144, 2015.
3. Lynch, C., Big data: How do your data grow? *Nature*, 455, 28–29, 2008.
4. Jin, X., Wah, B.W., Cheng, X., Wang, Y., Significance and challenges of big data research. *Big Data Res.*, 2, 2, 59–64, 2015.
5. Kitchin, R., Big Data new epistemologies and paradigm shifts. *Big Data Soc.*, 1, 1, 1–12, 2014.
6. Philip, C.L., Chen, Q., Zhang, C.Y., Data-intensive applications, challenges, techniques and technologies: A survey on big data. *Inf. Sci.*, 275, 314–347, 2014.
7. Kambatla, K., Kollias, G., Kumar, V., Gram, A., Trends in big data analytics. *J. Parallel Distrib. Comput.*, 74, 7, 2561–2573, 2014.
8. Del. Rio, S., Lopez, V., Bentez, J.M., Herrera, F., On the use of mapreduce for imbalanced big data using random forest. *Inf. Sci.*, 285, 112–137, 2014.
9. Kuo, M.H., Sahama, T., Kushniruk, A.W., Borycki, E.M., Grunwell, D.K., Health big data analytics: Current perspectives, challenges and potential solutions. *Int. J. Big Data Intell.*, 1, 114–126, 2014.
10. Dulhare, Uma N and Ayesha, Extraction of Action Rules for Chronic Kidney Disease using naïve bays classifier. *2016 IEEE conference on Computational Intelligence & Computing Research*, 2016.
11. Huang, Z., A fast clustering algorithm to cluster very large categorical data sets in data mining. *SIGMOD Workshop on Research Issues on Data Mining and Knowledge Discovery*, 1997.
12. Das, T.K. and Kumar, P.M., Big data analytics: A framework for unstructured data analysis. *Int. J. Eng. Technol.*, 5, 1, 153–156, 2013.
13. Das, T.K., Acharjya, D.P., Patra, M.R., Opinion mining about a product by analyzing public tweets in twitter. *Int. Conf. Comput. Commun. Inf.*, 1–4, 2014.
14. Zadeh, L.A., Fuzzy sets. *Inf. Control*, 8, 338–353, 1965.
15. Pawlak, Z., Rough sets. *Int. J. Comput. Inf. Sci.*, 11, 341–356, 1982.
16. Molodtsov, D., Soft set theory first results. *Comput. Math. Appl.*, 37, 4/5, 19–31, 1999.
17. Peters, J.F., Near sets. General theory about nearness of objects. *Appl. Math. Sci.*, 1, 53, 2609–2629, 2007.
18. Wille, R., Formal concept analysis as mathematical theory of concept and concept hierarchies. *Lect. Notes Artif. Intell.*, 3626, 1–33, 2005.

19. Arif, Faiza, Dulhare, Uma N *et al.*, A Machine learning based approach for Opinion Mining on Social Network Data. *3rd International conference on Computer and Communication Technologies (IC3T)*, 2019.

20. Al-Jarrah, O.Y., Yoo, P.D., Muhaidat, S., Karagiannidis, G.K., Taha, K., Efficient machine learning for big data: A review. *Big Data Res.*, 2, 3, 87–93, 2015.

21. Changwon., Y., Ramirez, Luis., Liuzzi, Juan., Big data analysis using modern statistical and machine learning methods in medicine. *Int. Neurol. J.*, 18, 50–57, 2014.

22. Singh, P. and Suri, B., Quality assessment of data using statistical and machine learning methods, in: *Computational Intelligence in Data Mining*, vol. 2, Jain, L.C., Behera, H.S., Mandal, J.K., Mohapatra, D.P. (Eds.), pp. 89–97, 2014.

23. Jacobs, A., The pathologies of big data. *Commun. ACM*, 52, 8, 36–44, 2009.

24. Zhu, H., Xu, Z., Huang, Y., Research on the security technology of big-data information. *International Conference on Information Technology and Management Innovation*, pp. 1041–1044, 2015.

25. Hongjun, Z., Wenning, H., Dengchao, H., Yuxing, M., Survey of research on information security in big data. *Congresso da sociedada Brasileira de Computacao*, Conference Proceedings, 1–6, 2014.

26. Merelli, I., Perez-sanchez, H., Gesing, S., Agostino, D.D., Managing, analysing, and integrating big data in medical bioinformatics: Open problems and future perspectives. *BioMed Res. Int.*, 2014, 1–13, 2014.

27. Mishra, N., Lin, C., Chang, H., A cognitive adopted framework for iot big data management and knowledge discovery prospective. *Int. J. Distrib. Sens. Netw.*, 2015, 1–13, 2015.

28. Chen, X.Y. and Jin, Z.G., Research on key technology and applications for internet of things. *Physics Procedia*, 33, 561–566, 2012.

29. Assuno, M.D., Calheiros, R.N., Bianchi, S., Netto, M. a. S., Buyya, R., Big data computing and clouds: Trends and future directions. *J.Parallel Distrib. Comput.*, 79, 3–15, 2015.

30. Hashem, I.A.T., Yaqoob, I., Badrul Anuar, N., Mokhtar, S., Gani, A., Ullah Khan, S., The rise of big data on cloud computing: Review and open research issues. *Inf. Syst.*, 47, 98–115, 2014.

31. Wang, L. and Shen, J., Bioinspired cost-effective access to big data. *Int. Symp. Next Gener. Infrastruct.*, Conference Proceedings, 1–7, 2013.

32. Shi, C., Shi, Y., Qin, Q., Bai, R., Swarm intelligence in big data analytics, in: *Intelligent Data Engineering and Automated Learning*, Yin, H., Tang, K., Gao, Y., Klawonn, F., Lee, M., Weise, T., Li, B., Yao, X. (Eds.), pp. 417–426, 2013.

33. Nielsen, M.A. and Chuang, I.L., *Quantum Computation and Quantum Information*, Cambridge University Press, New York, USA, 2000.

34. Herland, M., Khoshgoftaar, T.M., Wald, R., A review of data mining using big data in health informatics. *J. Big Data*, 1, 2, 1–35, 2014.

35. Huang, T., Lan, L., Fang, X., An, P., Min, J., Wang, F., Promises and challenges of big data computing in health sciences. *Big Data Res.*, 2, 1, 2–11, 2015.
36. Ingersoll, G., Introducing apache mahout: Scalable, commercial friendly machine learning for building intelligent applications, White Paper. *IBM Developer Works*, 1–18, 2009.
37. Li, H., Fox, G., Qiu, J., Performance model for parallel matrix multiplication with dryad: Dataflow graph runtime. *Second International Conference on Cloud and Green Computing*, pp. 675–683, 2012.
38. Acharjya, D.P., Dehuri, S., Sanyal, S., *Computational Intelligence for Big Data Analysis*, Springer International Publishing AG, Switzerland, USA, 2015.
39. Balachandar, S. and Chinnaiyan, R., Centralized Reliability and Security Management of Data in Internet of Things (IoT) with Rule Builder, in: *Lecture Notes on Data Engineering and Communications Technologies*, vol. 15, pp. 193–201, 2018.
40. Balachandar, S. and Chinnaiyan, R., Reliable Digital Twin for Connected Footballer, in: *Lecture Notes on Data Engineering and Communications Technologies*, vol. 15, pp. 185–191, 2018.
41. Balachandar, S. and Chinnaiyan, R., A Reliable Troubleshooting Model for IoT Devices with Sensors and Voice Based Chatbot Application. *Int. J. Res. Appl. Sci. Eng. Technol.*, 6, 2, 1406–1409, 2018.
42. Swarnamugi, M. and Chinnaiyan, R., IoT Hybrid Computing Model for Intelligent Transportation System (ITS). *IEEE Second International Conference on Computing Methodologies and Communication (ICCMC)*, pp. 15–16, Feb. 2018.
43. Swarnamugi, M. and Chinnaiyan, R., Cloud and Fog Computing Models for Internet of Things. *Int. J. Res. Appl. Sci. Eng. Technol.*, December 2017. International Conference on Mathematical Impacts in Science and Technology (MIST-17), November 2017.
44. Sabarmathi, G. and Chinnaiyan, R., Envisagation and Analysis of Mosquito Borne Fevers: A Health Monitoring System by Envisagative Computing Using Big Data Analytics, in: *Lecture Notes on Data Engineering and Communications Technologies book series (LNDECT*, vol. 31, pp. 630–636, Springer, Cham, 2019.
45. Balachandar, S. and Chinnaiyan, R., Internet of Things Based Reliable Real-Time Disease Monitoring of Poultry Farming Imagery Analytics, in: *Lecture Notes on Data Engineering and Communications Technologies book series (LNDECT*, vol. 31, pp. 615–620, Springer, Cham, 2019.
46. Swarnamugi, M. and Chinnaiyan, R., IoT Hybrid Computing Model for Intelligent Transportation System (ITS). *Proceedings of the Second International Conference on Computing Methodologies and Communication (ICCMC 2018)*, pp. 802–806, 2019.
47. Sabarmathi, G. and Chinnaiyan, R., Big Data Analytics Research Opportunities and Challenges - A Review. *Int. J. Adv. Res. Comput. Sci. Software Eng.*, 6, 10, 227–231, 2016.

48. Sabarmathi, G. and Chinnaiyan, R., Investigations on big data features research challenges and applications. *IEEE Xplore Digital Library International Conference on Intelligent Computing and Control Systems (ICICCS)*, pp. 782–786.
49. Dulhare, Uma N, Prediction system for heart disease using Naive Bayes and particle swarm optimization. *BioMed. Res.*, 29, 12, 2646–2649, 2018.
50. Nambiar, R., Sethi, A., Bhardwaj, R., Vargheese, R., A look at challenges and opportunities of big data analytics in healthcare. *IEEE International Conference on Big Data*, pp. 17–22, 2013.

6

Pattern Recognition Concepts

Ambeshwar Kumar, R. Manikandan* and C. Thaventhiran

School of Computing SASTRA Deemed University, Thanjavur, India

Abstract

The area of pattern recognition is concerned with the discovery of regularities in data by using machine learning algorithms. Make use of these regularities patterns to take an action for classifying the object in different categories. A pattern might be physically visible or it can be derived mathematically using algorithms. Consider an example to determine the two categories of fish like rohu and catla both looks similar but its pattern gives an idea to classify (i.e., head pattern of those fishes were different). The small changes in pattern are not able to classify easily and then it solved by using algorithms. In biomedical, image classification task to distinguish the matching pattern image and unmatched pattern is handled by pattern recognition techniques. Pattern recognition gives better ideas to further development of computational technology, with the help of machine learning and big data analytics to make a smarter system. As per the security purpose, it is more essential to track the forgery in bank, biometric tracking, and left luggage at the airport; these can be done easily by pattern recognition techniques. Learning a new knowledge or experience and linked it with the old or existing knowledge, sometimes, it might be new patterns got generated. Consciously learning patterns merged with the newly generated patterns give new results. Likewise, climate change and weather forecast are based on previous year pattern that helps the researcher to predict the future weather forecast or any natural calamities.

Keywords: Pattern recognition, classifier, clustering, explanation-based learning, texture analysis

Corresponding author: srmanimt75@gmail.com

Uma N. Dulhare, Khaleel Ahmad and Khairol Amali Bin Ahmad (eds.) Machine Learning and Big Data: Concepts, Algorithms, Tools and Applications, (131–152) © 2020 Scrivener Publishing LLC

6.1 Classifier

The problem of classifying or segregating the same pattern of object is a very relevant topic in the machine learning and big data analytics. The classifier is one of the effective methods intended to solve the large datasets in efficient manner. It is easy to find and retrieve the object of same feature when the data is classified in well-planned ways. The classified data play an important role for solving many real time problems such as risk management, security, legal discovery, compliance, price list, and recommendation system, etc.

6.1.1 Introduction

In machine learning, classification is a supervised learning technique to classify or categorize the large labeled dataset into a set of same feature of class. It determines the class label from an unlabeled test case. For understanding and validating a classifier, it requires analyzing its performance, accuracy, and ROC Curve. The classification implementation first needs to train the classifier, consider an example of brain images "tumor" or "no tumor" brain images would be used as a training data. After successfully train the classifier, it is able to detect the brain tumor images. Classifier separates the training dataset into group of same decision objects. A common way to classify the classifier behavior is to plot a graph of the training set color code according to the defined class labels. This helps to show how decision boundaries are separating the one class to other class. The goal in the classifier is to decide an input variable "x" and to allocate it to one of the K discrete classes where the value of K is to be assign 1, 2,..., k. In many cases, the classes are taken to be disjoint so that input should be assigned to one and only one class. The boundary which divides the input space is known as decision boundaries. The various machine learning algorithms have been developed to classify the objects from small or large datasets.

Some machine learning classification algorithms are as follows:

> ➤ Support vector machine (SVM)
> ➤ Logistic regression
> ➤ Random forest
> ➤ Naïve Bayes theorem
> ➤ Decision tree

6.1.2 Explanation-Based Learning

Explanation-based learning (EBL) is a powerful learning technique that exploits a strong and perfect domain theory in order to make a generalization and formal concept from training examples. It logically gives two distinct components: The explanation-based learning using preceding knowledge to examine or explain the training example, in order to refer that which example is applicable to the target function and which is not relevant to the target function. The system attempt to learn from a single example consider as "y" by explaining why the considered example "y" is an example of target function [1].

Learning by Generalizing Explanation

> ➢ Target example: what program or system seen in real world.
> ➢ A goal concept: A high level explanation of what the program is believed to learn.
> ➢ Operationally criterion: A narrative of which concept are useful.
> ➢ Domain theory: set of rules that illustrate the relationship between object and action in domain.

As we seen in Figure 6.1, the first step the domain theory is to reduce away all the irrelevant aspects of training data. What is left is "enlightenment" of why training example is an instance of goal concept, this clarification is expressed in terms that satisfy the operation criterion and the final step is to simplify the clarification as far as possible to recitation the goal concept.

The EBL unification-based generalization explains an interconnected collection of knowledge which contains inference rule, rewrite rule, analytical rule, etc. These rules are connected with each other using unification as in PROLOG-EBG. The general unifier allows the knowledge to be connected together when it is possible to connect. The prolog concept is explained as follows:

PROLOG-EBG (Target Concept, Training Examples, Domain Theory)

- • Learned Rules ← {}
- • Pos ← it contains the positive examples from Training Examples.

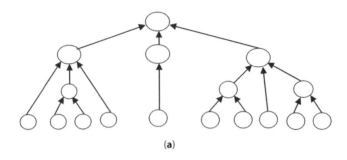

(a)

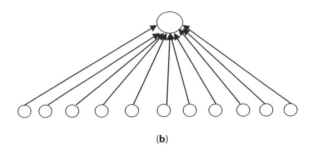

(b)

Figure 6.1 Explanation of EBL. (a) Standard approach to explanation-based learning and (b) Detailed proof of goal after learning go directly from fact to solution.

- For each Positive Example in Pos that is not covered by Learned Rules, do
  - ➢ Explain: Explanation of (proof) in terms of the Domain Theory that Positive Example satisfies the Target Concept.
  - ➢ Analyze: it analyze the adequate conditions of the most common set of features of Positive Example adequate to satisfy the Target Concept according to the Explanation.
  - ➢ Refine: Learned Rules ← Learned Rules + new horn clause where the new horn clause in the form of Target concept ← Sufficient Conditions
  - ➢ Returned: Learned Rules

The EBL architecture to explain the solving of problem to reach out of the goal of the solution is explained as follows:

As we seen in Figure 6.2, the specific goal problem is given to the problem solver system, sometime, external solution also helpful to solve the problem but in partial way not fully solve the problem. At next step in

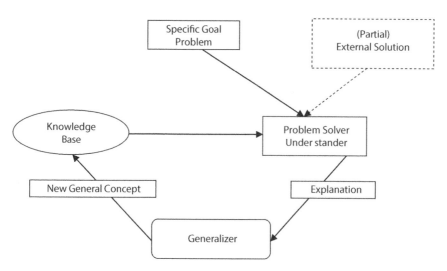

Figure 6.2 EBL architecture.

solving the problem, it needs to get the clear explanation of the problem. The Generalizer generalizes the problem using new concept and the knowledge base using prior knowledge to refine the goal and finally the output generates from the problem solver system.

6.1.3 Isomorphism and Clique Method

Isomorphism is a mathematical concept which is generally used for pattern recognition due to its matching behavior. The word isomorphism derives from Greek name "iso" that means "equal" and "morphosis" that means "form" or "shape". Generally, it preserves the set and relation among the same element. It is achieved by matching the pattern or pair of the graph. Imagine all substance is different so that their equivalent graphs are distinct and then provides a new graph the algorithm efficiently finds an isomorphic stored graph if it exists [2, 3]. The isomorphism graph algorithm contains of three phases defined as follows:

> ➤ Preprocessing phase: this phase computes the degree of nodes and other information which is used to generate new label creation for each node in both graphs. Additionally, the new label contains the degree of the node itself, degrees and labels of each child of this node. To reduce the confusion, we name as a "label" to the original label that are given with the

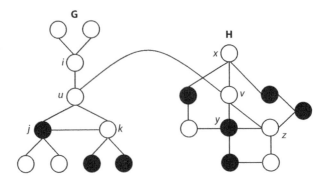

Figure 6.3 Node u that belongs to G is locally compatible with node v that belongs to H.

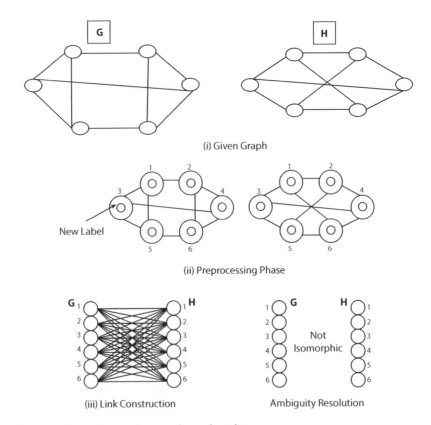

Figure 6.4 Three phases of isomorphism algorithm.

graph and "new label" for the generated labels after preprocessing steps.

➢ Link Construction: Connect all pair of nodes that have identical new label across the graph. In Figure 6.3, where the creative labels are assumed to be "lack" or "white", node u in graph G is linked to node v in graph. The connection between the nodes because the new label of u matches the new label of v, i.e., label and degree of node "u" match those of node v and each child of u, namely, i, j, and k, has a consequent child of node v that is equivalent to its label and degree. Here, the offspring i, j, and k in G correspond to the offspring x, y, and z in H, respectively. Clearly, the graphs G and H are not isomorphic.

➢ Ambiguity Resolution: This phase is a leading portion of the isomorphic algorithm phase. This phase resolves the ambiguity that may have resulted from the link connection phase. The goal of this phase to try and make a decision whether one to one mapping from node of the first graph to the node of the second graph is possible.

The graphs G and H have three phases of the algorithm steps shown in Figure 6.4, every node in G is connected to each node of H by the connection phase, and finally, the links are disconnected in ambiguity resolution phase since the graphs are not isomorphic.

Clique Method

The clique method is a popular approach in pattern recognition for analyzing the overlapping community structure of networks. It usually defined as a group of node that is more densely connected to each other. The clique method builds up from k-clique method which corresponds to fully connected sub-graph. It allowed the overlapping between the communities in natural ways through the color coded vertices. It is mainly used in real world problem to classify the object and its behavior. Most popular example in social networking application is to match the mutual friends of friend, let consider the people's profile represent as a vertices of a graph and mutual friends represent as an edge of graph so, the clique method is used to represent the subset of people who all know each other and suggest a people to add new friends in their profile list. The clique percolation method is to find the overlapping communities in the sub-graph, and internal edges of community are likely to form clique. The main advantage of clique method is that it allows the overlap between the communities. The k-clique method used to solve the problem using the defined "k" value in the graph. It directed the node with higher order to the lower order. The CPM algorithm is more likely for pattern matching rather than finding communities, they aspire to search a precise localized structure in network.

6.1.4   Context-Dependent Classification

The classification in which a feature vector is assigned depends on its own value, on the value of the other feature vector, and on existing relation among various classes. It is a robust phenomenon that has been observed with a variety of stimulus manipulations under incidental encoding conditions. This can be achieved by adopting different transition costs, which are not necessarily related to probability densities. These types of problem occur in image processing, speech recognition, and to establish a communication between the human work-force. The context-dependent classification is performed using all feature vectors simultaneously and in the same sequence in which they occurred from the experiment. The context-based classification refers with the feature vector as observing occurring in sequence from x_1 to x_n. It is introduced by hidden Markov model (HMM) and Markov chain model. HMM is one of the most widely used models for describing the underlying class dependence. MCM are applied for speech recognition and communication purpose. The context-dependent classification is explained using Bayes classifier; let us consider the sequence of observation X_1 to X_n as a feature vectors and $\omega_{i=1,...,M}$ the classes in which the vector is to be classified. Let Ω_i: ω_{i1}, ω_{i2}, ω_{i3},....., ω_{in} be the possible sequences of the classes corresponding to the observation of sequence. Total number of class sequence is M^N. The class sequence is decided by the classification task and the observation correspond to X. The observed specific X Bayes rule is assign to Ω_i. The Markov chain is widely used for describing dependence classes. It is limited only within two successive classes. It is conceptually quite intuitive and very accessible. They can be implemented without the use of any advanced statistical or mathematical concepts. General scenario we can take a prediction of weather is sunny or cloudy. It is directly observed by noticing the climate condition. When we have to predict for tomorrow's weather, then it need a calculation of weather data of several years and conclude that tomorrow is sunny or cloudy. The hidden Markov chain developed with mathematical concepts, because in Markov chain, the state is directly visible to the observer, but in the hidden Markov chain, the state is not directly visible but the output depends on the state is visible. HMM is suitable for dealing with recognizing the object which is based on sequence of features. Let us consider an example of tossing a coin: when we toss a single coin behind the

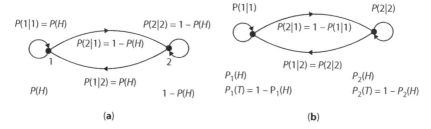

Figure 6.5 (a) Showing single coin and (b) showing two coins.

door, we don't know the exact output but the outcome of the experiment we know that it is either head or tail; thus, the crucial probabilistic part is hidden to us. It provides the state forward outcome H or T. When we consider the two coins tossed behind the door, it can't be modeled by single parameter. To process, the outcomes to this example assume two states corresponding to the two coins [4]. The states of this example are not observable, since we have no access to the information related to which coin is tossed each time. The illustration is shown in Figure 6.5.

P (i|j) indicates the transition probability from state s_j to state s_i once the coin has been tossed and an inspection has been made accessible to us. Thus, an HMM model consists of a number of, say, K states and the observation string is generated as a result of successive transitions from one state i to another j.

6.1.5   Summary

This chapter defines the briefly introduction of classifier and explain the classification method using the different method of classifiers. The major points to recall are as follows:

  ➢ The classifier is an effective methodology which intended to solve the large datasets problems in efficient manner.
  ➢ Explanation-based learning techniques used for understanding an element and improving the performance of element.
  ➢ Isomorphism is a mathematical technique to solve the classified homogenous data. It is achieved by matching the pattern or pair of the graph.
  ➢ Clique method is used to deal with social networking problem. It is very useful and efficient method to find the mutual connection. It suggests growing the networks on the basis of available data.
  ➢ Context-dependent classification is robust techniques. It works on feature vector that is assigned depending on its

own value, on the value of the other feature vector, and on existing relation among various classes.

6.2   Feature Processing

The feature processing is technique which is useful after getting to know about the data visualization and summary of data; to make it more meaningful, it needs further transformation of variable, and this process is known as feature processing. Consider an example to replace the invalid or missing data with more meaningful value. A common approach used to allocate missing values is to substitute missing values with the mean or median value. It is imperative to understand your data before choosing an approach for substituting missing values.

6.2.1   Introduction

The feature of any object can be defined as typical aspect like character, symbol, number, and quality. The main objective of the feature processing is to increase the result of classification and decrease the probability of misclassification. It will simplify the classifier both in learning stage and running stage. The feature processing quality criteria are defined in two categories: direct methods and indirect methods.

Direct Methods: reducing the probability of misclassification, it is an optimal solution but doesn't necessary to imply a better classification. The solutions are complex due to link to the used classifier.

Indirect Methods: increasing the independency of instances between the classes, it has less number of features which implies worse separable but it provides easier solution.

Explaining the feature processing with example like forming Cartesian product of one variable with another, consider we have two variables such as population density (urban, semi-urban, and rural) and state (Maharashtra, Andhra, Karnataka), there might be a useful information in the features formed by a Cartesian product of these two variable resulting in features (urban_ Maharashtra, semi-urban_ Maharashtra, rural_ Maharashtra, urban_ Andhra, suburban_ Andhra, rural_ Andhra, urban_ Karnataka, suburban_ Karnataka, rural_ Karnataka).

Considering more relevant features helps to increase the prediction authority. Clearly, it is not always possible to know the features with "signal" or predictive influence in advance. So, it is good to include all features that can potentially be related to the target label and let the model training algorithm pick the features with the strongest correlations.

6.2.2 Detection and Extracting Edge With Boundary Line

Edge detection and extraction is a fundamental concept of computer vision and image processing. It is an algorithm which is typically followed by the connecting and other recognition procedure; it is deliberate to accumulate the edge pixels into meaningful boundary lines. There are two types of detecting and extracting the edge line, which are local processing and global processing. Analyzing of image pixel in small neighborhood where every point has gone through edge detection, all points are similar and linked with each other. They are sharing common properties like direction of gradient and strength of response of gradient operator used to produce edge pixel. Many edge detection algorithms have been developed such as canny edge detection, Sobel edge detection, Prewitt edge detection, and Laplacian detection, in the existence and pixel locations of intensity transitions among adjacent pixels in a sub-window. Edge extraction is categorized in two subsets: true edge, which corresponds to the edges in the scene, and false edge, which do not correspond to the edges in the scene. False edge is also known as false positive edge, and false negative edge is defined as those edges in the scene that should have been recognized or a set of missing edges. Extraction of edges with boundary line presents two motivated ideas: boundary line to evaluate the edge extraction not only builds the problem well defined but also avoids overly sacrificing of the generality of the evaluation [5]. To maintain the performance gap, edge extraction technique has been introduced to deal with real time images and evaluate their effects on subsequent boundary line detection. Hough transforms is a technique which can be used to segregate features of a particular contour within an image. It is most commonly used to recognize the circle, eclipse, line, etc. The advantage of this technique is tolerance of gaps in feature boundary descriptions and is relatively unaffected by image noise. The main objective of this technique is to search the points of intersection in the curves, each of which corresponds to a line. Ratio-contour algorithm has been implementing for boundary grouping component. This algorithm works with boundary saliency. It is measured by an unbiased combination of three important Gestalt laws: closure, proximity, and continuity. Closure requires the boundary to be complete. Proximity requires the gap between two neighboring fragments to be small. Continuity requires the resulting boundary to be smooth. It always detects the global optimal boundary in terms of its boundary-saliency measure.

6.2.3   Analyzing the Texture

Texture provides information about the spatial arrangement of color or intensities in a respective image. It helps in segmentation of images into region or area of interest and to classify those regions. Analyzing the texture refers to the characterization of regions in an image by their texture content. It plays an important role in pattern recognition, defect detection medical image analysis. It attempts to enumerate spontaneous qualities described by terms likewise rough, smooth, silky, or bumpy as a function of the spatial variation in pixel intensities. More recently, texture analysis has been implemented to other imaging modalities, such as elastosonography, positron emission tomography/computed tomography (PET/CT), and MRI. Analyzing the texture used in various application including remote sensing, an automatic inspection of system, and medical image processing [6]. The texture analysis is usually categorized into four types as follows:

- ➢ Structural analysis
- ➢ Model-based analysis
- ➢ Statistical analysis
- ➢ Transform analysis

Structural analysis approaches represent texture by well-defined primitives and hierarchy of spatial arrangements of those primitives. It provides a high-quality symbolic description of the image; however, this feature is more useful for synthesis than task analysis. It is useful for bone image analysis, e.g., for the detection of changes in bone microstructure.

Model-based analysis approaches are using fractal and stochastic models, attempt to interpret an image texture by use of, respectively, generative image model and stochastic model. The fractal model has been useful for modeling some natural textures. It is deficient in orientation selectivity and not appropriate for describing local image structures.

Statistical analysis approaches is not effective to understand explicitly the hierarchical structure of the texture. It represents the texture indirectly by the non-deterministic properties that govern the dissection and connection among the grey levels of an image.

Transform methods of texture analysis like Gabor, wavelet, and Fourier transforms represent an image in a space whose coordinate system has an interpretation that is closely related to the characteristics of a texture. Fourier transform execute inadequately in practice, due to its deficient in of spatial localization. Moreover, Gabor filter presents an improved spatial localization. Wavelet transform provides a better feature extraction analysis compared to Gabor and Fourier, and it represents the texture with most suitable scale with wide range of choice for wavelet function.

6.2.4   Feature Mapping in Consecutive Moving Frame

In today's real world scenario, the main concern is the time complexity which depends on the number of features. The amount of data is increasing day to day and concerning features also increase exponentially. Feature mapping is a process of representing features along with the relevant feature on the graph to ensure that the features are visualized and their corresponding information is available [7]. Only relevant features are included and irrelevant features are excluded from the scene. Feature mapping is explained using four principles which are as follows:

- ➢ Explain
- ➢ Illustrate
- ➢ Explore
- ➢ Challenge

Rule to explain the scenario, example to elaborate the rules, steps taken to investigate the example arise question in example challenge everything. Consider one example to explain the feature mapping: I have 50,000 in my account and I live in Bangalore. Next month, I am planning for holiday tour to Singapore, but in available balance, I can afford Darjeeling, Dehradun, or Manali. Find a rule to define a solution to illustrate and explore the trip to Singapore but the consequences are as follows: there is not enough money, the long travel is also not prescribe by doctor, food is also not as per my health, and passport mandatory, these all variations become challenges which are not mapping, and the trip to Singapore will get cancel.

Feature mapping in consecutive frame is an exigent task because it entails understanding the motion of image in consecutive frame. The solution of this task is to understand the object in motion. It is challenging task due to object occlusion and noise at the time of transferring the image pixel to pixel from one frame to other frame. Recent technology uses optical flow to provide an optimal solution for motion image. Optical flow is the pattern of

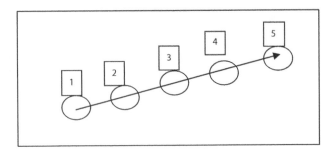

Figure 6.6 Ball moving in five consecutive frames.

apparent motion of image object between two consecutive frames caused by the movement of camera or movement of the object. Recover an image motion at each pixel, from spatial temporal image brightness variation. It tries to calculate the motion between two image frames which are taken at time "t" and "Δt" at every voxel position. It is a 2D vector field where each vector is a displacement vector showing the movement of points from one frame to another frame.

In Figure 6.6, the arrow that is shown is a displacement vector of the consecutive moving of ball. Pixel intensity of an object does not change between consecutive frame neighboring pixels that have several motions. Consider pixel in 1st frame and its moving distance (dx, dy) in next frame in time taken dt. It implies that the pixels are identical and the intensity is also similar to the previous frame. The calculation is as shown in Equation (6.1).

$$I(x, y, t) = I(x+ dx, y+ dy, t+ dt) \qquad (6.1)$$

Approximation of right-hand side is taken by Taylor series to eliminate the common terms and divide it by dt to get Equation (6.2).

$$f_x u+ f_y v+ f_t = 0 \qquad (6.2)$$

Where in Equation (6.2), $f_x = \frac{df}{dx}, f_y = \frac{df}{dx}, u = \frac{dx}{dt}, v = \frac{dy}{dt}$

Equation (6.2) is the optical flow equation where f_x and f_y are image gradient and f_t is the gradient along time. "u" and "v" are the unknown variables so, we can't solve this equation with two unknown variables. Several methods are provided to solve this problem but the Lucas-Kanade method is applied to provide a better solution.

6.2.5   Summary

This chapter includes the introduction of feature processing and explains the feature processing methods. The major points in this chapter are recall as follows:

> ➢ The main objective of the feature processing is to boost the effect of classification and diminish the probability of misclassification.
> ➢ Edge extraction with boundary line using Hough transform techniques to segregate features of a particular contour within an image.
> ➢ Analyzing the texture submit the characterization of regions in an image by their texture content, using structural analysis, model-based analysis, statistical analysis, and transform analysis.
> ➢ Feature mapping in consecutive frame is a difficult task because it entails understanding the motion of image in consecutive frame. The solution of moving object from one frame to another is solved using Lucas-Kanade method to provide optimal solution.

6.3   Clustering

Similar data or objects group together to form a single set that is known as a cluster. Object in one set is slightly different when compared from the object available in another set. Clustering is an unsupervised machine learning approaches used in analysis of statistical and exploratory data. Clustering is a general task that can be solved be means of several algorithms. The goal of clustering technique is to identify the inherent grouping in a set of unlabeled data [8]. Clustering techniques satisfy the scalability, interpretability, usability, and ability to deal with the noisy data. Clustering is used in many fields like marketing, insurance, city-planning, medical, library, etc.

6.3.1   Introduction

The clustering algorithm helps us to find the hidden relationship between the data points in dataset. It arranges and organizes the data according to the similar type of data or objects. Recognize the similar kind of pattern in medical image data to detect the affected part in an image to diagnose the disease. It distributes the data into meaningful groups which describe the objects and their relationships. The goal of clustering is to identify the useful groups of objects, i.e., useful for the analysis of large datasets. The clustering is divided into two subcategories: hard clustering and soft clustering.

Hard Clustering: The clustering is said to be hard clustering when every data point is either belong to a single cluster or not. To elaborate the meaning, just take an example of rental store: our wish is to understand the customer's preference to build our business and increase the profits. It is not possible to look into each customer in details, but we can distribute it in 10 groups to monitor the purchasing habits of customer, and based on their preference, we will recommend our products to customers.

Soft Clustering: The clustering is said to be soft clustering when a probability or likelihood of that data points is assigned to a cluster, instead of putting the each data point in separate cluster. Consider an example of a retail store where every customer has purchased two or more items which are similar in all baskets. So, just calculate the probability of the items and assigned to the available cluster to recommend the items to the customer.

6.3.2   Types of Clustering Algorithms

The goal of clustering algorithms is to identify and segregate the homogenous data in one group; it is a subjective task and plenty of algorithms have been implemented to identify the objects in multivariate datasets. Different types of clustering are as follows:

> Hierarchical clustering
> Partitioning method clustering
> Fuzzy clustering
> Centroid-based clustering

Hierarchical Clustering: it is also known as hierarchical cluster analysis; this clustering groups an identical object or data into groups called cluster. The output of hierarchical clustering is a tree-based representation of data also known as dendrogram. It has been categorized in two approaches: top-down approach or divisive and bottom-up approach or agglomerative. The divisive approach is starting in one cluster and splits the data performance recursively as move down towards the hierarchy, whereas in bottom up or agglomerative approach, each data or object starts in a single cluster at the outset, and then, each pair is moving upward in successively merge pair of clusters till all clusters have been merged or join together in a single cluster

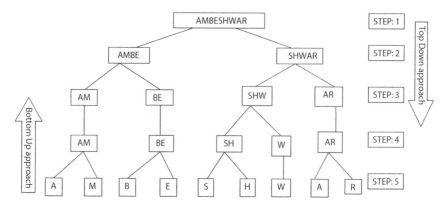

Figure 6.7 Hierarchal clustering methods

containing all data or objects in same cluster [9]. Consider an example to show the approach of hierarchical clustering in two ways in Figure 6.7.

Partitioning Method Clustering: Clustering of data is the fundamental technique in scientific analysis to retain the pattern recognition and identify the homogenous objects. Partition method clustering distributes the object into non-overlapping cluster. It should maintain that each object should be exactly in subset based on their similarity. The common algorithms used for the partitional clustering are k-means clustering, k-medoids clustering, and Clara algorithm. The main objective of this clustering method is two adaptive distances used to compare the vector of interval between the object distance and the comparison, which is based on the lower boundaries and upper boundaries of the interval assumed by symbolic variables. It also helps in evaluating the heterogeneity of data: intra-cluster and inter-cluster heterogeneity [10].

Fuzzy Clustering: Fuzzy clustering is also called as soft K-means clustering, where each data point belongs to more than one cluster. In fuzzy clustering, the points are very near to the center of cluster or may be in the cluster to a superior degree than points in the edge of a cluster. The degree, to which an object belongs to a cluster, is a numerical value range from 0 to 1. The fuzzy clustering is categorized in two parts: classical fuzzy clustering algorithms and shape-based fuzzy clustering algorithms.

Centroid-Based Clustering: it is a clustering method in which each cluster is represented by a central vector and the data points are assigned to the cluster based on the immediacy such that the squared distance from the central vector is diminished. It is also known as iterative clustering algorithm in which the clusters are formed by the nearness of data points to the centroid of clusters. When the number of clusters is set to k, the k-means clustering provides a formal description as an optimization problem: identify the k cluster centers and assign the objects or data to the nearest cluster center, such that the squared distances from the cluster are diminished.

6.3.2.1 Dynamic Clustering Method

The dynamic clustering method is the key technique in pattern recognition, its main objective to unwrap the hidden structure underlying a given collection of data. It is the clear awareness to investigate the novel approaches for solving the new clustering problem arising and it requires special treatment. It is more relevant to many other clustering situations like large data, data streams, incomplete data, noisy data, unbalanced data, and structured data. It is quite interesting to accept the challenges because clustering can also be just one step in a multi-step complex system. Dynamic clustering considers two perceptions: augmentation of the learning methods to devise the clustering model and self-adaptation of the learned model [11]. Two stages of dynamic-based clustering are distance and density-based clustering. The first stage of clustering is taking the data input and creating the "μ" clusters by merging the data samples that are close enough in the sense of distance between each other. The "μ" clusters contain the summarized details in the form of statistical and temporal information. The second stage takes place by analyzing the distribution of "μ" clusters. The density of "μ" cluster is consider as low, medium, and high which are used to create the final clusters using density-based approach. The "μ" cluster in density based is close enough that belongs to same cluster [12]. The illustration of dynamic-based clustering is shown in Figure 6.8.

6.3.2.2 Model-Based Clustering

Model-based clustering is an efficient approach of cluster analysis. It is generated to overcome the disadvantages of hierarchical clustering algorithms,

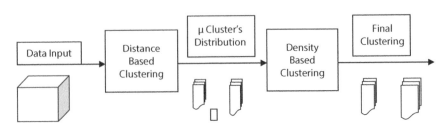

Figure 6.8 Dynamic-based clustering.

k-means algorithm, and not based on formal models. Where the formal inference is not possible, model-based clustering is providing ideas to deal with the data arise from the distribution, i.e., a mixture of two or more components. Model-based clustering allows assessing the difference between clusters using a sound statistical framework. Each component is described by the density function and contains a weight in the mixture. The main agenda of the model-based clustering is to fit the suitable data in given cluster shape by following the subsequent steps. It is to define the allotment of a cluster and to decide how the cluster sizes are scattered. The meaning of the cluster allocation can also be known as the specification of the clustering kernel. It is depending on the available of the data and its identical characteristics; different kernels are suitable. The cluster analysis and characteristics help to guide the choice of the clustering kernel. The prerequisite that a cluster distribution needs to be particular makes model-based clustering techniques more transparent with respect to the other clustering solutions [13]. The flexibility of model-based clustering approach stems from the fact that any statistical distribution or model can be used for the components. This permits us to come up with clustering techniques for any kind of data where a statistical model is available.

6.3.3   Application

Clustering is a powerful technique for segregating the unlabeled data. Many powerful algorithms have been implemented by the scientist and researcher and some of them are explained above. Here, we are discussing the innovative ideas generated by clustering to deal with the real world problems [14]. The applications are as follows:

> Social Network Analysis: In today's world, the social media is growing rapidly. Many organizations, private or public sector, are communicating using the social media networks. Sometimes, videos and messages are going viral on social media, to identify that the content is real or fake, clustering techniques are used to identify the fake articles by examining the words used in the content. The cluster helps to identify genuine or fake news. Sensitive or inflammatory words are used in fake article very rapidly. When it shows the high percentage of such terms, it declares as a fake news or article.

> Market Segmentation: The clustering techniques are very essential and useful in business sector to increase the sale and profit of the organization. To recommend the product

to target people in a right way is done the clustering algorithms. It groups the similar and likelihood product purchased by the customer. Once we group identical purchase of several customers. We can test each group with marketing copy that will help in future to target the relevant customers.

➢ Anomaly Detection: To detect the unauthorized access of card or any other unauthorized behavior. Normally, surfing is highly experienced activity during day time compare to night; this provides the correlation to spot the anomalies, but when the correlation is not present, it become difficult to detect the anomalies. K-means clustering is efficient to detect the anomalies by separating the normal signal with the noisy signal. It defined minimum and maximum thresholds value. The noisy signal should be within those limits; if not, this is an anomaly. It also defined the noise signal as being normally distributed with a mean of zero. If it suddenly changes into another distribution, something unusual or anomalous is appending.

➢ Document Analysis: If the data and record is small, it is easy to maintain, but if the data size is large, then it becomes difficult to organize the data quickly and efficiently. Hierarchical clustering technique has been used to solve this problem. This algorithm is able to come across at the data and group it into different argument. Using this technique, we can cluster and organize similar documents in one cluster quickly, using the characteristics, it helps to identified in the large dataset.

6.3.4   Summary

This chapter provides the knowledge about the clustering techniques. The explanation of different types of clustering techniques is explained with the real world application. The major points in this chapter are recall as follows:

➢ Clustering distributes the data into meaningful groups which describe the objects and their relationships.
➢ Hierarchical clustering is also called as hierarchical cluster analysis; this clustering groups an identical object or data into groups called cluster.
➢ Partitioning method clustering should maintain that each object should be exactly in subset based on their similarity.

- ➤ Dynamic clustering method is the key techniques in pattern recognition, its main objective to unwrap the hidden structure underlying a given collection of data.
- ➤ Model-based clustering is generated to overcome the disadvantages of hierarchical clustering algorithms, k-means algorithm.

6.4   Conclusion

The aim of this chapter has been contributed toward understanding the concept of classifier and clustering to recognize the object and data for categorizing the relevant data. The major points of the overall conclusion are as follows:

- ➤ Classifier: The classifier techniques provide a quick basic descriptive statistics, ideas to recognize the relevant pattern or data in efficient ways. The goal of the pattern recognition that is to find the relevant pattern for classifying data in easiest manner is discussed.
- ➤ Feature Processing: A feature processing is a technique to visualize the relevant data and to make the data more meaningful. Analyzing the data using area of interest to find the relevant pattern in data. It is useful in understanding the motion of images in the consecutive frames.
- ➤ Clustering: The clustering algorithms to distribute the data or objects into meaningful homogenous group with their relationships. It is also helpful in finding the hidden data points in large dataset. The main objective is to recognize the group of objects to analyze the large datasets. It is useful in social networking, market segmentation, anomaly detection, etc.

References

1. Timperley, M., Mokhtar, M., Bellaby, G., Howe, J., Explanation-based learning with analogy for impasse resolution. *Expert Syst. Appl.*, 61, 181–191, 2016.
2. Abdulrahim, M.A. and Misra, M., A graph isomorphism algorithm for object recognition. *Pattern Anal. Appl.*, 1, 3, 189–201, 1998.

3. Mendivelso, J., Kim, S., Elnikety, S., He, Y., Hwang, S. W., Pinzón, Y. Solving graph isomorphism using parameterized matching. In *International Symposium on String Processing and Information Retrieval*, pp. 230–242, Springer, Cham, 2013.

4. Yang, C., Feinen, C., Tiebe, O., Shirahama, K., & Grzegorzek, M. Shape-based object matching using interesting points and high-order graphs. *Pattern Recognit. Lett.*, 83, 251–260, 2016.

5. Ge, F., Edge Detection Evaluation in Boundary Detection Framework, [PDF File] Retrieved from http://citeseerx.ist.psu.edu/viewdoc/download?-doi=10.1.1.121.5788&rep=rep1&type=pdf, 2015.

6. Materka, A. and Strzelecki, M., Texture analysis methods–a review. Technical university of lodz, institute of electronics, COST B11 report, Brussels, 10(1.97), 4968, 1998.

7. Cheng, R., Jain, R., Muthakana, H., risub.me [PDF File]. retrieved from http://rishub.me/feature-flowframe.pdf., 2017.

8. Aggarwal, C.C., *Data classification: Algorithms and applications*, CRC press, New York, 2014.

9. Wei, W., Liang, J., Guo, X., Song, P., Sun, Y., Hierarchical division clustering framework for categorical data. *Neurocomputing*, 341, 118–134, 2019.

10. De Carvalho, F.D.A. and Lechevallier, Y., Partitional clustering algorithms for symbolic interval data based on single adaptive distances. *Pattern Recog.*, 42, 7, 1223–1236, 2009.

11. Bouchachia, A., Dynamic Clustering. Evolving Systems, UK, 3, 133–134, 2012. https://doi.org/10.1007/s12530-012-9062-5.

12. Barbosa, N.A., Travé-Massuyès, L., Grisales, V.H., A novel algorithm for dynamic clustering: properties and performance. In *2016 15th IEEE International Conference on Machine Learning and Applications (ICMLA)*, pp. 565–570, 2016.

13. Grün, B. Model-based clustering. Handbook of mixture analysis, pp. 163–198, CRC Press, Austria, 2018.

14. Claire Whittaker, Datafloq, [Blog post] retrieved from "https://datafloq.com/read/7-innovative-uses-of-clustering-algorithms/6224", 2019.

Section 3

MACHINE LEARNING: ALGORITHMS & APPLICATIONS

7

Machine Learning

Elham Ghanbari* and Sara Najafzadeh

*Department of Computer, Islamic Azad University, Yadegar-e-Imam Khomenini
(RAH) Shahre Rey, Tehran, Iran*

Abstract

Inspired by algorithmic and computational learning theory, machine learning examines the study and construction of algorithms that can learn and predict based on data—such algorithms do not just follow program instructions and Through modeling of sample input data, they predict or decide. Machine learning is used in computational tasks where the design and programming of explicit algorithms with good performance are difficult or impossible; some applications include email filtering, Internet intrusion detection, or internal malware intended to cause information breaches, learning ratings, and machine vision.

Keywords: Machine learning, concept learning, version space, supervised learning and unsupervised learning

7.1 History and Purpose of Machine Learning

7.1.1 History of Machine Learning

Machine learning exceeds the scope of artificial intelligence. In the early days of developing artificial intelligence as a science, the researchers found that machines learn from the data. They tried to solve this with a variety of symbolic methods and what then called "neural networks"; these methods were often perceptron and other models that were later determined to redesign the generalized linear models [1].

However, the growing emphasis on logical and knowledge-based methods made a gap between artificial intelligence and machine learning.

---

*Corresponding author: el.ghanbari@iausr.ac.ir

Uma N. Dulhare, Khaleel Ahmad and Khairol Amali Bin Ahmad (eds.) Machine Learning and Big Data: Concepts, Algorithms, Tools and Applications, (155–208) © 2020 Scrivener Publishing LLC

Probabilistic systems are filled with theoretical and practical issues about obtaining and displaying data. By the 1980s, the expert systems overtook AI and then statistics were not considered. Working on symbolic/knowledge-based learning, within the scope of AI, led to deductive logical programming. However, the statistical trajectory of the research was beyond the scope of AI and was found in the literature and retrieval of information [2].

Machine learning began to shine in the 1990s after resuscitation as a separate subject. It changed its aim at achieving artificial intelligence, engaging with resolution problems that have a practical nature, and transferred its focus from the symbolic methods it inherited from artificial intelligence, to methods and models borrowed from statistics and probabilities. It also benefited from the digital information that grew more and more on the internet, and the possibility of their distribution.

7.1.1.1   What is Machine Learning?

The word "learning" is, in fact, the acquisition of knowledge, or understanding, through reading, training, or experience, as well as learning to improve performance through experience. Machine learning is a relatively new field of artificial intelligence that is now growing and evolving. It is a very active research field in computer science. Various sciences are associated with machine learning, including artificial intelligence, psychology, and information theory. There are many definitions for machine learning, in this section; some of the most important ones are mentioned [1].

Machine learning is actually programming to optimize a performance using past data and experiences. Machine learning is how to write a program that can learn through experience and improve its performance. Learning might result in changes in program structure or data. In fact, it can be said that machine learning is seeking a way to create a program that automatically promotes performance according to experiences.

Tom M. Mitchell [3] provided a more formal definition of the algorithms studied in the machine learning domain: "It is said that a computer program learned from the experience of E in relation to a class T of tasks and the size of the function of P, whilst having the experience of E its performance as measured by P improved in the tasks of class T." It's a definition of what the machine learning is involved; it's a fully operational definition, not just a cognitive definition. This definition followed Alan Turing, replacing the question, "Can the machines think?" with the question "Can the machines do what we (as thinking beings) can do?"

7.1.1.2   When the Machine Learning is Needed?

Since computers were built, humans have always been looking for ways to program computers for their own purposes so that they can enhance their experiences over time. For example, one can imagine a day when homes are smart or personal software offers the best life plan. In addition, many things are beyond human control for instance. For example, there may be a great deal of important data that human beings cannot identify (data mining), or that it may not be known when designing a system of all its features while the machine can learn them as they work. Also, the environment may change over time when a machine can adapt to them by learning these changes [4].

In general, writing a program to diagnose is not easy in some cases, for example, identifying a face can be a difficult task, as there is no exact definition for it, and even if it exists, that is difficult to write a program based on it. As a result, instead of writing a program manually, it can be produced by providing a large amount of correct sample and applying it to a program machine learning algorithm that does the job. This program will be very different from what was supposed to be handwritten. If programmed correctly, it can also generate output for instances it has not seen before. So, in fact, where the program cannot be written directly, the learning needs to be done with the help of training data or experiences in the form of learning algorithms. In general, the need for machine learning can be summarized as follows [2].

1. Where the expert is not available.
2. When a human is unable to analyze the data because of large volume.
3. When a problem changes over time and depends on the ambient conditions, such as routing in computer networks.

In recent years, many advances have been developed in machine learning algorithms and related theories and many new research fields have emerged [5]. For example, in the exploration of information, the use of machine learning algorithms is very common, generally in the areas of data processing, these algorithms are much more than expected. It seems that the knowledge of machine learning algorithms is gradually maturing. So, it can be said that machine learning plays an important role in computer science.

7.1.2 Goals and Achievements in Machine Learning

A fundamental purpose of the machine learning is to generalize the experience. To generalize in this context, the learning machine's ability to perform precisely the new and unseen activities and examples is based on that machine's experience with the training dataset. The instructional examples come from a typically unknown distribution (considered to represent the space of the event), and for this space, the learner must generate a general model that will allow the predictor to be sufficiently accurate in new cases.

Computational analysis of machine learning algorithms and their function as a computational learning theory forms a branch of theoretical computer science. Since the training data sets are finite and the outcome is not certain, the learning theory generally does not give us a confirmation of algorithm success. Alternatively, probabilistic performance limitations are very common [4].

The sophistication of the inference must be as complex as the function of the data field for the best performance in the generalization process. If the assumption is less complex than the function, then the model under fit the data. If in response, the model complexity increases, then the training error is reduced; but if the assumption is too complex, the model is subject to over fit and generalization is weak.

In addition to functional boundaries, theorists also study computational learning, time complexity, and learning feasibility. In computational learning theory, a computation is called possible whenever it can be done in polynomial time. There are two types of results in terms of time complexity: positive results demonstrate that, in polynomial time, a certain class of functions can be learned, and negative results indicate that, in polynomial time, other classes cannot be learned.

7.1.3 Applications of Machine Learning

Machine learning has many applications in modern life, and the importance of machine learning technology has been recognized by most companies working with vast quantity of data [5].

Financial Services
Banks and other financial industry firms are using machine learning technology for two main purposes: to recognize valuable insights into data and to mitigate risk. These insights can identify investment

opportunities or help investors find the right time for trading. Data mining can also recognize high-risk customers or use cyber analytics to detect warnings of fraud.

Health Care
Machine learning has a high-speed trend in the health industry, which has been achieved thanks to the invention of sensors and wearable devices that can use data for real-time health assessment of a patient's health. This technology can help medical experts analyses the data to identify trends and alarming symptoms that may result in an improvement in diagnosis and treatment [6].

Oil and Gas
Finding new sources of energy, analysis of minerals in the ground, prediction of refinery sensor failure, facilitating oil distribution to increase productivity and cost. There are numerous uses for machine learning in the industry and it is still expanding.

Government
Government organizations need machine learning, such as community safety and infrastructure services companies, because they have various data sources that can be evaluated for insight. For example, sensor data analysis identifies ways of increasing efficiency and saving money. Machine learning can also help to define fraud and minimize theft of identity.

Marketing and Sales
Sites that suggest prospective items you may want based on your previous purchases use machine learning to analyze your purchase records and promote other items that may interest you. It is the ability to capture, evaluate, and use data to tailor a shopping experience of the future (implementing a marketing campaign).

Transport
Analyzing data to identify trends and patterns plays an important role in the transportation industry, helping streamline routes and anticipating potential profitability-enhancing issues. For freight forwarding companies, public transport and other transport organizations, data analysis and modeling of machine learning aspects are important tools.

7.1.3.1   Practical Machine Learning Examples

The following are some practical examples in the area of machine learning.

Spam Detection

Spam detection, which is constantly evolving, is one of the old uses of machine learning. At Email Service When we see a message; the service asks you if you believe the message is worthless after the message is found to be worthless. Ultimately, it is up to us to make the spam message available to the service and enhance its experience.

Robotics

By using machine learning, robots can acquire many skills that they learn either through the robot itself or through human intervention, as well as learning to adapt to the environment in which they work. With the increase in the number of sensors used in robots, other algorithms can be used outside the robot for further analysis [7].

Health Care

The competition today is to use machine learning for analysis in the medical field. Many different startups are looking for the benefits of machine learning with bulk data to provide the most professional medical care with the common goal of making the most sensible decisions. Nowadays, countless consumers, even with their smart phones, can measure a wide range of health information on a regular basis. Machine learning systems can provide a model of one's health status and use the recommendations the system updates to improve one's health [6].

Advertising

As long as the products were industrialized and the services provided by the companies were trying to have the greatest impact on the buyers to buy the product. In year 1995, the Internet offered retailers the chance to advertise directly on screens without the help of television or large companies. It should be remembered that the thought of using cookies on our computer keeps track of us? The competition is about disabling cookies from browsers and gaining control of them. Log file analysis is another tactic used to see things of interest. They will be able to categorize the results and categorize the group of users who are most interested in a particular product; in this way, mobile couple location information and highly targeted advertising will be sent directly to you. When this type of advertising was used, there was a concern that an invasion of privacy was taking place, but it was gradually used and made many people happy to check their status and sign in. If you think your friend is the only one you can see, you have to think again. In fact, many companies learn from or analyze their activities.

Internet of Things (IoT)
Connected devices are able to cope with the ubiquitous form of data. Device-to-device communication is a new issue, but it hasn't really been on the mind until recently. With the low cost of production and distribution, devices are now used at home only as long as they are present in the industry [8].

Home automation includes shopping and smart scaling to measure energy consumption. These things are in their infancy and there are many concerns about the security aspects of the devices. Likewise, the location of the phone device is worrying because the company is able to pinpoint the devices with its unique ID and eventually become dependent on a user.

On the other hand, rich data will have the opportunity to put machine learning in the data center and gain information from the machine output. For example, monitoring the hot or cold temperatures of a home's environment can be an example. It is too early for the IoT these days, but it happens in many areas that lead to interesting results. With the likes of the relatively inexpensive Arduino and Raspberry Pi computers, one can start to measure motion, temperature and sound, and then extract the data for analysis.

7.1.4   Relation to Other Fields

Machine learning is a multidisciplinary field, and in fact, there is a close connection between this field and other sciences, for example below, some of the important fields and functions of machine learning are discussed below.

7.1.4.1   Data Mining

Machine learning and data mining are using the same techniques and overlaps, but while machine learning focuses on statement based on the characteristics started to learn from training data, data mining concentrates on finding (formerly) unknown data properties. (This is the knowledge extraction step in the database). Data mining uses many machine learning methods but with different goals; on the other hand, machine learning also uses data mining methods as "unattended learning" or as a preprocessing step to improve learner accuracy [9].

In machine learning, performance is usually evaluated by the ability to reproduce known knowledge, whereas in knowledge discovery from data (KDD), the key activity is the discovery of previously unknown knowledge. Compared to known knowledge, a supervised method (an uninformed method) easily outperforms other supervised methods, whereas in a typical KDD activity, supervised methods cannot be used because of lack of access to training data.

7.1.4.2 Artificial Intelligence

According to the Collins Dictionary, artificial intelligence is the simulation of humans and their mental behaviors by a computer program. Artificial intelligence consists of two words, "intelligence" and "artificial". Something that is not natural and created by man is called artificial. Intelligence is also the ability to understand, reason, plan, and so forth; in other words, a code, technology, or algorithm that can mimic the category of cognitive understanding that emerges in itself or in its achievements is artificial intelligence. In fact, artificial intelligence has found the branch of machine learning. The main problem with the development of new artificial intelligence technology was: How to train large and complex models? In the field of computer science and artificial intelligence, the development and training of stronger subclasses of artificial intelligence was also a question mark on the path to answer these questions that machine learning emerged. So, in fact, machine learning is a major subset of artificial intelligence, and it can enable machines to make their experiences more quality and accurate by using statistical methods. This enables computers and machines to execute commands based on their data and learning. These programs or algorithms are designed so that they can learn more over time and get better with new data.

7.1.4.3 Computational Statistics

The machine learning is closely related to computational statistics (and often overlaps with it); the focus of this branch is also predicted by the computer and has a solid link to mathematical optimization, which also enters into the field theories, theories, and applications. Machine learning is sometimes merged with data mining; the focus of this subcategory is based on the exploratory analysis of the data and is known as unsupervised learning. Machine learning can also be monitored and used to learn and understand the basic form of behavior of various organisms and then to find meaningful anomalies.

7.1.4.4 Probability

Statistics and machine learning and statistics are closely related disciplines. According to Micheal L. Jordan, the ideas of machine learning, from the principles of methodology ranging from theoretical tools, have a long history of statistics. He also proposed the term data science for the general naming of the field. Leo Breiman proposed two statistical paradigms: the data model and the algorithmic model, where algorithmic "algorithmic" model is more or less the meaning of machine learning algorithms such as random forest.

7.1.5 Limitations of Machine Learning

Machine learning is not without limitations. The algorithms differ in the ability to generalize over large categories of patterns and the pattern that has never been seen by any algorithm may be different. In case humans have a broad knowledge of training and experience to act accordingly. It is also capable of detecting similar conditions when making decisions about new information. Machine learning methods can only deal with the generalization of what they have seen so far [10]. Even in this case, there are many limitations. The way a spam can be filtered can be based on the appearance of words or terms regardless of their meaning in the sentence and sentence structure. Although in theory it is possible to build an algorithm that can detect grammars in writing, it is rarely the case in practice. This is because much effort is needed to improve the algorithm's ability to analyze and compare large data sets. Understanding the meaning of words and their relationship to a person's life is much more than the information the spam filter system has and can visualize. In addition, although each of them has a different tendency to do so, all machine learning methods suffer from the possibility of extreme generalization. In most things in life, the general universality is less correct, based on a few examples. One common thing that may happen is that you get a very important email from a friend that contains the words "online pharmacy". In this case, you should be able to tell the algorithm that this email is not spam and the algorithm may infer that email from that friend is acceptable. The nature of most machine learning algorithms is that they can learn more with new information.

7.2   Concept of Well-Defined Learning Problem

7.2.1   Concept Learning

The concept is actually a subset of objects or events defined on a larger set and each of these subsets has common features and properties [11]. For example, a large set of all things (living, inanimate, man-made) can be defined as having a subset of animals that are made up of a small part, such as birds. If we can correctly identify the concepts in our issues, we can help classify them into objects and events. To learn a concept, one must emphasize common features and remove unrelated features. There are many definitions for learning the concept, some of which are mentioned below.

Suppose a set of tagged examples exists as members of a particular concept set and is intended to learn a model. So, in this definition, the goal is to create conceptual learning by having examples labeled as members of a concept set, including the automatic deduction of a general definition of the concept [12].

In another definition, concept learning is a binary function estimation of input and output training samples that determines whether each sample is a member of the concept set. In this model, we obtain a function that specifies membership and non-membership data for each sample [3].

In the third definition that is closest to us, learning the concept by examining positive and negative examples (positive examples: those who are members of our concept and negative examples are those who are not members of this concept) in the space of hypotheses. We may be looking for a hypothesis that best fits the training data.

So, in sum, from the labeled examples, we are looking for a hypothesis (function) that, based on the characteristics of the elements, can determine whether or not membership has the best performance in terms of evaluation criteria. To better understand, consider an example that illustrates the concept of "the days a person enjoys sports." Table 7.1 shows a few different days with features. The purpose of learning is to predict the amount of EnjoySport by knowing other features of a day.

In short, learning the concept of EnjoySport is finding and describing the days that Enjoysport = yes. So, in general, any conceptual learning problem can be identified by examples that have a purpose function defined (objective function: a set of existing hypotheses that the learner considers). For the example above, the general concept learning problem is set out in the table below.

Table 7.1 Positive and negative training examples for the target concept EnjoySport [3].

Data	Sky	AirTemp	Humidity	Wind	Water	Forecast	EnjoySport
1	Sunny	Warm	Normal	Strong	Warm	Same	Yes
2	Sunny	Warm	High	Strong	Warm	Same	Yes
3	Rainy	Cold	High	Strong	Warm	Change	No
4	Sunny	Warm	High	Strong	Warm	Change	Yes

Attributes   ← Concept

7.2.1.1   Concept Representation

Different symbols may be used to illustrate conceptual learning problems, but the simplest form used in this book is as follows. The data set that defines the concept is called a "set of instance" and is represented by X.

For example, as seen in the table above, X is all possible days that each day can be specified by a set of properties. The concept we are learning is called the "target concept" and is represented by C. That is, C is essentially a Boolean function defined on sample X. C: X → {0,1}. The above example in Table 7.1 is the objective function $c(x) = 1$, if Enjoysport = yes and $c(x) = 0$ if Enjoyspot = no. When learning a concept, a set of training data is needed, in fact each sample $x \in X$ needs to be defined by c (x) for each sample. Now, if this in the dataset is $c(x_i) = 0$ then x_i is a negative sample (sample for which the objective function is incorrect), and if $c(x_i) = 0$ means x_i is a positive sample.

Now with the training data, the problem becomes to find hypotheses that can estimate the function c. The set of all possible hypotheses is represented by H; each hypothesis h in H ($h \in H$) is a logical function that, for each sample, X wants to predict the value of the objective function h: X → {0, 1}. So, the goal is to find the hypothesis h that can fit all the training example $c(x) = h(x)$. So, actually the learning input is a set of training examples x with their target values (x, c (x)) and the learning output: a hypothesis like h such that $c(x) = h(x)$ (for all x). The definition of the EnjoySport concept learning task in this general form is given in Table 7.2.

Table 7.2 The EnjoySport concept learning task.

Given	
Instance x:	A collection of attributes (Sky, AirTemp, Humidity, etc.)
Target function c:	Enjoysport: X → {0, 1}
Hypothesis h:	A conjunction of constraints on the attributes.

A constraint can be:
- a specific value (e.g., Water = Warm)
- don't care (e.g., Water = ?)
- no value allowed (e.g., Water = Ø)

Training example d: An instance xi paired with the target function c,
$$D = \langle X, c(X) \rangle_m^1 = \{\langle x_1, c(x_1) \rangle, .. \langle x_m, c(x_m) \rangle\}$$

$c(x_i) = 0$	negative example
$c(x_i) = 1$	positive example

Determine

A hypothesis h in H with $c(x) = h(x)$ for all x in D

7.2.1.2   Instance Representation

As mentioned earlier, in constructing a proper hypothesis, training data is of great importance as training data is a set of instances in which each instance x is a set of attributes that define the concept and for each The sample in the training data needs to identify the target concept, in fact the function to be learned. So, in fact, the training data is shown $D = \langle X, c(X) \rangle_m^1 = \{\langle x_1, c(x_1) \rangle, .. \langle x_m, c(x_m) \rangle\}$ where m represents the number D is the set of positive or negative examples that are defined as follows:

- The examples for which data $c(x) = 1$ are positive examples, or members of the objective concept.
- Examples for which are data $c(x) = 0$ are negative examples, or non-member examples.

7.2.1.3   The Inductive Learning Hypothesis

Any hypothesis that could be a good approximation of the objective function large enough for a training set will be able to approximate the objective function in the case of unobserved examples. So, in fact, the goal of learning is to find the hypothesis h that works for all $x \in X$ samples similar to the objective function, i.e., data $c(x) = h(x)$. Since this type of learning is the only information available in the training example set, therefore, at best, a learning algorithm can present a hypothesis that approximates the objective function on the training examples.

Using inductive learning algorithms, it tries to maximally guarantee that the value of the hypothesis is the same as the objective function value in all training samples, that is, it can estimate the objective function well for the unobserved samples. So, if we want to briefly define the inductive learning hypothesis, we can write: "Any hypothesis in a set of training data that is large enough to accurately estimate the objective function also has the ability to estimate well for other examples that it has not seen".

7.2.2   Concept Learning as Search

The concept learning problem can be seen as a search for a large space of hypotheses (search for hypothesis h from all hypotheses H) [12]. This space is defined by how the hypotheses are presented. Choosing how a hypothesis is presented will determine the scope of the hypotheses that can be learned and learned. So, the purpose of this search is to find a hypothesis that best estimates the behavior of the target function for the training

Table 7.3 The EnjoySport concept learning as a search.

Instances X: Possible days, each described by the attributes	
Attribute	Values
Sky	Sunny, Cloudy, Rainy
AirTemp	Warm, Cold
Humidity	Normal, High
Wind	Strong, Weak
Water	Warm, Cool
Forecast	Same, Change

Hypotheses H: Each hypothesis is described by a conjunction of constraints on the attributes "Sky, AirTemp, Humidity, Wind, Water, and Forecast". The constraints may be "?" (any value is acceptable), "0 (no value is acceptable), or a specific value.

samples. Consider the EnjoySport example, all the hypotheses are represented by H and the training examples by X in Table 7.3. Each x ∈ X sample has six attributes in which the sky attribute three values and the rest of the attributes double values. So, the total number of distinct and possible samples for the above example is 3*2*2*2*2*2 = 96.

The number of hypotheses is also equal to 5120 = 5*4*4*4*4*4, since features (?) and (null) are added to each case. If any of these hypotheses are eliminated null, since the null will have a negative value for all examples, the number of meaningful hypotheses are: 1+ (4*3*3*3*3*3) = 973. This example is a very simple one for concept learning and has relatively few hypotheses in total, while most actual and practical learning tasks have a much larger and sometimes unlimited hypothesis space.

If we look at learning as a search problem, then it is natural that studying learning algorithms will actually explore different strategies to search the hypothesis space, and so, we will look for algorithms that are able to find very large or infinite hypothesis space. Search for the hypothesis that best fits with training data.

7.2.2.1 Concept Generality

A concept P is more general than or equal to another concept Q if the set of instances represented by P includes the set of instances represented by Q. For example in Figure 7.1, mammal is more general that dog.

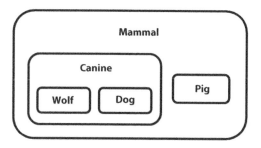

Figure 7.1 Concept generality example.

7.3   General-to-Specific Ordering Over Hypotheses

7.3.1   Basic Concepts: Hypothesis, Generality

The model built should be somehow displayed in the official languages that the computer can run, and each learner can have a set of these models capable of learning, which is called the hypothesis space learning hypothesis space. It is quite natural, if the classification is not in the hypothesis space, it cannot be learned! The symbol H is used to indicate the set of all possible hypotheses that the learner might consider when identifying the concept of purpose. In general, each hypothesis h of H represents the Boolean function defined on X. The goal of a learner is to find the best hypothesis in this space of hypotheses that can maximally resemble the objective function, that is to say, its training and experimental error is minimal [1].

In some cases, many hypotheses may be found to have minimal error and even zero. The purpose of learning is to choose the most appropriate one from all the correct hypotheses. The most appropriate hypothesis is to provide the best answer for new specimens to be considered in the future. The following describes how hypotheses are presented, evaluated, and constructed.

7.3.2   Structure of the Hypothesis Space

This section deals with the definition and presentation of the hypothesis, the evaluation, and the hierarchy of the hypothesis.

7.3.2.1   Hypothesis Notations

What representation of hypotheses should be used in this learning? In fact, each hypothesis can be defined simply by the definition of several properties as stated. For example, for EnjoySport problem showed in Table 7.1, features are considered as regular hex values that specify the values of these attributes. Each attribute can have one of the following states:

- Show it with "?" If any value is acceptable (don't care).
- Show it with "Φ" if no value is acceptable.
- Display it with a specified value (such as warm) if this value is certain.

If a sample x satisfies all the constraints of the hypothesis h, it can be said that the hypothesis h classified sample x as a positive (h(x) = 1).

7.3.2.2 Hypothesis Evaluations

The hypothesis is represented by h: $X \rightarrow c(X)$ where X is a data set that has a specific purpose function, so in fact, as stated above, each hypothesis h is a logical function that, for each sample, X wants to predict the value of the objective function. So, the goal is to find the hypothesis h that can fit all the training data $c(x) = h(x)$. So, actually the learning input is a set of training examples x with their target values (x, c (x)) and the learning output: a hypothesis like h such that $c(x) = h(x)$ (for all x). Now, to evaluate the hypothesis, the error rate of this hypothesis must be measured with the real objective function, which is defined as L where $L(c, h) = D(x: c(x) \neq h(x))$. Now, the goal is to find the hypothesis $h \in H$ so that it has the least error $\underset{h \in H}{\operatorname{argmin}} L(c, h)$ [13].

7.3.3 Ordering on Hypotheses: General to Specific

Many learning algorithms have based their search on the sorting structure, generally based on some hypotheses. Using this method, algorithms can be designed that can test all the hypotheses and choose between them without examining each hypothesis.

This method is particularly useful when the space of the hypothesis H is infinite. Consider the following three hypotheses, for EnjoySport example:

$$h_1 = \langle Sunny, ?, ?, Strong, ?, ? \rangle$$
$$h_2 = \langle Sunny, ?, ?, ?, ?, ? \rangle$$
$$h_3 = \langle Sunny, ?, ?, ? \, Cool, ? \rangle$$

In these hypotheses, since h_2 has less constraint, it evaluates more samples as positive, and in fact, any sample that is h_1 positive will also consider h_2 and h_3 positive, so h_2 is more general than h_1 and h_3. In general, the "general or equal" inherent relationship between hypotheses can be defined as follows [3]:

Definition: h_j is more general than or equal to h_k iff :

$$h_j \geq_g h_k \equiv (\forall x \in X)[(h_k(x) = 1) \rightarrow (h_j(x) = 1)] \qquad (7.1)$$

Definition: h_j is strictly-more general than to h_k iff :

$$h_j >_g h_k \equiv (h_j \geq_g h_k) \wedge (h_k \not\geq_g h_j) \qquad (7.2)$$

To better understand this concept, consider the three hypotheses defined above. These hypotheses are illustrated below. The left square represents X or all samples, and the right square represents H or the hypothesis space.

Each hypothesis is a subset of X (the same subset that satisfies it). The arrow shows the relationship between the hypotheses being more specific. Now, we want to see what the relationship between these three hypotheses is. As previously mentioned, h_2 is more general than h_1 Similarly, h_2 is more general than h_3. But, it should be noted that none of the hypotheses h_1 and h_3 are more general than the other. Although they share examples, they do not include any others. The relation $\geq_g$ and $>_g$ are defined independently of what the purpose concept is and are based solely on which examples fall within the hypothesis and not on the purpose function. The $\geq_g$ relation creates a special order within the H-space of the hypothesis. Unofficially when we say a partial order versus the general structure, we mean that there may be a pair of hypotheses such as h_1 and h_2 that $h_3 \not\geq_g h_1$ and $h_1 \not\geq_g h_3$ do not exist.

As can be seen in Figure 7.2 in the space of H hypothesis, there are generally two hypotheses that are: Most general hypothesis: $\langle ?,?,? ,? ,?, ?\rangle$ and Most specific hypothesis: $\langle \emptyset,\emptyset, \emptyset , \emptyset ,\emptyset, \emptyset\rangle$. Now, if there are two similar hypotheses in the hypothesis space that do not always have a relationship, $h_2 \geq_g h_1$ or $h_1 \geq_g h_2$, then the most specific generalized or most general specialized hypotheses can be defined. This is discussed in more detail below.

7.3.3.1 Most Specific Generalized

This case is in fact the most general hypothesis, assuming that the set G contains two hypotheses h_1, h_2, which is not null, and contains all the

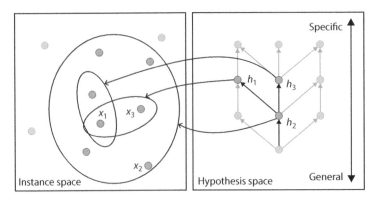

Figure 7.2 Instances space, hypotheses space, and the more general relation [14].

hypotheses that are more general than the two. In this case, the most general hypothesis is any hypothesis that is a member of the set and is larger than any particular hypothesis (as shown in Figure 7.3). This definition is detailed below.

Definition: the most specific generalized, $MSG(h_1, h_2)$ is generality relationship in H, when for h_1, h_2 given $(h_2 \geq_g h_1)$ or $(h_1 \geq_g h_2)$ is not always true and $G(h_1, h_2) = \{h_g \mid h_g \geq_g h_1 \text{ and } h_g \geq_g h_2\}$ is non-empty, So,

$$MSG(h_1, h_2): h_g \text{ in } MSG(h_1, h_2) \text{ and } \acute{h} < h_g \Rightarrow \acute{h} \text{ not in } MSG(h_1, h_2)$$

(7.3)

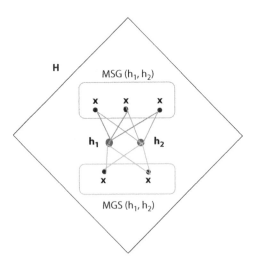

Figure 7.3 Most specific generalized and most general specialized relation.

7.3.3.2   Most General Specialized

This is the opposite of a high relationship, and in fact, the most general hypothesis. In this case, it is assumed that the set S contains two hypotheses h_1, h_2, which is not null, and contains all the hypotheses that are more specific than the two. In this case, the most general specific hypothesis is any hypothesis that is a member of the set and is more specific than any general hypothesis (as shown in Figure 7.3). This definition is detailed below:

Definition: the most specific generalized, MSG(h_1, h_2) is generality relationship in H, when for h_1, h_2 given ($h_2 \geq_g h_1$) or ($h_1 \geq_g h_2$) is not always true and S(h_1, h_2) = {h_S | $h_1 \geq_g h_S$ and $h_2 \geq_g h_S$} is non-empty, so

$$\mathrm{MGS}\big(h_1,h_2\big): h_s \text{ in } \mathrm{MGS}\big(h_1,h_2\big) \text{ and } h_s < h' \Rightarrow h' \text{ not in } \mathrm{MGS}\big(h_1,h_2\big)$$

(7.4)

7.3.3.3   Generalization and Specialization Operators

Demonstrating the generality of a hypothesis can be demonstrated by the Closing interval operator, Hierarchy Tree Ascent op, Conjunction abandon op, Alternative addition, etc., and its privatization can also be reversed. In general, the G_{set} operator representing the general set of assumptions and S_{set} representing the private set are defined as follows: (it should be noted that H convex for $\leq$. If h_1 and h_3 in H and $h_1 \leq h_2 \leq h_3$, then h_2 in H and H bounded, if there is a maximal element g and a minimal element s for generalization) [15].

Definition: The general boundary G, with respect to hypothesis space h and training data D, is the set of maximally general members of H consistent with D if H is convex and bounded, then:

$$G_{set} = \{h \text{ in } H \mid h \text{ coherent and } (if\ h' > h \text{ then } h' \text{ not in } G_{set})\} \quad (7.5)$$

Definition: The specific boundary S, with respect to hypothesis space H and training data D, is the set of minimally general (i.e., maximally specific) members of H consistent with D if H is convex and bounded, then:

$$S_{set} = \{h \text{ in } H \mid h \text{ coherent and } (if\ h' < h \text{ then } h' \text{ not in } S_{set})\} \quad (7.6)$$

7.3.4 Hypothesis Space Search by Find-S Algorithm

Find-S algorithm is a method for searching between hypotheses and finding the best hypothesis. The structure of this algorithm is that it starts from the most specific hypothesis within the space of H and proceeds to generalize it so that it can no longer cover the samples. (As mentioned, a hypothesis covers a positive sample when it can be included). At each stage of the algorithm, the hypothesis only becomes sufficiently general to cover the new sample. So at each step, the hypothesis h is the most specific hypothesis built on the previous positive examples (the word S is also found in the name of the Find-S specific word. The pseudo-code of this algorithm is shown in Table 7.4) [3].

Next, to better understand this algorithm, suppose training data in (as shown in Table 7.1) is available to learn the concept of EnjoySport. The steps of the Find-S algorithm to learn this concept are as follows:

According to the algorithm, the first step is to initialize the hypothesis as the most specific one. So, the hypothesis is $h_0 \leftarrow \{\varnothing, \varnothing, \varnothing, \varnothing, \varnothing, \varnothing\}$. It then goes to the first training data in the $x_1 \leftarrow$ {Sunny, Warm, Normal, Strong, Warm, Same}, because the label of this sample is positive, so for each attribute of this sample, the hypothesis h_0 should cover this sample. The first hypothesis is then replaced by the values of this sample and the second hypothesis is defined $h_1 \leftarrow$ {Sunny, Warm, Normal, Strong, Warm, Same}. This hypothesis is very specific because it does not satisfy any other positive sample except the first one. In the second step, the second training sample $x_2 \leftarrow$ {Sunny, Warm, High, Strong, Warm, Same} is inserted because the label of this sample is also positive, so the existing hypothesis should cover this sample as well. Therefore, the algorithm is forced to generalize the hypothesis h_1, by observing that the third attribute is created with the "?" new hypothesis (because this behavior was not covered by the

Table 7.4 Find-S algorithm.

1. Initialize h to the most specific hypothesis in H
2. For each positive training instance x
For each attribute constraint a_i in h
If the constraint a_i in h is satisfied by x
do nothing
Else
replace a_i in h by the next more general
constraint that is satisfied by x
3. Output hypothesis h

previous hypothesis). The new hypothesis is equal to $h_2 \leftarrow$ {Sunny, Warm, ?, Strong, Warm, Same}.

In the third step, by entering the third sample, since the label of this sample is negative, there is no need to change the hypothesis h_2. So, the hypothesis generated in this step is the same as the previous hypothesis, namely, that $h_3 = h_2$ does not actually do the Find-S in the presence of negative samples. While this algorithm behavior sounds a bit strange, the hypothesis that works for this sample is negative (in fact the hypothesis categorizes this sample correctly).

In step 4, to complete the fourth prototype algorithm $x_4 \leftarrow$ {Sunny, Warm, High, Strong, Cool, Change} also have to be entered, it can be seen that to cover the fourth prototype by the hypothesis h_3 the last two properties must be changed, the hypothesis becomes more general, and finally, the final hypothesis in the form $h_4 \leftarrow$ {Sunny, Warm, ?, Strong,?, ?} can be made. All of these steps can be seen in Figure 7.4.

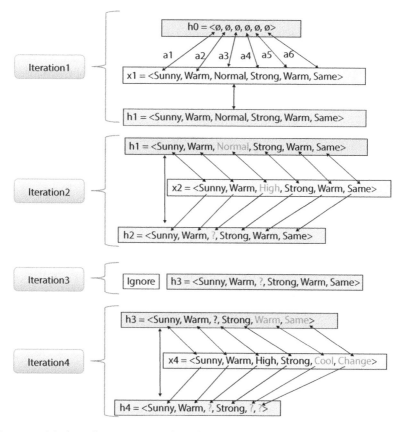

Figure 7.4 The hypothesis space search performed by Find-S algorithm.

7.3.4.1   Properties of the Find-S Algorithm

The Find-S algorithm is actually an example of using a more general feature to search for hypothesis space to find the optimal hypothesis. The search starts from a very specific hypothesis and goes on to generalize it. So that, at each stage just to cover the new sample, it needs to be generalized. The key feature of this algorithm is that it guarantees to represent the most specific hypothesis based on positive examples in the space of hypotheses (H). Assuming that the samples are correct and C is present in H, the output of this algorithm is zero for negative samples.

7.3.4.2   Limitations of the Find-S Algorithm

This algorithm is unable to answer the following questions [12].

- Has the algorithm come to the right concept? Is there another compatible hypothesis? Although this algorithm finds a hypothesis that is consistent with all the training examples, it does not guarantee that the hypothesis found is unique and there may be other hypotheses in the H space that match the samples.
- Is the most specific hypothesis good? When given to the Find-S algorithm, the output of the most specific hypothesis is likely to be output, and it is not clear why it does not follow the most general hypothesis or anything in between, but only the most specific hypothesis.
- Is there always an error-free training sample? In many learning issues, there is a possibility of errors or noise in the training samples. The search samples error find the Find-S. In other words, the algorithm is highly sensitive to noise. Therefore, it is preferable to use algorithms that recognize the error of the samples and be able to adapt itself to these errors. The find that the Find-S algorithm does not have the ability to do so.
- What if there were multiple maximal proprietary hypotheses or none? If in some spaces the hypothesis was not the most specific one, then the Find-S algorithm would have to be refined in such a way to consider other options.

7.4   Version Spaces and Candidate Elimination Algorithm

7.4.1   Representing Version Spaces

To define the concept of version space (VS), we first need to define the concept of compatibility. "Consistent" means a hypothesis consistent with training examples if they correctly classify samples.

Definition: The hypothesis h is consistent with a set of training examples D if and only if h (x) = c (x) for each example x, c(x) in D.

$$Consistent\ (h, D) \equiv (\forall\ \langle x, c(x)\rangle \in D)\ h(x) = c(x) \qquad (7.7)$$

It should be noted, however, that the concept of consistency and satisfy is not the same, for example, suppose the hypothesis h satisfies the sample x if h (x) = 1 while x does not differ from the positive or negative sample. While the sample x is consistent with the hypothesis h when h (x) = c (x).

The concept of consistency is shown in Figure 7.5. According this figure, h_1 covers a different set of examples than h_2. h_2 is consistent with training set D, and finally, h_1 is not consistent with training set D.

Hypotheses compatible with training examples are called version space, since all accepted versions include the concept of purpose. Version space is dependent on the space of hypotheses H and training examples D. Version Space, represented by $VS_{H,D}$, actually contains all the H hypotheses that are compatible with D examples, given the H hypothesis space and D training examples [3].

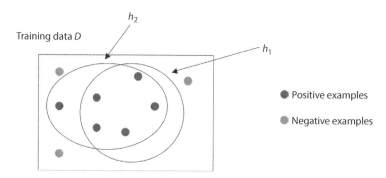

Figure 7.5 Consistent hypothesis in a set of training examples.

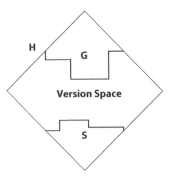

Figure 7.6 Version space bade on general boundary and specific boundary.

Definition: The version space, denoted $VS_{H,D}$, with respect to hypothesis space H and training examples D, is the subset of hypotheses from H consistent with the training examples in D.

$$VS_{H,D} \equiv \{h \in H \mid Consistent\ (h,\ D)\} \qquad (7.8)$$

Each VS can be specified by its most specific and general members, which are further defined by the general boundaries of G and the specific S, and it can be proved that the only VS can be determined using these two boundaries (as shown in Figure 7.6).

7.4.1.1   General Boundary

Definition: The general boundary G: For hypothesis space H and training data D, G is the set of H members that are maximally general with D compatible [16].

$$G \equiv \{g \in H \mid Consistent\ (g,D) \wedge (\nexists g' \in H)[(g' >_g g) \wedge consistent(g',D)]\} \qquad (7.9)$$

7.4.1.2   Specific Boundary

Definition: The specific boundary S: For hypothesis space H and training data D, S is equal to the set of H members that are maximally specific to D [16].

$$S \equiv \{s \in H \,|\, Consistent\ (s,D) \wedge (\nexists s' \in H) \big[(s >_g s') \wedge consistent(s',D) \big] \}$$

(7.10)

7.4.2 Version Space as Search Strategy

One can look at the problem of learning, the concept as a search for a large space of hypotheses. This space is defined as non-explicit by the way hypotheses are presented. Choosing how a hypothesis is presented will determine the scope of the hypotheses that can be learned and learned. Since most learning tasks have a large set of hypotheses, it is important to select a set of these hypotheses to find hypotheses consistent with working examples. In fact, the learning problem can be regarded as a problematic problem, and since the hypotheses that are consistent with the training examples are defined as VS, then VS can be used as a method to search for appropriate hypotheses in the whole set [15]. Hypotheses knew.

7.4.3 The List-Eliminate Method

The simplest way to specify VS is to specify each of the hypotheses that are part of this set; this type is specified by a method called List-Eliminate defined in Table 7.5. This method lists all H hypotheses and then any hypotheses which are inconsistent with the training examples will be removed [3]. The remainder will be VS. (Practical for small H only).

In this algorithm, it is initially assumed that all the assumptions in the H space are consistent with the training examples D, that is, it actually initializes VS = H. It then removes any hypothesis that is inconsistent with the training examples. This elimination is done by examining the consistency of each of the hypotheses with the individual training data. If the amount of training data is sufficient, ultimately only one hypothesis remains in the VS set, but if the number of data is insufficient, there is more than one

Table 7.5 The List-Eliminate method.

1. $VS_{H,D} \leftarrow$ a list containing every hypothesis in H
2. For each training example, x, c(x)
remove from $VS_{H,D}$ any hypothesis that is inconsistent with the
training example $h(x) \neq c(x)$
3. Output the list of hypotheses in $VS_{H,D}$

hypothesis in this space, and the same set of hypotheses are consistent with the training data.

7.4.4 The Candidate-Elimination Method

The Candidate-Elimination algorithm works the same as the List-Eliminate algorithm. Except that it uses another display to display the special space (VS). In this representation, VS is represented by its most general G and its most specific S hypotheses. It actually considers the hypotheses between the two sets of general and partial hypotheses. These two boundaries encompass all the hypotheses in the hypothesis space, since all hypotheses are more general than S_0 and more specific than G_0. Now, each sample is examined, and based on S and G, it becomes more general and specific to eliminate hypotheses that are inconsistent with the sample from VS. After

Table 7.6 The Candidate-Elimination method.

G ← maximally general hypothesis in H
S ← maximally specific hypothesis in H
For each training example x, c(x)
      <u>(modify G and S so that G and S are consistent with d)</u>
 	
    If d is a positive example
          • Remove from G any hypothesis that is inconsistent with d
          • For each hypothesis s in S that is not consistent with d
               • Remove s from S.
               • Add to S all minimal generalizations h of s such that
                  h consistent with d
                  Some member of G is more general than h
               • Remove from S any hypothesis that is more
                 general than another hypothesis in S
 	
    If d is a negative example
          • Remove from S any hypothesis that is inconsistent with d
          • For each hypothesis g in G that is not consistent with d
               • Remove g from G.
               • Add to G all minimal specializations h of g such that
                  h consistent with d
                  Some member of S is more specific than h
          • Remove from G any hypothesis that is less general than
             another hypothesis in G

examining the entire sample, the VS is determined. Of course, positive and negative samples affect S and G in different ways (symmetrically) [17]. This algorithm is summarized in Table 7.6.

It is important to note that the algorithm stops when either the examples are finished or the number of hypotheses remaining is zero. In general, the number of remaining hypotheses may be as follows:

- 0 Hypothesis: There is no compatibility definition for the algorithm.
- 1 Hypothesis: Algorithm Converged.
- More than two hypotheses: all generalizations found.

7.4.4.1 Example

For example, the EnjoySport problem that data are presented in Table 7.1 is used to calculate VS using the Candidate-Elimination algorithm so that it is compatible with all existing training examples. First, according to the structure of the algorithm, the most general hypothesis is $G_0 \leftarrow \{?,?,?,?,?,?\}$ and the most specific equation is $S_0 \leftarrow \{\emptyset,\emptyset,\emptyset,\emptyset,\emptyset,\emptyset\}$. Then, in duplicates with the number of training data samples, S and G become more general and specific. For example, when the algorithm reaches the first prototype, no change is made to G, since G_0 is the most general hypothesis and therefore covers this sample, then $G_1 \leftarrow \{?,?,?,?,?,?\}$. So, the algorithm goes to S and checks S_0 and finds that S_0 is too specific so it doesn't cover this sample so it needs to change to S_0.

So, the particular hypothesis is defined as $S_1 \leftarrow$ {Sunny, Warm, Normal, Strong, Warm, Same}. Now, in the second step, enter the second sample which is again positive and so no change in G_1 is given and the next general hypothesis is equal to the previous one, so $G_2 \leftarrow \{?,?,?,?,?,?\}$. Now, the hypothesis S_1 should cover this example so the algorithm is forced to generalize it, so the new hypothesis equals $S_2 \leftarrow$ {Sunny, Warm, ? , Strong, Warm, Same}; If you look closely you can see that up to this point, it is very similar to the Find-S algorithm.

In the third step, entering the third sample because it is negative should first be examined. Does hypothesis S_2 cover this data? It can be seen that this hypothesis covers the sample so that in this step S_2 remains unchanged, and hence, the next hypothesis equals $S_3 \leftarrow$ {Sunny, Warm, ? , Strong, Warm, Same}. Now, we have to go to the G_2 hypothesis, we find that this hypothesis is too general and we have to make it specific because without specifying it is predicted that this example is a positive example. So, G_2

must be specified to the point that this sample is true and negative, as there are many specifics for the G_2 hypothesis as shown below, all of these new hypotheses become part of the new G_3 boundary set.

Why is it that while six more specific hypotheses can be defined for G_2, only three are added to G_3? For example, the hypothesis h ← {?,?, Normal,?,?,?}. That you deny the negative sample correctly and a general but more specific hypothesis than the previous one has not been added?

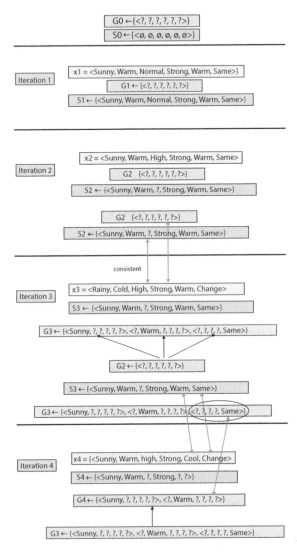

Figure 7.7 An example for Candidate-Elimination method.

The answer is that this hypothesis is not consistent with the previous two positive examples.

The algorithm understands this by comparing the hypotheses with S because S stores a summary of the previous positive samples and it can be determined whether the general hypothesis that is specific is consistent with the positive samples or No. That is, any hypothesis that is more general than S is consistent with any previous positive sample. In contrast, G stores a summary of negative samples.

In the fourth, last step, the sample is positive, so in step G_3 it should be checked whether the sample is covered by each of the hypotheses or not. This hypothesis is equivalent to h ← {?,?,?,?,?}, same, since the fourth sample is the last attribute of "Change" and does not cover this sample. Then, G_4 ←{(Sunny,?,?,?,?,?,) (?, Warm, ?,?,?,?)}. Now, S_3 should cover the sample observed to be more general and therefore equal S_4 ← {Sunny, Warm, ?, Strong,?, ?}. Now, as shown in Figure 7.7, after 4 iterations, S_4 and G_4 are calculated and each hypothesis is VS.

7.4.4.2   Convergence of Candidate-Elimination Method

One of the important debates in the Candidate-Elimination algorithm is the convergence of this algorithm in the sense of whether the algorithm is moving towards the correct hypothesis [17].

The answer to this question is yes, provided that 1. There is no error in the training examples. 2. H contains a hypothesis that can properly describe the concept of purpose. In this case, it can be expected that the output of the algorithm tends to the hypothesis that the objective concept is correctly described. When the two boundaries S and G reach a unified set of words, in other words, converge to a single hypothesis, the concept of purpose is fully learned.

What if the training samples are not correct and there is an error in which the noise is available? Unfortunately, in such examples, the right target algorithm is removed from the specific space and in other words, the objective concept is removed from the specific space, because, for instance, if a sample is to be positive instead of positive, it causes the algorithm to eliminate all the hypotheses it takes. In such situations, however, with sufficient samples S and G, the set S and G does not exist, meaning there is no hypothesis in H that matches all the training samples. Therefore, if the examples have errors, it may eliminate the target algorithm from the VS and eventually converge to the empty set if possible. Therefore, we assume that all samples are correct and the target concept is present in H.

7.4.4.3 Inductive Bias for Candidate-Elimination

One feature of inductive learning is that it must have an institutional assumption about the hypothesis space; otherwise, learning will be impossible. A learning system that has no presupposition about the nature of the target function will not be able to categorize the observed data. In fact, the only reason the Candidate-Elimination algorithm was generalizable was that it assumed that the target function could be combined with the feature-specific combination. The assumption that applies to the hypothesis space is bias. For example, the Find-S bias of space H is defined as a combination of properties and has the concept of C [3].

As stated, the Candidate-Elimination algorithm will converge to the correct concept if the learning examples are correct and the hypothesis space contains the concept. But if the hypothesis space does not include the concept of purpose, can the hypothesis space be chosen to encompass all possible hypotheses to avoid the above problem? And what are some examples of tutorials? These are simple questions about induction in general. Here are some questions about the Candidate-Elimination algorithm. However, it can be seen that the results of this study are applicable to all conceptual learning systems.

A Biased Hypothesis Space
Suppose we want to include the hypothesis space, the concept of purpose that is unknown. The first and easiest way is to put all possible hypotheses in the hypothetical space [17]. For example, consider EnjoySport problem in Table 7.1. In this example, a hypothetical case involving all the hypotheses was considered. Because of this limitation, it does not encompass a very simple nonlinear hypothetical space such as h ← {sky = suuny or sky = cloudy}. In this case, the most specific hypothesis or the most general hypothesis may be too general or specific because we bias the space of the H hypothesis and consider only the conjunctive components needed to solve this problem. To use a more general or specific hypothesis space.

An Unbiased Hypothesis Space
One way to ensure that the goal in space is to consider this space so large that all possible hypotheses can be covered. This large space can be viewed as the power set of the number of training samples. For this, assume that if X is all examples of learning, the set of all subsets of X can be used to set up. For example, in Table 7.1 (EnjoySport), all states of one day, characterized by six attributes, is 96, which is the strength set of 296 members. Overall, 296 the hypotheses can be defined, whereas in the examples that

were resolved, h had only 973 billion, which represents a small portion of the above set, suggesting that we actually bias our space [3].

The learning function in the previous example can be done this time with the new hypothesis space that is actually expanding the previous space, so that H ', which is the hypothesis space without bias (actually the power set X). A method of constructing the hypothesis space H ' is constructed so that H can be modified to include all reversible, seasonal, and contradictory states. Then, the hypothesis h ← {sky = suuny or sky = cloudy} can be written as h ← {(suuny,?,?,?,?,?) or (cloudy,?,?,?,?,?)}.

By adding such hypotheses, one can confidently turn to the Candidate-Elimination algorithm and be sure that the hypothesis space encompasses the target concept. Despite the success of the Candidate-Elimination algorithm in learning some examples using bias-free learning, the algorithm is not capable of generalization and will only retain instructional examples. In other words, solving this problem itself creates another problem, which is that with this hypothesis space, it is impossible to predict new samples. For example, if the training set contains positive examples x_1, x_2, x_3 and negative examples x_4, x_5, the VS space will be converted to the following set.

$$G \leftarrow \left\{ \neg \langle x_4 \rangle \vee \langle x_5 \rangle \right\} \qquad \Leftarrow \ VS \ \Rightarrow \qquad S \leftarrow \left\{ \langle x_1 \rangle \vee \langle x_2 \rangle \vee \langle x_3 \rangle \right\}$$

Such a hypothesis would not be able to categorize ignored examples. The above discussion specifies a fundamental property of inductive learning, that is, a learning system that has no presupposition about the nature of the objective function will not be able to categorize unobserved data. In fact, the only reason the candidate deletion algorithm had the power to generalize to the ignored examples was that it was assumed that the objective function could be represented by a custom combination of features.

7.5   Concepts of Machine Learning Algorithm

In this section, the general types of learning algorithms and issues related to machine learning are discussed.

7.5.1   Types of Learning Algorithms

The learning algorithms can be divided into different categories, which are basically based on the way learning is done in these categories.

7.5.1.1 Incremental vs. Batch Learning Algorithms

Based on the complete or gradual availability of training data, machine learning algorithms can be divided into two categories: "batch" and "incremental".

In batch learning algorithms, the training data is fully available and accessible to the learning agent from the beginning, and after the training phase, new training data cannot be added to the system. In these algorithms, if the training data is too large, the training period will be long and time-consuming, and in some cases, there may be a lack of space to store the entire training data [18].

In incremental learning algorithms, the training data may not be definite or complete from the beginning or may be added over time. In other words, it is possible for these algorithms to enter new training data after the training phase. The purpose of these algorithms is to preserve the results of previous stages of training and improve the performance of the learning agent only by learning new patterns [19]. In fact, these algorithms adapt and update themselves with the arrival of new ones without having to re-train old ones that may no longer be available.

Incremental learning is one of the important issues in machine learning. A variety of definitions and interpretations of incremental learning can be found in texts including online learning, incorrect reclassification of previous examples, or the development and pruning of cluster architecture.

Incremental learning is defined as: "An incremental learning is said to be provided if the required training data is not readily available and provided to the learning agent over time." In fact, an incremental learning-based system is a system that updates its previous assumptions and information when new samples are introduced, without reusing previous ones.

In fact, such a system, when presenting new samples, does not forget the results of the training of its previous phases on the old samples, but improves its past knowledge with respect to the new samples. In other words, such a system teaches the concept of Y based on the set of samples X_1, then teaches the concept of Z on the basis of the concept of Y and set of samples X_2, and continues the process.

An incremental learning is called incremental learning if it has the following characteristics [19]:

- Ability to gain additional knowledge when introducing new data.
- Ability to keep the information learned from previous learning stages.

- Ability to learn a new class when presented with a new sample.

Based on the studies on algorithms with incremental learning capability, these algorithms can be categorized according to different criteria. For example, these algorithms can be divided into three categories based on their ability to hold educational data:

- Complete data: This set of algorithms is capable of storing all training data without losing old data. The benefits of these algorithms can be to refurbish and update efficiently and to achieve accurate accuracy, but because of all the training data, these algorithms require a lot of storage space.
- Partial data: These algorithms only hold specific data. They thus reach a degree of agreement between accuracy and memory usage.
- No data: In this category, algorithms only store statistical information about the data and discard all data. Therefore, the accuracy of these algorithms is lower than the two categories above, depending on the type of data stored. The memory usage of such algorithms is also low.

There are other categories for incremental learning algorithms that divide these algorithms into two categories: strong and weak algorithms.

- Strong Algorithm: A learning approach is called strong incremental learning if the memory and computation required for the algorithm is not dependent on the number of training samples. In other words, with the introduction of the new tutorial, there is no need for more memory and computing.
- Weak Algorithm: These incremental algorithms require more memory and computation with the introduction of new tutorials. Among the weak incremental algorithms are ID5R and k-nearest neighbor.

Most classification algorithms are not capable of making changes to add incremental learning, but rather have algorithms that are incremental. The designed algorithms have certain advantages and disadvantages and are designed for a variety of purposes.

7.5.1.2   Offline vs. Online Learning Algorithms

Offline learning in this machine model learns over time using data enhancement. In other words, it has to learn using the data it already has. Of course, this model consumes a great deal of time and resources and usually does its job offline [20]. First the machine learns, then runs to reach the market and runs in a way that no longer learns.

In online learning, the machine learns using data that is given in mini-batch. Each learning stage is fast and inexpensive, so the machine gathers data and quickly learns it.

The difference between the two types of learning can be explained by a simple example. Suppose a student wants to learn statistics and probabilities. In the first type of learning, this student can produce, read, and learn multiple sets of statistics and probabilities. After learning from this set of statistics, he no longer learns anything new and only uses his own knowledge from now on. It's a kind of offline learning. In this learning method, all data is available during the training and after the training phase, we will no longer have the learning, but second learning, or online learning, is such that the student first reads and reads their books. Learn, and then, while using his knowledge, whenever he finds a new book on statistics and probabilities, reads, and improves his learning by reading it.

Most algorithms are offline, meaning that at the time of the train, all the data was in the algorithm and the algorithm could somehow perform the learning operation on the data, but there is another type of learning. Sometimes, data comes in the form of data flows or needs to be learned on a regular basis [20].

So, offline learning is like you have a set of books and you have to learn them because you have to try tomorrow. All of your sources are these books, and in fact, you have all the data, but suppose you are on the road to life and with the new information you are given every day you have to learn new things and add to your previous knowledge. This is the second case of online learning, when not all data is currently available. An online learning model is built and then updated as newer data arrive [1].

The online learning model or online learning has two major advantages:

1. This method can train very high volume data. For example, data that is not in memory due to its large volume.
2. Changes that may occur in the nature of the data are covered in this way. Suppose Google has developed an algorithm for its email system that intelligently detects spam emails with machine learning algorithms. As you might expect, the

content of spam emails is constantly changing, and people who send spam emails are optimizing themselves against these Google algorithms every day. So, Google's spam email detection algorithm can do online learning to detect spam emails that have changed over time. In fact, algorithm learning is updated and strengthened by the modification of the content and shape of spam emails.

7.5.1.3   *Inductive vs. Deductive Learning Algorithms*

The learning algorithms by type of construction can be categorized as induction and deduction. However, inductive algorithms have a stronger leverage than deductive algorithms. The following is a brief description of each.

Inductive algorithms are algorithms where learning is based on multiple examples, such as decision trees. In these algorithms, the constructed model is such that if it can enlarge a good approximation of the objective function to a sufficiently large set of training sets, it can approximate this objective function in the case of unobserved examples [21]. In this learning, the only information available is the training example set, so at best, a learning algorithm can present a hypothesis that approximates the objective function on the training examples.

In contrast to deductive algorithms, the model is built on general states, which means that a series of rules is attempted to reach a particular state. The following figure illustrates the difference [21].

The overall structure of machine learning algorithms is that by using a data set, a model is built to generate output for new entries that have not been seen before. One of the differences between ranking learning algorithms is how data is used to model the training data used to build the model, whether or not to use their labels [22]. So, a framework for learning ratings can include: data (training and testing), the algorithm used to construct the model, and finally the model evaluation to generate the appropriate output, which will be explained in each case.

7.5.2   A Framework for Machine Learning Algorithms

The general structure of machine learning algorithms is that, using a set of data, a model is made to produce an output for new inputs that have not yet been observed. One of the differences between learning algorithms is how to utilize data in order to utilize the training data used to build the model if they use their tag. A framework for learning learning, that showed in

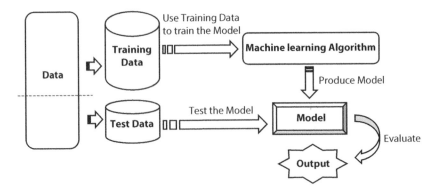

Figure 7.8 The framework for machine learning algorithms.

Figure 7.8, can include: Data (training and testing), the algorithm used to build the model and finally assess the model for output production, which will be explained later on each.

7.5.2.1   Training Data

Machine learning algorithms use training data to build models. In fact, the data used in the simplest case is divided into two parts: training data and test data [23]. There are several ways to access training data. In the simplest way, for example, 75% of the data is used as training data and 25% is used to test and evaluate the constructed model [24]. The training data is used for some algorithms with the class tag and for others without the tag. The test data is also provided to the models completely without class [9].

So in fact, if we want to define precisely, the training data is shown as $D = \left(X, Y_m^1 \right) = \left\{ \left(x_1, y_1 \right), .. \left(x_m, y_m \right) \right\}$ where m represents the number of data that is educational. In this respect, x_i represents the feature vector and y_i represents the label. For example, x_i can be a vector of features related to a disease and y_i is a diagnosis of that disease.

7.5.2.2   Target Function

The objective function in ranking learning algorithms is actually the class and the label that must be predicted or described. In fact, suppose a ranking learning algorithm has produced an f model using the training data, but for each sample, x must be able to produce the desired output, namely, y, that is, $f : X \leftarrow Y$ in the following sense.

7.5.2.3   Construction Model

Modeling actually involves several steps, first extracting the appropriate features from the dataset and then selecting some of them based on the objective function and then making a decision maker for the other samples based on machine learning algorithms. To be. This is the final output decision of the model [25].

7.5.2.4   Evaluation

There are many evaluation criteria to compare the performance of machine learning algorithms. This section introduces these criteria. The categorization used can be subdivided depending on the machine learning algorithm.

Supervised Learning
Confusion matrix is a table showing the performance of a machine learning model based on actual and predicted labels. Suppose, for example, that the 100 data sample is available. This data is modeled individually and each class receives an output [9]. The class predicted by the model and the actual data class can be displayed in a table. For example, Table 7.7 is a confusion matrix for data containing n labels or classes. The rows represent the exact class of the samples, and the columns represent the predicted class of the model.

This matrix shows what examples are categorized correctly and which ones are incorrectly categorized. The samples in the original diameter of this matrix are actually samples that have the same true and predicted class and are called accuracy.

Table 7.7 Confusion matrix for multiple classes.

		Prediction				
		Class 1	Class 2	Class 3	...	Class n
Actual	Class 1	Accurate				
	Class 2		Accurate			
	Class 3			Accurate		
	...				Accurate	
	Class n					Accurate

Table 7.8 Confusion matrix for binary class.

		Prediction	
		Positive	Negative
Actual	Positive	TP	FN
	Negative	FP	TN

Consider Table 7.8, for example. The table depicts a model that has two outputs, one positive and one negative. These two outputs actually represent the class of each instance. Since there are only two outputs, the model for this matrix is called a binary classifier. In these issues, there are four states that these four modes are as follows:

- True Positives: The cases in which we predicted YES and the actual output was also YES.
- True Negatives: The cases in which we predicted NO and the actual output was NO.
- False Positives: The cases in which we predicted YES and the actual output was NO.
- False Negatives: The cases in which we predicted NO and the actual output was YES.

These four states can be defined as separate criteria such as false positive rate, true positive rate, etc., or a combination of criteria such as accuracy, accuracy, recall, and so on [1]. In the following, both categories will be introduced. False positive rate criteria and true positive rate are as follows:

$$False\ Positive\ rate\left(Specifictly\right)=\frac{FP}{FP+TN} \qquad (7.11)$$

$$True\ Positive\ rate\left(Sensitivity\right)=\frac{TP}{FN+TP} \qquad (7.12)$$

Correctness and error are important criteria in evaluating binary categories. The accuracy criterion, which represents part of the data that is correctly classified, is defined as follows:

$$Accuracy = \frac{TP+TN}{TP+TN+FP+FN} \qquad (7.13)$$

In general, accuracy means how well the model predicts output correctly. Looking closely, one can immediately see whether the model is properly trained and how it performs in general, but this criterion does not provide detailed information about the model's performance. Error similarly expressive is part of the data that is incorrectly categorized. In addition, other criteria such as accuracy and recall can also be defined. The definitions of these two criteria are as follows:

$$Precision = \frac{TP}{TP+FP} \qquad (7.14)$$

$$Recall = \frac{TP}{TP+FN} \qquad (7.15)$$

In fact, when the model predicts a positive result, to what extent is the result true? When false positives are high, this value will be a good criterion. Suppose we have a model for cancer diagnosis and this model has a low Precision. The result is that this model misdiagnoses many people's cancer by mistake. The result will be a lot of stress, a lot of testing, and a huge cost to the patient.

Conversely, when the value of false negatives is high, the Recall criterion is a good criterion. Suppose we have a model for the diagnosis of a fatal Ebola disease. What would happen if this model had a low Recall? This model considers many people who are infected with this deadly disease healthy and this is a disaster.

In order to combine the two precision and recall criteria, the F_β criterion is one of the most commonly used criteria, and is accurately obtained by assigning the β weight. In most cases, the value of $\beta = 1$ is accepted as the acceptable value, which is called the F_1 criterion The F_1 criterion is at best one and at worst zero.

$$F_1 = \frac{Recall \times Precision}{Precision + Recall} \qquad (7.16)$$

The last criterion that is most suitable for evaluating learning algorithms is the use of ROC diagrams. This chart is very useful for domains that have unequal batch distribution or unequal classification error cost. The ROC diagram shows the true positive rate versus the false positive rate when the prediction threshold is changed to the limit of its possible values.

Unsupervised Learning
As mentioned, the supervised part is much easier to evaluate because the categories are specific and we can perform the evaluation depending on whether the specified category is correct for the test data. But evaluation is not easy for the unsupervised. Because the algorithm performs the classification according to the parameters it selects. For human beings, the same data may be categorized differently. The efficiency can be defined as a number. For example, we can determine how much we want to have for a given data set of a class, or how much we want to do for the data set of elements in the data set. This way, we can create a recursive relationship between the learning model and the evaluation model to get the value of the given number to our desired value.

7.5.3   Types of Machine Learning Algorithms

Machine learning algorithms can be categorized into different perspectives from different perspectives, for example, based on the presence or absence of instructional data in a specific form for learning into four categories of "supervised learning", "unsupervised learning", "semi-supervised learning", "reinforcement learning", and "deep learning" are divided, which are summarized below. Figure 7.9 shows this segmentation along with some important algorithms in each domain.

1. Supervised learning: A type of learning which he dataset contains labeled examples and there is a so-called supervisor who provides information to the learner, thereby trying to learn a function from input to output.
2. Unsupervised learning: Unlike supervised learning, there is unlabeled examples in dataset and the purpose is to classify them.
3. Semi-supervised learning: It is also a type of learning that uses both labeled and unlabeled examples to learn a model.

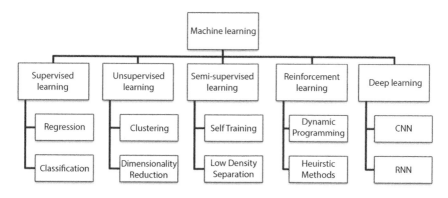

Figure 7.9 Categorization of machine learning algorithm.

4. Reinforcement learning: In this type of machine learning, there is no supervisor to teach models, and algorithms called Agents learn from and develop their experiences.

To better understand the difference between these methods, consider the following: Suppose you just bought a robot that can view the outside world, hear the sounds with its microphones, talk to you with speakers (let's take a bound), and move its footer. There is also a remote control box in the robot that you can give different types of instructions to the robot. In the following paragraphs, you will find some examples of these commands.

The first thing you want to do is shoot the robot if it sees you, but if it sees a stranger, it will shout aloud. We currently assume that the robot is capable of producing those sounds, but has not yet learned your face. So what you do is you stand in front of his eyes and command him with the help of a remote control to associate the face he sees with a snort.

You do this for a few different angles to your face to make sure the robot doesn't behave like strangers if it sees you in the profile. You also show him some stranger faces and identify the stranger's face with the order of passing. In this case, you tell the robot computer what input to output. Notice that both input and output are specified and labeled as output. This way of learning is called supervised learning.

There may be another way that, unlike the previous time you told your robot what drive to output and what to output, this time you want your robot to learn this. If you see and snore, somehow reward him (for example, with the same control over you) and punish him if he mistakenly punishes you (again with the same control over you). In this case you are not telling the robot what is appropriate for each situation, but rather letting the robot explore itself and only encouraging or punishing the end result. This way of learning is called reinforcement learning.

In two cases, the robot was supposed to connect the input to the output, but sometimes, we just want the robot to be able to detect what it sees somehow relate to what it saw before without knowing exactly what was seen. Is something or what to do when seeing it. Your intelligent robot must be able to differentiate between a chair and a human without telling him that these are examples of chairs and those of other humans. Here, as opposed to learning, objective control is not the input-output relationship, but the only categorization. This type of learning, which is called unrestrained learning, is very important because the robot world is full of entrances that no one is assigned a label on but are clearly part of a category.

Since you are busy, you can only play with your robot for a limited time a day, show him things and label them, but the robot is clear throughout the day and receives a lot of data. Here, the robot can learn both by itself and without supervision, and when you guide it, try to use those personal experiences and make the most of your training. A combination of intelligent agents using both unlabeled and unlabeled data is called semi-supervised learning.

7.5.3.1   Supervised Learning

In this learning, a set of similar problems is used to solve a problem called training data. One of the subsets of learning with the instructor is categorization. The process in these algorithms is divided into two phases: In the first step called training, the training data is analyzed by the classification algorithm and by extracting the features, a model for the classification is provided [26].

Secondly, the algorithm uses this model to classify a sample that it has not seen before. In these methods, therefore, educational data is an essential and important source of learning for classifiers [27]. So in fact, in supervised learning, we use labeled data to train the algorithm. Labeled data means that data is available along with the result and the desired response.

For example, if we want to teach a computer to recognize a dog image of a cat, we use data labeled for training. The algorithm is taught how to classify the image of dog and cat. After training, the algorithm can classify new unlabeled data to determine whether the new image is a dog or a cat.

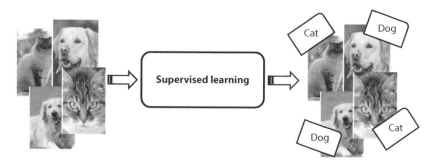

Figure 7.10 The supervised algorithms.

Machine learning will work better with monitoring for complex issues (as shown in Figure 7.10).

One of the applications of supervised learning is to recognize images and letters. Writing the letter A or number 2 differs from person to person. The algorithm learns letter and number patterns by learning by labeling datasets with the types of letters A or number 2. Today, computers are more accurate and robust in recognizing handwriting patterns than humans. The following are some of the algorithms used in supervised learning

Decision Tree
Decision tree structure in machine learning is a predictive model that links the observed facts about a phenomenon to the inferences about the purpose of the phenomenon [28]. The decision tree as a method will allow you to systematically consider the issues and be able to draw reasonable conclusions from them.

Naive Bayes Classifier
Machine Learning Naive Bayes Classifier Method in machine learning: a group of probability-based simple classifiers is applied with the assumed independent random variables between different states and based on the Bayesian theorem. The Bayesian method is simply a method of classifying phenomena based on the probability of occurrence or non-occurrence of a phenomenon [28].

Minimum Squares
The ordinary minimum squares machine learning, linear regression in statistics, ordinary least squares, or ordinary least squares is a way to estimate the unknown parameters in the linear regression model by minimizing the

difference between the observed variables in the dataset. This method is widely used in economics, political science, and electrical engineering and artificial intelligence.

Logistic Regression

Logistic regression machine learning: When using our logistic regression, we have to use logistic regression when our dependent variable is bi-directional (such as gender, disease, or non-disease). Measuring the success of an election campaign, predicting the sale of a product, or predicting an earthquake in a city are some examples of logistic regression applications.

Support Vector Machines

Machine learning - support vector machine is one of the supervised learning methods that they use for classification and regression. The basis of the SVM classifier is linear data categorization, and in the linear division of data, we try to select a line that has more reliable margins. SVM can solve big and complex issues such as identifying humans and bots on sites, displaying user-favorite ads, identifying people in photos, and more.

7.5.3.2   Unsupervised Learning

In this type of algorithm, we do not have a target variable and the output of the algorithm is unknown. The best example of this type of algorithm is the automatic clustering of a population. For example, by automatically sharing personal information and customer purchases, we automatically divide them into identical and equivalent groups. In unsupervised learning, algorithms use inferential statistics-based estimation methods to identify patterns and correlate and correlate between raw and unlabeled data [29].

For example, suppose it is given an image having both dogs and cats which have not seen ever. Thus, the machine has no idea about the features of dogs and cat so we can't categorize it in dogs and cats. But it can categorize them according to their similarities, patterns, and differences, i.e., we can easily categorize the above picture into two parts. First may contain all pictures having dogs in it and second part may contain all pictures having cats in it. Here, you didn't learn anything before, means no training data or examples (as shown in Figure 7.11).

Once patterns are identified, the algorithm uses statistics to identify the boundaries within the dataset. Data with similar patterns is categorized into one group. As the data classification process continues, the algorithm

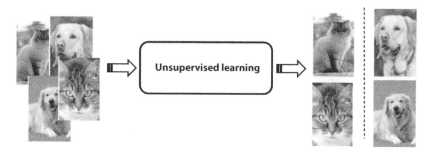

Figure 7.11 The unsupervised algorithms.

understands the data set pattern and makes predictions for new data [30]. Here are some of the algorithms used in non-supervised learning.

Clustering Analysis
Machine learning clustering algorithm clustering or cluster analysis in statistics and machine learning is one of the branches of learning that is a process in which the samples are divided into classes whose members are similar to each other, called clusters; A cluster is therefore a set of objects in which the objects are similar to each other and are not identical to the objects in the other clusters.

Principal Component Analysis
Machine learning is the non-supervised learning of principal component analysis in vector space, which is mostly used to reduce the size of the data set. Principal component analysis is an orthogonal linear transformation that drives the data into the new coordinate system so that the largest variance of the data lies on the first coordinate axis, the second largest variance on the second coordinate axis. It thus preserves the components of the dataset that have the greatest impact on variance.

Machine Learning - Face Detection Decomposition is a fundamental step in many scientific and engineering calculations. The first face recognition systems were developed using the Single Value Analysis (SVD) and Principal Component Analysis (PCA) algorithms.

Singular Value Decomposition
Independent Component Analysis Machine Learning Independent component analysis is a method of dividing a signal into a sum of several other signals such that the resulting signals are independent and have a non-Gaussian

distribution. This is a case of blind source separation. The problem is usually considered simpler, with no delay in receiving the signals.

Independent Component Analysis
Machine learning - Analysis of independent components analysis is a method for separating the signal to a sum of several other signals so that the resulting signal is non-Gaussian distribution. This method is one of the sources of source - source isolation or source - source blind. Usually, the problem is simplified in simpler mode, where there is no delay in receiving signals.

7.5.3.3   Semi-Supervised Learning

In this learning, tutorials include tagged and unlabeled samples that try to build a model output that can estimate examples that they have not yet seen. Semi-supervised learning is used in areas where unlabeled data is readily available and abundant and data labeling is costly [31]. The goal of this learner is to use the distribution of unlabeled data available to the learner to achieve a better performance than the supervised algorithms [27].

7.5.3.4   Reinforcement Learning

These algorithms exploit the observations collected by interacting with the environment to increase the benefits and reduce the risk. These algorithms learn about the environment with continuous iterations. Perhaps, the best example of reinforcement learning are some computer games that, while playing the game, learn the man's style of play, reinforce himself against him, and ultimately defeat him. In this type of machine learning, there is no supervisor to teach models, and algorithms called Agents learn from and develop their experiences [32].

They are trained by trial-and-error and always consider the long-term benefits. There are different types of reinforcement learning that include [5]:

- Positive reinforcement: Positive reinforcement occurs when a behavior triggers an event and increases that event's intensity, frequency, and frequency of behavior.
- Negative reinforcement: Reinforcing a behavior by stopping or preventing certain situations from happening is called negative reinforcement.

The main difference between reinforcement learning and other machine learning methods is that in reinforcement learning, the agent is never told what is the right thing to do in each situation, and only the criterion is understood by the agent. That's how good or how bad an Action is. It is the task of the Learner to learn what is best in each situation by having this information. This is part of the specific strengths of reinforcement learning. In this way, complex decision-making problems can often be resolved by providing the least amount of information needed to solve the problem. In many animals, reinforcement learning is the only way of learning. Reinforcement learning is also an essential part of human behavior [13]. When our hands burn in the face of heat, we quickly learn not to repeat this again. Pleasure and pain are good examples of the rewards that make up our behavior patterns and that of many animals. In reinforcement learning, the primary purpose of learning is to do something or achieve a goal, without being fed by external direct information. Component of Reinforcement Learning are present follows:

Policy: Determines how you deal with each action and how you decide in each of the different situations. In fact, Policy determines how the Agent behaves in a given time and guides the intelligent agent to better modes.

Reward Function: Specifies the target in the learner function. This objective function is to reward one agent for each action so that the target approaching increases the reward. The reward function is important if it is poorly defined. Reward is short term and long-term value means it may not have a home bonus but it makes us closer to the goal so it has higher value.

Value Function: For each state, a set amount that the more the target closer, as if in a game, let the opponent screw you out in this case does not reward yourself but otherwise you are going to better than previous modes.

Model: The problem of reinforcement learning is probabilistic and stochastic and the states or states are non-deterministic; that is, for one action, it can go to all states but with one probability. Every action is a possibility and it is possible to move from one state to another. The goal of the learner is to maximize long-term rewards. In a problem of reinforcement learning, we are faced with a factor that interacts with the environment through trial and error and learns to select the optimal action to achieve the goal. Reinforcement learning is therefore considered as a way to train agents to perform an action through reward and punishment without having to specify how the agent performs the action.

7.5.3.5   Deep Learning

Machine Learning Mastery describes deep learning as follows: A subset of machine learning that has artificial neural networks that can function similar to the brain [33]. Deep learning is a particularly specialized area of machine learning that is designed based on the brain's functionality and has its own neural system called the artificial neural network. Input works: After passing the "input" section, the data is entered into another layer called the hidden layer and finally the data output. Each layer of this system is equipped with one or more neurons.

Suppose a machine with deep learning has the task of detecting an animal; for example, it must determine whether the image in question is the image of a dog or a cat (as shown in Figure 7.12).

In this example, factors such as the presence of a mustache, the presence of a tail, and other capabilities obtainable from the image must be collected. Next, more important indicators are examined to consider the animal category. Deep learning has the ability to identify which index or feature is more important than others and look for it in the image. Such a capability we would have had to manually computerize machine learning technology, but this would be done automatically in systems equipped with deep learning.

The simplest way to understand the difference between the two branches of machine learning and deep learning is the "DL IS ML" method. Here are some of the important parameters of this method [33].

Data Independence
The first and most important difference between machine learning and deep learning is how systems work with increased data rates. The following table shows that the deep learning system does not produce the desired results in the case of low volume data, but why? Because deep learning algorithms require high volumes of data to better understand how data

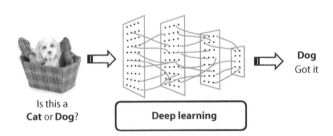

Figure 7.12 Deep learning.

relates to each other. Machine learning, but with a small amount of data, also works well.

Capabilities Engineering
This step involves using the information received to reduce the complexity of the data and to clarify the patterns of the training algorithms. This is a costly and difficult step and requires a great deal of time and expertise. In the case of machine learning, most capabilities must be identified by an expert and then coded with that feature or feature. The accuracy of the process of identifying features by the expert has a great impact on the performance of the system, but in deep learning, the system needs to be trained and able to automatically understand the data, features, and capabilities required. The same process prevents deep learning from machine learning.

Problem-Solving Methods
When using machine learning to solve the problem, it is recommended to break the problem into several smaller smaller layers first and present each part individually to the system. Finally, the results are combined, and the end result is presented, but in-depth learning does the whole process itself without the need for human expert intervention. What is the object and where is the image. Let's see how machine learning solves this problem: In machine learning, the problem should be divided into two parts: object detection and object location detection. We use an algorithm that can identify all the objects in the image first and then identify each compartment. By combining the data obtained from both algorithms, we obtain both the object type and the location of the object. Deep learning does all of these steps on its own. Simply present the desired image to the system and the system declares the result using algorithms.

Operation Time
Developing and training deep learning algorithms takes a lot of time because many parameters have to be studied and system training is time consuming, but machine learning takes much less time. However, in the case of data queries, the problem of time is exactly the opposite: when testing, deep learning algorithms work much faster than machine learning algorithms.

7.5.4 Types of Machine Learning Problems

Various problems can be solved by machine learning which can be divided into the following categories:

7.5.4.1 Classification

Databases are a very rich source of hidden information that can be used to make intelligent decisions. Classification and estimation are two forms of data analysis that can be used to derive a model for describing the data or to provide some direction for subsequent data. This will allow better understanding of high volume data [28].

Supervised methods, such as classification and estimation, attempt to discover the relationship between input attribute attributes (sometimes called independent variables) with one or more target attribute attributes (sometimes called dependent variables). Finally, this relationship with a structure is shown as a model.

With the help of this model and by providing the input attribute attributes, we can estimate the value of the target attribute; in other words, we are able to assign the specimens to one of several defined classes or to assign a value to the attribute attribute. Set a goal. The model building process is a two-step process that is modeled in the first step with the help of a training dataset whose class labels identify all the examples [14]. This is known as the learning phase. In the second step, the model is validated with the help of experimental data sets, where the class labels are usually unknown. In fact, the model evaluation is calculated based on how many classes of sample experimental data are correctly estimated.

7.5.4.2 Clustering

The process of grouping datasets into categories is called clustering. A cluster is a set of data that is similar to other data in the same cluster but different from other clustered samples. Cluster analysis is one of the most important human activities. In fact, man learns in childhood how to differentiate between different objects.

This is due to the continual increase in unconscious schemes of object classification in his mind. Cluster analysis has many different applications, including pattern recognition, data analysis, image processing, and commercial analysis. In this way, we can identify the densely populated areas and thus find interesting dispersions and correlations between the data properties [34].

In the process of knowledge discovery and extraction, clustering can also be used to process or prepare data. A clustering algorithm can have desirable features such as scalability, ability to extract clusters in any way, ability to handle data types, no need for input parameters, no sensitivity to data entry, noiseless data-based clustering capability. On the limitation and online, accepting high-dimensional data is understandable for the final results of the algorithm [35].

The main topic in the clustering and dissimilarity clustering techniques is data and examples. In each cluster, the samples are more similar. In other words, similar samples are to be grouped in one cluster and dissimilar samples in different clusters, so a scale or a criterion is needed to evaluate similarity. Since each sample can contain several attributes and each of these attributes is considered a data type, the similarity criteria for the types of data must be defined in the calculation or analysis of the similarity of the two samples.

7.5.4.3 Optimization

Machine learning is also closely linked to optimization: many learning problems are expressed as minimizing a loss function on a set of training examples. Harm functions represent the difference between the predictions of the model under learning and the actual evidence of the problem (for example, in the classification, the purpose is to assign the label to the evidence, and the models are trained to predict the label of examples). The difference between the two disciplines stems from their overarching goal: While optimization algorithms can minimize losses on a training set, machine learning tends to minimize losses on unobserved samples.

7.5.4.4 Regression

This powerful statistical technique can be applied to all stages of the data mining process. Linear regression and nonlinear multiple regression are one of its types. In linear regression, two different samples of data are modeled as a straight line. The regression line is a tool for predicting the value of a variable in terms of the dependent variable. In fact, for the linear model, we find that the two attribute values are close to all pairs of values of these two attributes. If there is an error paired for each pair and the regression line [13]. This line not being a straight line will somehow be selected to minimize the error. Minimizing the sum of squares of errors is a common method used in most cases.

Conclusion

In this chapter, we deal with issues such as machine learning definition and its goals and achievements and applications. Types of machine learning are categorized in five parts such as supervised learning, unsupervised learning, semi-supervised learning, reinforcement learning, and deep learning. All of these categories are discussed separately in this chapter. In other parts of the chapter, offline and online learning algorithms were discussed.

References

1. Ławrynowicz, A. and Tresp, V., Introducing machine learning, *Perspectives On Ontology Learning*, AKA Heidelberg/IOS Press, 2014.

2. Langley, P., *Elements of machine learning*, Morgan Kaufmann, San Francisco, CA, United States, 1996.

3. Mitchell, T.M. *et al.*, *Machine Learning*, 45, 37, 870–877, McGraw Hill, Burr Ridge, *IL*, 1997.

4. Brynjolfsson, E. and Mitchell, T.M., What can machine learning do? Workforce implications. *Science*, 358, 6370, 1530–1534, 2017.

5. Jordan, M.I. and Mitchell, T.M., Machine learning: Trends, perspectives, and prospects. *Science*, 349, 6245, 255–260, 2015.

6. Beam, A.L. and Kohane, I.S., Big data and machine learning in health care. *Jama*, 319, 13, 1317–1318, 2018.

7. Badal, V.D. *et al.*, Challenges in the construction of knowledge bases for human microbiome-disease associations. *Microbiome*, 7, 1, 1–15, 2019.

8. Mahdavinejad, M.S., Rezvan, M., Barekatain, M., Adibi, P., Barnaghi, P., Sheth, A.P., Machine learning for Internet of Things data analysis: A survey. *Digital Commun. Netw.*, 4, 3, 161–175, 2018.

9. Kononenko, I. and Kukar, M., *Machine learning and data mining*, Horwood Publishing, UK, 2007.

10. Sejnowski, T.J., *12 The Future of Machine Learning*, The Deep Learning Revolution, 171-194, Cambridge, 2018.

11. Shanahan, J.G., Machine Learning, *Soft Computing for Knowledge Discovery: Introducing Cartesian Granule Features*, 143–175, Springer US, Boston, MA, 2000.

12. Sammut, C., Concept learning. *Encycl. Mach. Learn.*, 205–208, Springer, Boston, MA, 2010.

13. Mohri, M., Rostamizadeh, A., Talwalkar, A., *Foundations of machine learning*, MIT press, Cambridge, 2018.

14. Michie, D., Spiegelhalter, D.J., Taylor, C.C., Machine learning. *Neural Stat. Classification*, 13, 1–298, 1994.

15. Hong, T.-P. and Tseng, S.S., A parallel concept learning algorithm based upon version space strategy, in: *Proceedings of the Ninth Annual International Phoenix Conference on Computers and Communications*. pp. 734–740, 1990.

16. Hirsh, H., Generalizing Version Spaces. *Mach. Learn.*, 17, 1, 5–46, 1994.

17. Mitchell, T.M., Version spaces: A candidate elimination approach to rule learning, in: *Proceedings of the 5th international joint conference on Artificial intelligence*, pp. 305–310, 1977.
18. Bouchachia, A., Gabrys, B., Sahel, Z., Overview of some incremental learning algorithms, in: *IEEE International Fuzzy Systems Conference*, pp. 1–6, 2007.
19. Gepperth, A. and Hammer, B., *Incremental learning algorithms and applications*, 2016.
20. Ben-David, S., Kushilevitz, E., Mansour, Y., Online learning versus offline learning. *Mach. Learn.*, 29, 1, 45–63, 1997.
21. Madala, H., Comparison of inductive versus deductive learning networks. *Complex Syst.*, 5, 2, 239–258, 1991.
22. Widmer, G., A tight integration of deductive and inductive learning, in: *Proceedings of the sixth international workshop machine learn.*, 11–13, 1989.
23. Zaremba, W., Mikolov, T., Joulin, A., Fergus, R., Learning simple algorithms from examples, in: *International Conference on Machine Learning*, pp. 421–429, 2016.
24. Witten, I.H., Frank, E., Hall, M.A., Pal, C.J., *Data Mining: Practical machine learning tools and techniques*, Morgan Kaufmann, San Francisco, CA, United States, 2016.
25. Thrun, S. and Pratt, L., *Learning to learn*, Springer Science & Business Media, New York, USA, 2012.
26. Singh, A., Thakur, N., Sharma, A., A review of supervised machine learning algorithms, in: *3rd International Conference on Computing for Sustainable Global Development (INDIACom)*, pp. 1310–1315, 2016.
27. Zhu, X. and Goldberg, A.B., Introduction to semi-supervised learning. *Synth. Lectures Artif. Intell. Mach. Learn.*, 3, 1, 1–130, 2009.
28. Kotsiantis, S.B., Zaharakis, I., Pintelas, P., Supervised machine learning: A review of classification techniques. *Emerging Artif. Intell. Appl. Comput. Eng.*, 160, 3–24, 2007.
29. Hastie, T., Tibshirani, R., Friedman, J., Unsupervised learning, in: *The elements of statistical learning* 485–585, Springer, 2009.
30. Barlow, H.B., Unsupervised learning, *Neural Comput.*, 1, 3, 295–311, 1989.
31. Chapelle, O., Scholkopf, B., Zien, A., Semi-supervised learning. *IEEE Trans. Neural Networks*, 20, 3, 542, 2009.
32. Sutton, R.S. and Barto, A.G., *Introduction to reinforcement learning*, vol. 2, 4 MIT press, Cambridge, 1998.
33. Zhang, L., Tan, J., Han, D., Zhu, H., From machine learning to deep learning: progress in machine intelligence for rational drug discovery. *Drug Discovery Today*, 22, 11, 1680–1685, 2017.
34. Ayodele, T.O., Introduction to machine learning. *New Advances in Machine Learning*, 1–9, IntechOpen, London, UK. 2010.
35. McGregor, A., Hall, M.A., Lorier, P., Brunskill, J., Flow clustering using machine learning techniques, in: *Proceedings of the International workshop on passive and active network measurement*, pp. 205–214, 2004.

8

Performance of Supervised Learning Algorithms on Multi-Variate Datasets

Asif Iqbal Hajamydeen* and Rabab Alayham Abbas Helmi

Faculty of Information Sciences & Engineering, Management & Science University, Shah Alam, Selangor, Malaysia

Abstract

Supervised Machine Learning (SML) algorithms stands on the principle of generating theories on the existing data instances to make predictions on the upcoming data instances. Typically, a supervised learning algorithm is provided with a set of labelled instances from which the algorithm generates a model to categorize/predict future instances. Supervised learning algorithms are used in multidisciplinary research due to its capability in predicting and classifying data accurately, provided the algorithms were sufficiently trained. Therefore, this chapter concentrates on evaluating the performance of supervised algorithms namely Support Vector Machine, Naïve Bayes, Bayesian Network, K-Nearest Neighbour, Hidden Markov Models and Neural Networks. Multi-variate datasets were tested using the aforesaid algorithms to substantiate the suitability of an algorithm and its performance in terms of training time and accuracy with diverse datasets.

Keywords: Machine learning, supervised algorithm, classification, labelled data, accuracy, multi-variate datasets, training time

8.1 Introduction

The initiative for machine learning starts from the straightforward incompetence of the human to learn, comprehend and evaluate large number of features and instances instantaneouslyand relate it to previous data, to decide on the outcome of the data. Although human beings possess

---

*Corresponding author: asif@msu.edu.my

Uma N. Dulhare, Khaleel Ahmad and Khairol Amali Bin Ahmad (eds.) Machine Learning and Big Data: Concepts, Algorithms, Tools and Applications, (209–232) © 2020 Scrivener Publishing LLC

natural/evolutionary intelligence to relate and analyse, difficulties exist in the ability to consider voluminous data together. Therefore, learning algorithms or programs for machines were written to handle data collectively in a faster pace giving a new pathway for the era of machine learning.

Machine learning (ML) is an artificial intelligence (AI) based application providing the facility to learn automatically from existing knowledge without being hardcoded. The existing knowledge includes data or observations from samples, direct experience or instruction which is scrutinized to make better decisions on new or future data. ML applications usually involvesbigger storage and extensive computation time as it is process intensive. All the samples could not be loaded into the memory, when handling very larger datasets which necessitates a reduction in feature vector size that is commonly accomplished through feature selection and transformation approaches.

Machine learning algorithms that are supervised enables AI systems to draw conclusions faster and more accurate than humans. But then, effectively constructing, scaling, and deploying precise supervised models requires extensive time and expensive technical expertise. Supervised learning problems starts with a data set containing labelled training samples with correct labels. In other words, the algorithm is given a set of inputs with their anticipated output, and in common all algorithms presented in this work aims to find the closest solution compared to the given output.

This chapter introduces supervised learning algorithms in Section 8.2 and explain the details of the dataset and the related preprocessing to enable learning process. Section 8.3 introduces classification together with the measurements used to validate, and the performance (accuracy) of the classification algorithms and the training time consumed with the datasets. Neural Network and the details of the Artificial Neural Network are discussed in Section 8.4, followed with the performance comparison of classification and forecasting algorithms in Section 8.5. Section 8.5 summarises and concludes the chapter.

8.2   Supervised Learning Algorithms

Majority of the real-world circumstances offers a lesser number of labelled instances to learn and a huge number of unlabelled data that need to be classified or labelled based on the previously supplied instances. In such situations, supervised learning algorithms comes conveniently to handle the situation. Supervised learning problems are classified as regression and classification problems. Classification is used to get categorical value as output and regression is used when the output needed is a continuous value. An added difficulty is that, the learning methods perform correctly-with one criterion may not perform well on the other. For example, SVMs and boosting are devised to enhance accuracy, while neural nets usually optimize squared error or cross entropy.

8.2.1   Datasets and Experimental Setup

This section provides the details of the datasets used, especially on the choice of datasets and the nature of features in the dataset. To assess the capability supervised algorithms, five publicly available datasets (https://www.kaggle.com/datasets) [1] of varying instances and features were chosen. The details of the datasets used for the experiments are tabulated in Table 8.1, which specifies the number of features, the number of classifications the instances in a dataset has been labelled and the nature of the data.

The experiments were conducted using the existing machine learning tool, i.e., Weka (Waikato Environment for Knowledge Analysis) [2]. Weka is a popular collection of machine learning algorithms written in Java which can be applied directly to a dataset or called from your own Java code and is well-suited for developing novel machine learning schemes. It supports several data mining tasks and particularly data preprocessing, classification, regression, clustering, feature selection, and visualization. As

Table 8.1 Details of the used datasets.

Datasets	Features (excluding class labels)	Classification	Instances	Remarks
Chord Progressions	4	20	28	4 Numeric
Zoo	17	7	101	1 Nominal, 16 Numeric
Spine	12	2	310	12 Numeric
Flavors	1	28	856	1 Nominal
NIDS-1	41	2	5000	38 Numeric, 3 Nominal
NIDS-2	41	2	10000	38 Numeric, 3 Nominal

this tool constitutes the algorithms being tested, Weka was used to execute the experiments with different datasets. Despite the availability of various tools, MatLab was chosen for its capability to process both medium and large data in a timely manner.

8.2.2   Data Treatment/Preprocessing

The datasets comprise of data having numerous features and classifications to support the evaluation on the capability of an algorithm. Datasets were carefully treated without spoiling the integrity of the data contained. As stated in Table 8.1, there are five different datasets, whereas NIDS-1 and NIDS-2 are the subsets of NIDS containing 5000 and 10000 instances respectively. The entire dataset of NIDS contained 25,192 instances, and therefore two subsets of 5000 and 10000 instance were created. The reason behind this subset creation is to evaluate the performance of the algorithms in handling similar datasets of varying size. The class label of the dataset (Zoo) is changed from numeric to nominal taking reference from the supporting dataset (Class) containing the equivalent nominal values for the numeric values. This is due to the restriction by the machine learning tool (Weka) allowing to use only nominal class labels.

8.3   Classification

Classification is method or a technique to learn and discover the way by which a set of instances (Test data) can be categorised based on set of instances (Training data) that were already classified and labelled. The instances of a dataset are given labels evaluating all the features it contains, which is then used to classify new data. In line with that, the datasets used for experiments were trained and tested on all the machine learning algorithms chosen for this study.

A true positive (TP) decision classifies two similar events in the same class whereas a true negative (TN) decision classifies two dissimilar events in different classes. Failure to classify the events in the appropriate class is measured using false positive (FP) and false negative (FN). All these four measurements decide the classification accuracy and therefore the accuracy of classification is calculated using the formula: *Accuracy = (TP + TN) / (FP + FN + TP + TN)*. The experiments were conducted using Weka experimenter with a 10-fold cross- validation to test the effectiveness of the algorithm. 10-Fold enables less biased model and ensures that every instance from the original dataset has the chance of appearing in training and test set. The performance of the algorithm is assessed by the accuracy of prediction, and therefore TP, TN, FP and FN were measured to calculate the accuracy.

8.3.1   Support Vector Machines (SVM)

SVM [3, 4] is a supervised learning algorithmwhich uses Margin Maximization to the ideal separator line amongst classes that is utilised for classification and regression problems and is generally used for classification. The algorithm plots each data points in n-dimensional space, i.e., n is number of features. Classification is performed on the data points to find the hyperplane to segregate the classes where hyperplanes serve as decision boundaries to categorize the data points. Data points falling on either side of the hyperplane can be attributed to different classes. The hyperplane is a line for 2 input features and the hyperplane develops a two-dimensional plane for 3 input features. The data points nearer to the hyperplane are called support vectors which affect the position and alignment of the hyperplane and removing such vectors changes the position of the hyperplane.

The accuracy achieved (Figure 8.1) with multivariate datasets shows that, the accuracy deteriorates with the increase in the number of classification labels by which the instances were classified in a dataset. This was apparently exhibited by the lower accuracy achieved with *Chord Progressions* and *Flavors*, irrespective of the smaller volume of events compare to the other datasets tested. Accuracy with a similar dataset (*NIDS-5000, NIDS-10000*) improved

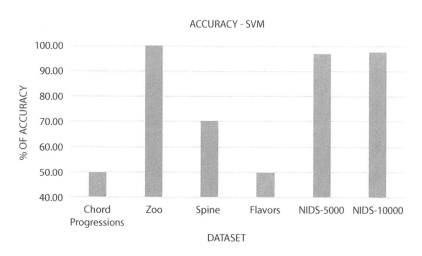

Figure 8.1 Classification accuracy - SVM.

with the increase in volume of the instances, reflects the ability of SVM to predict precisely when more instances were given during training.

8.3.2   Naïve Bayes (NB) Algorithm

Naive Bayes is a group of classification algorithms which assumes that features are statistically independent and shares a common principle grounded on Bayes' Theorem [5, 6]. Bayes' Theorem (Probability theory) assumes that all the features predicting the target value are independent of each other and the algorithm is based on this assumption and hence getting the name Naïve Bayes. A feature depends on the other feature to determine the target. Naïve Bayes can handle voluminous datasets with fast training and prediction and performs well on categorical input variables.

As shown in Figure 8.2 Naïve Bayes classification accuracy is influenced by the number of classification labels in a dataset. Accuracy of NB is maintained despite the number of instances were doubled with in similar datasets (*NIDS-5000, NIDS-10000*), exposes the stability of NB and its dependency on the features and classification and not on the volume of instances.

8.3.3   Bayesian Network (BN)

Bayesian networks or belief networks are probabilistic graphical models where the graphical structures characterize the knowledge on an uncertain domain [7, 8]. Every node in the model denotes a random variable and

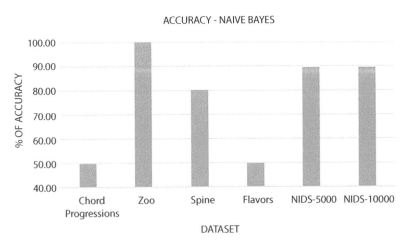

Figure 8.2 Classification accuracy - NB.

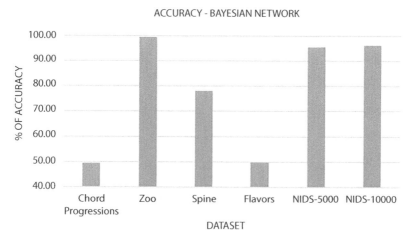

Figure 8.3 Classification accuracy – BN.

the edges among the nodes represent probabilistic dependencies between the corresponding random variables. Bayesian network can determine the effects of several variables on an outcome and perform well even in those situations where other methods fail.

Like SVM and NB, the accuracy of BN is very much dependent on the classification labels and it exposes an increase in accuracy when the volume of instances increases with a dataset as shown Figure 8.3.

8.3.4   Hidden Markov Model (HMM)

Hidden Markov Model (HMM) is a statistical Markov model where the model is assumed to be a Markov process with hidden or unnoticed states [9–11]. Markov process hypothesize that the prediction of future states does not require past state, provided the current state is known. HMM deals with observed states and the hidden states that are fundamental to the observed states.

HMM models process with different stages that occurs in fixed or certain order and the processes containing unobservable states. This nature of HMM reflects on the accuracy of classification on the chosen dataset, where it achieved the same accuracy (50%) on all the datasets tested shows that the tested datasets have less or no unobserved states. This mentions the limitation of HMM in handling multivariate data and the factors to be considered before choosing HMM for a dataset as shown in Figure 8.4.

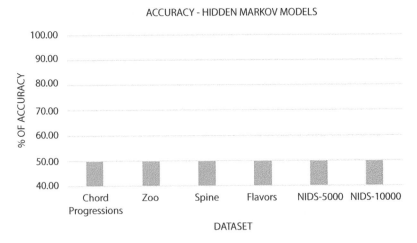

Figure 8.4 Classification accuracy - HMM.

8.3.5   K-Nearest Neighbour (KNN)

The KNN algorithm is designed based on the assumption that things alike exist near to each other [12]. Apart from the nearness of data points, the algorithm also calculates the distance between data points. The K value given decides the accuracy of predictionsand the number of errors, therefore choosing the right K gains critical significance. The process is significantly slower with higher volume of data makes the method as impractical choice inenvironments where rapid predictions are needed.

KNN achieved a better accuracy as shown Figure 8.5 with larger datasets (*NIDS-5000, NIDS-10000*) consisting of more features compared to other datasets. The accuracy remained stable even when the number of instances were doubled.

8.3.6   Training Time

All machine learning algorithm requires training using a sample set of data, before it can be used for classification or prediction. Therefore, all the datasets were trained with various machine learning algorithms and the training time were tabulated (Table 8.2). The training time taken by the algorithm with various datasets are verified to assess the effect of the instances, features and classifications on the training time.

SVM took a longer time with the dataset (*Flavors*) having more classifications (28) despite the lesser number of instances (856) and feature (1) compared to NIDS-2 having 41 features and 10000 instances. This

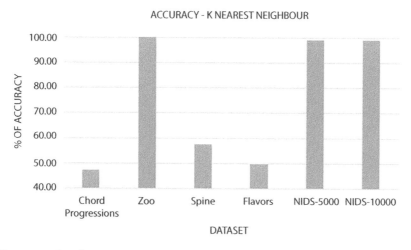

Figure 8.5 Classification accuracy – KNN.

symbolizes SVM training time is affected by the number of classification labels significantly rather than instance and the features.

Although HMM consumed very lesser training time compared to SVM, in the same way as SVM, classification labels influence the training time of HMM. On the other hand, training time is influenced by volume of the instances and features for NB, BN and HMM.

8.4 Neural Network

Artificial Neural Network (ANN) is a nonlinear model, inspired by the biological neural systems. The name ANN refers to a network as a combination of an interconnected and communicating unit, i.e., those units emulate the role of neurons in the nervous systems in living creatures. The way, the ANN work is based on the idea of reaching a model through simulating the data, thus eliminating the need for developing a model for the data. This is achieved through training the network with previous data and this property of self-learning provides high accuracy in the solution. Moreover, it provides the network with the ability to solve any model, whether linear, semi-linear or non-linear and therefore providing the ability in finding solutions for various types of highly complex problems [13].

The main aim of modelling is to improve a given system through the analysis of the systems behaviour components and environment circumstances. A secondary objective is to find an optimal form for future systems. Developing models is one of major issues facing researchers in

Table 8.2 Training Time for the datasets for different Algorithms.

| Data set | Training time (Secs) | | | | | Dataset details | | |
	SVM	NB	BN	HMM	KNN	Features (excluding class labels)	Classification	Instances
Chord Progressions	90	1	1	8	1	4	20	28
Zoo	21	1	1	4	1	17	7	101
Spine	2	1	1	1	2	12	2	310
Flavors	8029	1	4	12	4	1	28	856
NIDS-1	825	11	14	6	72	41	2	5000
NIDS-2	4151	18	32	8	305	41	2	10000

developing models for any problem or data series, due to the incapability of quantitative methods to solve or estimate the coefficient of a model unless the model represents the problem coefficient in sound detailed way during model development, thus reaching sound results. In the same sense, it is a continuing research effort for researchers in Artificial Neural Networks (ANN) to evaluate their efficiency, in order to propose ANN as a methodology to solve such problems with higher efficiency [14, 15].

8.4.1 Artificial Neural Networks Architecture

The increasing attention and focus on ANN are due to its high flexibility in the data model learning process as well as storing and distribution of data, in comparison with other mathematical methods used in the process. In this sense, ANN isdescribed as a data processing system whereas artificial neural networks are defined as information processing systems based on simple mathematical models that have certain performance characteristics in a manner that mimics the biological neural network. The "nervous system" is composed of processing units that are computational elements called Nodes or Neurons. This has a neurological property that stores practical knowledge and experimental information to make it accessible to the user by adjusting weights [13].

Figure 8.6 illustrates the pattern of the biological neuron and how it inspired the artificial model in which the following is applicable:

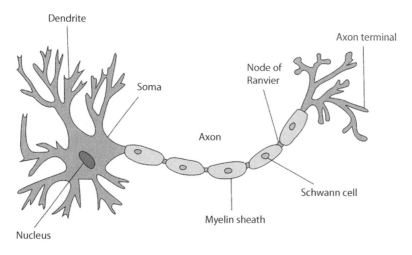

Figure 8.6 Neural cell.

- Dendrites: represents the receipt of signals or data.
- Cell Body: Represents signal or data processes.
- Axon: represents the transfer of processed information to other neurons.
- Synapse: represents aninteraction between the end of Axon and Dendrites of other neurons.

The methodology of ANN is based on simple mathematical techniques, to achieve certain performance aspects similar toa biological neural network, like the nervous system. The ANN is considered one of the non-linear models. Thus, they are represented by the perception, which is a simulation of the paleogeonal neural cell, was proposed in 1958. The perceptual consists of neurons, nodes or input units that mimic the signals entering the paleogenic neuron. Each line binds to a specific weight, multiplying the signals entering the node with these weights and then combining the weighted inputs in the nodes or neurons, after which the output of each node is processed by a non-linear function with a threshold known as the Activation Function.

For artificial neural networks,interest in neural networks was delayed in the 1970s due to the limited use of single-layer neural networks, but the discovery of the idea of reverse error propagation for multilayer network training by a number of researchers in the late 1980s played a key role in the re-emergence of neural networks as a tool for solving many problems on a large scale. Although single-layer networks are very limited in corresponding "interview" processes, they can learn, but multi-layer neural networks "with one or more hidden layers" can learn any continuous interview process for optional accuracy. This network can be defined as a gradient descent to find the minimum value of the total error square of the output value computed by the network.

The reverse error neural network is based on the concept of error-based network training, where weights occur between layers. As the weight contributes to the formation of the error, the network continues to update the weights until the optimal weights are achieved to reach the best alignment of the model. This is shown in Figure 8.7, where (X1 X2... Xp) receives input from neurons or another environment. The input feedcomes through links with 'weights', total contribution is the total input weight from all the input sources. Meanwhile Conversion Function or Activation Function converts inputs to outputs that is then going to other neurons or environment.

The neural network consists of minimal of three levels and in each level includes several nodes, where the first level represents the input and the

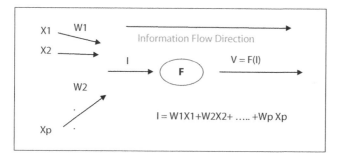

Figure 8.7 ANN architecture and data flow.

second level represents the outputs and the other level represents the hidden layer. All three are attached and each attachment is attached to a specific weight. The structure of ANN is illustrated in Figure 8.8. The role of the hidden layer is crucial to the success of the network; its main task is to "distil", in the contest of a refinement process, thus important patterns can be highlighted from the previous layer, in order to be passed to the next layer. This will improve the network performance in terms of efficiency and speed of processing, with the introduction of a simple recognition of important information to pass on to the next layer and reduction of redundant information [15, 16].

Meanwhile the non-linear characteristic of the network's relations is represented through the conversion function, so that this non-linearism in the relation is incorporated in the transaction of input to the output. This unique architecture gives ANN as a method some equally unique features

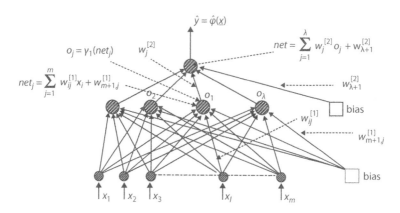

Figure 8.8 ANN structure [17].

that makes them applicable in solving many real lives as well as simulated problems. Some of the key features of ANN are:

1. Self-learning ability.
2. Scalability.
3. Generalise ability.
4. Reduction of data entry restriction.
5. Ability to represent linear, semi-linear and non-linear phenomena.

Those characteristics have increased the popularity of using ANN solution among researches, academicians as well as decision makers.

8.4.2 Application Areas

There is no dispute among researchers that ANN is an important tool that is applicable in various fields with great potential of even more opportunity for novel applications in erstwhile areas. When it comes to applications of the different types of ANN, researchers and practitioners report the use of ANN as a method in solving various kinds of problems, such as image processing, disease diagnoses, hand writing recognition, sales' predictions, weather forecast, speech recognition and Optical Character Recognition (OCR) among other. Such an approach in reviewing the applicability of ANN although is shows the vastness of its solution application domain, but it does not properly classify those application domains. This paper advises a more structural approach in reviewing those application area, firstly to identify the type of solution in Machine Learning (ML) which the application falls under, secondly to classify according to the major approaches in the application techniques as shown in Figure 8.9, the figure shows three major categories based on the application technique in accordance to the type of solution in ML.

From the Figure 8.9, not only supervised learning can employ ANN but also unsupervised learning, this include several applications where ANN is used to solve highly complex problems, hence finding optimal solutions to real life problems such as complex scheduling and route optimization.

Never the less, the main focus of this paper is on supervised learning algorithms, in this category two major classes are defined, classification which generally deal with labelled data, the key indicator on efficiency in this type of approach is accuracy in classification, this type of supervised learning is covered in the earlier parts of this work, covering various algorithms.

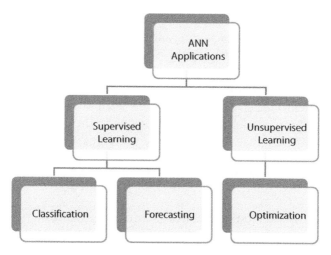

Figure 8.9 ANN Application areas.

On the other hand, the third type which is using ANN for forecasting shows both efficiency and potential. When solving forecasting problems researchers and decision makers need to analyse time series that represent certain information on a long-time interval, based on the "historic" or previous data instances, future data instances need to be interpreted. Classical time series forecasting is done using method similar to the one by Box and Jenkins (), those methods have been used for a long time, although the use of ANN has proven to be much more efficient, the main reason for the superior performance of the ANN as a tool in forecasting is due to its learning ability, thus enabling the network to learn from the past data to refine outputs, but that is nothing but the face value, since this is a general attribute of ANN. On a more specific level, the Neural Networks excellence as a forecast tool is a tribute of two very significant aptitudes.

Firstly, the ability of ANN to process the time series data without the constrain of needing a model to represent the phenomena that the data is portraying, although this as also due to the fact that the network has the ability to learn from the previous data that has been processed, but it also provide it with a unique quality that other classic solution do not provide. This quality was only made useful with the advancement in computational power available at the disposal of those working on ANN analysis. The same quality of learning from data without the need for a pre-existing model was at some point a liability that hinders the process of releasing ANN at a forecasting tool to its full potential. The reason behind that is the processing power and time needed to complete the iterations needed to achieve the networks' training with the amount of data that time series provide, this made it expensive, time consuming and therefore not feasible as a solution, which explains the delay in adopting ANN as a forecasting tool.

Secondly, the ability to represent almost all kinds of models, accordingly as a tool it can represent a wide range of models, regardless that they are linear, semi-linear or non-linear. This attribute is especially important in non-linear models. This feature is due to the quality of Multilayer Perceptron (MLP) that is available in a special category of Feedforward Artificial Neural Networks, which employ the Backpropagation technique for the ANN training. Therefore, facilitating to solve non-linear problems.

8.4.3   Artificial Neural Networks and Time Series

Neural networks are gaining increasing importance in the processing and analysis of time series for their ability to self-learn and train. All hypotheses are based on the method of displacement of the chain to one degree or more to determine the inputs of ANN for forecasting time series using artificial neural networks. Simulation is one of the important practical methods used to determine the behaviour of a system. In this aspect, the models are applied through simulation to monitor and detect errors, process them and gain experience. Simulations are often used to monitor the model before it is applied in an actual scenario, it is a wildly used technique not only in time series but in many other cases when the system involves a high degree of risk, when is represents a rare phenomenon that is highly unrepeatable, when the experiment cannot be repeated in a controlled environment or when it is too costly to repeat.

Many evidences exist that clearly show the high efficiency in using ANN for forecasting when weigh against to the classical method, in this case efficiency is not measured in terms of accuracy but rather in terms on error in the forecast. Few error measures can be used to assess the efficiency of the forecast, such as:

- Mean Absolute Error (MAE).

$$MAE = \frac{\sum |et|}{n} \quad ..... (1)$$

- Mean Square Error (MSE)

$$MSE = \frac{\sum et^2}{n} \quad .....(2)$$

- Mean Absolute Percentage (MAP).

$$MAP = \frac{\sum \frac{et}{Xt}}{n} * 100 \ \ .....(3)$$

- Root Mean Squared Error (RMSE).

$$RMSE = \sqrt{\frac{\sum_{i=1}^{n} e_t^2}{n}} \ \ ...(4)$$

Where
　　Xt: actual value
　　X^t: forecasted value
　　Et: error (difference between actual and forecasted value)
　　N: sample size.

- Coefficient of determination (R^2).
  $R^2 = SSR/SST$ ....(5)

Where:
　　SST = Total sum of square = $\Sigma (y(i)-\mu(y))^2$;for i=1,2, ..., n
　　SSR = Regression sum of square = $\Sigma (\hat{Y}(i)-\mu(y))^2$;for i=1,2, ..., n
All the error measures can be used simultaneously to assess the effectiveness of the forecasting method used. This paper select MAP and RMSE as a measure of efficiency of the networks, due to their compatibility with the cases selected.

8.5   Comparisons and Discussions

The performance of classification and forecasting is compared to evaluate the accuracy and efficiency of the algorithms.

8.5.1   Comparison of Classification Accuracy

The accuracy of classification achieved by various algorithms with the datasets are presented in Figure 8.10. The accuracy of all the tested algorithms were influenced by the number of classifications which is exposed by the accuracy achieved with *Chord Progressions* (20 labels) and *Flavors*

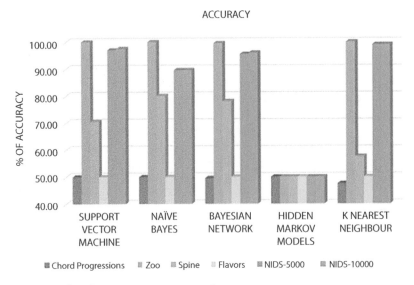

Figure 8.10 Classification accuracy - comparison.

(28 labels). In *Chord Progressions*, there were 20 classifications for 28 instances which is a small sample to enable proper and adequate learning that affected the accuracy. In *Flavours*, there is only one nominal feature to predict the class label which affected on the accuracy.

Overall, SVM performed better with all the datasets presents its ability in handling multi-variate datasets, but then it consumed a longer learning time with all the datasets compared to the other algorithms tested.

8.5.2   Forecasting Efficiency Comparison

In this part a few types of ANN will be discussed along with their forecasting efficiency withseveral data sets. The ANN performance was compared to that of the classical methods; the classical methods in this research are the Autoregressive Integrated Moving Average (ARIMA) [18] method and the Generalized Autoregressive Conditional Heteroscedastic (GARCH) [19, 20] method.

8.5.3   Recurrent Neural Network (RNN)

This type of networks can be classified under the dynamic ANN, due to a special characteristic of their nodes which enables them to interconnect the network, connecting back to themselves and other nodes as well. This means the output of a node (neuron) becomes the input of the same node and other nodes as well. This behaviour is responsible of making the flow of the information in the network multidirectional, therefore the input of the node from a node is connected to the output of the same node from pervious iteration. This ability provides the backward feed of the information flow through the network above the usual forward flow that is inherited from it being a neural network. This significant ability of backward feed is made possible through a "loopback connection", which is displayed clearly in Elman Neural Network, one of the most widely recognised networks in this type. The feedback loop is established through a hidden layer with a delay feedback ability, infact making this the only distinguished feature from normal feed forward network, that is the additional delay (memory) node that enables the local feedback [20]. The results of the comparison of the RNN with the classical method, in this case represented by the ARIMA method, is presented in Figure 8.11.

The forecasted date set for this case is the oil production to the United Arab Emirates is calculated based the crude oil production data acquired from United States Energy Information Administration, which shows the time series for crude oil production for the United Arab Emirates for the period 1980-2012. The Same data set was used for the forecast of both ARIMA and RNN methods. The results from Figure 8.11 clearly shows higher efficiency in the forecast performed by the RNN in comparison with the classical method. Where the results of both MAPE and RMSE are respectively for ARIMA are (23,8.3) on the other hand the results from

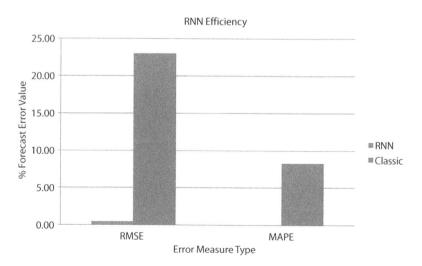

Figure 8.11 RNN efficiency analysis.

RNN for both MAPE and RMSE are respectively (0.46, 0.02) this shows clearly the supremely higher efficiency of the RNN in the forecast of the data set at hand.

8.5.4   Backpropagation Neural Network (BPNN)

This type of ANN must have at least a backpropagation sequence, as the case of other networks in this type it is able to include one or more layer, the output from each node, is passed as input to all other nodes. Moreover, it consists of auto backpropagation, thus with the implication that a node's output is send back as input for the same node. The basic steps of the Back-Propagation Methodology (BPM) is to calculate the error in the output layer, then use it to update the weightage for the hidden-output layer. Similarly, the error for the hidden layer is calculated to update weightage for the input-hidden layer. After that the output for the network using the new weightage is calculated and the same process steps of calculating error and updating weightage are repeated until minimal error for the network is reached [21]. The efficiency of this type of network was compared to GARCH method representing the classical method. The same data set was used for forecasting results of both methods, Figure 8.12 shows the results comparison.

The data set used is for Egyptian currency (Egyptian Pound) exchange rate for the period (1/1/2009 – 4/6/2013), this is because of the changes that took place within the interval of that period of time in Egypt in general and the financial market in specific, making the forecasting process both

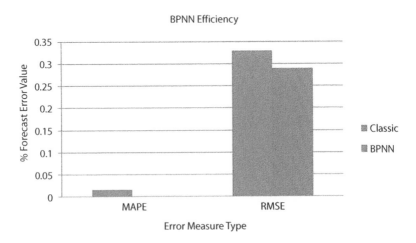

Figure 8.12 BPNN efficiency analysis.

challenging and extremely important. The results for the GARCH model for both MAPE and RMSE are respectively (0.015, 0.33). While for the same data, the BPNN shows error results of (0.0008, 0.29) for both MAPE and RMSE are respectively. It is clear from RMSE results that there is less error indicator in the results of BPNN but the comparison of MAPE leave no room for any doubt on the difference in efficiency.

8.5.5   General Regression Neural Network

This type of ANN is considered a front feed neural networks, they were developed by Donald Specht 1991, for system modelling and diagnosis, it actual can be considered as the probabilistic ANN main-stream and is generally referred to using the short form GRNN. Apart from the general purpose of pattern classification for the probabilistic neural network, the GRNN have a lot of other different applications. The basic idea behind developing General Regression Neural Network (GRNN) is based on the ability to approximate any function that is given inputs and data pair outputs [21]. Similar to the case of BPNN the results of the GRNN is compared to the results of a classical method represented by GARCH, once more the same data set is used as in the previous section, the results of the comparison are provided in Figure 8.13.

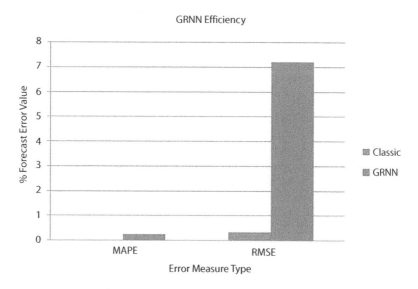

Figure 8.13 GRNN efficiency analysis.

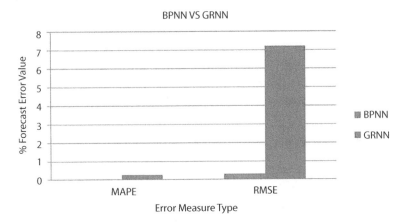

Figure 8.14 Efficiency comparison of BPNN and GRNN.

The results clearly show that for the case of GARCH model for both MAPE and RMSE are respectively (0.015, 0.33) as in the previous case due to the data set being one and the same. While for the same data the GRNN shows error results of (0.25, 7.2) for both MAPE and RMSE are respectively. It is clear from the results that GARCH show better forecast error results from GRNN, the comparison of the results of comparing CRNN and BPNN is shown in Figure 14, which clearly show the betterment of forecasting error results for BPNN.

8.6   Summary and Conclusion

In this chapter, six machine learning algorithms (SVM, NB, BN, HMM, KNN, ANN) were utilized with five different datasets which are univariate and multi variate. The training time taken by an algorithm with the datasets and the accuracy of the algorithm in classifying the instances were evaluated. The accuracy achieved with various datasets represents the fact that, the choice of the machine learning algorithm depending nature and volume contained in a dataset plays the significant role in the outcome expected. Forecasting outcomes demonstrates evidently an improved efficiency in forecasting in case of BPNN and RNN,as in both cases the output is used to improve the input. On the contrary, forward-feed networks represented by GRNN results in less forecasting efficiency than the classical methods. More algorithms need to be tested with datasets containing instances of different features and data types with varying volume to ascertain the applicability of the algorithm for a data.

References

1. Datasets | Kaggle., https://www.kaggle.com/datasets, Accessed on 01-08-2019.
2. Hall, M., Frank, E., Holmes, G., Pfahringer, B., Reutemann, P., Witten, I.H., The Weka data mining software: An update. *ACM SIGKDD Explorations Newsletter*, 11, 1, 10–18, 2009.
3. Cortes, C. and Vapnik, V., Support-vector networks. *Mach. Learn.*, 20, 3, 273–297, 1995.
4. Platt, J., Fast training of support vector machines using sequential minimal optimization, in: *Advances in Kernel Methods—Support Vector Learning*, pp. 185–208, AJ, MIT Press, Cambridge, MA, 1999.
5. John, G.H. and Langley, P., Estimating continuous distributions in Bayesian classifiers, in: *Proceedings of the Eleventh conference on Uncertainty in artificial intelligence*, Morgan Kaufmann Publishers Inc., pp. 338–345, 1995.
6. Rish, I., An empirical study of the naive Bayes classifier, in: *IJCAI 2001 workshop on empirical methods in artificial intelligence*, vol. 3, 22, pp. 41–46, 2001.
7. Heckerman, D., A tutorial on learning with Bayesian networks, in: *Innovations in Bayesian networks*, pp. 33–82, Springer, Berlin, Heidelberg, 2008.
8. Buntine, W., Theory refinement on Bayesian networks, in: *Proceedings of the Seventh conference on Uncertainty in Artificial Intelligence*, Morgan Kaufmann Publishers Inc., pp. 52–60, 1991.
9. Rabiner, L.R. and Juang, B.H., An introduction to hidden Markov models. *ieeeassp Mag.*, 3, 1, 4–16, 1986.
10. Eddy, S.R., Hidden markov models. *Curr. Opin. Struct. Biol.*, 6, 3, 361–365, 1996.
11. Ghahramani, Z., An introduction to hidden Markov models and Bayesian networks, in: *Hidden Markov models: applications in computer vision*, pp. 9–41, 2001.
12. Aha, D.W., Kibler, D., Albert, M.K., Instance-based learning algorithms. *Mach. Lear.*, 6, 1, 37–66, 1991.
13. Galushkin, A.I., *Neural networks theory*, Springer Science & Business Media, Berlin, Germany, 2007.
14. Allende, H., Moraga, C., Salas, R., Artificial neural networks in time series forecasting: A comparative analysis. *Kybernetika*, 38, 6, 685–707, 2002.
15. Palit, A.K. and Popovic, D., *Computational intelligence in time series forecasting: theory and engineering applications*, Springer Science & Business Media, Berlin, Germany, 2006.

16. Donate, J.P., Li, X., Sánchez, G.G., de Miguel, A.S., Time series forecasting by evolving artificial neural networks with genetic algorithms, differential evolution and estimation of distribution algorithm. *Neural Comput. Appl.*, 22, 1, 11–20, 2013.

17. Ashour, M.A.H. and Abbas, R.A., Improving Time Series' Forecast Errors by Using Recurrent Neural Networks, in: *Proceedings of the 2018 7th International Conference on Software and Computer Applications*, ACM, pp. 229–232, 2018.

18. Box, G.E., Jenkins, G.M., Reinsel, G.C., Ljung, G.M., *Time series analysis: forecasting and control*, John Wiley & Sons, Hoboken, NJ 07030-5774, 2015.

19. Hung, J.C., Lee, M.C., Liu, H.C., Estimation of value-at-risk for energy commodities *via* fat-tailed GARCH models. *Energy Econ.*, 30, 3, 1173–1191, 2008.

20. Muhammed, M.J., *The Use of GARCH Model for Saudi Financial Market Forecasting*, Al-Rafidain University Second Scientific Conference Baghdad-Iraq, 2010.

21. Ashour, M.A.H., Jamal, A., Abbas, R.A., Effectiveness of Artificial Neural Networks in Solving Financial Time Series. Proceedings of Al-Rafidain University Second Scientific Conference. *Int. J. Eng. Technol.*, 7, 99–105, 2018.

9

Unsupervised Learning

M. Kumara Swamy[1]* and Tejaswi Puligilla[2]

[1]Department of Computer Science & Engineering, CMR Engineering College, Kandlakoya (V), Hyderabad, Telangana, India
[2]Deloitte Consulting, Madhapur Hyderabad, Telangana, India

Abstract

Machine learning (ML) algorithms train an automated system with an existing data and the trained system is expected identify the class label of the new item. In the ML, the existing data is used to train the system. Hence, the systems are called the supervised learning. In ML, there existing another type of systems called unsupervised learning. In case of unsupervised learning, the training data does not exist to train the automated system. In this chapter, we explain the various ML algorithms/approaches in the area of unsupervised learning. We explain parametric and non-parametric approaches. We also concentrate on Dirichlet process mixture model and X-means algorithms in ML approaches.

Keywords: Machine learning, data sciences, data mining, algorithms, data

This chapter enlighten about various unsupervised learning approaches in machine learning.

- Basic algorithms such as parametric and non-parametric algorithms.
- Dirichlet process mixture model and X-means algorithms in machine learning.

9.1 Introduction

Machine learning (ML) is one of the applications of artificial intelligence (AI) which provides the flexibility to find out from the present data and

---

Corresponding author: m.kumaraswamy@cmrec.ac.in

Uma N. Dulhare, Khaleel Ahmad and Khairol Amali Bin Ahmad (eds.) Machine Learning and Big Data: Concepts, Algorithms, Tools and Applications, (233–250) © 2020 Scrivener Publishing LLC

identify the unknown object from the training. The method of learning starts with observations from the data, like samples, patterns, rules, etc., and uses this learning for better decisions within the future. This gives an opinion that a computer/system learns from the existing data, finds some kind of patterns and rules, and takes a decision in future from the patterns and rules. Generally, ML algorithms are categorized as supervised and unsupervised [1, 2].

In supervised learning, the algorithm learns from the past data and predicts the class label of the new data which is not seen. This means that some data is provided to the ML algorithm called the *training* data and this ML algorithm then identifies the class label of the unknown data called *test* data.

In case of unsupervised learning, the ML algorithms are employed when there's neither the data is assessed nor labeled. In unsupervised learning, algorithms can figure out the patterns from unlabeled data to describe an unseen structure. But the algorithm does not determine the right output. In this chapter, we focus on unsupervised learning algorithms. The goal of unsupervised ML technique is to identify similarities together, within the set of same data points and a data point. Generally, the method of grouping data points together is named as clustering [3–6].

Classification of data with similar objects together forms a cluster. When compared to other clusters objects are found to be dissimilar to each other. Several algorithms have been proposed in clustering.

In the rest of the chapter, first, we explain the related work on unsupervised learning. In addition, unsupervised algorithms, its classification, and algorithms with ML are explained respectively in Sections 9.3, 9.4, and 9.5. We conclude the chapter with summary and conclusions.

9.2 Related Work

In this section, we explain various unsupervised learning approaches proposed in the literature. The unsupervised learning (clustering) is one of the age-old problems. It has been addressed in several ways. In Hartigan [3], the clustering is defined as the grouping of similar objects. The book explains that the naming of minor planets and the classification of sightings are typical clustering problems. Further, it has mentioned that two objects are similar if, considering measurement error, the sightings could plausibly be of the same item.

In Kaufman and Rousseeuw [7], the clustering is analyzed as "finding groups in data is a clear, readable, and interesting presentation of a small number of clustering methods. The book discusses various types of data such as interval-scaled and binary variables as well as similarity data and explains how these can be transformed prior to clustering."

In Jain *et al.* [8], it is explained that the "clustering analysis is the organization of a collection of patterns into clusters based on similarity, intuitively, patterns within a valid cluster are more similar to each other than they are to a pattern belonging to different cluster."

Several variations are reported in Berkhin [5], such as hierarchical clustering methods, partitioning methods, gird-based methods, constraint-based clustering, scalable clustering algorithms, algorithms for high dimensional data, etc. In this chapter, we will explain few of the approaches using ML perspective.

9.3   Unsupervised Learning Algorithms

In this section, we formally define the unsupervised learning and provide various techniques in ML. In a ML perspective, the clustering is related to identifying a set of patterns hidden in the correspond data. Clustering is defined as forming same set of data points (same patterns, tuples, cases, observations, objects, instances, transactions) in groups. Data objects are found to be dissimilar when compared to other cluster data objects, yet they are similar if they are compared from same cluster, which is also called cluster analysis. Different clusters are generated from different clustering algorithms and on the same data set. Normally, clustering is done by clustering algorithms but not performed by humans. In this way, clustering leads to previously unknown groups in the data. Therefore, the clustering analysis is being studied as part of the ML.

The process of clustering analysis is shown in Figure 9.1. In the set of data points, based on the similarity, the data is clustered. Each data point similarity is compared with other data points in the data. Data points are clustered based on the similarity. The data points with high similarity are grouped into a cluster. So, the data points in the figure are grouped into three clusters.

Generally, the clustering process depends on similarity. Suppose, there are

M data points where $1 \leq I \leq M$.

Let i and j are two data points. The distance of two data points can be measure using $d(i,j)$ function.

The following are the properties of the similarity.

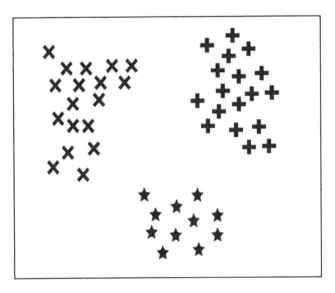

Figure 9.1 Clustering analysis.

- Non-negativity: The distance between i and j is always positive.
  d (i, j) $\geq$0.

- Identity of indiscernible: The distance from i to i should be zero.
  d (i, i) = 0.

- Symmetry: Distance is a symmetric function.
  d (i,j)=d (j,i), distance from i to j and j to i should be same.

- Triangle inequality: Making a tour with object K in space is almost equivalent going directly from object ito object j.
  d (i,j)$\leq$d (i,k)+d (k,j)

Any measure is termed as metric only if it satisfies the above conditions. It can be noted that the non-negativity property can be implied by result of the three properties.

- Both *Euclidean* and *Manhattan* distances satisfy the mathematical properties.

The length of the line segment is the Euclidean and distance between points p and q.

For Cartesian coordinates, the p to q distance or q to p distance is given by Pythagorean formula. In Euclidean space p=(p1,p2,.pn), q=(q1,q2,.qn).

$$d(p,q) = d(q,p) = \sqrt{\left(q_1 - p_1\right)^2 + \left(q_2 - p_2\right)^2 + \cdots + \left(q_n - p_n\right)^2}$$

$$= \sqrt{\sum_{i=1}^{n} \left(q_i - p_i\right)^2}$$

Each position in Euclidean n-space is known as a Euclidean vector. The Euclidean space starts from initial point p and ends at terminal point q, in which p and q are Euclidean vectors. The length of vector is measured by *Euclidean length or Euclidean norm.*

$$\left\|\mathbf{p}\right\| = \sqrt{p_1^2 + p_2^2 + \cdots + p_n^2} = \sqrt{\mathbf{p} \cdot \mathbf{p}},$$

The above expression has the dot product.

Vector is defined as a line segment from the origin of Euclidean space to a point in that space. Euclidean distance between tail to tip is known as Euclidean Norm.

When there is a direction from points p to q, then its relationship can be represented by a vector, given by $\mathbf{q} - \mathbf{p} = (q_1 - p_1, q_2 - p_2, \cdots, q_n - p_n)$. In a two- or three-dimensional space (n = 2, 3), this can be visually represented as an arrow from p to q. Vector can be visually represented by an arrow from p to q in an two- or three-dimensional space (n = 2, 3). In any space, it can be regarded as the position of *q* relative to *p* called as displacement vector if *p* and *q* represent two positions of some moving point.

The Euclidean length (Euclidean distance) of displacement vector between *p* and *q* is $\left\|\mathbf{q} - \mathbf{p}\right\| = \sqrt{\left(\mathbf{q} - \mathbf{p}\right) \cdot \left(\mathbf{q} - \mathbf{p}\right)}$. This equation is equal to 1st equation and can be equalized to $\left\|\mathbf{q} - \mathbf{p}\right\| = \sqrt{\left\|\mathbf{p}\right\|^2 + \left\|\mathbf{q}\right\|^2 - 2\mathbf{p} \cdot \mathbf{q}}$.

Over the dimensions of the vectors, Manhattan distance between two vectors is defined as $\sum_i \left|a_i - b_i\right|$, and this is also known as Manhattan distance.

This is also known as the L^1 norm because the L^p norm is defined as

$\|x\|_p = \left(|x_i|^p + |x_2|^p + \cdots + |x_n|^p \right)^{\frac{1}{p}}$. You can see how p = 1 and x = a – b leads to the first formula.

In competitive programming, a common trick is to convert the L^1 norm to the $L\infty$ norm by rotating the plane by 45° and appropriately scaling. This is so common that it's one of the first things you should think of if you see the words "distance in a city", "cows walking along a grid", etc.

The $L\rightarrow\infty, L\rightarrow\infty$ norm, where $p\rightarrow\infty, p\rightarrow\infty$, is defined as $\|x\|_\infty = \max\left\{ |x_1|, |x_2|, ..., |x_n| \right\}$. This representation is considerably more powerful since many standard sweep-line algorithms and 2D data structures can now be used.

9.4   Classification of Unsupervised Learning Algorithms

As we explained previously, all the clustering algorithms are referred as unsupervised learning algorithms. Now, we explain the classification of clustering algorithms in the following. Generally, the categorization of clustering algorithms is not straightforward similar to classification algorithms. For the convenience of the reader, we provide a classification. In reality, some of the groups below are overlapped. The list is not limited to the following.

9.4.1   Hierarchical Methods

The tree of clusters together forms a hierarchical cluster called as *dendrogram*. Every cluster node helps in exploring the data on different levels of granularity as it contains child clusters, and the sibling clusters partition the points covered by their common parent. The two hierarchical clustering methods are bottom-up (agglomerative) and top-down (divisive) in Figure 9.2. The clustering which begins with single point and recursively merges two or more appropriate clusters is called as bottom-up clustering. The top-down clustering emerges with one cluster of all data points and recursively splits the most appropriate cluster. Until an end point of criteria is achieved to stop the clustering process, this is continued. That is the requested K number of clusters are achieved.

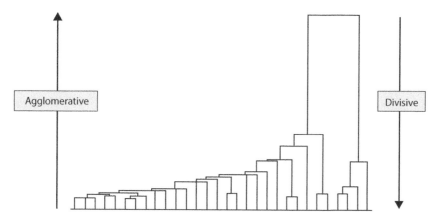

Figure 9.2 Agglomerative and divisive hierarchical clustering.

Creating clusters which have predetermined order from top to bottom is called hierarchical clustering. For instance, hard disk folders and files are arranged in hierarchy. Divisive and agglomerative are two types of hierarchical clusters.

9.4.2   Partitioning Methods

Partitioning algorithms divide the data into several small subsets. Because it is not feasible to check all the subset systems computationally, few other methods are used.

The data is classified through a certain number (i.e., K) of clusters. For each cluster, primary thing is to define K centers. These centers are placed in alternate way as different locations provide different results. So, placing them very far from each other will be the better choice. Early grouping is considered as completed only when there is any point in data left pending and got associated with its nearest center which also indicates completion of first step. Now, we have to re-compute k new centroids clusters which results from the previous step. In between same data points and nearest new center, the new binding has to be created and loop must be generated. K centers change their locations step by step according of the loop. In precise, the centers do not move anymore.

The partitioning algorithms are majorly of two types: *k-medoid* and *k-means*. The *K-medoid* is the suitable algorithm for representing the clusters within a cluster that represents it. This algorithm has two advantages. First, the attribute types do not have any limitations. The points inside the cluster dictate the medoids choice. So, to the outliers, this approach is not sensitive. Therefore, this approach does not seem to be sensitive to the outliers. The center in K-means is represented by clustering virtual centroid. Within the cluster weighted average of data points is known as mean of cluster. This approach is more convenient to the numerical attributes and not suitable for single outliers. On the other hand, the centroids of the clusters give more advantage to identify the geometric and statistical meaning to each cluster.

We consider an example to explain the k-medoid clustering approach. Consider the data in Table 9.1. The data consist of X and Y coordinates of 10 data points from 0 to 9. The cost function of the k-medoid algorithm is as follows.

$$c = \sum_{Ci} \sum_{Pi \in Ci} |Pi - Ci|$$

The data points in Table 9.1 can be plotted on a graph and can be produced in Figure 9.3.

We explain the clustering processing as follows. Let us consider the number of clusters, k be 2 (i.e., k = 2). Let the randomly selected medoids

Table 9.1 Sample dataset.

#	X	Y
0	7	6
1	2	6
2	3	8
3	8	5
4	7	4
5	4	7
6	6	2
7	7	3
8	6	4
9	3	4

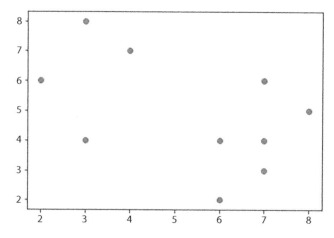

Figure 9.3 Data points in the graph.

be C1 (3, 4) and C2 (7, 4). Now, let us calculate the cost of clustering. The dissimilarity of each non-medoid point with the medoids is calculated and tabulated in Table 9.2. Each point is assigned to a cluster of that medoid whose dissimilarity is less. The points 1, 2, 5 go to cluster C1 and points 0, 3, 6, 7, 8 go to cluster C2. The cost C = (3 + 4 + 4) + (3 + 1 + 1 + 2 + 2) which is C = 20. Now, let us select randomly one non-medoid point and

Table 9.2 Dissimilarity computation for sample data.

#	X	Y	Dissimilarity from C1	Dissimilarity from C2
0	7	6	6	2
1	2	6	3	7
2	3	8	4	8
3	8	5	6	2
4	7	4	4	0
5	4	7	4	6
6	6	2	5	3
7	7	3	5	1
8	6	4	3	1
9	3	4	0	4

Table 9.3 Dissimilarity computation for sample data second time.

#	X	Y	Dissimilarity from C1	Dissimilarity from C2
0	7	6	6	2
1	2	6	3	7
2	3	8	4	8
3	8	5	6	2
4	7	4	4	0
5	4	7	4	6
6	6	2	5	3
7	7	3	5	1
8	6	4	3	1
9	3	4	0	4

recalculate the cost. Let the randomly selected point be (7, 3). The dissimilarity of each non-medoid point with the medoids C1 (3, 4) and C2 (7, 3) is calculated and tabulated in Table 9.3. Each data point is assigned to that cluster whose dissimilarity is less. So, the points 1, 2, 5 go to cluster C1 and points 0, 3, 6, 7, 8 go to cluster C2. The cost C = (3 + 4 + 4) + (2 + 2 + 1 + 3 + 3) C = 22. Swap Cost = Present Cost – Previous Cost = 22 – 20 = 2 > 0. As the swap cost is not less than zero, we undo the swap. Hence, (3, 4) and (7, 4) are the final medoids. The clustering is shown in Figure 9.4.

The same process would be taken place for k-mean. However, the centroid points will not be existing in case of k-mean. Computation of clustering is almost similar the approach shown in k-medoid approach.

9.4.3   Density-Based Methods

The problem with the *hierarchical* and *partitioning* methods is that the data points are clustered in circular or rectangular shaped manner. This is due to an open set in the Euclidean space which divides into a set of linked data points from existing data points. For The implementation of partitioning to the finite set of points requires concepts of nearest neighbors such as density, connectivity, and boundary. The density-based algorithms have ability to turn up the clusters in

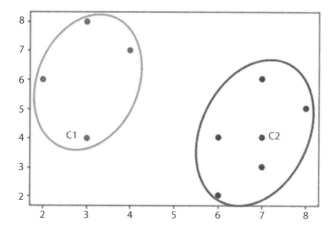

Figure 9.4 Final Clusters for the sample data.

arbitrary shapes that are defined as a linked dense unit which grows in any of direction and lead the way to density. This also provides natural protection counter to outliers. In Figure 9.5, we have shown few cluster shape partitioning clustering problem (e.g., k-means). However, they are solved accordingly by density-based algorithms. The problems in cluster shapes are because of partitioning clustering algorithm but it is handled by the density-based algorithm.

Figure 9.5 Dense-based clustering.

Clusters which are dense in regions are separated by density points which are from lower regions. This algorithm is based on this accustomed knowledge of noise and clusters. The fundamental idea is that, for a given boundary, there should be at least minimum number of points in the neighborhood for each point of the cluster. In substantial life, there are irregularities seen in such as data may contain noise and clusters and that are of arbitrary shape like ones displayed in the figure below. Figure 9.6 depicts data points which contain outliers and nonconvex clusters. For that data in Figure 9.6, it is difficult to identify the arbitrary shaped clusters with k-means/k-medoid algorithms.

The DBSCAN algorithm has two parameters. The first one is epsilon value, which defines the data points in neighborhood. Two data points are called neighbors when the distance between them is equal or lower to eps. The large part of the data is considered as outliers when the eps value is too small. There might be a consequence of having eps value very large that is, clusters will get merged and maximum data points will come in to the same cluster. One way to find the *eps* value using k-distance graph and other way is using minimum number of points (*MinPts*). If the dataset is larger, then the larger values of *MinPts* must be chosen. Generally, number of facets D in the dataset helps in deriving the *MinPts*as, *MinPts*>= D+1. At least three numbers of minimum values must be chosen. We have three types of data points in this algorithm.

A) Core Point: Within eps, the point which has more than *Minpts* points is called as core point.

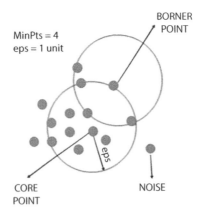

Figure 9.6 Clustering process using DBSCAN algorithm.

B) Border Point: If a point is neighborhood of a core point and fewer than *MinPts* points within *eps*, then it is called as border point.

C) Noise or outlier: The point which neither a core point nor a border point is a noise or outlier.

9.4.4   Grid-Based Methods

In the dense-based clustering, significant notions of density have used which require elaborate definitions. The other way of addressing the issue is to acquire the study from existing attribute scope which is available inherently. In order to curb the search combinations, multi-rectangular segments are chosen. The direct Cartesian product of sub-ranges of individual attributes is known as segment (cube, cell, region). As such, binning is an approach which is used for numerical attributes. The grid-based applications are employed to partition space frequently. Comparing to single-value sub-ranges, the portion is called as elementary segment.

This shows that our attention has been changed to space partitioning instead of data partitioning. The data partitioning is induced by the data points membership in the segments resulted from space partitioning; on the other hand, the space partitioning is based on input data points which are accumulated from grid-characteristics.

9.4.5   Constraint-Based Clustering

In current applications, the consumers are sporadically interested in immortal result. In this clustering, these groupings are generally concerned with few specific constraints which are excessively appropriate for certain business actions. These conditioned cluster partitions help in active research [9].

This framework is introduced in Tung *et al.* [10]. The classification of clustering constraints includes parameter constraints that are addressed by preprocessing or external cluster parameters and constraints on parameters of individual objects. There are also constraints on individual clusters which are described in terms of bounds on functions called aggregate functions such as min, avg, etc., over each one of the clusters. Since they may require a new methodology, these constrains are generally essential.

9.5   Unsupervised Learning Algorithms in ML

As discussed in previous section, many algorithms were proposed in the area of clustering. The clustering algorithms were also used in ML to classify the data in an unsupervised method. In Roberts [11], the classification made as parametric and non-parametric unsupervised cluster. Furthermore, we also discuss the other major unsupervised clustering algorithms such as Dirichlet process mixture model (DPMM) and X-means.

9.5.1   Parametric Algorithms

In parametric algorithms, the probabilistic finite mixture modeling [12, 13] is commonly used parametric clustering methods which is well known. Various probabilistic approaches were existed in the literature such as Gaussian Mixture Model (GMM) [12] and Latent Dirichlet Allocation [14]. These techniques are demonstrated as strong and triumphant in great range of functions regarding the examination of constant and discontinuous data points. These designs provide main ways to mark the problems such as the amount of cluster, missing element esteems, and so on. Parametric blend models are compelling, just when dissemination of information in underlying distribution is either known or can be intently approximated by appropriation which is accepted by that model. This is an inadequacy due to the fact that it is surely understood that groups of clusters in genuine real data are not generally of a similar shape and seldom follow a decent distribution such as Gaussian Jain and Dubes [4]. In general, every single cluster would follow its unique unknown data distributions, which confines the presentation of parametric blend models. Comparative shortcomings can be credited to squared mistake-based grouping algorithm, for instance, K-means. K-Mean is one among the most well-known clustering algorithm due to its empirical performance and its effortlessness of implementation.

9.5.2   Non-Parametric Algorithms

As explained in the previous sections, that approach is aimed to divide the given n data points represent as n × n similarity matrix and in **d** dimensional space as data points. Since, the non-existence of a cluster and its data dependent nature has generate in publication of a very large number of clustering algorithms, each with different assumptions about the cluster structure [15].

The shortcomings of above parametric models can be overcome by algorithms that can be exploited by non-parametric density estimation methods. Several non-parametric clustering algorithms have been proposed in the literature such as Jarvis-Patrick Jarvis and Patrick [16], DBSCAN: Ester *et al.* [17], Mean- shift: Comaniciu and Meer [18]. These methods find a single kernel density estimate of the entire data points and then identify the clusters by detecting regions of heavy density in the predicted density [18]. In spite of success of these approaches, most of those approaches are not always fruitful in finding group of density data points in high-dimensional datasets, due to the fact that it is difficult to find the neighborhood of a data points in a high-dimensional space when the existing sample size is small [19]. Because of this reason, all non-parametric density-based algorithms have applied to low-dimensional issues such as image segmentation [18]. Furthermore, in these methods, it may not be possible to *a priori* specify the preferred number of clusters.

9.5.3   Dirichlet Process Mixture Model

This process is another non-parametric Bayesian model that is generally used for design selection or averaging, density estimation and semi-parametric modeling. The Dirichlet processes are known as non-parametric as they have numerous numbers of parameters. They are treated in a Bayesian approach, we can create huge models with infinite number of parameters which we combine out to circumvent the problem of excess-fitting. It can also be shown that the Dirichlet processes can be represented in different mathematically equivalent ways.

For performing clustering in a set of data points, DPMMs are constructed. The numbers of mixture components are infinite with DPMMs with which we build one mixture model. So, the DPMM is not required for us to define from the beginning the number of clusters in which case it is uncountable, and it allows us to adapt the number of busy clusters as we input more data points to our model over period.

The DPMMs have become popular both in Statistics and in ML. Similarly, they are used in huge number of applications. Wood *et al.* [20] have used DPMMs to perform spike sorting and identify the number of different neurons that were monitored by a single electrode. Suddath *et al.* [21] have used this model to achieve Visual Scene Analysis and detect the number of features, objects, and parts that a particular image contains.

9.5.4 X-Means

Generally, k-means [22, 23] algorithm has been used for numerical data points. The advantage of k-means is local-minimum convergence properties and its simplicity. The major issues in k-means are not so fast and measures slowly in order with time taken to complete, k has to be supplied as input and due to k value, and it empirically finds worse local optima.

X-means is a new algorithm that quickly estimates k value. After each iteration of K-means, it goes into an action, making the decision about which subset of the current centroids should split themselves in order to find the data points.

9.6 Summary and Conclusions

ML algorithms are used to train a system and it is expected to identify the class label of the new item. Unsupervised learning is one of the methods to find the classification of data when the class label is not available. In this chapter, we explain the various ML algorithms/approaches in the area of unsupervised learning. We explain parametric and non-parametric approaches. We also concentrate on DPMM and X-means algorithms in ML approaches.

References

1. Russell, S. and Norvig, P., *Artificial Intelligence: A Modern Approach*, 3rd edition, Prentice Hall Press, Upper Saddle River, NJ, USA, 2009.
2. Han, J., Kamber, M., Pei, J., 3rd edition, Morgan Kaufmann Publishers Inc., Data Mining: Concepts and Techniques San Francisco, CA, USA, 2011.
3. Hartigan, J.A., *Clustering Algorithms*, 99th edition, John Wiley & Sons, Inc., New York, NY, USA, 1975.
4. Jain, A.K. and Dubes, R.C., *Algorithms for Clustering Data*, Prentice-Hall, Inc, USA, 1988.
5. Berkhin, P., Survey of clustering data mining techniques, in: *Grouping Multidimensional Data*, J. Teboulle M. Kogan and C. Nicholas (Eds.), pp. 25–71, Springer, Berlin, Heidelberg, 2006.
6. Everitt, B.S., Landau, S., Leese, M., *Cluster Analysis*, 4th edition, Wiley Publishing, UK, 2009.
7. Kaufman, L. and Rousseeuw, P.J., *Finding Groups in Data: An Introduction to Cluster Analysis*, John Wiley, New Jersey, 1990.

8. Jain, K., Murty, M.N., Flynn, P.J., Data clustering: A review. *ACM Comput. Surv.*, 31, 3, 264–323, 1999.

9. Han, J., Kamber, M., Tung, A.K.H., Spatial clustering methods in data mining: A survey, in: *Geographic Data Mining and Knowledge Discovery, Research Monographs in GIS*, H.J. Miller and J. Han (Eds.), Taylor and Francis, Abingdon, 2001.

10. Tung, A.K.H., Ng, R.T., Lakshmanan, L.V.S., Han, J., Constraint-based clustering in large databases, in: *Proceedings of the 8th International Conference on Database Theory, ICDT'01*, pp. 405–419, Springer-Verlag, Berlin Heidelberg, 2001.

11. Roberts, S.J., Parametric and non-parametric unsupervised cluster analysis. *Pattern Recogn.*, 30, 2, 261–272, 1997.

12. Figueiredo, M.A.T. and Jain, A.K., Unsupervised learning of finite mixture models. *IEEE Trans. Pattern Anal. Mach. Intell.*, 24, 3, 381–396, 2002.

13. Mallapragada, P.K., Jin, R., Jain, A., Non-parametric mix- ture models for clustering, in: *Proceedings of the 2010 Joint IAPR International Conference on Structural, Syntactic, and Statistical Pattern Recognition, SSPR& SPR'10*, pp. 334–343, Springer-Verlag, Berlin Heidelberg, 2010.

14. Blei, D.M., Ng, A.Y., Jordan, M.I., Latent dirichletallocation. *J. Mach. Learn. Res.*, 3, 993–1022, 2003.

15. Jain, A.K., Data clustering: 50 years beyond k-means. *Pattern Recogn. Lett.*, 31, 8, 651–666, 2010.

16. Jarvis, R.A. and Patrick, E.A., Clustering using a similarity measure based on shared near neighbors. *IEEE Trans. Comput.*, 22, 11, 1025–1034, 1973.

17. Ester, M., Kriegel, H.-P., Sander, J., Xu, X., Adensity-based algorithm for discovering clusters a density-based algorithm for discovering clusters in large spatial databases with noise, in: *Proceedings of the Second International Conference on Knowledge Discovery and Data Mining, KDD'96*, pp. 226–231, AAAI Press, USA, 1996.

18. Comaniciu, D. and Meer, P., Mean shift: A robust approach toward feature-space analysis. *IEEE Trans. Pattern Anal. Mach. Intell.*, 24, 5, 603–619, 2002.

19. Bishop, C.M., *Pattern Recognition and Machine Learning (Information Science and Statistics)*, Springer-Verlag, Berlin, Heidelberg, 2006.

20. Wood, F., Goldwater, S., Black, M.J., A non-parametric Bayesian approach to spike sorting, in: *Proceedings of the International Conference of the IEEE Engineering in Medicine and Biology Society*, IEEE, USA, 2006.

21. Sudderth, E.B., Torralba, A., Freeman, W.T., Willsky, A.S., Describing visual scenes using transformed objects and parts. *Int. J. Comput. Vis.*, 77, 1-3, 291–330, 2008.

22. Bishop, C.M., *Neural Networks for Pattern Recognition*, Oxford University Press, Inc., New York, NY, USA, 1995.

23. Duda, R. O., Hart, P. E., *Pattern classification and scene analysis*, Wiley, New York, 1973.

Manish Devgan, Gaurav Malik and Deepak Kumar Sharma*

*Department of Information Technology, Netaji Subhas University of Technology,
New Delhi, India*

Abstract

Semi-supervised learning is a machine learning paradigm which combines both labeled and unlabeled data to increase the performance accuracy of the machine. Unlike the supervised and the unsupervised approaches [1] that rely solely on labeled and unlabeled data respectively, semi-supervised learning uses a collective set of labeled data and unlabeled data and tries to converge to an absolute perfection for predicting the data points. The motivation behind using both types of data is due to the readily available unlabeled data that exists in enormous amount, whereas labeled data is hard to find and is a very expensive task to label the unlabeled data. Semi-supervised learning emerged as an improvisation to the unavailability of labeled data for natural systems as well as a strong potential quantitative tool to model the substantial unlabeled data around. It starts with understanding the unlabeled data by the means of labeled data and then training the machine of the natural system [1, 2].

This chapter provides a great introduction for learners exploring the field of semi-supervised learning including self-training, generative models, and co-training along with Multiview learning algorithms, graph-based algorithms, and more. The discussion on generative models comprises of image classification, text classification, speech recognition and Baum-Welch algorithm.

Keywords: Semi-supervised learning, machine learning, generative models, unlabeled data, self-training, s3vms, Baum-Welch algorithm, graph-based algorithm

---

**Corresponding author*: dk.sharma1982@yahoo.com

Uma N. Dulhare, Khaleel Ahmad and Khairol Amali Bin Ahmad (eds.) Machine Learning and
Big Data: Concepts, Algorithms, Tools and Applications, (251–280) © 2020 Scrivener Publishing LLC

10.1   Introduction

10.1.1   Semi-Supervised Learning

In today's world, technology has taken a long jump thanks to machines and their abilities. Advanced systems are capable of deriving solutions to the problems without being explicitly programmed for the same. The machines have grown smart and have already outdated a large number of technologies that worked on primitive methodologies. Machines are able to think and arrive at a conclusion, but what drives the machines to do this work? It is the data that allows the systems to think. Machine learning works in not so mysterious ways and has applications ranging from the smallest to the largest use case. It not just reduces the computation required to perform a certain task but also allows us to gather a deep insight about the data which otherwise would have not been considered. Some of the most famous areas in which machine learning has its application are *self-driving cars, online recommendation systems, spam detection* of emails, *facial recognition* systems, *text-to-speech (TTS)* and *speech-to-text (STT)* systems, and a lot more.

The machines that run these amazing and once deemed computationally impossible tasks all have one constituent in common, i.e., data. All these systems require data to make or gather insight information about the context that they are dealing with. Therefore, it is completely logical to say that without data, a staggering 100% of all the machine learning systems would render useless. But what actually is *data*? Data can be defined as any unprocessed value, or collection of values. These values need not be in text every time. The term data is *type-agnostic*, i.e., any kind of format can presumably be data. Data in the form of text, images, multimedia, sound, videos, graphics, and even game and log data from systems and servers running online. The major use of data is to mine information. This information is what makes the amazing machine learning systems perform tasks that are capable of performing right now. The collected information from the unstructured data should have a definite meaning, the processed information should be structured perfectly so that it fits the model or the system perfectly. The information need not necessarily be collected from the raw data initially but can also be generated and collected from the past experiences of the machine. In any machine learning environment the data can be split into three important categories: *training data*, this is the portion of the data that the model uses to train; *validation data*, this part of the data is used to evaluate the trained model by improving the hyper parameters associated to the model running inside the machine learning environment; and finally, the *testing data*, this data is separated out in the beginning before model training and is used to evaluate the correctness and accuracy of the trained model by correctly predicting the values corresponding to each data values and then checking the target value and computing the loss incurred.

The world around us is overflowing with data streams, if we can capture them, then we can possible store and capture huge tons of data to train a model efficiently. But not all data is valuable to us, i.e., not all data can be simply used for training purposes. Training data can further be classified as *labeled* and *unlabeled* data. Labeled data, as the name suggests, is the data which is perfectly labeled. Each and every individual data point in the labeled dataset contains the target value corresponding to itself. Unlabeled data on the other hand is not labeled, i.e., the data exists but bears no label corresponding to individual datapoint. Unlabeled data is available to us in abundance, whereas labeled data is scarce in the world. It is because the overhead of labeling the data correctly is a task that must be carried out either by a human or under the supervision of a human therefore making labeling the unlabeled data a huge and painful task for most of us. Unlabeled data normally includes pictures, audio, videos, tweets, articles, medical data, etc. Most of the models working inside a machine learning environment are trained using labeled data only since it is easy to rely on them since there is a less chance that the data will be corrupt or wrongly labeled, although it can happen but it still has a lower probability when done by or under the supervision of a human. Machines use the labeled data to establish the sense of knowledge over the data and try to converge to a point where it predicts almost nearly perfectly thereby improving its accuracy. The training data is used to train and validation data to validate, whereas the model accuracy is evaluated by the use of the test data available.

Now that we know about labeled and unlabeled data, let us have an overview of the two most popular machine learning approaches, *supervised* and *unsupervised* learning.

Supervised learning is "Train Me!" learning. In simpler words, it is a learning mechanism where the machine tends to *"learn under the guidance of a teacher"*, i.e., the machine has a set of input defined using the labeled data and its corresponding output or the target value is used to help train the machine and the error signals are generated and the machine takes countermeasures by adjusting the parameters, often the associated weights to generate positive results. Supervised learning also learns to predict data from its history. For example, train the model with every fruit individually and then get all the fruits from a given fruit basket. On the other hand, unsupervised learning is *"I am self-sufficient in learning"*. The algorithm is used to train the machine without using any classified or labeled data and act on that unlabeled information without any guidance. Unlike supervised learning there is no prior knowledge or training given to the machine. For example, suppose there are lots of images of dogs and cats given and the machine won't be able to detect that any image is either a dog or a cat but it will be able to categorize them into two clusters of dogs and cats according to their features and patterns [1].

Supervised learning is mainly used for classification problems where we know the target data value and the incoming input data is to be classified into either of the given discrete classes [2]. It is also used for regression where the output is a real value defined on a weighted graph normally corresponding but not limited to height, currency value, etc. Unsupervised learning is mainly used to process the problems dealing with the clustering of data values in which the inherent similarities of different data points are clustered together to be identified as a separate unit, and association, which defines a problem where one wants to discover rules that describe large portions of the data such as people that buy a certain item are also observed to buy a certain item.

The next approach that we are going to discuss is not much well known like the aforementioned two approaches. It is slowly gaining popularity. It is a mixture of the above-mentioned methods, i.e., supervised learning and unsupervised learning. Semi-supervised learning [1, 2] is partly between supervised and unsupervised learning methods. It means that Semi supervised learning makes use of both labeled and unlabeled data to develop a learning method that is not restricted to the use of only one type of information. Here, a machine learning algorithm is trained on a labeled dataset in which each record contains an output metric. This will help the algorithm to understand the patterns and relationships between the target and the input data. After that, the algorithm is fed with the unlabeled data to predict its decisions. The unlabeled data with the most confidence scores is then again added back to the labeled data which is continually used up by the machine to retrain itself and to converge itself.

Semi supervised learning or *SSL* models are becoming popular in the industry including Google. Some of the well-known examples are: speech

SEMI-SUPERVISED LEARNING   255

analysis to label the audio files, classifying protein sequences with the function of proteins, classification of web-based content to organize the web pages and their knowledge etc. There are many other scenarios for semi-supervised learning models but not all AI situations can be handled by SSL. Here are some criteria that a scenario should contain to be effectively handled by SSL, like:

- Sizable unlabeled dataset: the size of the domain of unlabeled dataset should be relatively much bigger than the labeled dataset otherwise the problem can be solved by supervised learning.
- Input-output proximity symmetry
- Relatively simple labeling and low dimension nature of the problem

10.1.2   Comparison With Other Paradigms

We now know that *SSL* can be defined as a mixture of the other two majorly used learning approaches. But what makes it so special is that none of the aforementioned algorithms are efficiently using the entire available data.
   Here are some of the disadvantages of supervised learning,

- The decision boundary can be over trained. In other words, if the training set does not include some examples which one want to have in the output domain, after training it is impossible to get that result.
- When there is an input which does not belong to any class, then it might get a wrong label after classification.
- One has to select a lot of good example or training data from each class while training the classifier. Inclusion of big data can be hefty task or in some other cases too, training needs a lot of computation time.

Unsupervised learning also possesses disadvantages

- It is quite impossible to gather information about the nature of data and its output such as is it sorted etc. It is because the data used to model an unsupervised learning approach is not labeled and hence not known.
- The inability to achieve higher accuracy is due to the fact that data used in unsupervised learning is unlabeled. It requires human effort to sit in front of the computer screen

and correctly classify each and every individual data point into correct classes.

- The change in spectral properties of data can render data useless, and hence, the machine needs to have updated data after some span of time.

Thus, taking note of these disadvantages, a new learning approach has been defined. The idea is to make appropriate use of both labeled as well as the abundantly available unlabeled data to train the machine so as to empower it to produce even better results. The primary work is to train the model using the readily available labeled data and then use this trained model to classify the unlabeled data into defined discrete classes that correspond to the labeled data. Now, the unlabeled data with the most *confidence score* is added to the set of labeled data and is again used to train the model or refine the model's accuracy. We use labeled data and augment it with the unlabeled data since the amount of labeled data available is very less when compared to the abundance of unlabeled data available all around us at any instance. Moreover, unlabeled data is easier to obtain and gather, whereas labeled data is tough to acquire. So, the goal is to overcome one of the problems of supervised learning—having not enough labeled data. The solution to this problem is semi-supervised learning in which we add cheap and abundant unlabeled data, in a hope to build a model with better accuracy than simple supervised approach or unsupervised approach. *SSL* aims at getting the best out of both worlds.

In order to make proper use of unlabeled data, some assumptions are made while using semi-supervised learning to maintain a structure of the distribution of data.

- Continuity: The assumption about continuity states that the data that lies closer to each other on the plane are highly likely to share a common label. Such assumptions in the supervised learning approach helps in attaining a simpler boundary or decision line. In the particular case of *SSL*, the assumption about smoothness additionally yields a preference for decision boundaries generated in the low-density regions, so that there are fewer points close to each other but in different categories of labels.
- Cluster: Clustering assumes that the available data tends to form clusters as it shares common behavioral points with the

nearby data. Therefore, the data that lies together is more likely to form a cluster. This is a special case of the smoothness assumption and gives rise to feature learning with clustering algorithms.

- Manifold: The data lie approximately on a manifold of much lower dimension than the input space. The attempt is made to learn the manifold making use of both the unlabeled data and the labeled data so as to avoid dimensionality problems. The distances and densities defined on the manifold can be used to carry on the learning.

10.2 Training Models

In this section, we shall study the various training models associated to semi-supervised learning, namely, self-training, co-training, and generative models.

10.2.1 Self-Training

As discussed so far, semi-supervised learning is a machine learning paradigm which makes use of both labeled data and unlabeled data to improve the performance of model. A machine learning model, based on any paradigm, aims at solving classical problems such as classification, regression, and clustering, etc. Here, we focus primarily on classification problems. Self-training is a semi-supervised learning model that employs heuristic approach and is the oldest approach in the history of semi-supervised learning which began surfacing during the early 1960s. It is also referred to as self-teaching or bootstrapping.

Self-training algorithm uses both unlabeled and labeled data to provide a much better accuracy than the labeled data alone [2, 3]. Let L be the set of labeled data and U be the set of unlabeled data from a total set S, such that S comprises of both L and U. In a standard training algorithm, we train a classifier, say H, on the labeled data L and then classify the unlabeled data U. But in self-training algorithm, we train the classifier H on the labeled data L and classify the unlabeled data U with H. After classification, we obtain a set U', where U' is a subset of unlabeled data U. U' contains the classified data with the most confidence score. Confidence score is the trust value of a prediction.

Now, we add *U'* to *L* and remove *U'* from *U*. We keep on repeating this procedure until convergence.

• Initialize the labeled data, mark it as *L*.
• Initialize the unlabeled data, mark it as *U*.
• Repeat until model converges
  o Using the labeled data *L*, train the classifier *H*
  o Use H to classify the unlabeled data *U*
  o Find a subset U' of U with the most confident scores.
  o Update the labeled set as $L = L + U'$
  o Update the unlabeled set as $U = U - U'$
• End

Algorithm 10.1 Self-training algorithm.

In every iteration of self-training, we add *U'* to *L* which contains the most confidence score. This method allows the model to increase the labeled data count by classifying the unlabeled data by itself. Since we are classifying the unlabeled data *U*, there is no way to validate the correctness; hence, we use confidence score of the model as the only metric to find *U'* from *U*. Self-training allows us to develop a machine learning model that can predict with high accuracy with a small dataset.

In Figure 10.1, the circle denotes the labeled data, which increases on every iteration when *U'* is added to *L*, whereas *U* decreases since labeled data increases.

Advantages of self-training.

- Self-training is the simplest form of semi-supervised learning method.

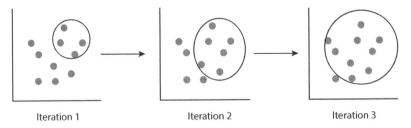

Iteration 1   Iteration 2   Iteration 3

Figure 10.1 Self-training in progress. Circle representing the classified data, which increases with every iteration.

- It is a wrapper method, i.e., can be applied to existing classifiers with ease.
- Frequently used in real time tasks in NLP.

Disadvantages of self-training.

- Mistakes can re-enforce themselves.

If the model makes a mistake then the mistakes will cumulate over time and lead to an incorrect model [4].

10.2.2   Co-Training

We have discussed how self-training can be a method to improve the model accuracy by feeding in both labeled and unlabeled data. The unlabeled data U is used for prediction and improving the model accuracy by gradually expanding L, the labeled data. With every step of training, U decreases and L increases thereby improving the labeled data [3].

Co-training is not very different from self-training [5]. In co-training, the data is considered using two views. An assumption is formed that defines that the data D is described using two features $f1$ and $f2$, such that $f = f1 + f2$, or in other words, we say that the two features $f1$ and $f2$ complement each other. The two views corresponding to the features $f1$ and $f2$ are created, let us call them $v1$ and $v2$, respectively. The views are chosen in a way that they are conditionally independent and a single view v_k, for $k = \{1,2\}$ is self-sufficient. Now, using each view v_k, we generate a classifier H_k for $k = \{1,2\}$. Each classifier is trained over the already labeled data L_k, where L_k denotes the labeled data for the view v_k. The further steps are similar to self-training where the unlabeled data U_k is used to iteratively construct or expand the labeled data L_k, as can be seen from Figure 10.2.

Co-training was first proposed in a paper which described an experiment that classified web pages from the internet into two categories. The purpose of the experiment was to classify the homepages of web pages into *academic* or *non-academic* homepages. Co-training was used with an original labeled data set of 12 web pages. Out of the 788 pages, the model was successfully able to classify 95% of the pages using only the 12 initially labeled web pages. This is considered to be one of the finest experiments using co-training and has been cited more than one-thousand times.

Given below is a simple co-training algorithm.

- Start with data *D*.
- Divide them into views v_1 and v_2.
- Initialize labeled data *L* and unlabeled data *U*.
- Repeat until model converges
  - o   Generate classifiers H_1 and H_2 corresponding to v_1 and v_2.
  - o   Predict unlabeled data and construct more labeled data.
- End

Algorithm 10.2 Co-training algorithm.

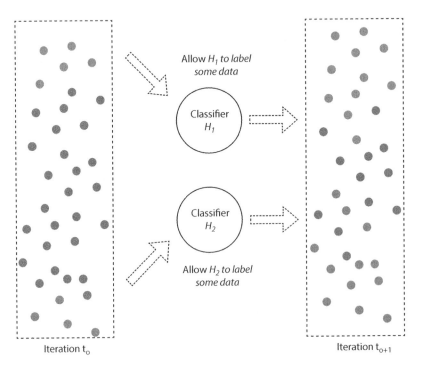

Figure 10.2 Co-training in progress. Green and red are two classes and blue is unlabeled data.

With such great accuracy with small amount of dataset initially, one must think that co-training can help ease out the work by a lot extent but it is in-fact not the truth. The major drawback that co-training has is the important clause of *conditionally independent views*. Using views that are not *conditionally independent* may actually worsen the accuracy of the model and lead to bad results. If both the classifiers H_1 and H_2 agree on all the unlabeled data *U*, then it means that the views are not independent, and labeling the data generates no new information.

10.3   Generative Models—Introduction

It is well known that a model, let's consider a classification model, will be able to perform better if fed with quality labeled data. The data used for training must be correct, concise and properly labeled to allow the model or the classifier to work well. The wellness of a model is defined by its *accuracy*. Accuracy is measured as the model's ability to perform correctly on a properly curated testing data.

The limitation to the above-mentioned scheme is the unavailability of huge amount of labeled data. Therefore, we use semi-supervised learning as it aids us in achieving the *prediction accuracy*. *Generative Model (GM)* is a powerful method to mine *knowledge* from available data [8]. Generative models employ unsupervised learning to learn almost any kind of distribution. These models have proved to be very precise and offer great accuracy. In *Generative Models*, the aim is to learn the true nature of the data and its distribution. The purpose is to generate more data points, corresponding to the training dataset, which are generated by making slight variations. *Generative Models* are used to fit a known distribution to the sample data or in other words *it uses neural networks to approximate a function that fits a non-linear distribution to match the true nature of data,* refer to Figure 10.3 for the same. Typically, *GANs (Generative Adversarial Networks)* [7] and *VAE (Variational Auto-Encoders)* are the two most common approaches associated to *GM*.

In the coming topics, we shall study about various applications of *Generative Models*. Given below is an algorithm associated to *GM*.

- Given labeled training data *L*.
- Divide *L* into training classes, say C_1 & C_2.
- Look for the most likely
  - *Prior probability* $P(C_i)$.
  - *Class dependant probability* $P(L|C_i)$.
  - $P(L|C_i)$ is a gaussian parameterized by μ^i and Σ
- The unlabeled data *u* will help re-estimate the value of $P(C_1)$, $P(C_2)$, μ^1, μ^2, Σ

Algorithm 10.3 *Generative Models* for classification.

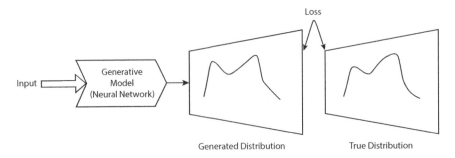

Figure 10.3 Depicting generative models predicting a distribution based on the true distribution.

A. Generative Models

In this section, we shall further explore about the generative models [8].

Use and Advantages

As discussed so far, there exist two approaches to building a classifier, in statistical classification of data, namely, discriminative and generative approach. The major difference is seen in the degree of *statistical modeling*. The two approaches differ in the context of statistical approach. Let us assume θ as the set of observed values and E as the set of targets or the expected values. Discriminative modeling is the approach of creating a model of the conditional probability ($P(A|B)$, defined as the probability of occurrence of A given B) of expected values E, given the observed values in the set θ, or simply P $(E|\theta = \phi)$. Generative modeling, on the other hand, is essentially the approach of creating a model of the conditional probability of observed values θ, given the expected values or the targets E, or simply P $(\theta|E = \phi)$, where ϕ is some number. In mathematical terms, generative models are used to generate a distribution which is identical to the expected distribution.

There are various different kinds of generative models. Given below are a few examples:

- HMM, or Hidden Markov Model [16]
- RBM, or Restricted Boltzmann Machine
- NB Classifier, or Naïve Bayes Classifiers
- PCFGs

- Autoencoders
- GANs, or Generative Adversarial Models [9]
- Gaussian Mixture Model, or GMM

Uses of Generative Models

Generative models can be put to use at places where we require to produce data. The primary aim of generative models is to generate data or distributions [9]. Given below are some of the uses of Generative Models.

- Speech Recognition
- Handwriting Recognition
- Gesture Recognition
- Image Classification [7]
- Text Categorization
- GANs are the most commonly used Genetic Models. They are used primarily for the following purposes.
  o   Generating realistic images
  o   Developing computer characters
  o   Designing game levels
  o   Game player modeling
  o   Human image synthesis
  o   Transfer map styles
  o   Generate protein molecules
  o   3D model construction
- Identifying presence of subpopulations in the sample
  o   Identifying a subpopulation in a group of identities is equivalent to clustering problems. Normally, a population consisting of various different groups together is known as a mixture, and more often the generative model used for such task is the Gaussian Mixture Model.
- Autoencoders are another important kind of generative model. They have the following uses.
  o   Reducing dimensionality of data
  o   Information Retrieval
  o   Semantic Hashing
  o   File Compression
  o   Detecting Anomalies
  o   Medicine and Drug discovery
- And other categorization problems.

Advantages and Disadvantages
Advantages of Generative models lie in the fact that it focuses on the following [10].

- Output
- Explanation of the sample
- Missing Values
- Value of Information
- Validation
- Background Knowledge

Disadvantages associated with Generative Models and its applications are given below.

- It tends to be slower than its discriminative counterpart.
- Concerns about the use of GANs for Human Image Synthesis have drawn a lot of attention recently.

In the next sections of this chapter, we shall study how generative models can be used for image classification, text categorization, and speech recognition.

10.3.1 Image Classification

Generative models have found their use in various different fields. The most prominent one of them is using these generative models for classifying images under different labels or categories. Normally, a discriminant-based approach is applied where the classifier constructs a *decision boundary* or *decision hypersurface*, which is a line or a hyperplane that partitions the sample into small population sizes and categorizes them based on their features. The concept of decision boundary is not present in the generative approach. Figure 10.4 shows decision boundary being used for

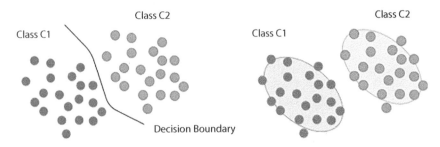

Figure 10.4 Discriminative (left) vs generative (right) approach.

discriminative approaches whereas generative approaches do not have the concept of decision boundary. The conventional approach can be challenged using the generative models. Generative models can be used for classification of the image dataset, refer to Figure 10.5.

This section explores image classification, namely, classifying handwritten digits using generative approach. The aim of the classifier is to recognize the given handwritten digit and categorize it into one of the known classes. Let us aim at classifying handwritten images of digits 0, 1, 2, 3, 4, 5, 6, 7, 8, and 9. In generative model approach, we associate a model corresponding to each class or category. The categories C_i in this case will be the numeric values 0, 1, 2, 3, 4, 5, 6, 7, 8, and 9 and the model associated with them be M_i, i = {0, 1, 2, 3, 4, 5, 6, 7, 8, 9}.

Divide the entire sample S, into two parts S_{train} and S_{test}. The process of identifying the category for the handwritten digit is closely related to finding the correct model. The approach is to identify the model that is most likely to have generated the handwritten digital image I. The aforementioned approach has an advantage, i.e., in addition to providing a class or a label it can also explain the image I chosen from S_{test}.

Revow et al. [11] explains an approach for recognition of handwritten digits by fitting generative models. The method is built using deformable

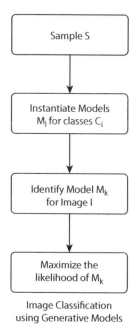

Image Classification
using Generative Models

Figure 10.5 Image classification using generative models.

B-splines with Gaussian ink-generators spaced along the length of the B-spline curve. The model adjustment is carried out using the *expected maximization,* and algorithm that tries to maximize the likelihood of the model generating the data. The approach has various advantages as listed below.

- The model identification produces not just the class or category of the digit but also a rich analysis of associated parameters which can yield valuable information about the model or the class.
- During image explanation the model can also perform *recognition drive segmentation.*
- Training the models is fast as the training steps involve relatively lower number of parameters.
- The aforementioned approach is robust to arbitrary scaling, translations, and also to a limited degree of rotated images.

The only disadvantage of [11], as mentioned, is that it requires more computation power than most of the standard OCR processors.

10.3.2   Text Categorization

Text categorization is not the same as image classification as discussed above. An image is generally a matrix of size $n \times m$ containing, whereas a text is a string containing n words. One of the basic types of text categorization using generative probabilistic approaches is using the *Naïve Bayes classification* [12]. Naïve Bayes classifier is a generative model which is easy to implement and generates quite effective results. It uses probabilities to identify the class associated to a particular text. In the following section, we will discuss how we can perform text categorization based with an example of *spam-classifier* as depicted in Figure 10.6. Let the sample of text be denoted by D, and the sample be further divided into classes D^s and D^h. The classes D^s and D^h denote the classes *spam* and *ham*, respectively. The first step is to create a *word-table* which contains the words corresponding to sentences and their respective class or category.

Let us assume a sentence S from the sample D. The sentence S can be written as a composition of words such that it can be expressed as $S = w_1 + w_2 + w_3 + \dots w_n$ where w_i denotes the i-th word in the sentence S. The aim of the classifier is to predict the accurate class to which the sentence S may belong. The classifier uses probabilities related to the individual words in the sentence to determine the class in which the sentence may belong. The

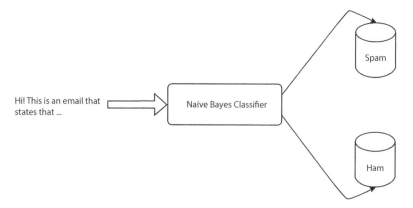

Figure 10.6 Workflow of text categorization using naïve Bayes.

process consists of computing $P(w_i|C_k)$, i.e., the conditional probability of a word w_i given the probability of class C_k. The conditional probabilities of each individual word in the sentence S is computed assuming the probability of class C_k. The basic approach toward this method is to compute the conditional probability like it is computed normally.

But the aforementioned process may lead to wrong results and to avoid them the process of calculating the conditional probability can be changed to the following. The probability $P(w_i|C_k)$ can be computed as

$$P\left(w_i|C_k\right) = \frac{n_i + 1}{n + |voc|}$$

where,

- n_i is the occurrences of word w_i.
- n is the total number of words with repetition corresponding to C_k class.
- $|voc|$ is the total number words.

The final answer for classes C_k is computed as $\Pi\, P(w_i|C_k)$. Comparing the answers for different C_k gives us the final class or category that corresponds to the input sentence S.

Generative text classification has also been performed using various different neural network techniques such as the one illustrated in [12, 13]. For further study, please refer to the references section.

10.3.3   Speech Recognition

Speech recognition is a field that is a subject of wide research. The topics such as speech recognition, synthesis, *STT* and *TTS* conversions are trendy research domains. Generative models have shown quite extraordinary performance in the *speech-domain*, the domain includes all of the aforementioned topics.

Performing speech recognition is a heavy as well as complex task. Systems performing speech recognition use HMM [16] (Hidden Markov Model) to maximize the likelihood, as is required in the generative model approach. HMM can also be used discriminatively to perform speech recognition and often give good performance. A speech sample contains many things and often contains variable length data sequences. These sequences generally arise from the variations in speaker rate, also due to difference in word sequence and accent as well. HMM are preferred for this task as they handle such variation in data sequences very well.

Oord *et al.* [14] describes WaveNet, an audio generative model based on the architecture of PixelCNN. The WaveNet is capable of not just recognizing speech but also to produce speech, i.e., speech synthesis on its own. The architecture has been proposed to tackle the problem of speech synthesis but it shows string results when tested on a sample data of speech recognition. WaveNet has also shown amazing results in the field of music generation as well. Smith and Gales [15] proposes an approach using HMM and SVM for the task of speech recognition. The topics of speech recognition are very heavily researched area with on-going research; for further information on this topic, please refer to the references at the end of the chapter.

10.3.4   Baum-Welch Algorithm

HMM [16] or Hidden Markov Models for generative modeling were first used to serve as a model for speech recognition by James K. Baker in 1975. HMM allows for continuous speech recognition in an easy and fast manner. The first step is feature analysis done on spectral and/or temporal features of the speech signal hence generating an *observation vector*. Every individual unit of speech recognition system is fed with this observation vector. Similar to the approach of *lexicon decoding*, the next steps in this chain are followed by a strict grammar and rule-set. Finally, the semantic analysis of the generated output is done and the final output or the recognized utterance is generated. *Baum-Welch* is an *expectation-maximization* algorithm that is used to find or tune the hidden parameters of the HMM.

HMM defines the joint probability of a collection of hidden and observe. Baum-Welch algorithm is a dynamic programming approach to the *expectation-minimization* algorithm. It works on the assumption that the *k-th* hidden variable, in the KMM given, the *(k-1)-th* hidden variable is independent of the previous hidden variables, i.e., the current hidden variable can only be dependent on the current hidden state in question. Before moving toward the algorithm, let us first define some terms that will be used excessively below. *A* is the state transition matrix, *B* is the emission matrix which contains the probabilities of a state *i* resulting in an observed value *j* and the initial state distribution is given by π. There are three phases to this algorithm apart from the *initial phase* they are *forward phase, backward phase* and the *update phase*. In the initial phase, we initialize the values of *A*, *B*, and π, respectively.

In the *forward phase*, we calculate the *alpha* function recursively, where the *alpha* function is defined as the joint probability of the observed data up to the time *t* and the state at that time *t*.

$$\alpha\left(X_t\right) = P\left[Y_{0:t}, X_t\right] = \sum_{X_{t-1}} \alpha\left(X_{t-1}\right) P\left(X_t | X_{t-1}\right) P(Y_t | X_t)$$

to begin with the computation the initial required value of *alpha* is given as

$$\alpha(X_0) = P[Y_0, X_0] = P(Y_0 | X_0)\, P(X_0)$$

Next is the *backward phase*, here, we calculate the *beta function* also known as the conditional probability of observed data starting from the time *t + 1* given the state at any time *T = t*. It is also calculated recursively and uses the state transition probability as derived from *A* and the emission probability from the emission matrix *B*.

$$\beta\left(X_t\right) = P\left[Y_{t+1:T}, X_t\right] = \sum_{X_{t+1}} \beta\left(X_{t+1}\right) P\left(X_{t+1} | X_t\right) P(Y_{t+1} | X_{t+1})$$

the base case for the *beta function* is given by

$$\beta(X_T) = 1$$

The use of *alpha function* and *beta function* is also termed as *filtering* and *smoothing*. Next comes the *update phase*, in which we compute the hidden variables.

$$\gamma\left(X_t\right) = P(X_t|Y_{0:T}) = \frac{\alpha\left(X_t\right)\beta\left(X_t\right)}{\displaystyle\sum_{X_t}\alpha\left(X_t\right)\beta\left(X_t\right)}$$

$$\varepsilon\left(X_t, X_{t+1}\right) = P(X_t, X_{t+1}|Y_{0:t}) = \frac{\alpha\left(X_t\right)\beta\left(X_{t+1}\right)P\left(X_{t+1}|X_t\right)P(Y_{t+1}\,|\,X_{t+1})}{\displaystyle\sum_{X_t}\alpha\left(X_t\right)\beta\left(X_{t+1}\right)P\left(X_{t+1}|X_t\right)P(Y_{t+1}\,|\,X_{t+1})}$$

The value of $\gamma(X_t)$ defines the probability distribution of a state at time t provided all the observed data available and $\varepsilon(X_p, X_{t+1})$ is the joint-probability of two stated provided the data available. We use these values to determine the values of the hidden variables of the HMM.

$$\pi_0^* = \gamma\left(X_0\right)$$

$$a_{ij}^* = P(X_t = j\,|X_{t-1} = i) = \frac{\displaystyle\sum_t \varepsilon(X_t = j, X_{t-1} = i)}{\displaystyle\sum_t \gamma(X_{t-1} = i)}$$

$$b_{ij}^* = P(Y_t = j\,|X_t = i) = \frac{\displaystyle\sum_t \gamma(X_t = i) \times 1_{Y_{t=j}}}{\displaystyle\sum_t \gamma(X_t = i)}$$

Baum-Welch algorithm is known as an optimized *EM* algorithm. It can be broken into two parts, the calculation of *alpha* and *beta* functions, *forward* and *backward phase* is the *E-part* and the *update phase* is the *M-part* of the algorithm.

10.4   S3VMs

In recent times, there has been a drastic increase in the amount of data generated through various devices all over the world. Numerous technologies and ways to collect this data efficiently have been introduced throughout this time. But this collection of data consists of large chunks of data with no label, which requires tremendous work and time to label all of it. Since semi-supervised learning techniques usually work on combining the labeled data with the unlabeled data the make the learning behavior better, this algorithm was tried to be combined with support vector machines (SVMs) to achieve better results.

SVMs are machine learning methods based on statistical learning theory. They are helpful in a lot of fields such as solid theoretical foundation, global optimization, the sparsity of the solution and generalization. They have proved to be advantageous in practical engineering fields. The limitation of SVM is that it is applicable to only labeled data and hence, with supervised learning only. It is very rare to have a learner model which is able to perform with a limited labeled data. Thus, semi-supervised learning can be a good option to use with SVM when there is a scarcity of labeled data but unlabeled data is sufficiently enough.

The main task of SVM is to obtain an optimal classification hyperplane which satisfies the requirements of classification. In Figure 10.7, let the black dots represent one sample class and the white dots represent the other sample class. H represents the classification hyperplane and H_1 and H_2 are the hyperplanes containing the sample points (also known as support vectors) and have the nearest distance to H. H_1 and H_2 are parallel to H and the distance between them is called the maximum margin. The aim of SVM is not only to separate the sample points by the classification hyperplane but to maximize the margin as well.

Hyperplanes are defined such that,

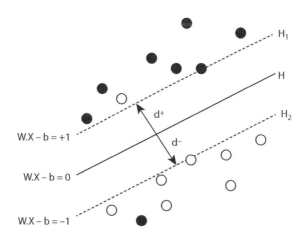

Figure 10.7 SVM.

$$x_i{}^*w + b >= +1 \text{ when } y_i = +1 \quad \text{and} \quad x_i{}^*w + b <= -1 \text{ when } y_i = -1$$

Where,

d^+ is the shortest distance to the closest positive point,

d^- is the shortest distance to the closest negative point,

H_1 and H_2 are the hyperplanes with their equations,

The points on the planes H_1 and H_2 are the support vectors,

The margin of the linear separator is $d^+ + d^-$ which is to maximized.

S3VMs were proposed by Bennett and Demiriz in 1999 with an aim to build a classifier using a limited amount of labeled data along with a surplus amount of unlabeled data whereas in case of SVMs, the machines worked solely on supervised learning algorithms. The idea of an S3VM is to build one basic SVM for every labeling and finally pick the SVM with the greatest margin. These are developed with the same working as SVM with a slight change in their parameters and including a penalty term in the objective function.

The challenge still remains in the optimization of the S3VM developed. While the objective of SVM is convex in shape, that semi-supervised SVM has non-convex objective (mostly hat shaped) as shown in Figure 10.8.

Different optimization techniques for S3VM can be great area of research. Some famous implementations are: SVM^light, ∇S3VM, continuation S3VM, deterministic annealing, CCCP, Branch and Bound, SDP convex relations, etc.

S3VMs can be advantageous for use in the following ways:

- These are applicable everywhere where SVMs are used. Thus, always improving the performance of SVMs.
- Faster in speed with less computational time as it is built on a clear mathematical framework.

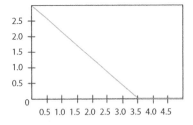 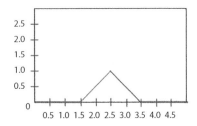

Figure 10.8 SVM has hinge loss (left) and S3VM has hat loss (right).

Few disadvantages of S3VMs include:

- Sometimes optimization of one can be a confusing task. It is difficult to choose a perfect optimization technique for a particular S3VM.
- At some points, it is possible that workflow is trapped in a bad local optimum and further provides incorrect results.
- It is a more modest assumption than generative model or graph-based methods (to be discussed), which further provides potentially lesser gain.

Unlabeled Instances Selection

S3VMs have been popular these days because of their better performance than SVMs due to their exploitation of unlabeled data. Though, they have provided to be helpful but there might arise a condition where it may result in even poor performance than using labeled data only. To avoid these kinds of problems, it can be done that instead of exploiting all the unlabeled data, only those instances should be selected which are likely to be helpful and not those instances which can degrade the overall performance of the machine.

There can be two possible approaches to simplify these problems, namely, S3VM-c and S3VM-p. S3VM-c works on the fact only when the component density sets are visible or noticeable, then unlabeled data can be helpful. In this, label (lb) and confidence (cf) are calculated for each cluster in both SVM and S3VM which can be calculated as:

$$lb^i_{S(3)VM} = \text{sign}\left(\sum_{j \in C_i} (x_j) y_{S(3)VM} \right)$$

$$cf^i_{S(3)VM} = \sum_{j \in Ci} (x_j) y_{S(3)VM}$$

S3VM-p, on the other end, is mostly based on confidence estimation in graph methods like when confidence can be measured as a risk involvement of unlabeled instances. In both these cases, if the results by S3VM contain the same bias of label propagation with a high value of confidence, S3VM prediction results are chosen; else, prediction of SVM is used.

Using S3VM-c and S3VM-p might reduce the chances of performance degradation, but usage if these techniques also contain some deficiencies.

Like S3VM mostly explore in a local manner and there is no consideration about the relationship between two clusters. This can further lead to not exploiting some useful unlabeled instances. In S3VM-p, if the label initialization is imbalanced, the estimated confidence might produce incorrect results with label propagation. Also, both S3VM-p and S3VM-c are highly dependent on S3VM predictions and can be harmful if S3VM itself is providing degraded performance.

Due to these deficiencies, hierarchical clustering was taken into consideration which resulted into a new method S3VM-us (S3VM with unlabeled instances selection). Hierarchical clustering was chosen due its greedy and iterative manner. It starts with initializing each single instance as a cluster and starts merging two clusters having the shortest distance at every step. In this, cluster relations are taken into consideration and there does not exist and label initialization problem as this works in an unsupervised manner. In hierarchical clustering, if p_j and n_j are the distances from the current instance x_j to its nearest positive and negative labeled instances, the difference between p_j and n_j is taken as an estimation of the confidence of x_j. The confidence of x_j is directly proportional to the difference between these two distances. The results of S3VM show that it avoids the wrong prediction instances of S3VM and inherits only the good ones.

10.5 Graph-Based Algorithms

In semi-supervised learning techniques, graph-based algorithms are often employed to define the approach of learning. In graph-based methodologies, the entire system or the dataset can be described as a graph in which individual nodes are the labeled and unlabeled datapoints in the dataset and the edges connecting the nodes to each other are weighted and their weight defines the similarity between the two samples connected together through the edge. For the algorithms to work an assumption about label smoothness over the graph is established. Graph parameters can be categorized as discriminative, nonparametric, and transductive in nature.

These graph-based algorithms all work on a principle of optimizing an objective function often denoted as f. The important properties of the objective function f are that it must be as close as possible to the target label L_t on the nodes that are labeled and it must remain smooth on the entire graph. The closeness of labels is termed as loss function and the *smoothness* is often termed as *regularizer*. Various methods of graph-based algorithm discussed below differ to each other only in terms of the loss function and regularizer associated to them.

10.5.1   Mincut

As defined in graph theory, a mincut is described as a subset of the original graph normally obtained by creating a partition of vertices into two disjoint sets and the aim of doing so is to minimize the graph in some or the other sense. Chawla and Baum [17] proposed a model that employed the use of mincut algorithm to solve semi-supervised learning problems. In the case where the classification problem is binary in nature, i.e., there exist only two categories into which the data could fall into then the positive label is defined as the source and the negative label or the complimentary label is defined as the sink in the graph. The primary goal of the algorithm is to find the set of edges removing which will isolate the source and the sink completely or in other words the aim is to block the flow from the source to sink by removing minimum number of edges from the graph. After the mincut is observed, the nodes connected to the source are then labeled as positive or the corresponding category and the nodes connected to the sink are then labeled correspondingly with the negative label. The associated loss function is the quadratic loss function with infinite weight.

$$\infty \sum_{i \in L} \left(y_i - y_{i|L} \right)^2$$

and the regularizer is given as

$$\frac{1}{2} \sum_{i,j} w_{ij} \left| y_i - y_j \right| = \frac{1}{2} \sum_{i,j} w_{ij} \left(y_i - y_j \right)^2$$

Adding the two together, since y_i takes only two binary values as 0 and 1.

$$\infty \sum_{i \in L} \left(y_i - y_{i|L} \right)^2 + \frac{1}{2} \sum_{i,j} w_{ij} \left(y_i - y_j \right)^2$$

Pang and Lee [18] uses the graph mincut algorithm to categorize sentences into two categories considering the fact that the sentences close to each other on a directed graph belong to the same category.

10.5.2   Harmonic

Zhu *et al.* [19] mentions about harmonic functions and Gaussian random fields. It states that it is a continuous relaxation to the already difficult Boltzmann machine or the discrete Markov random fields. The harmonic function relaxes the discrete labels to continuous values in R. Hence, the harmonic function is bound to satisfy the following properties.

- $f(x_i) = y_i$ for $i = 1 \dots l$
- f must minimize the energy

$$\sum_{i \sim j} w_{ij} \left(f(x_i) - f(x_j) \right)^2$$

- the mean of the Gaussian random field
- average of neighbors

$$f(x_i) = \frac{\sum_{j \sim i} w_{ji} f(x_j)}{\sum_{j \sim i} w_{ij}}$$

$$\forall x_i \in X_u$$

The algorithm to compute harmonic function is given below.

- Start with
- Initially, set the value of $f(x_i) = y_i$ for $i = 1 \dots l$ and $f(x_j)$ arbitrarily for $x_i \in X_u$.
- Continually find the average of neighbors until the function converges.

$$f(x_i) = \frac{\sum_{j \sim i} w_{ji} f(x_j)}{\sum_{j \sim i} w_{ij}}$$

$$\forall x_i \in X_u$$

- End

Algorithm 10.4 Computing harmonic function.

Local and Global Consistency

As described in Zhou *et al.* [20], the local consistency and global consistency method proposes the loss function and the *normalized Laplacian* described by the following:

$$\sum_{i=1}^{n}\left(f_i - y_i\right)^2$$

and

$$D^{-\frac{1}{2}}\triangle D^{-\frac{1}{2}} = I - D^{-\frac{1}{2}}WD^{-\frac{1}{2}}$$

respectively in the regularize given below.

$$\frac{1}{2}\sum_{i,j}w_{ij}\left(f_i / \sqrt{D_{ii}} - f_j / \sqrt{D_{jj}}\right)^2 = f^T D^{-\frac{1}{2}}\triangle D^{-\frac{1}{2}} f$$

10.5.3 Manifold Regularization

The manifold regularization as stated in Belkin *et al.* [21] has two terms for regularization.

$$\frac{1}{l}\sum_{i=1}^{l}V\left(x_i, y_i, f\right) + \gamma_A \left\|f\right\|_K^2 + \gamma_I \left\|f\right\|_I^2$$

In which V is an arbitrarily defined loss function, K is the base kernel, and the regularization term defined by both labeled and unlabeled data is given by I.

10.6 Multiview Learning

Multiview learning is a learning method that solves the problem of knowledge mining from the data that is depicted in a lot of dimensions. The data is question often contains multiple different and distinct feature sets. Multiview learning came into existence owing to the changing nature of data. The current data available for training is often described by different "views" of different feature sets. For example, a movie may be described by individual frames and their video and sound component. These serve as the different views of the movie. This method also shows effective improvement in the performance even when there exists no natural split in the data. A split is what allows the data to have different feature sets. Multiview learning is a promising research topic [23].

The application of multiview learning ranges from supervised, ensemble, transfer learning, active learning, dimensionality reduction, and finally in the field of semi-supervised learning [24].

10.7   Conclusion

In this chapter, we have studied primarily about semi-supervised learning paradigm. The chapter also contained a detailed discussion about the other paradigms of machine learning and compared them to semi-supervised learning comparing their benefits and defects the advancements that semi-supervised learning brings to the table. We have also learned about the two important learning techniques associated with semi-supervised learning, namely, self-training and co-training with emphasis on understanding and developing an insight into the topic with the help of algorithms. The chapter also discussed about the two approaches to solving classification problems, the discriminative and the generative approach. A detailed discussion about generative models and its usage has been discussed by explaining its application that ranges from image classification, speech recognition to text categorization using the generative approaches. The chapter contains a perfect mixture of examples alongside relevant algorithms and equations to help the reader understand the topic well. Another topic covered is S3VM and how it has helped improve semi-supervised learning in the recent past. The chapter also tries to cover the graph-based approaches along with their respective regularizer functions. Various graph-based approaches discussed in the chapter are the mincut algorithm, harmonic, local and global consistency, and the manifold regularization. The chapter ends with a brief discussion about multiview learning since it is a new field and is a topic of research interest. The chapter concludes with a set of references that the reader can refer to anytime for gaining a better understanding of the topics covered above in the chapter.

The purpose of the chapter is to impart knowledge about semi-supervised learning and the readers are encouraged to read more the topic to gather insights about the research prospects that lie ahead.

References

1. Zhu, X., *Semi-Supervised Learning Literature Survey*, Technical, Report 1530, Univ. of Wisconsin-Madison, 2005.
2. Zhu, X. and Goldberg, A.B., *Introduction to Semi-Supervised Learning*, Synthesis Lectures on Artificial Intelligence and Machine Learning, vol .3, no. 1, pp. 1–130, 2009.
3. Zhu, X., *Semi-Supervised Learning Tutorial*, International Conference on Machine Learning (ICML), pp. 1–135, 2007.
4. Azmi, R., Norozi, N., Anbiaee, R., Salehi, L., IMPST: A New Interactive Self-Training Approach to Segmentation Suspicious Lesions in Breast MRI. *J. Med. Signals Sens.*, 1, 2, 138–148, 2011.
5. Sousa, R. and Gama, J., Comparison Between Co-training and Self-training for Single-target Regression in Data Streams using AMRules., IoT Large Scale Learning from Data Streams 2017, Vol-1958, http://ceur-ws.org/Vol-1958/IOTSTREAMING6.pdf
6. Wang, W. and Zhou, Z.-H., On Multi-View Active Learning and the Combination with Semi-Supervised Learning, in: *ICML 2008*, pp. 1152–1159, 2008.
7. Kong, Q., Tong, B., Klinkigt, M., Watanabe, Y., Akira, N., Murakami, T., Active Generative Adversarial Network for Image Classification, in: *AAAI 2019*, 2019.
8. Adiwardana, D.D.F., Matsukawa, A., Whang, J., Using Generative Models for Semi-Supervised Learning, *Med. Image Comput. Comput. Interv. – MICCAI 2016*, 106–114, 2016.
9. Kingma, D.P., Mohamed, S., Rezende, D.J.,, Welling, M., Semi-supervised learning with deep generative models, in: *Advances in Neural Information Processing Systems*, pp. 3581–3589, 2014.
10. Advantages of Generative Model Approach http://ai.stanford.edu/~moises/tutorial/sld159.htm
11. Revow, M., Williams, G.K.I., Hinton, G.E., Using generative models for handwritten digit recognition. *IEEE Trans. PAMI*, 18, 592–606, 1996.
12. Yogatama, D., Dyer, C., Ling, W., Blunsom, P., Generative and discriminative text classification with recurrent neural networks. Thirty-Fourth International Conference on Machine Learning (ICML 2017), 2017.
13. Sarkar, S., Goswami, S., Agrwal, A., Aktar, J., A Novel Feature Selection, Technique for Text Classification Using Naïve Bayes, International, Scholarly Research Notices, vol. 2014, no. 717092, p. 1–10, Apr. 2014
14. Oord, A., Dieleman, S., Zen, H., Simonyan, K., Vinyals, O., Graves, A., Kalchbrenner, N., Senior, A., Kavukcuoglu., K., WaveNet: A Generative Model for Raw Audio, 2016. In Arxiv. https://research.google/pubs/pub45774/
15. Smith, N. and Gales, M., Speech recognition using SVMs, in: *Proc. NIPS*, pp. 1197–1204, 2001.

16. Eddy, S.R., Hidden Markov Model, Curr. *Opin. Struct. Biol.*, 6, 361–365, 1996.

17. Blum, A. and Chawla, S., Learning from labeled and unlabeled data using graph mincuts. *Proc. 18th International Conf. on Machine Learning*, 2001.

18. Pang, B. and Lee, L., A sentimental education: Sentiment analysis using subjectivity summarization based on minimum cuts, in: *Proceedings of ACL*, 2004 2004.

19. Zhu, X., Ghahramani, Z., Lafferty, J., Semi-supervised learning using gaussian fields and harmonic functions, in: *ICML*, 2003.

20. Zhou, Dengyong, Bousquet, Olivier, Lal, Thomas Navin, Weston, Jason, Sch¨olkopf, Bernhard, Learning with local and global consistency, in: *Advances in Neural Information Processing Systems 16*, S. Thrun, L. Saul, B. Sch¨olkopf (Eds.), MIT Press, Cambridge, MA, 2004.

21. Belkin, M., Niyogi, P., Sindhwani, V., Manifold regularization: A geometric framework for learning from examples. *J Mach Learn Res Arch.*, 7, 2399–434, 2006.

22. Li, Y.-F. and Zhou, Z.-H., Improving semisupervised support vector machines through unlabeled instances selection, in: *Proceedings of 25th AAAI Conference on Artificial Intelligence*, pp. 386–391, 2011a.

23. Sun, S., A survey of multi-view machine learning. *Neural Comput Appl*, 23, 7–8, 2031–2038, 2013.

24. Sindhwani, V., Niyogi, P., Belkin, M., A co-regularization approach to semi-supervised learning with multiple views. *Proceedings of the Workshop on Learning with Multiple Views*, pp. 824–831, 2005.

11

Reinforcement Learning

Amandeep Singh Bhatia[1]*, **Mandeep Kaur Saggi[2]**, **Amit Sundas[1]**
and **Jatinder Ashta[1]**

*[1]Chitkara University Institute of Engineering and Technology, Chitkara University,
Punjab, India*
*[2]Department of Computer Science & Engineering, Thapar Institute of Engineering
& Technology, Patiala, India*

Abstract

Reinforcement learning (RL) has gradually become one of the most active research areas in the field of artificial intelligence and machine learning (i.e., agent learns to interact with the environment to achieve reward, robotics, and many more). It is a sub-area of machine learning. Due to its generality, it has been studied widely in many other disciplines such as operations research, control theory, game theory, swarm intelligence, and multi-agent systems. In this chapter, the model-free and model-bases RL algorithms are described. There exist several challenges that need to be addressed. One of challenges that arise in RL is trade-off between exploration and exploitation. The dilemma of exploration-exploitation has been intensively presented.

Keywords: Machine learning, reinforcement learning, Q-learning algorithm, Monte Carlo method, SARSA learning, R-learning, temporal difference, dyna-Q learning

11.1 Introduction: Reinforcement Learning

It is defined as a computational method for compassionating and automating purposive behavior learning and decision making. It represents to solving sequential and to control a stochastic dynamical system by simulation and trial-and-error. There are two algorithms for solving reinforcement learning (RL): (use models and planning called) model-free RL algorithms and (that explicitly trail-and-error learners called) model-based RL algorithm [1]. It is applicable for the problems where the decision making is step-wise process

*Corresponding author: amandeep.9807@chitkara.edu.in

Uma N. Dulhare, Khaleel Ahmad and Khairol Amali Bin Ahmad (eds.) Machine Learning and Big Data: Concepts, Algorithms, Tools and Applications, (281–304) © 2020 Scrivener Publishing LLC

and objective is long-term, such as game playing, robotics, resource management, or logistics.

Delayed reward and trial and error search are the two crucial elements of RL. Similar to several areas such as quantum computing, mountaineering, and machine learning, which are ending with "ing" [2]. It can be called a class of solution procedures that are executed on some tasks and the area that studies the task and its solution procedures. In other words, RL is a learning what to do and how to map solution procedures to the problems enlarge a reward signal [3]. The trade-off between exploitation and exploration is a major challenge in RL, which do not exist in other forms of learning [4]. For many decades, the dilemma of exploitation-exploration has been extensively studied by mathematicians, but it is still unresolved. The key characteristic is that RL focuses on the complete task of an agent correlating with an ambivalent environment [5].

Recently, the exhilarating features of RL came into existence after its fruitful and substantive interconnections with other scientific areas. Besides of machine learning and artificial intelligence, it shows greater integrity with optimization and statistics [6]. It has shown substantial advantages after interconnected with neuroscience and psychology [7]. The RL models have the ability to learn with parameterized approximators. RL is one of the forms of machine learning, which is very close to the learning of humans and animals [8]. Several RL methods are inspired by learning of biological systems. The best way to get insight of RL is to focus on applications and examples that lead its development [9].

- A chess player plays a move. The choice is made according to planning that is predicting possible replies and counter replies that is made by instinctive discernment of possible moves and positions [10].
- The real-time adaptive controller sets the operational parameters of a petroleum refinery. The quality trade-off quality and cost is optimized by controlled based on the marginal cost rather than the values set by operators [11].
- After being born, a gazelle calf tussles to its feet. But, after half an hour later, the calf is running at 25 miles per hour [12].
- A mobile robot is searching to collect more trash. It decides to enter a new room or move back to recharge its battery. The decision is based on the present status of its battery and past record that how expediently it has been able to locate the charger earlier [13].

11.1.1   Elements of Reinforcement Learning

Agent is an intelligent programs and their use is defined by reward function. The environment is an external condition. Figure 11.1 shows the elements of reinforcement learning. At the other side of agent and environment, the following are the four components of RL [14, 77]:

- *Policy:* It is the core element of RL. It signifies the mapping associated with perceived states of an external condition to actions to be placed.
- *Reward:* The main function of reward element is to map the states of an external condition to a number. It indicates the essential value of that state. It must be unchanged by the agent. Nevertheless, it can be employed to change the policy. It is given directly by an environment.
- *Value:* The main objective of approximating the values is to attain more reward. So, there could be no values without rewards. It defines the total reward that agent can anticipate to amass in the future. It is most crucial element in planning and decision-making process. But, it is quite hard to investigate the values as compared to investigate the rewards. The value function is determined from the chain of inspections that an agent performs in lifetime [15].
- *Model:* It is an optional element of RL. It mimics the behavior of an external condition [16]. Figure 11.2 shows the representation of model-based and model-free RL

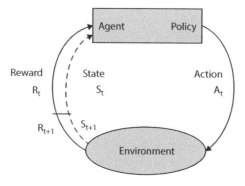

Figure 11.1 Elements of reinforcement learning.

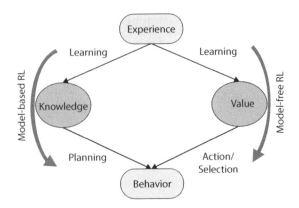

Figure 11.2 Model-based and model-free RL.

11.2   Model-Free RL

In a model-free RL approach, it is directly using data to find a close to the optimal policy. By directly interconnecting with an environment, it learns optimal behavior *via* trial-and-error search. In this context, the learner has no direct knowledge of the state transition or the reward function [17]. The steps of Q-learning algorithm are described in Figure 11.3 The systems in model-free RL do not have an idea about the changes in an environment due to single action. The model-free popular methods are Q-learning and R-learning.

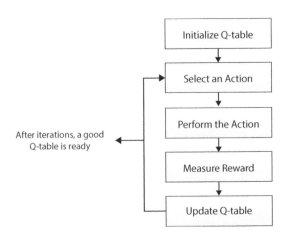

Figure 11.3 Steps of Q-learning algorithm.

11.2.1   Q-Learning

Q-learning [18] is a form of model-free RL and optimizing discounted reward, making far-future rewards less prioritized than near-term rewards. The Q-value Q^{π} (s, a) denotes the expected (discounted) value of return for starting in state s, taking action a, and following policy π thereafter [19].

$$Q^{*}(s, \alpha) = \max_{\pi} Q^{\pi}(s, \alpha), \forall\, s \in A(s) \tag{11.1}$$

Q-learning is more efficient due to off-policy learning. In any RL algorithm, there are two types of policies for a learning agent [20]:

- On Policy: According to the action obtained from the presently used policy, the learning agent learns the value. In this, the learning agent learns the value function according to the current action derived from the policy currently being used.
- Off Policy: According to the action obtained from another policy, the learning agent learns the value.

Consider an example illustrating the working of Q-learning algorithm. Suppose an automaton has to move and cross the puzzle, where starting and ending point is mentioned. Moreover, bombs are planted on some points and automaton can move in all four directions [21]. If automaton comes in contact with the bomb, then it is dead. The automaton has to reach the final destination *via* shortest path. The rules for scoring/reward are as:

- The 100 points are reduced if the automaton comes in contact with the bomb and then the game comes to an end.
- If the bomb reaches the final destination, it gains 100 points.
- At each step, it loses one point. If the automaton gains energy while moving across the puzzle, it gains one point.

The Q-function takes two inputs action (*a*) and state (*s*) and uses the Bellman equation as

$$Q^{\pi}(s_{t}, \alpha_{t}) = E[R_{t+1} + \gamma\, R_{t+2} + \gamma^{2}\, R_{t+3}.. + s_{t}, a_{t}]$$

Initially, model the environment in Q-table, where rows are the states and columns define the actions:

Actions	↑	→	←	↓
Start	0	0	0	0
Blank	0	0	0	0
Energy	0	0	0	0
Bombs	0	0	0	0
End	0	0	0	0

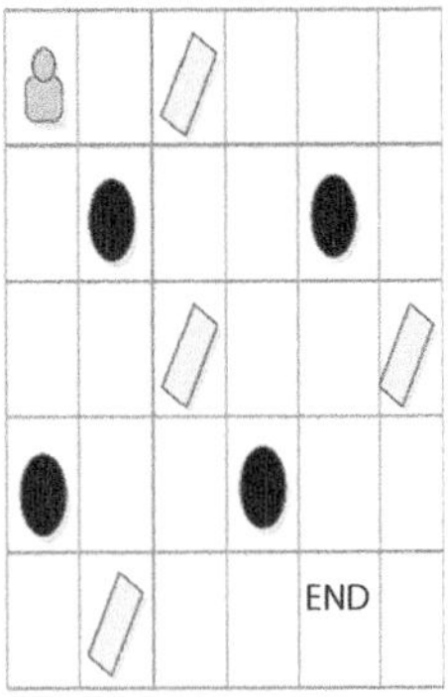

Figure 11.4 The status of initial Q-table and the puzzle.

After initialization of the Q-table, next step is to select and perform an action (move toward left, right, up, or down direction) [22]. Figure 11.4 shows the initial status of Q-table and the puzzle. The second and third steps are performed for undefined amount of time. It will run until we stop the training process. The automaton does not about the environment, so it will move randomly, suppose toward the right direction [23].

Further, update the Q-values and moving right using the Bellman equation. Finally, observed an outcome and the reward. The updates equation is as:

$$Q\,(s_t, \alpha_t) = Q\,(s_t, \alpha_t) + \alpha[\gamma_{t+1} + \gamma \max_{\alpha} Q(s_{t+1}, a) - Q(s_t, a_t)]$$

The process of updating of Q-table continues until the automaton does not reach the end point or it step up the bomb [24].

11.2.2 R-Learning

R-learning [25] is a method for optimizing average reward, weighing both far-future and near-term reward the same. It is an off-policy control technique for the problems in which one neither divides nor discounts experience into definite episodes with finite returns. R-learning is designed to arrive at the T-optimal policies for undiscounted performance criteria. The name R-learning is an alphabetic descendant to Q-learning, but it is an allusion to *relative* values learning [26]. The access-control queuing example was suggested by Carlstrom and Nordstrom [27].

In every step, the main objective is to maximize the average reward. The value functions (π) for a policy are described according to the average expected reward as follows:

$$\overline{r}(\pi) = \lim_{n \to \infty} \frac{1}{n} \sum_{t=1}^{n} E_{\pi}[R_t]$$

The value of an average expected reward does not depend on the initial state. During long run, the average reward remains same, but transient should be there. Sometimes, some states received better or worse than average rewards [28]. Thus, the transient signifies the value of a state as

$$v_{\pi}(s) = \sum_{k=1}^{n} E_{\pi}[R_{t+k} - \overline{r}(\pi) | S_t = s]$$

the value of a state-action is equivalent to the transient variability in reward when beginning in that state and action is taken [29]:

$$q_{\pi}(s,a) = \sum_{k=1}^{n} E_{\pi}[R_{t+k} - \overline{r}(\pi) | S_t = s, A_t = a]$$

R-learning is a basic temporal difference (TD) control algorithm like Q-learning, based on off-policy. It preserves the two policies, an estimation and behavior policy in addition to an average reward and an action-value function [30]. The experience is generated by behavior policy, and action-vale function is determined by the ε-greedy policy. The description of an R-learning algorithm is given in Table 11.1.

11.3   Model-Based RL

Model-based RL algorithms are used very less practically. The working is based on a transition table which can be assume as a life hack book consisting information the person needs to become successful and powerful in the world [31].

Table 11.1 Steps of R-learning algorithm.

Initialize $\bar{R}$ and $Q(s, a)$ $\forall s \in S, a \in A(s)$
Do forever: i. $S \leftarrow$ current state (non-terminal)   ii.   Select action A in S using behavior policy   iii. Take action A and determine R, S' iv. $\delta \leftarrow R - \bar{R} \max_a Q(S',a) - Q(S,A)$ v. $Q(S, A) \leftarrow Q(S, A) + \alpha\delta$ vi.   If $Q(S, A) \leftarrow \max_a Q(S, A)$, then $\bar{R} \leftarrow \bar{R} + \beta\delta$, the scalars α β are step-size parameters.

Model-Based vs Model-Free Learning

It is known that dynamic programming is used for solving the problems when the basic model of an environment is already known (i.e., model-based learning). RL is concerned with the learning from exposure in playing games [32]. In dynamic programming algorithms, a complete model of the external condition includes all the state transition probabilities [33]. Although, the model of an environment or the state transition probabilities is not known earlier in most real-life situations [34, 78].

Take an example to train automaton to learn how to play chess. Figure 11.5 represents the 8*8 chess board. First step is to convert the environment of chess into a model-based dynamic programming (MDP) [35]. The complete environment can have more than 1,050 states and numerous actions

Figure 11.5 8*8 chess board.

depending upon the position of pieces. Thus, such environment is not possible to create [36]. The only solution is to play a chess game number of
times and assign a negative reward for losing and positive for winning the
game at the end. The whole repeated process is called learning from the
experience [37].

11.3.1   SARSA Learning

SARSA learning can be achieved by small alterations in the Q-learning algorithm. Q-learning method is based on off-policy method, where the greedy
algorithm is applied to learn the Q-value. SARSA is based on on-policy
approach, where the actions are applied by the present policy to learn the
Q-value [38]. The illustration of SARSA learning is shown in Figure 11.6. The
distinction between Q-learning and SARSA learning can be seen in the update
statements:

- Q-learning

$$Q\,(s_t, \alpha_t) = Q\,(s_t, \alpha_t) + \alpha(\gamma_{t+1} + \gamma \max_\alpha Q(s_{t+1}, a) - Q(s_t, a_t))$$

- SARSA

$$Q\,(s_t, \alpha_t) = Q\,(s_t, \alpha_t) + \alpha(\gamma_{t+1} + \gamma\, Q(s_{t+1}, a_{t+1}) - Q(s_t, a_t))$$

It is noted that the update statement relies on the present state, action performed, reward achieved, resultant state, and next action to be performed [39].
Therefore, the name SARSA is defined as collection of five tuples $(s, \alpha, r, s', \alpha')$,
i.e., stands for State Action Reward State Action.

SARSA method is also known as an on-policy algorithm due to its update
policy is based on the actions performed [40]. The description of SARSA algorithm for an estimating $Q \approx q^*$ is given in Table 11.2.

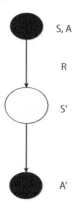

S, A

R

S'

A'

Figure 11.6 Illustration of SARSA method.

Table 11.2 The pseudocode of SARSA-learning algorithm.

Initialize $Q(s, \alpha)$, $\forall s \in S$, $\alpha \in A(s)$, arbitrarily and Q(terminal-state)=0

Do forever:-
 	
 i. Initialize $S \leftarrow$current state
 ii. $A \leftarrow \varepsilon$-greedy(S, Q)
 iii. Repeat (for each step of episode):
 	
     • Take action A and determine A, S'
     • Select A' from S' using policy (e.g., ε-greedy)
     • $Q(s, \alpha) = Q(s, \alpha) + \alpha[R + \gamma Q(S', A') - Q(S, A)]$
     • $S \leftarrow S'$, $A \leftarrow A'$
     until S is terminal.

By taking account the action, the Q-value is updated. In SARSA, the actions with the highest Q-value are performed in the next state and *S*1 is used to make changes in Q-table [41].

11.3.2   Dyna-Q Learning

Dyna-Q is an example model-based RL method, which interplays simulations offline and implement actions to modify Q functions [42]. The feature values are predicted in next state and domain values from the data directly. It generates a world model and uses it to train Q functions, which accelerates the learning policy [43]. It is also tabular-based method to create the Dyna-Q model. But, many samples of simulated experience are needed to estimate the environment correctly. It is often used to speed-up the learning process in RL. It is a variant of model-based RL, called Dyna Architecture [44]. It is also capable to update the value functions, instead of using the real experience. It is a simple and effectively powerful algorithm that productively blends Q-planning and Q-learning, where planning is executed during the interaction with an environment online [45]. Dyna-Q extends the idea of other models to improve or generate a policy as shown in Figure 11.7.

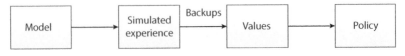

Figure 11.7 Generate a policy using Dyna-Q model.

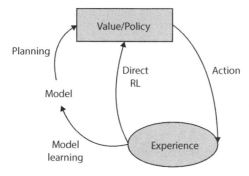

Figure 11.8 Illustration of Dyna-Q model.

The processes such as model learning, planning, action, and direct RL occur frequently in Dyna-Q model, as shown in Figure 11.8.

- *Planning:* It is random one-step tabular Q-planning random method.
- *Direct RL:* It is one-step tabular Q-learning.
- *Model learning:* It is tabular-based method for the deterministic environment.

The Dyna-Q algorithm begins by initializing the Q and Model (*M*) and then goes into the main loop. It starts at the current state, chooses an action according to a policy, implements an action, determines the reward *R*, and the newstate *S'* is observed [46]. It modifies the $Q(S,A)$ and the Model (*M*). Now, the observed state *S'* is the present state. Further, it enters the planning phase. The algorithm comes into a second loop, where iteration is performed *n* times [47]. It chooses a state and correlated action randomly, put into the model. Further, it output the associated reward and the new state from the model. Finally, it updates the $Q(S,A)$ as in the outer loop [48]. The pseudocode of Dyna-Q algorithm is given below.

Dyna-Q is well-suited for financial market applications where historical/real data is unable to generate efficient models. Thus, it a type of RL algorithm that can proceed with both simulated and real experience [49].

11.3.3   Temporal Difference

TD is an agent learning from an environment through episodes. It does not have any previous knowledge of an external condition. It follows an unsupervised learning approach or mode-free model. It can be learning from trial and error [50].

Table 11.3 Steps of Dyna-Q learning algorithm.

Initialize $Q(s, a)$ and Model $M(s, a)$ $\forall s \in S$, $\alpha \in A(s)$

Do forever:
 	
 iv. $S \leftarrow$ current state (non-terminal)
 v. $A \leftarrow \varepsilon$-greedy(S, Q)
 vi. Implement an action A, determine resultant state S' and reward R.
 vii. $Q(S, A) \leftarrow Q(S, A) + \alpha[R + \gamma \max_\alpha Q(S', \alpha) - Q(S, A)]$
 viii. $M(S, A) \leftarrow R, S'$ (deterministic external condition)
 ix. Repeat the following steps n times:
 	
     • $S \leftarrow$ observed previous state randomly
     • $A \leftarrow$ action performed in S randomly
     • $R, S' \leftarrow M(S, A)$
     • $Q(S, A) \leftarrow Q(S, A) + \alpha[R + \gamma \max_\alpha Q(S', \alpha) - Q(S, A)]$

The steps of Dyna-Q learning algorithm are described in Table 11.3. It consists three different algorithms, namely, TD (0), TD (1), and TD(λ). Before, we discuss them, it is necessary to define some notations, which will be used in the algorithms.

- *Gamma* (γ): It defines the rate of discount and it varies between 0 and 1. The higher the value the less you are discounting.
- *Lambda* (λ): It signifies the credit assignment variable and varies between 0 and 1. The higher the value the more credit can be given to action and state.
- *Alpha* (α): It denotes the learning rate. A small value adjusts conservatively and higher value adjusts aggressively.
- *Delta* (δ): It signifies a difference or any change in value.

11.3.3.1   TD(0) Algorithm

TD(0) is simple and easy to understand. It focuses on the immediate reward (R_{t+1}) and estimate discount value of only 1 step before $V(S_{t+1})$, as shown in the equation [51].

$$V(S_t) = V(S_t) + \alpha(R_{t+1} + \gamma V(S_{t+1}) - V(S_t))$$

The only difference between the TD(0) and TD(1) algorithms is an update step. It should be noted that the value of (G_t) is stepped out with one step ahead estimation. The process of estimation to update estimate value is called bootstrapping [52]. It has higher bias than TD(1) algorithm, due to creating the estimates from estimates itself as compared to creating estimates after perceiving an entire episode. Thus, it leads to lower variance [53]. The main advantage of TD (0) algorithms is that it has the ability to learn external conditions which do not have terminal states, but TD(1) cannot learn [78].

11.3.3.2   TD(1) Algorithm

TD(1) follows the same approach of Monte Carlo method to update the values at the end of the episode. So moving toward the left or right direction randomly, until coming into "A" or "G". On the completion of an episode, then update the values of previous states [54]. It is noted that TD(1) and Monte Carlo method only applicable in episodic external conditions because they make an update on finish line of the episode. Aforementioned that the higher the value of lambda, then the credit can be assigned and in the extreme case it is equal to 1 [55, 56].

The value of G_t denotes the summation of discounted rewards seen in an episode. Therefore, we need to keep track of all the rewards and their summation with discount (γ). At any time ($t + 1$), the instant reward (R) adds to the discount (γ) of a future reward (R_{t+2}) and so on [57]. The summation of discounted rewards is determined as

$$G_t = R_{t+1} + \gamma R_{t+2} + ... + \gamma^{T-1} R_T$$

Next step is to update the estimated values $V(S)$. Initially, we don't have an idea about the perfect starting estimate [58]. So, better to start with all zeros or take random values and then perform changes to that estimated value [59].

Take the summation of discounted rewards (G_t) and subtract it from the previous estimate $V(S_t)$, as shown in equation [60]. It is called as TD error. The user estimated value minus the prior estimate value. Further, it is multiplied with a scalar (α) for tuning that how much error the user like to update [61]. Finally, makes an update by adding it to prior estimated value $V(S_t)$ to an adjusted error as shown

$$V(S_t) = V(S_t) + \alpha (G_t - V(S_t))$$

It is one episode, where the random walk and summation of rewards are selected. This process is repeated again to make TD(1) update [62].

11.3.3.3   TD(λ) Algorithm

Suppose, if user wants to update the value before the completion of the episode TD (1), then it adds one more step before TD(0) for estimation [63]. Thus, the TD(λ) comes into an action. There exist two steps of execution of TD(λ), namely, forward and backward view. The forward view looks at the n-steps before and utilizes λ to decay the crucial future estimates. The backward view changes the values at every step. Thus, it makes update to all previous steps just after completion of each step in an episode. The eligibility traces (ETs) is used to assign weight to previous steps appropriately [64].

The main purpose of ET is to keep record the number of times the state enters into an equation. The weight is assigned to the states which are entered recently and frequently concerning to terminal state.

The gamma (γ) and lambda (λ) are used to discount the traces.

$$E_0(s) = 0$$

$$E_t(s) = \gamma\lambda E_{t-1}(s) + 1(S_t = s)$$

It should be noted that if state "F" is visited recently and more frequently concerning to terminal state "G" and it receives many updates [65]. Thus, the more credit is assign to state "F" in proportion to the TD error. If the state "B" is not visited as often concerning to final state "G", so its value cannot be updated and remains close to 0, i.e., an initial value. The continuous updates to previous estimates is performed as

$$\delta_t = R_{t+1} + \gamma V(S_{t+1}) - V(S_t)$$
$$V(s) \longleftarrow V(s) + \alpha\delta_t E_t(s)$$

11.3.4   Monte Carlo Method

Monte Carlo method needs experience-trial chain of states, actions, and recompense from simulated or real interconnection with an external condition. The learning from real experience is notable due to the previous knowledge about an environment is not required. But, still, it can obtain an optimal behavior [66]. The learning from simulated experience is also strong. While, it requires model, which can produce only sample transitions rather than probability distribution of transitions, which is needed for dynamic programming. Therefore, any method can be categorized as Monte Carlo if capable of solving the problem *via* producing suitable numbers randomly and determining the numbers satisfying some feature or features [67].

Monte Carlo method solves the problem of RL by calculating the average sample returns. It is defined for only episodic tasks to ensure well-defined returns as an outcome. Thus, suppose the experience is partitioned into episodes [68]. Further, no matter what actions are chosen, all the episodes are terminated eventually. After the completion of the episode, the policies and values are updated. It is mostly used for approximation method where the operations are performed with randomly selected element.

For an example, we try to calculate the value of *pi* manually. Firstly, a square of unit length is drawn consisting a quarter circle of unit radius [69]. The task is assigned to bot to put the dots as many possible ($n = 3,000$ times) on square randomly as shown in Figure 11.9.

Each time, the bot counts the dot after put it inside the circle. Thus, the value of *pi* is calculated as:

$$pi = 4 * \frac{N}{3000}$$

where N denotes the number of times a dot put inside the quarter circle. The need is to determine the number of dot falls inside the circle randomly and then take the ratio to approximated value of *pi* [70].

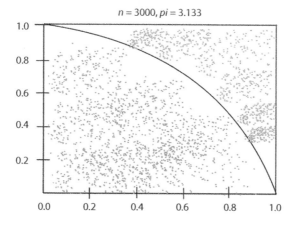

Figure 11.9 A square of unit length consisting quarter circle of unit radius.

11.3.4.1   Monte Carlo Reinforcement Learning

The learning phase of Monte Carlo method occurs from episodes of experience directly without having any previous knowledge of MDP transitions. The associated return or reward is the random. The alarming bell is that it can be applicable to episodic MDPs only [71]. The reason is that before determining the returns, we have to terminate the episode. Thus, rather than each episode, the update process cannot be performed after each action. It follows the simple rule, i.e., to take the mean return of all sample trajectories for every state. There exist two steps policy evaluation and improvement. The policy evaluation is used to determine the value function for a given policy randomly. The policy improvement is used to investigate the optimum policy [72].

11.3.4.2   Monte Carlo Policy Evaluation

Under a policy pi, the main objective is to learn the value function $V_\pi(s)$ from episodes of experience. It should be noted that the return denotes the discounted reward [73].

$$S_1, A_1, R_2, \ldots, S_k \sim pi$$

The value function is the expected return calculated as:

$$V_\pi(s) = E_\pi[G_t|S_t = s]$$

The expected value can be estimated by summing all the samples and dividing with the total number of samples as

$$\overline{V}_\pi(s) = \frac{1}{N}\sum_{i=1}^{N} G_{i,s}$$

where i denotes an index of episode and s is an index of the state. The question arises here is that how do these samples returns? The answer is that, we need to play a group of episodes and produce them. We have a chain of rewards and state for each episode. After determine the rewards, we can investigate the return, i.e., calculated by accumulating the future rewards [74].

First visit Monte Carlo: It returns only an average on visiting the episode first time. The steps of first visit Monte Carlo algorithm are described in Table 11.4. The working of first visit Monte Carlo algorithm is given as

Table 11.4 Steps of first visit Monte Carlo algorithm.

1. *Initialization* of the policy and state value function
2. Following the current policy, produce an episode
2.1 During generating episodes, keep track of states
3. Choose a state produced in step 2.1
3.1 After first occurrence of the state, sum up the list of returns
3.2 Take average over all returns
3.3 Give the computed average to that state
4. Repeat step 3
5. Repeat steps 2 to 4 until satisfied

Table 11.5 Computation for two samples of episodes.

First visit Monte Carlo	Every visit Monte Carlo
$V(A) = \dfrac{1}{2}(2+0) = 1$	$V(A) = \dfrac{1}{4}(2-1+1+0) = \dfrac{1}{2}$
$V(B) = \dfrac{1}{2}(-3-2) = \dfrac{-5}{2}$	$V(B) = \dfrac{1}{4}(-3-3-2-3) = \dfrac{-11}{4}$

Every visit Monte Carlo: It takes an average of returns on visiting an episode every time. The only difference lies in step 3.1 of the above algorithm, sum up the list of returns after every occurrence of same state. Table 11.5 shows the computation for two samples of episodes. Let's there exist an environment consisting two states (A and B) and two samples of episodes are observed as

$$A+3 \rightarrow A+2 \rightarrow B \rightarrow 4 \rightarrow A+4 \rightarrow B-3 \rightarrow T$$

$$B-2 \rightarrow A+3 \rightarrow B-3 \rightarrow T$$

where T stands for terminating, $A+3\rightarrow A$ signifies that state A is changed to state A with a reward $+3$. Let's find out the value function using both methods.

11.3.4.3　Monte Carlo Policy Improvement

After determining the value function for a random policy, the crucial task is to investigate the optimum policy using the concept of Monte Carlo.

The formula used for policy improvement in dynamic programming is given as

$$\pi'(s)=\arg\max_{a}\sum_{s',r}p(s',r|s,a)[r+\gamma v_{\pi}(s')]$$

It is used to find the optimum policy by calculating actions that augment the sum of rewards. Thus, a major caution is that the transition probabilities are used, which is not present in model-free RL [75].

The state transition probabilities $p(s', r|s, \alpha)$ *are not known and look-ahead search is not possible like dynamic programming.* Therefore, the required information can be obtained by exploring the environment or experience of playing the game [76].

11.4　Conclusion

RL is placed in between supervised learning and unsupervised learning, which deals with the learning in subsequent decision making tasks with restricted feedback. In this chapter, the model-based and model-free RL algorithms are described. It has provided the necessary background of RL with its elements. The core elements of several solution algorithms are discussed. Furthermore, a new type of learning algorithm, i.e., temporal-difference (TD) learning is shown that how it can be applied to the real-life RL situations. It is combination of ideas of dynamic programming and Monte Carlo. The situation is divided into prediction and control. TD methods are used to perform predictions for long-term about the dynamic systems. Still, there are lots of issues, which are needed to be resolved before applying in various industries. It should understand the consequences of different strategies and assist the human to take actions to achieve a common goal.

References

1. Song, Z. and Sun, W., Efficient model-free reinforcement learning in metric spaces, 2019. arXiv preprint:1905.00475, 1–17.

2. Abbeel, P. and Ng, A.Y., Apprenticeship learning *via* inverse reinforcement learning, in: *Proceedings of the twenty-first international conference on Machine learning*, ACM, p. 1, 2004, July.

3. Kaelbling, L.P., Littman, M.L., Moore, A.W., Reinforcement learning: A survey. *J. Artif. Intell. Res.*, 4, 237–285, 1996.

4. Mnih, V., Kavukcuoglu, K., Silver, D., Graves, A., Antonoglou, I., Wierstra, D., Riedmiller, M., Playing atari with deep reinforcement learning, 2013. arXiv preprint:1312.5602, 1–9.

5. Sutton, R.S. and Barto, A.G., *Reinforcement learning: An introduction*, Cambridge University Press, United Kingdom, MIT press, 2018.

6. Mnih, V., Badia, A.P., Mirza, M., Graves, A., Lillicrap, T., Harley, T., Kavukcuoglu, K., Asynchronous methods for deep reinforcement learning, in: *International conference on machine learning*, pp. 1928–1937, 2016, June.

7. Lillicrap, T.P., Hunt, J.J., Pritzel, A., Heess, N., Erez, T., Tassa, Y., Wierstra, D., Continuous control with deep reinforcement learning, In: *Proceedings: 4th International Conference on Learning Representations*, San Juan, Puerto Rico, 2016. arXiv preprint arXiv:1509.02971.

8. Van Hasselt, H., Guez, A., Silver, D., Deep reinforcement learning with double q-learning, in: *Thirtieth AAAI conference on artificial intelligence*, 2016, March.

9. Tan, M., Multi-agent reinforcement learning: Independent vs. cooperative agents, in: *Proceedings of the tenth international conference on machine learning*, pp. 330–337, 1993.

10. Dayan, P. and Hinton, G.E., Feudal reinforcement learning, in: *Advances in neural information processing systems*, pp. 271–278, 1993.

11. Sutton, R.S., Generalization in reinforcement learning: Successful examples using sparse coarse coding, in: *Advances in neural information processing systems*, pp. 1038–1044, 1996.

12. Crites, R.H. and Barto, A.G., Improving elevator performance using reinforcement learning, in: *Advances in neural information processing systems*, pp. 1017–1023, 1996.

13. Baird, L., Residual algorithms: Reinforcement learning with function approximation, in: *Machine Learning Proceedings 1995*, Morgan Kaufmann, pp. 30–37, 1995.

14. Ziebart, B.D., Maas, A., Bagnell, J.A., Dey, A.K., Maximum entropy inverse reinforcement learning. In: *Proceedings of the Twenty-Third AAAI Conference on Artificial Intelligence*, Chicago, Illinois, 2008.

15. Wiering, M. and Van Otterlo, M., Reinforcement learning. *Adapt. Lear. Optim.*, 12, 3, 2012.

16. Sutton, R.S., McAllester, D.A., Singh, S.P., Mansour, Y., Policy gradient methods for reinforcement learning with function approximation, in: *Advances in neural information processing systems*, pp. 1057–1063, 2000.

17. Hu, J. and Wellman, M.P., Nash Q-learning for general-sum stochastic games. *J. Mach. Learn. Res.*, 4, Nov, 1039–1069, 2003.

18. Watkins, C.J.C.H., Learning from delayed rewards, PhD Thesis, Cambridge University, United Kingdom, 1989.

19. Vrancx, P., *Decentralised reinforcement learning in Markov games*, ASP/VUBPRESS/UPA, Vubpress Brussels University Press, Brussels, Belgium, 2011.

20. Littman, M.L., Markov games as a framework for multi-agent reinforcement learning, in: *Machine learning proceedings 1994*, Morgan Kaufmann, pp. 157–163, 1994.

21. Dayan, P. and Balleine, B.W., Reward, motivation, and reinforcement learning. *Neuron*, 36, 2, 285–298, 2002.

22. Ormoneit, D. and Sen, Ś., Kernel-based reinforcement learning. *Mach. Learn.*, 49, 2–3, 161–178, 2002.

23. Hu, J. and Wellman, M.P., Multiagent reinforcement learning: Theoretical framework and an algorithm, in: *ICML*, vol. 98, pp. 242–250, 1998, July.

24. Ramachandran, D. and Amir, E., Bayesian Inverse Reinforcement Learning, in: *IJCAI*, vol. 7, pp. 2586–2591, 2007, January.

25. Schwartz, A., A reinforcement learning method for maximizing undiscounted rewards, in: *Proceedings of the tenth international conference on machine learning*, vol. 298, pp. 298–305, 1993.

26. Ng, A.Y., Coates, A., Diel, M., Ganapathi, V., Schulte, J., Tse, B., Liang, E., Autonomous inverted helicopter flight *via* reinforcement learning, in: *Experimental robotics IX*, pp. 363–372, Springer, Berlin, Heidelberg, 2006.

27. Carlstrom, J. and Nordstrom, E., Control of self-similar ATM call traffic by reinforcement learning, in: *Proceedings of the International Workshop on Applications of Neural Networks to Telecommunications*, vol. 3, pp. 54–62, 1997.

28. Zoph, B. and Le, Q.V., Neural architecture search with reinforcement learning, In: *Proceedings of 5th International Conference on Learning Representations*. Toulon, France, 2017. arXiv preprint arXiv:1611.01578.

29. Boyan, J.A. and Littman, M.L., Packet routing in dynamically changing networks: A reinforcement learning approach, in: *Advances in neural information processing systems*, pp. 671–678, 1994.

30. Szepesvári, C., Algorithms for reinforcement learning. *Synth. Lect. Artif. Intell. Mach. Learn.*, 4, 1, 1–103, 2010.

31. Boyan, J.A. and Moore, A.W., Generalization in reinforcement learning: Safely approximating the value function, in: *Advances in neural information processing systems*, pp. 369–376, 1995.

32. Kearns, M. and Singh, S., Near-optimal reinforcement learning in polynomial time. *Mach. Learn.*, 49, 2–3, 209–232, 2002.

33. Barto, A.G. and Mahadevan, S., Recent advances in hierarchical reinforcement learning. *Discrete Event Dyn. Syst.*, 13, 1–2, 41–77, 2003.
34. Taylor, M.E. and Stone, P., Transfer learning for reinforcement learning domains: A survey. *J. Mach. Learn. Res.*, 10, Jul, 1633–1685, 2009.
35. Guestrin, C., Lagoudakis, M., Parr, R., Coordinated reinforcement learning, in: *ICML*, vol. 2, pp. 227–234, 2002, July.
36. Bu, L., Babu, R., De Schutter, B., A comprehensive survey of multiagent reinforcement learning. *IEEE Transactions on Systems, Man, and Cybernetics, Part C (Applications and Reviews)*, vol. 38, 2 pp. 156–172, 2008.
37. Singh, S.P. and Sutton, R.S., Reinforcement learning with replacing eligibility traces. *Mach. Learn.*, 22, 1-3, 123–158, 1996.
38. Wang, Z., Schaul, T., Hessel, M., Van Hasselt, H., Lanctot, M., De Freitas, N., Dueling network architectures for deep reinforcement learning, in: *Proceedings of the 33rd International Conference on Machine Learning*, New York, NY, USA, 2016. arXiv preprint arXiv:1511.06581.
39. Džeroski, S., De Raedt, L., Driessens, K., Relational reinforcement learning. *Mach. Learn.*, 43, 1–2, 7–52, 2001.
40. Busoniu, L., Babuska, R., De Schutter, B., Ernst, D., *Reinforcement learning and dynamic programming using function approximators*, CRC Press, United States, 2017.
41. Sutton, R.S., Barto, A.G., Williams, R.J., Reinforcement learning is direct adaptive optimal control. *IEEE Control Syst. Mag.*, 12, 2, 19–22, 1992.
42. Doya, K., Samejima, K., Katagiri, K.I., Kawato, M., Multiple model-based reinforcement learning. *Neural Comput.*, 14, 6, 1347–1369, 2002.
43. Klucharev, V., Hytönen, K., Rijpkema, M., Smidts, A., Fernández, G., Reinforcement learning signal predicts social conformity. *Neuron*, 61, 1, 140–151, 2009.
44. Moriarty, D.E. and Mikkulainen, R., Efficient reinforcement learning through symbiotic evolution. *Mach. Learn.*, 22, 1–3, 11–32, 1996.
45. Ernst, D., Geurts, P., Wehenkel, L., Tree-based batch mode reinforcement learning. *J. Mach. Learn. Res.*, 6, Apr, 503–556, 2005.
46. Smart, W.D. and Kaelbling, L.P., Effective reinforcement learning for mobile robots, in: *Proceedings 2002 IEEE International Conference on Robotics and Automation*, vol. 4, IEEE, pp. 3404–3410, 2002, May, Cat. No. 02CH37292.
47. Duan, Y., Chen, X., Houthooft, R., Schulman, J., Abbeel, P., Benchmarking deep reinforcement learning for continuous control, in: *International Conference on Machine Learning*, pp. 1329–1338, 2016.
48. Peters, J., Vijayakumar, S., Schaal, S., Reinforcement learning for humanoid robotics, in: *Proceedings of the third IEEE-RAS international conference on humanoid robots*, pp. 1–20, 2003.
49. Dietterich, T.G., Hierarchical reinforcement learning with the MAXQ value function decomposition. *J. Artif. Intell. Res.*, 13, 227–303, 2000.

50. Moore, A.W. and Atkeson, C.G., Prioritized sweeping: Reinforcement learning with less data and less time. *Mach. Learn.*, 13, 1, 103–130, 1993.
51. Li, J., Monroe, W., Ritter, A., Galley, M., Gao, J., Jurafsky, D., Deep reinforcement learning for dialogue generation, in: *Proceedings of the Conference on Empirical Methods in Natural Language Processing*, pages 1192–1202, Austin, Texas, 2016. arXiv preprint arXiv:1606.01541.
52. Gambardella, L.M. and Dorigo, M., Ant-Q: A reinforcement learning approach to the traveling salesman problem, in: *Machine Learning Proceedings 1995*, Morgan Kaufmann, pp. 252–260, 1995.
53. Kohl, N. and Stone, P., Policy gradient reinforcement learning for fast quadrupedal locomotion, in: *IEEE International Conference on Robotics and Automation, 2004. Proceedings. ICRA'04. 2004*, vol. 3, IEEE, pp. 2619–2624, 2004, April.
54. Lin, L. J., Self-improving reactive agents based on reinforcement learning, planning and teaching. *Mach. Learn.*, 8, 3–4, 293–321, 1992.
55. Stone, P., Sutton, R.S., Kuhlmann, G., Reinforcement learning for robocup soccer keepaway. *Adapt. Behav.*, Cambridge, United States, 13, 3, 165–188, 2005.
56. Barto, A.G., Reinforcement learning, in: *Neural systems for control*, pp. 7–30, Academic Press, 1997.
57. Strehl, A.L., Li, L., Wiewiora, E., Langford, J., Littman, M.L., PAC model-free reinforcement learning, in: *Proceedings of the 23rd international conference on Machine learning*, ACM, pp. 881–888, 2006, June.
58. Peters, J. and Schaal, S., Reinforcement learning of motor skills with policy gradients. *Neural Netw.*, 21, 4, 682–697, 2008.
59. Zhang, W. and Dietterich, T.G., A reinforcement learning approach to job-shop scheduling, in: *IJCAI*, vol. 95, pp. 1114–1120, 1995, August.
60. Strens, M., A Bayesian framework for reinforcement learning, in: *ICML*, vol. 2000, pp. 943–950, 2000, June.
61. Chrisman, L., Reinforcement learning with perceptual aliasing: The perceptual distinctions approach, in: *AAAI*, pp. 183–188, 1992, July 1992.
62. Singh, S., Jaakkola, T., Littman, M.L., Szepesvári, C., Convergence results for single-step on-policy reinforcement-learning algorithms. *Mach. Learn.*, 38, 3, 287–308, 2000.
63. Littman, M.L., Value-function reinforcement learning in Markov games. *Cognit. Syst. Res.*, 2, 1, 55–66, 2001.
64. Humphrys, M., Action selection methods using reinforcement learning. *Anim. Animats*, 4, 135–144, 1996.
65. Whitehead, S.D., A Complexity Analysis of Cooperative Mechanisms in Reinforcement Learning, in: *AAAI*, pp. 607–613, 1991, July.
66. Whitehead, S.D. and Ballard, D.H., Active perception and reinforcement learning, in: *Machine Learning Proceedings 1990*, Austin, Texas, pp. 179–188, Morgan Kaufmann, 1990.
67. Michels, J., Saxena, A., Ng, A.Y., High speed obstacle avoidance using monocular vision and reinforcement learning, in: *Proceedings of the 22nd*

international conference on Machine learning, ACM, pp. 593–600, 2005, August.

68. Barto, A.G., Sutton, R.S., Brouwer, P.S., Associative search network: A reinforcement learning associative memory. *Biol. Cybern.*, 40, 3, 201–211, 1981.

69. Wiering, M.A., Multi-agent reinforcement learning for traffic light control, in: *Machine Learning: Proceedings of the Seventeenth International Conference (ICML'2000)*, pp. 1151–1158, 2000.

70. Theodorou, E., Buchli, J., Schaal, S., A generalized path integral control approach to reinforcement learning. *J. Mach. Learn. Res.*, 11, Nov, 3137–3181, 2010.

71. Riedmiller, M., Neural fitted Q iteration–first experiences with a data efficient neural reinforcement learning method, in: *European Conference on Machine Learning*, Springer, Berlin, Heidelberg, pp. 317–328, 2005, October.

72. Ipek, E., Mutlu, O., Martínez, J.F., Caruana, R., Self-optimizing memory controllers: A reinforcement learning approach, in: *ACM SIGARCH Computer Architecture News*, vol. 36, 3 pp. 39–50, Beijing, China IEEE, Computer Society, 2008, June.

73. Baker, B., Gupta, O., Naik, N., Raskar, R., Designing neural network architectures using reinforcement learning, in: *Proceedings of 5th International Conference on Learning Representations*. Toulon, France, 2017. arXiv preprint arXiv:1611.02167.

74. Andre, D. and Russell, S.J., State abstraction for programmable reinforcement learning agents, in: *AAAI/IAAI*, pp. 119–125, 2002, July.

75. Littman, M. and Boyan, J., A distributed reinforcement learning scheme for network routing, in: *Proceedings of the international workshop on applications of neural networks to telecommunications*, Psychology Press, pp. 55–61, 2013, June.

76. Kulkarni, T.D., Narasimhan, K., Saeedi, A., Tenenbaum, J., Hierarchical deep reinforcement learning: Integrating temporal abstraction and intrinsic motivation, in: *Advances in neural information processing systems*, pp. 3675–3683, 2016.

77. Sutton, R.S. and Barto, A.G., *Reinforcement learning: An introduction*, Cambridge University Press, United Kingdom, 2011.

78. Chentanez, N., Barto, A.G., Singh, S.P., Intrinsically motivated reinforcement learning, in: *Advances in neural information processing systems*, pp. 1281–1288, 2005.

79. Baird, L.C., III and Moore, A.W., Gradient descent for general reinforcement learning, in: *Advances in neural information processing systems*, pp. 968–974, 1999.

Application of Big Data and Machine Learning

Neha Sharma[1], Sunil Kumar Gautam[2]*, Azriel A. Henry[2] and Abhimanyu Kumar[3]

[1]Tata Consultancy Services, Pune, Maharashtra, India
[2]Department of Engineering & Computing, Institute of Advanced Research, Gandhinagar, India
[3]Department of Computer Science & Engineering, NIT Uttarakhand, Srinagar, India

Abstract

Today, Machine Learning (ML) is apart of our daily life. It has major advancements in its applications and research as well. ML is the study in which a machine is trained with past data and examples and uses algorithms to build the logic. Important ML applicationsare speech recognition, computer vision, biosurveillance, robot or automation control, empirical science experiments, DNA classification, intrusion detection, astronomical data analysis, information security, transportation, etc.

According to a recent survey, computer-generated insurance advice is helpful to customers. Using ML, determination of cover for a certain customer can be predicted. Choice of the mode of transportation can also be benefited from ML. ML predicts the mode of transportation for an individual to make their travel better. Travel modes may include private car, public transport (bus or train), or soft mode (walking or cycling). The very first step in applying ML is to define a problem. This step includes three important processes to be considered, namely, problem identification, the motivation behind problem solving, and the solution itself.

This chapter presents the evolution of ML along with the purpose it serves. It also focuses on the ideas of concept learning along with the methods and algorithms therein.

Keywords: Big data, machine learning, healthcare, ecosystem conservation

*Corresponding author: gautamsunil.cmri@gmail.com

Uma N. Dulhare, Khaleel Ahmad and Khairol Amali Bin Ahmad (eds.) Machine Learning and Big Data: Concepts, Algorithms, Tools and Applications, (305–334) © 2020 Scrivener Publishing LLC

12.1   Introduction

Big data and machine learning are frequently used terminology that adopted by in researcher in this era. Nowadays, big data carry out is a field carry out data analysis and information extraction from datasets that are huge and complex. Afterwards, the machine learning (ML) technology come that represents machine learns certain from input data and predicts the specific output. Thus, it's helpful in insights of the data that is huge, complex, and cannot be analyzed by human analysts. Several companies used the ML technique for analyzing huge amount of dataset such as Giant used the technique for predicating the output [1, 2]. Since 2019, it saved $1 billion for Netflix by recommending shows and movies to its subscribers. It's also providing the time-effective processing due to this features an online company Amazons used this technique and save time in click-to-ship [3, 4].

Big data are not dependent on single factor called size but actually characterized by high velocity, high volume, and/or high variety data which require advanced techniques to have data insights. Data analytics plays a significant role in extracting value from huge amount of data [5]. Big data does not always means data in Giga or Tera bytes rather a small amount of data can also be called as big data for a given context. For example, if a user tries to send an attachment of 100 MB in a mail he/she will not be able to do so as the email system will not support that size. Therefore, this attachment with respect to an email can be referred to as big data. Similarly, if a user wants to process 20 TB of data using traditional system, he/she will not be able to process it in a given time due to insufficient computing power. Therefore, data can be also being referred to as big data in reference of the computing system.

Nowadays, there are various tools available on basis of data stores, namely, development platforms and tool, integration tool for reporting and analytics. Hadoop, Apache Spark, Apache Storm, Cassandra, Rapid Miner, etc., are examples of big data tools. In these tools, Hadoop is open source tool that is most popular tool in big data world. Many of application used the big data technique such as healthcare, media, agriculture, banking, and manufacturing, etc. In these applications, healthcare application is rapidly using the big data technique. In medical field, United State of America is collecting the Zetta bytes in data in healthcare section [6]. It is also more useful in banking sector by providing them disaster prevention, theft prevention, and methods to understand the behavior of customers [7].

ML has become a key mechanism for extracting knowledge and useful information from raw data and turning them to a piece of structured information which benefit the processes of analysis and predictions [8]. In this technique, humans train machines with the past data called training dataset. It categorize given data into favorable or unfavorable class.

ML is extensively used in search engines for suggestions for the query, spell correction, web indexing, and page ranking [9]. It can primarily be categorized into two groups, namely, supervised learning and unsupervised learning. Supervised ML uses input and gives predictions based on given targets. Unlike supervised learning, unsupervised training dataset does not have any targets for prediction [10]. Though unsupervised learning ML algorithm processes upon the data without the reference of pre-established labels. It is based on a qualitative understanding of the data. ML is applied in numerous fields including healthcare, banking, insurance, agriculture, education, etc. Among these areas, healthcare sector is one of the most benefited sectors where ML is applied. Its support large data about patient's medical history can predict diabetes risk, heart attack risk, or other health issues. It is playing a vital role in the medical imaging field which includes image fusion, image segmentation, computer-aided diagnosis, image registration, image-guided therapy, image database retrieval, and image annotation [11].

Now, in Section 12.2, we discussed on about motivation about the chapter. Section 12.3 highlighted the related work about application. In Section 12.4, we discussed about the different application of big data and ML. Section 12.5 describes the issues and challenges. At last, we present our conclusion in Section 12.6.

12.2   Motivation

In current scenario, big data play a vital role in research, and most of companies are using several techniques to extract information from huge dataset. Machine learning technique provides a platform for extracting useful information from large size dataset. Due to presence of huge amount of dataset in several applications, the demand of ML with big data will be increasing. In this chapter, we will discuss about various applications such as health sector, banking filed, agriculture, and media entertainment, etc., that are merging with ML with big data.

12.3   Related Work

The big data and ML are popular topic for research in these days. These techniques provide several opportunities that applied in different applications such as such as healthcare, banking, transportation, media, and entertainment industry, etc. [12]. In medical field, the patient's data have rapidly increased that provide a scope for research. The existing systems were used to deal with such data until modern technologies came into action [13]. The privacy and security of the data also need to be focused upon, but sadly, many who implemented these technologies have not considered them noticeable. Prableen Kaur *et al.* have discussed about development of smart and secure healthcare system using ML to handle big medical data [14]. In parallel, banking sector also deals with huge amount of data that needs to be accurately analyzed and structured to benefit their customers. In banking, customer profile depends upon generally two data types namely transactional and demographic data. Emad Dawood *et al.* proposed a system merging both data types to get a more accurate result and to minimize the risk [15].

These technologies have also big research opportunities in transportation. Researchers have developed ideas to understand traffic events and control them to make better decisions. Data used here originates from different sources, i.e., sensors, IoT, social media which create heterogeneity in the data. This idea has been successfully demonstrated on the arterial road network of Victoria, Australia [16]. Newly, there is a noticeable growth in the electric vehicle manufacturing sector. Companies are putting their efforts into making cars that run on electricity as it has less impact on the environment and is economically decent. Chung-Hong Lee *et al.* used ML and big data to analyze energy consumption and to estimate driving range for electric vehicles [17].

ML and big data have also played an essential role in benefiting education sector. Education is necessary for everyone no matter where they are. One of the important factors in education is the teaching strategy of teachers. Natalia Kushik *et al.* proposed a system which can predict and evaluate the student's level of ability or skill when certain teaching strategy is applied. This system can be brought to the education system to help teachers or the management system to efficiently educate students based on their goals and capabilities [18]. Big data and ML are helping the media and entertainment industries in areas like personalized marketing, customer sentiment analysis, real-time analytics, recommendation engines, media content usage analysis, etc. Companies like Netflix and Amazon are saving their money and time respectively with the help of these technologies.

Agriculture products need to be increased with an increase in the human population. It requires expansions of agriculture lands and farms. Countries around the globe are investing much in the agriculture sector to cope up with the need for agriculture products or food. By the reason of global warming, crops are damaged thereby making them poisonous. Smart systems have been developed to assess the condition of crops which can predict the damage. Fan-Hsun Tseng et al. proposed a system called Intelligent Agriculture platform which can monitor the farm environment, learn soil fertility conditions, and determine irrigation time and quantity [19]. The study [20] shows the system that provides drought monitoring and forecasting with the use of satellite remote sensing data (land cover type, soil moisture, and weather data).

ML and big data are also taking over manufacturing industries in many ways. These industries need much manpower that is now being replaced by machines or robots. These technologies play an ample role in replacing humans. Manufacturing industries also deal with a huge amount of data that need to be accurately analyzed. The study [21] shows a generic data analytics system for manufacturing production. This system can carry out analysis even if there is no prior knowledge or experience of data analytics. Chaoyang Zhang et al. proposed a system that helps to reduce the carbon emission from the manufacturing industries. Big data methods have been used to calculate and evaluate the carbon emissions of machine processes [22].

The following section will discuss the applications of ML and big data for various sectors in detail.

12.4   Application of Big Data and ML

12.4.1   Healthcare

Healthcare sector can be considered as the most essential sector of all. Any advancement in this sector is directly related to human interest to the extent of saving a life. There are different types of medical methods available to cure different types of diseases. In fact, in some cases, there is more than one method is available to cure the same disease or symptoms. Ayurveda, allopathic medicines, homeopathy, modern medicines, etc., are some of the healthcare methods. The study [23] shows that allopathic medicine system is the choice of treatment in chronic conditions. Another study [24] shows that in an emergency, allopathic medicine system is their choice of therapy. Modern computer science technologies such as big data and machine learning are helping such medical systems in a very constructive way. Healthcare data is growing so rapidly and is predicted to grow faster than any other sector in the coming years. This leaves the sector with the challenge to manage an extremely huge amount of data [25]. Big data techniques and ML algorithms have the potential to manage and analyze a huge amount of data. Therefore, these technologies are showing a ray of hope to all sectors that are dealing with large datasets and the healthcare sector is not left to be benefited by these modern technologies.

ML techniques help (shown in Figure 12.1) in benefits healthcare with its ability to predict diseases, future health conditions, etc., based on previous observations or data. Chronic diseases like cancer, diabetes is already on the table to be predicted by ML algorithms. According to [26], every year, 14 million new patients are diagnosed with cancer—the people who are uncertain about their survival. Doctors are pretty well in diagnosis and prognosis (prediction of the development of disease) with around 97% of success rate. Nevertheless, the prognosis accuracy rate is only 60%. This is where ML tools partners up with the doctors or pathologists in saving a life.

The applications of ML and big data are discussed here by dividing them into two categories based on treatment and data management which are as follows.

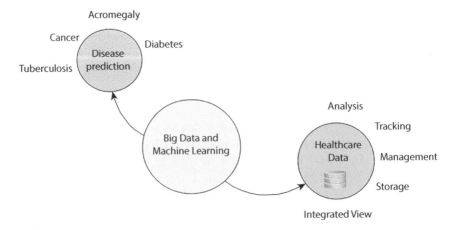

Figure 12.1 Overview of big data and machine learning application in healthcare.

In treating patients

- ML algorithms are used to predict the survivability rate of the patient suffering from lung cancer so that chemotherapy can be provided for such patients. Pradeep K R *et al.* have shown the use of Support Vector Machine (SVM), C4.5, and Naïve Bayes to predict the survivability rate. After the comparison, they concluded that the ML algorithm C4.5 performs better in predicting lung cancer [27].
- Diabetes is also one of the common chronic diseases and needs to be treated early for better and fast treatment. Prediction algorithms can be used to predict the occurrence of diabetes. According to Salman Ibrar *et al.*, Artificial Neural Network (ANN) provides the best accuracy rate than Random Forest and K-means clustering techniques to predict diabetes [28].
- ML methods can also detect Acromegaly which results from the excess growth hormone (GH). The symptoms of Acromegaly are enlargement of the hands, feet, forehead, jaw, and nose. Xiangyi Kong *et al.* proposed a system which can detect Acromegaly from facial photographs using ML algorithms like K-Nearest Neighbor (KNN), SVM, Random Tree (RT), etc.
- ML and Big data can also predict Breast Cancer based on gene expression (GE) or DNA methylation (DM) or combination of GE and DM. Sara Alghunaim *et al.* experimented with these types of data along with the combination and found that the SVM outperformed all other classifiers and the data based on GE has the lower error rate [29].
- Computational approach using ML can help clinicians to monitor patient's condition and to keep them away from inessential tests. Researchers from Princeton University have proposed such a system to benefit doctors as well as patients [30].

In data management

- Big data tools like Hadoop benefits the healthcare sector in storing big data while making it available for further processing or analysis [31].

- Big data can find ways to improve the performance and efficiency in the healthcare sector using the collection of data and analyzing them to reduce the growing healthcare costs [32].
- These technologies also help to create a holistic or 360-degree view of physicians, consumers, and patients [32].
- Big data also include data from the fitness tracker devices which keep track of the physical activity of an individual which can further be used to monitor his/her health conditions [33].

These technologies allow data to be managed, analyzed, and viewed even if it is from more than one source. José Pedro Almeida, a researcher, has proposed a software platform called HVITAL (Hospital surVeillance, moniToring and ALert) which is capable to show clinical and business information that is stored in different hospital systems [34].

12.4.2   Banking and Insurance

Banking and insurance are among the early adopters of ML technology. These technologies have benefited banking and insurance in a variety of applications. The 24x7 customer care chatbot is the one among many benefits. According to a recent report of PredictSense [35], 93% of Indian bankers choose decision-making algorithms using big data. ML and big data also benefit insurance companies in offering their customers policies that are focused on their needs and interests. It is nearly impossible for a bank to provide dynamic services to customers without using ML techniques dynamic services especially when their customers are order of 10 million or more. ML over big data has made this possible. Fair Isaac Corporation (FICO)-Cognitive Fraud Analytics Fraud-focused ML platform is one of the examples of machine learning products for banking that offers benefits like loss reduction, increased operational efficiencies, improved business agility, risk-aware growth, etc. [36, 37].

Banking sector gets affected by fraud activities like information stealing very often. Increase in the system information availability and advancement of technology has fueled these activities to another level [38]. To sustain under this constant fraudulent attacks banking sector needs to be highly accurate in detecting such frauds. ML has begotten ways to detect such fraud activities, thereby making banking secure. ML use past or existing data like past transactions, customer details, customer banking activities, etc., to detect fraud attempts.

There are several types of insurance policies available, and among them, four insurance policies are essential or important. These are health, life, property, and auto insurance policies. These policies give protection against unexpected [39]. ML use data about the necessities of an individual and recommend policies that are crucial for him/her. It can recommend health insurance policy to an individual based on the age, coverage (family members), cost, claim ratio, waiting period, etc. Similarly, ML can also recommend other policies to the people based on their needs making it profitable for the insurance companies as well. Moreover, it also keeps track of existing plans of customers to suggest them the renewal of their plans.

With the increase in the use of credit cards, there is a want for the credit score generator models. Credit score can tell the lenders whether the borrower will be able to pay the debts or not. This score is all based on the user's credit history, past transactions, etc. Therefore, ML is an efficient way to generate the credit scores of the customers. Hongmei Chena *et al.* in their study show how ML models are generating the credit scores. This study concludes that the Group Lasso method is better in interpretability and prediction accuracy [40].

Various Solutions in Banking and Insurance Sector

- N. Sun *et al.* have proposed a framework called Intelligent Customer Analytics for Recognition and Exploration (iCARE) which can analyze the behavior of the banking customers for a certain business scenario. It has been confirmed in a real case study of a particular bank in China [41].
- ML over big data can also predict the credit risk involved in lending. Dinesh Bacham *et al.* in their study show how ML assesses the credit risk of medium-sized and small borrowers. However, they found that the results by ML methods are sometimes hard to be interpreted [42].
- Chatbots in the banking sector has made things easier and fast. There are so many banks who have their chatbot to cope up with millions of their customers. K. Satheesh Kumar *et al.* proposed their chat bot called Artificial Intelligence Powered Banking Chatbot which includes services like steps to open an account, transaction limit,

etc., their chat bot was able to answer with more than 90% success rate [43].

- Moreover, it also provides services like Robo-Advisors for Financial Products, Personalized Financial Services, Smart Wallets, Emotion AI, etc. [44].

Security services like Fraud Detection and Prevention, Compliance Monitoring, etc., are also delivered by these modern technologies [44].

12.4.3   Transportation

Transportation is also one of the essential things that people in any country need. No transportation system or slow transportation system can affect many other sectors as well. There is a growing need for automobiles across the world. Economy and the standard of living of a country are influenced by the transportation system it has. Growth in the transportation sector has brought growth in its data too. Data analytics techniques like Machine learning and big data can fetch insights from transportation data which can lead to a safer transportation system. ML and big data have begotten so many benefits for the transportation sector in areas like passenger safety, vehicle safety, traffic monitoring and controlling, smart transport facilities, etc. [45, 46].

According to the Association for Safe International Road Travel (ASIRT) facts [47], nearly 1.25 million people die every year in road accidents that is approximately 3,287 deaths per day. Another report [48] from the World Health Organization—Estimated number of traffic deaths, China tops in the number of death followed India with 261,367 and 207,551 deaths, respectively. So, the increase in population is one of the causes of road accidents. Many countries have started taking actions against it and have proposed methods to have safer transportation. ML and big data play an important role for the betterment of the transportation system. These technologies have enhanced the transportation sector by improving traffic control and management, vehicle systems, transportation mode selection, etc., in Figure 12.2.

Applications of ML and big data in the transportation sector are divided into several categories, which are discussed as follows.

a.   Traffic Controlling and Management

Traffic congestion or bottleneck is one of the major problems in the transportation sector. ML and big data can help in regulating the traffic and organizing the proper signal system. Shiva S R [107] proposed a system

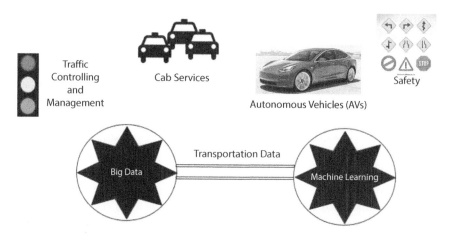

Figure 12.2 Overview of the applications of big data and machine learning in transportation sector.

that can detect traffic density through a unique number which further helps to maintain the waiting time of vehicles with respect to the traffic density [49]. Another system proposed by Rusheng Zhang *et al.* show the use of reinforcement learning an area of ML to reduce the waiting time for vehicles at an intersection [50]. ML and big data have lead traffic controlling effectively to newer heights in terms of accuracy and automation.

b.   Autonomous Vehicles (AVs)

Development of autonomous and intelligent vehicles is rapidly growing with remarkable achievements. Researchers have started to consider the behavior and habits of a human driver to develop effective automatic parking system, adaptive cruise control, etc. [51]. Electric car manufacturing company Tesla has approximately 500,000 vehicles equipped with the hardware that tesla claims to be a full self-driving system. Moreover, its sale is growing by approximately 5,000 cars per week [52]. Reliability and performance expectation are the factors that influence the adoption of this technology. ML and big data have played a major role in the development of such AVs. Big data and ML techniques analyze the data (about driving, cars, roads, etc.) and train the model to execute in a real environment.

c.   Cab Service

One of the biggest cab service companies, Uber, is available in 65 countries worldwide with 14 million trips per day [53]. These cab companies generate a large amount of data which make the analysis of the data next to impossible. But big data has the potential to analyze a large amount of data in a fraction of time. ML and big data analysis serve the companies as well as the customers in many different ways. Objectives like traffic avoidance, peak hour judgment, recognizing frequent customers to provide them with benefits, etc. [54].

d.   Safety

As mentioned above, thousands of people die every single day in road accidents. Road crash data can be analyzed and explored to prevent future accidents. Zhuoning Yuan *et al.* [55] have proposed a system using ML algorithms to predict traffic accidents with heterogeneous urban data. The bad road surface is also one of the causes that lead to road crashes and accidents. Researchers Yifan Pan *et al.* [56] have presented the use of the unmanned aerial vehicle (UAV) to identify the cracks, potholes, and damages on the road which is further used by the road maintenance department. Therefore, these advancements show how ML and big data can be used effectively to reduce road accidents and to make road journeys safer at large scale in the future.

12.4.4   Media and Entertainment

In the year 2013, a group called Farsite Group, Columbus, Ohio launched an open campaign to showcase the use of predictive analysis in forecasting the winners of the 85th Annual Academy Awards. According to Michael Gold, chief executive of the company, predicting Oscar winner would be a great way to have a platform that can showcase data science in a way people like. Farsite predicted five out of six major awards right missing only Ang Lee who got the Best Director award on that Sunday Oscar night [57, 58]. There are numerous other such examples of how big data and ML has its dwelling in the media and entertainment sector as well.

These technologies help the media and entertainment industry in a variety of ways. Media and entertainment industry can save its money by using big data and ML. These technologies help the sector majorly in recommendations. In Figure 12.3, media companies like Netflix and Amazon are a prime example that uses these technologies for recommending films and TV shows to their customers. Netflix figured out that the time when a user finds something of his/her interests is very less. So to grab subscriber's attention, Netflix has to be very fast. Using ML and big data, Netflix managed to provide good recommendations that fall in the area of the user's interest. This helped Netflix to save $1 billion or more every single year [4, 59].

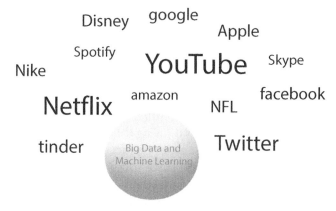

Figure 12.3 Well-known brands using big data and machine learning.

The gaming sector has witnessed major growth in recent times. According to a report [60] (2019), there are around 2 billion gamers in the world. Board games like chess and other games allow a single gamer to play two-player game with Computer or Artificial Intelligence (AI) playing as an opponent. ML and big data techniques have helped game developers to study the moves of a human player and train the artificial player in a way to beat any human player.

Google, one of the biggest companies in the world, is transforming its products with the help of ML. Google voice assistant is one of the major examples of such products. Google has used ML techniques to power the assistant to answer a variety of question and to perform diverse tasks. Apple's Siri and Amazon's Alexa are also among the products that are aided with ML. Recently, Apple has introduced Deep Fusion technology in its camera application that takes nine images which then is used by ML produce a master image with much detail [61].

Increase in the amount of data in the media and entertainment industry has created a need for an appropriate method to manage and analyze the data. ML and big data have satisfied this need. The use of ML and big data in this sector has reached new heights and is still growing rapidly [62–65].

12.4.5   Education

The education sector is a big sector consisting of universities, colleges, schools, and other private institutions. Before, this system was all unwritten and whereas writing was introduced much later which enabled people to share information [66]. With advancements in technology, the education sector has become highly organized. In recent years, there is a noticeable growth in the education sector. According to the National Center for Education Statistics [67], undergraduate enrollments in the United States has increased by 27% in the years between 2000 and 2017, i.e., 16.8 million students, and it is projected to 17.2 million students by 2028. Due to the growth, the data in the education sector has increased in great proportion.

B. Williamson in his work [68] regarding Digital Education Governance provides two detailed case studies of using this large amount of data. One of the case studies in Williamson's work focuses on the enablement to track and predict student's performance using digital data. Big data and ML techniques enable the education sector to perform analysis of the data and to draw prediction from the same. S. Kotsiantis [69] used a student's demographic characteristics and marks of some written assignments for training the ML algorithm to predict the performance of a new student.

Mathematics ability is becoming vital in our day-to-day life and works, thereby making it necessary for the education sector (in Figure 12.4) to improve mathematics learning in students. Florence Gabriel *et al.* have showcased the use of ML to address this necessity considering various aspects of mathematics learning such as psychological disposition and demographics [70].

Joshi, N.. in his article discusses about important ways in which big data is transforming the education sector such as in improving student result, customizing programs for each individual, reducing dropouts and enhancing recruitment strategies [71].

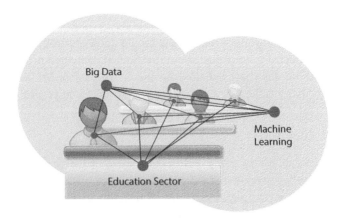

Figure 12.4 Big data and machine learning in education sector.

Another research proposed by Jiun-Yu Wu *et al.* demonstrates how ML techniques can be utilized to predict student's grades in final course and also to identify students with failure risk [72].

These advancements in the education sector are not the result of small-scale researches alone. Tech Giants like Apple, Google, and Microsoft are massively investing much in developing products of the education sector. Applications like "The classroom app", "School work", and "Handouts" are applications developed by Apple to benefit the education sector. Similarly, "Google classroom" and "Microsoft Language Translator" applications are developed by Google and Microsoft respectively for this sector. Moreover, Google has also developed its device called Chromebook which according to them is Simple, Secure, and Shareable device for students to achieve their goal [73].

E-learning is also increased in a fair amount in recent times which allows students to learn and educate themselves on the go. It holds a large amount of education data such as videos, assignments, and other reading materials. Big data techniques are able to manage and analyze this big data to present it to the students in a proper and required way.

12.4.6   Ecosystem Conservation

It is impossible to live without the ecosystem. The ecosystem provides water, clean air, food, medicine, and other cultural resources to human society. To protect the ecosystem is a big challenge to our generation [74]. There are many different ways in which ecosystems can be protected at small scale such as reducing the use of household chemicals and pesticides, reducing the waste, recycling the waste, etc. [75]. The best approach to protect the ecosystem is a large-scale approach [76]. Big data and ML techniques provide efficient ways to analyze the data of ecosystems and monitor and predict the conditions occurring in nature. These can help ecologists to take better and early measures to protect or conserve the ecosystem.

The classification task is widely applied in the study of ecology. Dealing with noisy and high-dimensional data is a bottleneck for ecologists. To overcome this issue, ML provides efficient ways to classify such a big ecology data [77].

It seems that there is a little consideration on the conservation of endangered species. According to the 2018 Living Planet Report, there is a decline of 60% in the population of wild vertebrates in around 40 years. Bland *et al.* [77] have shown the use of ML to predict the conservation status of data-deficient terrestrial mammals. This approach can help biologists and ecologists in taking measures to protect poorly known biodiversity [78].

In Figure 12.5, David J. Klein *et al.* [74] present a strategic vision with working case studies which use big data and ML to monitor ecosystems of the whole world. This approach shows how data-driven approaches and better information can lead to an effective mechanism of ecosystem conservation.

These technologies can also be used to calculate the use of certain ecological service. Simon Willcock *et al.* [108] demonstrate the use of ML techniques to identify the region where the use of firewood is within the first half of the year. Moreover, they also present the use of ML to identify biodiversity value [79]. ML techniques can also detect the growth of harmful species of plants and their spread over time [80].

Some other approaches to protect the ecosystem are discussed in [81] such as Earthcube Project, The Great Elephant Census, eBird, and Leafsnap. Earthcube Project creates a living 3D replica of the earth which can be used by scientists of numerous disciplines to study and monitor different ecosystems. The Great Elephant Census was developed by Microsoft co-founder Paul Allen in 2014 to have the insights of the number of elephants in Africa. eBird projects allow the user to record a bird sightings as they see them and input the data into the application. The aim behind this project is to develop useable datasets of birds for professionals. Lastly, Leafsnap is an application developed using ML that is able to identify

Figure 12.5 Ecosystem monitoring with big data and machine learning.

species of tree from their leaf images. The aim of the developers is to create appreciation and awareness of biodiversity.

12.4.7   Manufacturing

The higher the demand, the higher needs to be the production. In Figure 12.6, we observed that manufacturing industries have to cope with the need by developing new and appropriate strategies to optimize their production [83]. At the same time, the quality of the product should not be compromised. Currently, the manufacturing industry is experiencing an increase in the available data. To utilize this data productively, there has to be a system that can have better insights into the data available. Big data and ML can serve the manufacturing industry by providing them a better analysis of their data.

These technologies can be utilized to monitor product manufacturing in the industry. Thorsten Wuest *et al.* [82] have showcased the use of supervised ML to monitor the quality of the product based on its state suspending the conventional methods based on modeling cause-effect relations [83].

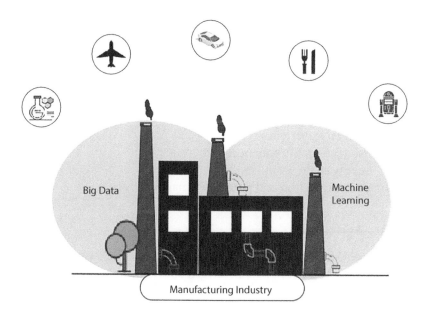

Figure 12.6 Overview of the sectors benefited by big data and machine learning.

ML techniques can also be used to detect damaged product to improve the overall production. Mehdi Namdari *et al.* have discussed how ML can be used for fault diagnosis in a chemical process [84].

To make major enhancements via investments in cooperate structure or new equipment is not economically and physically feasible. However, ML offers a promising way to deal with this issue. Karl Hansson *et al.* investigate ML classifiers to find the best possible model that can solve this issue [85].

Fei Tao *et al.* have raised the issue of the lack of convergence between product physical space and virtual space. They also discuss its possible solution by proposing digital twin–driven method with big data [86].

The aerospace industry generates a large amount of data continuously. Every part of a Boeing 787s aircraft from the engines to the landing gears is connected with the internet. According to the Virgin Atlantic IT director David Bulman, a single 787 aircraft generates half a terabytes of data in a single flight [87]. This a real challenge to the aerospace industry. However, big data accepts this challenge providing the industry with benefits like real-time aircraft monitoring and real-time monitoring of aircraft propulsion system [88].

Big data also benefits the food industry by keeping a watch over its supply chain. The Cheesecake Factory is using IBM's big data tools to analyze data generated from 175 of its locations. Using this technology restaurant can determine the cause of problems and take effective measures to prevent them from occurring in the future [89, 90].

In general, the applications of big data and ML in the manufacturing industry can be categorized as following [91, 92].

- Demand forecasting and inventory management
- Robotization
- Predictive analytics
- Product quality enhancement
- Supply chain optimization
- Fault prediction and preventive maintenance

12.4.8   Agriculture

Big data and ML have created opportunities in various sectors including one of the significant sectors named agriculture sector seen in Figure 12.7. These technologies have taken forward agriculture to new heights. There are several categories of agriculture sector in which big data and ML play a beneficial role. Some of the categories include disease detection, crop

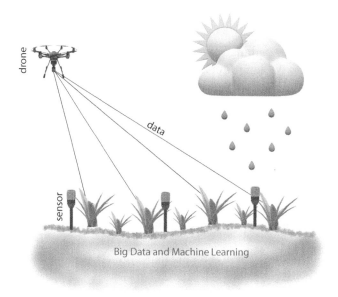

Figure 12.7 Big data and machine learning in agriculture.

management, yield prediction, water management, animal welfare, crop quality, etc. [93].

Agriculture sector requires accurate planning which depends upon the yield estimation. Farmers can efficiently plan to grow a particular crop if he knows about its yield. Big data and ML techniques can benefit farmers in predicting crop yield. Jharna Majumdar *et al.* perform the analysis of the agriculture data to obtain the optimal climate requirement to achieve higher production [94]. Van-Quyet Nguyen *et al.* have addressed big data problems like data collection, data storage, and data analysis and developed a platform for the solution of the same [95]. Another study [96] shows how big data can enhance farmer capabilities by predicting climate change effects, speeding up plant breeding, and delivering real-time farm knowledge.

These technologies can also be utilized to detect and predict plant diseases. A study [97] presents the detection of several diseases using ML such as HLB (Huanglongbing), HLB from Zinc deficiency, HLB on citrus trees, citrus HLB, powdery mildew, and tomato viruses. Another study [98] shows how ML can be used for High Throughput Stress Phenotyping in plants.

Selection of crops is an important step in agriculture planning. It also has its effect on the economy of the country. Several researchers from India have proposed a method called Crop Selection Method (CSM) using

ML. This proposed method can select the sequence of crops that are to be planted over a season [99].

ML is useful for soil management in understanding the soil conditions and their effects on agriculture. It can also be utilized for water management to estimate evapotranspiration and evaporation for the effective irrigation system. ML can be used to accurately classify the crops which can make its price to go high and waste to go low. Moreover, weed that are threats to the crop production can be distinguished well using these technologies [100].

According to Markets of Markets report global agriculture analytics market is estimated to touch $1.236 billion in 2023. The acceptance of the data-driven solutions provided by ML and AI is the fuel of this demand. These technologies have indeed made agriculture easy and highly productive [101].

Based on the above discussion big data and ML benefits for agriculture can be categorized as follows [101, 102].

- Increase in production
- Environment challenges management
- Cost saving
- Better supply chain management
- Yield prediction
- Food safety

12.5 Issues and Challenges

Big data and ML offer a variety of applications in different sectors as discussed above. To provide this, variety of benefits big data and ML technologies need to be highly proficient.

Big data is designed to deal with a huge amount of data that the traditional systems are unable to handle. But there are few challenges in big data as discussed in [103] like data complexity, computational complexity, system complexity, etc. Moreover, a study [104] shows how big data also faces issues like data privacy, data security, and data discrimination.

Information is rapidly increasing but the improvisation of the information processing systems is relatively slow. There are a limited number of tools available to completely address big data issues. Big data tools like Hadoop, MapReduce, Hbase, and Cassandra cannot solve real-time analysis problems ideally.

In a large amount of data, incomplete, inconsistent, and noisy data are susceptible. Therefore, several techniques are to be applied to filter the data. Each of such techniques faces a different challenge with respect to the use. In Figure 12.8, we have seen that privacy and security of the data are also important issues of big data. As the data increases, there is a greater possibility of security breaches. Policies which can cover all aspects concerning privacy and security of user's data needs to be developed [105].

Volume, variety, velocity, and veracity are the important characteristics of big data. High volume cause or adds computational complexity to computation methods, i.e., ML techniques. High volume also causes the computational algorithm to depend on the architecture used to store the data. Another challenge is that the data needs to be uniformly distributed in a large dataset to avoid class imbalance.

Another characteristic of big data, variety, also creates issues like data locality, data heterogeneity, and dirty and noisy data. ML needs to train the models with the training dataset to gain knowledge from the new data. These models need to be trained again (not with complete training data) every time a new data arrives which is referred to as incremental learning. Real-time processing of the data is also a big challenge as traditional ML approaches are not designed for that.

M. I. Jordan *et al.* [106] illustrate the challenge of ML by comparing the same with humans. They discuss how ML learns from a single source of

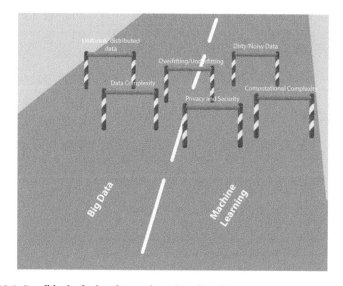

Figure 12.8 Roadblocks for big data and machine learning.

data, whereas human learn different types of knowledge and skills from multiple data around them. They have also raised the issue of data privacy and data security that are caused due to the increase in the size of the data.

Moreover, over fitting and under fitting are also considerable issues in ML which affects the performance of the model. Over fitting refers to when the model is trained too well that it also learns the noise in the data which delivers a negative impact on the performance. Unlike over fitting, under fitting occurs when the model fails to model the training data in a way it is supposed to do.

12.6   Conclusion

This chapter presents the application of big data and machine learning in various sectors in detail. Almost every sector, from healthcare to agriculture, is aided with these modern technologies. The ability to deal with humongous data and gain knowledge from the same has made these technologies to plant their roots in the sectors discussed above. Small-scale companies, as well as well-known companies, are putting their efforts to invest in big data and machine learning. Big data and machine learning are still growing and creating opportunities for researchers to beget yet more services.

However, the pathway to grow and enhance is not easy for big data and machine learning. Issues like complexity, privacy, security, etc., as mentioned and discussed in the previous section are challenging these technologies in many ways. By resolving such issues, these techniques can achieve even greater heights.

References

1. Bilyk, T., The verification's criterion of learning algorithm, in: *5th International Conference on Intelligent Systems Design and Applications*, pp. 90–93, IEEE, 2005.
2. Höchtl, J., Parycek, P., Schöllhammer, R., Big data in the policy cycle: Policy decision making in the digital era. *J. Org. Comp. Elect. Com.*, 26, 1–22, 147–169, 2016.
3. Song, H. and Liu, H., Predicting tourist demand using big data, in: *Analytics in smart tourism design*, pp. 13–29, Springer, 2017.
4. Moon, K.R., van Dijk, D., Wang, Z., Gigante, S., Burkhardt, D., Chen, S.W., Yim, K. *et al.*, Visualizing structure and transitions in high-dimensional biological data. *Nat. Biotechnol.*, 37, 12, 1482–1492, 2019.

5. L'heureux, A., Grolinge, K., Elyamany, H.F., Capretz, M.A.M., Machine Learning With Big Data: Challenges and Approaches. *IEEE Access*, 5, 7776–7797, April 24, 2017.

6. Dhayne, H., Haque, R., Kilany, R., Taher, Y., In Search of Big Medical Data Integration Solutions - A Comprehensive Survey. *IEEE Access*, 7, 91265–91290, July 9, 2019.

7. Srivastavaa, U. and Gopalkrishnan, S., Impact of Big Data Analytics on Banking Sector: Learning for Indian Banks. *2nd International Symposium on Big Data and Cloud Computing (ISBCC'15)*, Elsevier, pp. 643–352, 2015.

8. Xing, E.P., Ho, Q., Xie, P., Wei, D., Strategies and Principles of Distributed Machine Learning on Big Data. *Engineering*, 2, 179–195, 2016. Elsevier.

9. Boutaba, R., Salahuddin, M.A., Limam, N., Ayoubi, S., Shahriar, N., Estrada-Solano, F., Caicedo, O.M., A comprehensive survey on machine learning for networking: Evolution, applications and research opportunities. *J. Internet Serv. Appl.*, 9, 16, 2018. Springer.

10. Hyde, K.K., Novack, M.N., LaHaye, N., Parlett-Pelleriti, C., Anden, R., Dixon, D.R., Linstead, E., Applications of Supervised Machine Learning in Autism Spectrum Disorder Research: A Review. *Rev. J. Autism Dev. Disord.*, 6, 128–146, February 19, 2019. Springer.

11. Andreassen, A., Feige, I., Frye, C., Schwartz, M.D., JUNIPR: A framework for unsupervised machine learning in particle physics. *Eur. Phys. J. C*, 79, 102, February 1, 2019. Springer.

12. Yan, P., Suzuki, K., Wang, F., Shen, D., *Machine learning in medical imaging*, vol. 24, pp. 1327–1329, Springer, 2013.

13. Yu, Y., Li, M., Liu, L., Li, Y., Wang, J., Clinical Big Data and Deep Learning: Applications, Challenges, and Future Outlooks. *Big Data Min. Anal.*, 2, 4, 288–305, 2019.

14. Kaur, P., Sharma, M., Mittal, M., Big Data and Machine Learning Based Secure Healthcare Framework. *International Conference on Computational Intelligence and Data Science*, pp. 1049–1059, Elsevier, 2018.

15. Dawood, E.A.E., Elfakhrany, E., Maghraby, F.A., Improve Profiling Bank Customer's Behavior Using Machine Learning. *IEEE Access*, 7, 109320–109327, August 12, 2019.

16. Nallaperuma, D., Nawaratne, R., Bandaragoda, T., Adikari, A., Nguyen, S., Kempitiya, T., ... & Pothuhera, D., Online incremental machine learning platform for big data-driven smart traffic management, in: *IEEE Transactions on Intelligent Transportation Systems*, 20, 12, pp. 4679–4690, 2019.

17. Lee, C.H. and Wu, C.-H., A Novel Big Data Modeling Method for Improving Driving Range Estimation of EVs. *IEEE Access*, 3, 1980–1993, 2015.

18. Kushik, N., Yevtushenko, N., Evtushenko, T., Novel machine learning technique for predicting teaching strategy effectiveness. *Int. J. Inf. Manage.*, 1–9 2016.

19. Tseng, F.H., Cho, H.H., Wu, H.T., Applying Big Data for Intelligent Agriculture-Based Crop Selection Analysis. *IEEE Access*, 7, 116965–116974, 2019.

20. Deng, M., Di, L., Yu, G., Yagci, A., Peng, C., Zhang, B., Shen, D., Building an on-demand web service system for global agricultural drought monitoring and forecasting. *IEEE Geosci. Remote Sens. Symp.*, 958–961, 2012.

21. Zhang, H., Wang, H., Li, J., Gao, H., A Generic Data Analytics System for Manufacturing Production. *Big Data Min. Anal.*, 1, 160–171, 2018.

22. Zhang, C. and Ji, W., Big Data Analysis Approach for Real-Time Carbon Efficiency Evaluation of Discrete Manufacturing Workshops. *IEEE Access*, 7, 107730–107743, August 5, 2019.

23. Chatterjee, B., Biswas, P.C., Pancholi, J., Health awareness and popularity of alternative medicines among people of Jamnagar town: A cross - sectional study. *Int. Q. J. Res. Ayurveda*, 33, 1, 33–37, 2012.

24. Borde, M.K., Lalan, H.N., Ray, I.M., Sanjeeva Kumar Goud, T., Health Awareness and Popularity of Allopathic, Ayurvedic and Homeopathic Systems of Medicine Among Navi Mumbai Population. *World J. Pharm. Pharm. Sci.*, 3, 9, 783–788, 2014.

25. Big Data to See Explosive Growth, Challenging Healthcare Organizations. Retrieved From https://healthitanalytics.com/news/big-data-to-see-explosive-growth-challenging-healthcare-organizations

26. Cruz, J.A. and Wishart, D.S., Applications of machine learning in cancer prediction and prognosis. *Cancer Informatics*, 2 :117693510600200030, 2006.

27. Pradeep, K.R. and Naveen, N.C., Lung Cancer Survivability Prediction based on Performance Using Classification Techniques of Support Vector Machines, C4.5 and Naive Bayes Algorithms for Healthcare Analytics, in: *International Conference on Computational Intelligence and Data Science (ICCIDS)*, Elsevier, pp. 412–420, 2018.

28. Alam, T.M., Iqbal, M.A., Ali, Y., Wahab, A., Ijaz, S., Baig, T.I., Hussain, A., Malik, M.A., Raza, M.M., Ibrar, S., Abbas, Z., A model for early prediction of diabetes. *Inf. Med. Unlocked*, 16, 1–6, 2019.

29. Alghunaim, S. and Al-Baity, H.H., On the Scalability of Machine-Learning Algorithms for Breast Cancer Prediction in Big Data Context. *IEEE Access*, 7, 91535–91546, 2019.

30. Desautels, T., Calvert, J., Hoffman, J., Jay, M., Kerem, Y.,Shieh, L., Shimabukuro, D. et al. Prediction of sepsis in the intensive care unit with minimal electronic health record data: A machine learning approach. *JMIR Med. Inform.*, 4, 3, e28, 2016.

31. Alharthi, H., Healthcare predictive analytics: An overview with a focus on Saudi Arabia. *J. Infect. Public Health*, 11, 6, 749–756, 2018. Elsevier.

32. What is Healthcare Big Data? Retrieved from https://www.evariant.com/faq/what-is-healthcare-big-data

33. Healthcare Big Data and the Promise of Value-Based Care. Retrieved From https://catalyst.nejm.org/big-data-healthcare/

34. Almeida, J.P., A disruptive Big data approach to leverage the efficiency in management and clinical decision support in a Hospital. *Porto Biomed. J.*, 1, 1, 40–42, 2016.

35. Fossaceca, J.M. and Young, S.H., Artificial intelligence and machine learning for future army applications, in: *Ground/Air Multisensor Interoperability, Integration, and Networking for Persistent ISR IX*, vol. 10635, p. 1063507, International Society for Optics and Photonics, 2018.
36. Banking. Retrieved from https://www.fico.com/en/industries/banking
37. Chouiekh, A. and EL Haj, EL Hassane Ibn, Convnets for fraud detection analysis, in: *Procedia Computer Science*, vol. 127, pp. 133–138, 2018.
38. Morten, K., Biro, M., Messnarz, R., Johansen, J., Vohwinkel, D., Nevalainen, R., Schweigert, T., The SPI manifesto and the ECQA SPI manager certification scheme. *J. Softw-Evol.* Proc., 24, 5, 525–540, 2012.
39. Chena, H. and Xianga, Y., The Study of Credit Scoring Model Based on Group Lasso. *Inf. Technol. Quant. Manage. (ITQM), Procedia Comput. Sci.*, 122, 677–684, 2017. Elsevier.
40. Sun, N., Morris, J.G., Xu, J., Zhu, X., Xie, M., iCARE: A framework for big data-based banking customer analytics. *IBM J. Res. Dev.*, 58, 5/6, 4:1–4:9, 2014.
41. Zhao, J., Xie, X., Xu, X., Sun, S. Multi-view learning overview: Recent progress and new challenges. *Inform. Fusion*, 38, 43–54, 2017.
42. Kumar, K.S., Tamilselvan, S., Sha, B.I., Harish, S., Artificial Intelligence Powered Banking Chatbot. *Int. J. Eng. Sci. Comput.*, 16134–16137, 2018.
43. Artificial Intelligence for Banking, Insurance and Financial Services. Retrieved fromhttps://automationedge.com/artificial-intelligence-for-banking-insurance-and-financial-services/
44. Machine Learning in Transportation. https://www.hindawi.com/journals/jat/si/492310/cfp/
45. Neilson, A., Indratmo, B.D., Tjandra, S., Systematic Review of the Literature on Big Data in the Transportation Domain: Concepts and Applications. *Big Data Res.*, 17, 35–44, 2019. Elsevier.
46. Road Safety Facts. Retrieved from https://www.asirt.org/safe-travel/road-safety-facts/
47. Chan, M., *Global status report on road safety*, Technical Report, pp. 1–318, WHO Library Cataloguing, 2013.
48. Das, S.K., Chen, S., Deasy, J.O., Zhou, S., Yin, F.F., Marks, L.B., Decision fusion of machine learning models to predict radiotherapy-induced lung pneumonitis, in: *Seventh International Conference on Machine Learning and Applications*, pp. 545–550, IEEE, 2008.
49. Zhang, R., Ishikawa, A., Wang, W., Striner, B., Tonguz, O., Using Reinforcement Learning With Partial Vehicle Detection for Intelligent Traffic Signal Control, in: *IEEE Transactions on Intelligent Transportation Systems*, pp. 1–12, 2020.
50. Li, A., Jiang, H., Zhou, J., Zhou, X., Learning Human-Like Trajectory Planning on Urban Two-Lane Curved Roads From Experienced Drivers. *IEEE Access*, 7, 65828–65838, 2019.
51. Park, B., Kang, R., Eady, M., Deep Learning Methods for Classifying Shiga Toxin-producing E. coli with Hyperspectral Microscope Images. Annual Meeting. *IAFP*, 2019.

52. Iqbal, M., *Uber Revenue and Usage Statistics 2018*, Policy Research Project Report, pp. 1–15, 2019.

53. Sachapara, V., Shinde, H., Puri, A., Aggrawal, S., Wandre, Prof. S, Big Data Analytics on Cab DataSet Using Hadoop. *Int. J.Adv. Res. Comput. Commun. Eng. (IJARCCE)*, 7, 5, 281–284, 2018.

54. Yuan, Z., Zhou, X., Yang, T., Tamerius, J., Mantilla, R. Predicting traffic accidents through heterogeneous urban data: A case study, in: *Proceedings of the 6th International Workshop on Urban Computing*, Halifax, NS, Canada, vol. 14, 2017.

55. Pan, Y., Zhang, X., Cervone, G., Yang, L., Detection of Asphalt Pavement Potholes and Cracks Based on the Unmanned Aerial Vehicle Multispectral Imagery. *IEEE J. Sel. Top. Appl. Earth Obs. Remote Sens.*, 11, 10, 3701–3712, 2018, 2018.

56. Gold, M., Mcclarren, R., Gaughan, C., The Lessons Oscar Taught Us: Data Science and Media & Entertainment, in: *Big Data*, 1, 2, 105–109, 2013.

57. Alexander, H.D., Mack, M.C., Scott Goetz, M.M., Loranty, P.SA., Earl, K., Nucleation-driven regeneration promotes post-fire recovery in a Chilean. *Plant Ecol.*, 214, 5, 76–776, 2013.

58. Mcalone, N., Why Netflix thinks its personalized recommendation engine is worth $1 billion per year, https://www.businessinsider.in, 2016.

59. Maley, M., Video Games and Esports: *The Growing World of Gamers*. Greenhaven Publishing LLC, 2019.

60. Priye, A., Wong, S., Bi, Y., Carpio, M., Chang, J., Coen, M., Cope D. et al. Lab-on-a-drone: Toward pinpoint deployment of smartphone-enabled nucleic acid-based diagnostics for mobile health care. *Anal. Chem.*, 88, 9, 4651–4660, 2016.

61. Hayes, J., and Danezis, G., Machine learning as an adversarial service: Learning black-box adversarial examples. arXiv preprint arXiv:1708.05207, 2, 2017.

62. Purcărea, T., CMOs at the confluence of AI, CX, and Growth, pp. 1–12, 2018.

63. D'Amico, B., Myers, R.J., Sykes, J., Voss, E., Cousins-Jenvey, B., Fawcett, W., Richardson, S., Kermani, A., Pomponi, F., Machine learning for sustainable structures: A call for data, in: *Structures*, vol. 19, pp. 1-4, Elsevier, 2019.

64. Stanley, R.J., Stoecker, W.V., Moss, R.H., A relative color approach to color discrimination for malignant melanoma detection in dermoscopy images. *Skin Res. Technol.*, 13, 1, 62–72, 2007.

65. Trost, S.G., Zheng, Y., Wong, W.K., Machine learning for activity recognition: hip versus wrist data. *Physiol. Meas.*, 35, 11, 2183, 2014.

66. Georgiopoulos, M., DeMara, R.F., Gonzalez, A.J., Wu, A.S., Mollaghasemi, M., Gelenbe, E., Alnsour, A.J., A sustainable model for integrating current topics in machine learning research into the undergraduate curriculum. *IEEE T. Educ.*, 52, 4, 503–512, 2009.

67. Williamson, B, Digital education governance: Data visualization, predictive analytics, and 'real-time' policy instruments. *J. Educ. Policy*, 31, 2, 123–141, 2016.

68. Kotsiantis, S., Pierrakeas, C., Pintelas, P., Predicting Students' Performance in Distance Learning Using Machine Learning Techniques. *Appl. Artif. Intell.*, 5, 411–426, 2010.

69. Gabriel, F., Signolet, J., Westwell, M., A machine learning approach to investigating the effects ofmathematics dispositions on mathematical literacy. *Int. J. Res. Method Educ.*, 41, 3, 306–327, March 22, 2017.

70. Joshi, N. and Kadhiwala, B., Big data security and privacy issues—A survey, in: *Innovations in Power and Advanced Computing Technologies*, pp. 1–5, IEEE, 2017.

71. Wu, J.Y., Hsiao, Y.C., Nian, M.W., Using supervised machine learning on large-scale online forumsto classify course-related Facebook messages in predictinglearning achievement within the personal learning environment. *Interact. Learn. Environ.*, 28, 1, 65–80, 2020.

72. Anurag. How is Education Technology evolving with Time. https://www.newgenapps.com/blog/how-is-education-technology-evolving-with-time

73. Klein, D.J., McKown, M.W., Tershy, B.R., Deep Learning for Large Scale Biodiversity Monitoring. *Bloomberg Data for Good Exchange Conference*, September 28, 2015.

74. Padgalskas, V., How to Protect the Ecosystem. Retrieved from https://www.hunker.com/12221148/how-to-protect-the-ecosystem.

75. Why Ecosystem Conservation is so Important. Retrieved from https://www.greenlivinganswers.com/archives/175

76. Kampichler, C., Wieland, R., Calmé, S., Weissenberger, H., Arriaga-Weiss, S., Classification in conservation biology: A comparison of five machine-learning methods. *Ecol. Inf.*, 5, 441–450, 2010. Elsevier.

77. Bland, L.M., Collen, B., Orme, C.D.L., Bielby, J., Predicting the conservation status of data-deficient. *Conserv. Biol.*, 29, 1, 250–259, 2014.

78. Willcock, S., Martínez-López, J., Hooftman, D.A.P., Bagstad, K.J., Balbi, S., Marzo, A., Prato, C., Sciandrello, S., Signorello, G., Voigt, B., Villa, F., Bullock, J.M., Athanasiadis, I.N., Machine learning for ecosystem services. *Ecosyst. Serv.*, 33, 165–174, 2018. Elsevier.

79. Shiferaw, H., Bewket, W., Eckert, S., Performances of machine learning algorithms for mapping fractional cover of an invasive plant species in a dryland ecosystem. *Ecol. Evol.*, 9, 5, 2562–2574, 2019. Wiley.

80. Jia, Z., Zhan, J., Wang, L., Han, R., McKee, S.A., Yang, Q., Li, J. Characterizing and subsetting big data workloads, in: *International Symposium on Workload Characterization*, pp. 191–201, IEEE, 2014.

81. McKinnon, M.C., Mascia, M.B., Yang, W., Turner, W.R., Bonham, C., Impact evaluation to communicate and improve conservation non-governmental organization performance: The case of Conservation International. *Philos. T. R. Soc. B*, 370, 1681, 2015.

82. Wuest, T., Irgens, C., Thoben, K.D., An approach to monitoring quality in manufacturing using supervised machine learning on product state data. *J. Intell. Manuf.*, 25, 5, 1167–1180, 2013.

83. Namdari, M., Jazayeri-Rad, H., Hashemi, S.J., Process Fault Diagnosis Using Support Vector Machines with a Genetic Algorithm based Parameter Tuning. *J. Autom Control*, 2, 1, 1–7, 2014.

84. Hansson, K., Yella, S., Dougherty, M., Fleyeh, H., Machine Learning Algorithms in Heavy Process Manufacturing. *Am. J. Intell. Syst.*, 6, 1, 1–13, 2016.

85. Tao, F., Cheng, J., Qi, Q., Zhang, M., Zhang, H., Sui, F., Digital twin-driven product design, manufacturing and servicewith big data. *Int. J. Adv. Manuf. Technol.*, 2017. Springer.

86. Finnegan, M., Boeing 787s to create half a terabyte of data per flight, says Virgin Atlantic, 2013. https://www.computerworld.com/article/3417915/boeing-787s-to-create-half-a-terabyte-of-data-per-flight–says-virgin-atlantic.html.

87. Badea, V.E., Zamfiroiu, A., Boncea, R., Big Data in the Aerospace Industry. *Inf. Econ.*, 22, 1, 17–24, 2018.

88. Allouche, G., (n.d.). The Impact of Big Data on the Food Industry. Retrieved from https://datafloq.com/read/big-datas-impact-food-industry/96.

89. Farr, C., IBM uses 'big data' tech to keep track of your meatballs, 2013. https://venturebeat.com/2013/03/01/ibm-brings-big-data-tech-to-food-to-prevent-the-next-horse-meat scandal/?utm_source=datafloq&utm_medium=ref&utm_campaign=datafloq.

90. Bobriakov, I., Top 8 Data Science Use Cases in Manufacturing, 2019. Retrieved from https://medium.com/activewizards-machine-learning-company/top-8-data-science-use-cases-in-manufacturing-749256b8f1ee.

91. Datta, K., Big data potential to eradicate challenges in the manufacturing industry, November 13, 2108. Retrieved from https://www.capgemini.com/2018/11/big-data-potential-to-eradicate-challenges-in-the-manufacturing-industry/.

92. Liakos, K.G., Busato, P., Moshou, D., Pearson, S., Bochtis, D., Machine Learning in Agriculture: A Review. *Sensors, MDPI*, 18, 8, 2674, 2018.

93. Majumdar, J., Naraseeyappa, S., Ankalaki, S., Analysis of agriculture data using datamining techniques: application of big data. *J. Big Data*, 4, 1, 1–15, 2017. Springer.

94. Nguyen, V.Q., Nguyen, S.N., Kim, K., Design of a Platform for Collecting and Analyzing Agricultural Big Data. *J. Digital Contents Soc.*, 18, 1, 149–158, February 2017.

95. Rao, N.H. and Rao, K.L., Big Data and Climate Smart Agriculture - Status and Implications for Agricultural Research and Innovation in India. *Proc. Indian Natl. Sci. Acad.*, 83, 3, 625–640, February 13, 2018.

96. Yang, X. and Guo, T., Machine learning in plant disease research. *Eur. J. BioMed. Res.*, 3, 1, 6–9, March 31, 2017.

97. Singh, A., Ganapathysubramanian, B., Singh, A.K., Sarkar, S., Machine Learning for High-Throughput Stress Phenotyping in Plants. *Trends Plant Sci.*, 21, 2, 110–124, February 2016.

98. Kumar, R., Singh, M.P., Kumar, P., Singh, J.P., Crop Selection Method to Maximize Crop Yield Rate using Machine Learning Technique. *International*

Conference on Smart Technologies and Management for Computing, Communication, Controls, Energy and Materials (ICSTM), Chennai, T.N., India, May 6–8, pp. 138–145, 2015.

99. Walsh, T., Evatt, A., de Witt, C.S., Artificial Intelligence & Climate Change: Supplementary Impact Report, 2020.

100. Schlam, T.R., and Baker, T.B., Playing Around with Quitting Smoking: A Randomized Pilot Trial of Mobile Games as a Craving Response Strategy. *Games Health J.*, 9, 1, 64–70, 2020.

101. Tantalaki, N., Souravlas, S., Roumeliotis, M., Data-Driven Decision Making in Precision Agriculture: The Rise of Big Data in Agricultural Systems. *J. Arg. Food Inform.*, 20, 4, 344–380, 2019.

102. Jin, X., Wah, B.W., Cheng, X., Wang, Y., Significance and Challenges of Big Data Research. *Big Data Res.*, 2, 2, 59–64, June, 2015. Elsevier.

103. Ghosh, K. and Nath, A., Big Data: Security Issues, Challenges and Future Scope. *International Journal of Research Studies in Computer Science and Engineering*, 3, 3, 1–9, 2016.

104. Khan, N., Yaqoob, I., Abaker T Hashem, I., Inayat, Z., Ali, W.K.M., Alam, M., Shiraz, M., Gani, A., Big Data: Survey, Technologies, Opportunities, and Challenges. *Sci. World J.*, 2014, 1–18, 2014. Hindawi.

105. Jordan, M.I. and Mitchell, T.M., Machine learning: Trends, perspectives, and prospects. *Science*, 349, 6245, 255–260, 2015.

106. Brownlee, J., *Overfitting and UnderfittingWith Machine Learning Algorithms*, Machine Learning Mastery, 21, 2016.

107. Shiva S.R., *Traffic Control Using Machine Learning*, MIT Report, 2017.

108. Willcock, S., Martínez-López, J., Hooftman, D.AP., Bagstad, K.J., Balbi, S., Marzo, A., Prato, C. *et al.*, Machine learning for ecosystem services. *Ecosyst. Serv.*, 33, 165–174, 2018.

Section 4

MACHINE LEARNING'S NEXT FRONTIER

13

Transfer Learning

Riyanshi Gupta[1], Kartik Krishna Bhardwaj[1] and Deepak Kumar Sharma[2*]

[1]Department of Instrumentation and Control, Netaji Subhas University of Technology (formerly Netaji Subhas Institute of Technology), New Delhi, India
[2]Department of Information Technology, Netaji Subhas University of Technology (formerly Netaji Subhas Institute of Technology), New Delhi, India

Abstract

A rapid surge in applicative implementation of machine learning and artificial intelligence has been experienced in recent times. This has lead to a need for improvement in performance as well as resolution of commonly encountered obstacles in the learning paradigms. One such major obstacle faced in the learning and intelligence frameworks is the need for a data collection by an intelligent model to learn the assigned task. The resolution of task learning hurdles has motivated many new schemes in the learning paradigms for intelligent systems. The independence of learning from a prescribed learning data has long been coveted and worked toward, leading to the coinage of reinforcement learning. The idea behind reinforcement learning is inspired by the dynamic learning capacity of the human brain while performing various tasks. This idea is further extended toward learning through a different inference medium, similar in data to be inferred or the inferential model. The capacity of the human brain to use the knowledge gained during a previous task so as to learn to perform a new task, where the previous task had a similar input basis or was similar in the nature of inferenced output to the current task. The emulation of such an ideology lead to conceiving of transfer learning. In this chapter, we shall explore the theoretical principle, functionalities, methodologies, and applications of transfer learning, as well as its relationship with deep learning paradigms.

Keywords: Reinforcement learning, inductive transfer, transducive transfer, domain confusion, multitask learning, natural language processing, computer vision

*Corresponding author: dk.sharma1982@yahoo.com

Uma N. Dulhare, Khaleel Ahmad and Khairol Amali Bin Ahmad (eds.) Machine Learning and Big Data: Concepts, Algorithms, Tools and Applications, (337–360) © 2020 Scrivener Publishing LLC

13.1   Introduction

13.1.1   Motivation, Definition, and Representation

The contemporary world has seen a surge in machine learning and artificial intelligence-based applications, with their implementations affecting various fields. A significant amount of efficiency in the machine learning paradigm applications has been reached with successful employment of the same for applications ranging from healthcare-based problems to simple mail sorting programs. However, for a real time application, there is a huge scope of improvement in terms of efficiency, speed of perception, and data dependability of inference. The scalability of such paradigms is also an aspect that needs plenty of attention and improvement. The cost of building such systems due to the infrastructure involved for processing as well as data collection efforts also have the scope of revision.

Such a case presented in front of the data processing and machine learning community as a challenge resulted in the idea of transfer of knowledge from one model to another, given the similarity basis presented between them. This principle of transferring knowledge between similar perception paradigms, which came to be known as transfer learning, is based on the idea that two problems shall have a similar input or output basis which shall allow one model to emulate the ability to map between the input and output from another given the analogical relation between the two perception schemes.

To understand the transfer learning methodology, we shall take an example of learning the balancing of a bike. If the rider of a motorbike has the knowledge of riding and balancing a cycle, he may not need to learn the art of balancing a motorbike from scratch. Instead, he shall be able to emulate his experience and knowledge of riding a cycle, which is a different task than that on hand, using it as the starting point for the learning process for balancing a bike.

We shall learn more about transfer learning in the upcoming sections, covering the functionality, methodology, categories, relation with deep learning and applications that transfer learning may serve.

13.2   Traditional Learning vs. Transfer Learning

Traditional learning is a model-specific approach and works for definite tasks and data sets. The approach is used for the purpose of training independent exclusive models on those specific data sets. Here, no retention of knowledge for further use occurs. This means that the previously learned knowledge is never considered while the learning is performed on some other task. On the contrary, transfer learning enables us to retain knowledge from the previously trained models which could then be used for training other newer models having a slight similarity with the previous ones [1]. Hence, in the case of transfer learning, learning of a new task is dependent on the earlier learned tasks. This approach makes the learning or training process faster with a higher degree of accuracy, and also averts the requirement of a large-sized training dataset. Transfer learning works well with a smaller training data, thereby accelerating results. This is illustrated in Figure 13.1.

Let us understand the above-mentioned concept with the help of an example. In the traditional supervised learning scheme of machine learning, if we wish to identify objects in images, we assume that the labeled dataset for this task is given to us. We then train our model for this task and domain, say A, so that it can perform well on any unseen data from this domain A. Now, if we are given some other task or domain B, we again use the labeled data of this task or domain to train another model B and tune it to perform well on any data from this task and domain which can be seen in Figure 13.2. Given the model-specific approach of the traditional learning,

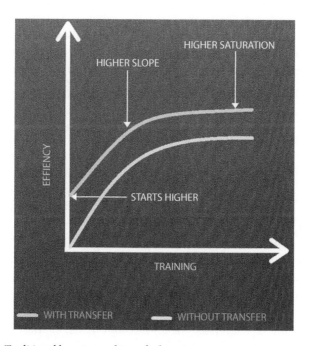

Figure 13.1 Traditional learning and transfer learning.

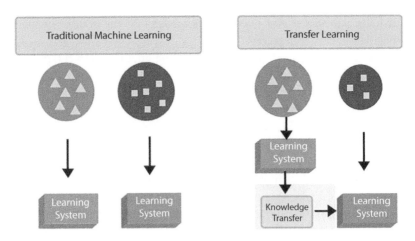

Figure 13.2 Traditional learning vs transfer learning.

this approach fails when the sufficient labeled data is not provided for the desired task in the given domain. Transfer learning helps us overcome this issue by reusing the existing data of some similar task or domain. This data can be stored as knowledge acquired from the source task or domain which could then be transferred to the target task or domain for learning or training purposes. This approach is also called as domain adaptation. In the above example, if the data provided for task A is more, we can train the model A and then use its learning for task B. Hence, transfer learning let us transfer the already existing knowledge from the source setting to act as a secondary input in a new target task setting.

13.3   Key Takeaways: Functionality

As an introduction to some of the common terms pertaining to the input and output functions of learning paradigms, we shall explore about the same and understand the functionality of transfer learning pertaining to these notations as introduced.

The basic requisite to describe any learning paradigm is the "domain" that it works on, which can be described as the input data that it shall learn from so as to get the know how of problem solving, and the "task" that it works toward, which is the application of the gained knowledge during the learning stage.

The domain is comprised of two components, namely, the "feature space" and the "marginal probability distribution". These two components define the model used for the perception and inference of the domain and hence carrying out the task as assigned. These two factors differentiate the domain space. For such differentiation, either there will be a difference in the feature spaces pertaining to the two domains or a difference in the marginal probability distributions for the two domains [2].

The feature space consists of various vectorized values of the learning samples. It represents the various parameters that can be used to describe an entity. They are a set of input entity properties that shall be employed toward solving a particular task. For understanding, take the example of description of a circle. A circle can be represented in form of the coordinates to its center and the measure of its radius. Here, two features are sufficient to represent a circle; however, more features like any three points on the circumference can be used to better describe it.

The marginal probability distribution is defined as the distribution of the data points pertaining to a particular feature constrained to a given subset of allowed (or chosen) values. In a simplified language, it is the probability description of feature vectors across different values allowed in the domain space which are independent of respective value set of other feature vectors.

A task is the problem assigned to the perception model. The function of the model then is to learn the solving methodology for the given task. This is done by learning the mapping criterion for the achievement of the task between the input feature values and the task output corresponding to a given input through the sample provided for learning [3].

Transfer learning uses the above described parameters for its functioning. In this description of learning parameters, the functionality of transfer learning shall be described as follows:

For the transfer of knowledge, given the source domain and learning task for the source, the target domain and target learning task shall aim toward the improvement of the predictability of target perception through imitation of methodology of gaining knowledge and emulation of knowledge gained by the source perceptor.

We shall learn more about how the learning between the domains occurs through the different methodologies applied for the same described in the next section.

13.4 Transfer Learning Methodologies

In the previous section, we have learnt some terminologies that pertain to the functionality of transfer learning paradigm. Given the importance of

TRANSFER LEARNING METHODOLOGIES

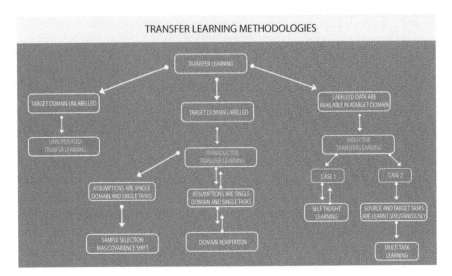

Figure 13.3 Summarization to the transfer learning methodologies.

domain, task at hand and data availability, the transfer learning methodologies can be differentiated into various categories on the basis of these parameters. On the basis of these parameters, the transfer learning methodologies can be categorized as [4]:

- Inductive Transfer learning
- Unsupervised Transfer Learning
- Transductive Transfer Learning

These paradigms are explained in detail in the upcoming sections, with a summarization to understand the categorization given in Figure 13.3.

13.5   Inductive Transfer Learning

The importance of recognition of similarity in the tasks that are carried out by the source as well as the target operatives and their respective domain of feature collective that they operate in has been exemplified in the previous sections. The basis of the methodology to be adopted to transfer the knowledge from one paradigm operative to another as well as the components that shall be chosen for successful transfer, and henceforth, a positive outcome on the target task. Here, we shall be dealing with the case of transfer where we shall find similarity in domain space while performing different tasks, though somewhat related due to the relation of functional domain of feature space.

The transfer of learning paradigm from one operative to another, that operate on a similar domain space, but are designed to perform tasks that are different from each other's perspective of utilization and inference of the said domain data, is known inductive transfer of knowledge.

So, the implementation of inductive transfer learning deals with a scenario where the functional domain shall be shared by the two operatives: the source and the transfer operatives, respectively. Here, we shall have a defined and labeled functional domain of feature space for the target operative. Hence, our aim in such a scenario is to relate the target domain with its predictive model values, mapping the functional predictive output with the corresponding operative input. The labeling of data in the source domain and its relational schema with the prediction model applied by the source operative shall be emulated by the target operative's predictive relational model, using the structure of the relational schema between input and output of source's prediction operative to its own advantage.

Given the importance of the labeling of source domain, inductive transfer learning is categorized, on the basis of availability of labels for source operative's domain, into two implementational variants. The variants are described below with their operational summarization [5]:

- In the first variant, along with a labeled target domain, a well-documented *labeling for source domain is available* too. In such a scenario, transfer of knowledge from source operative to the target and shaping of target's inferential/predictive mapping is quite straightforward, closely following the crude explanation of knowledge transfer as followed in inductive transfer paradigm as discussed before. Here, emulating the relational mapping between the domain feature space and the predictive paradigm's resulting inference for the source operative, the target operative learns the utilization of the common feature space toward building the inference scheme for task learning, so as to accomplish a better performance toward the designated target task. Such a scheme is very similar to multitasking of learning paradigm, where multiple tasks are designated to the same domain of feature space. The subtle difference between multitask learning and inductive transfer learning with labeled source domain is that, in the former, both the tasks and the learning process for their operations take place simultaneously, whereas, in the latter, a different task is attempted using the knowledge gained during the learning of a previously performed task, on a common domain of feature space.

- In the second variant, *data labeling is either not available or is inadequate for the source domain.* Such a scenario might occur either due to source domain being unlabeled, providing no example set for the target domain, or due to labeling of feature space being differently referred in the two domains. This form of inductive transfer works a bit differently than the above described methods. Here, given the labeled target domain, though with a rather unusable source domain, we are not left with much context for usability of source knowledge in the target task. Hence, the direct application of source domain is not possible in a traditional fashion as discussed before. This absence in transferable context is dealt in a manner of self-teaching methodology. Here, just like in a self-taught learning environment, we shall find contextual argument for source domain in an unsupervised mannerism for its own tasks, search for its feature labels through this self-learning paradigm, and then find a transferable feature set as well as the methodology for relation of the already labeled target domain with the prediction mechanism for the target task, emulating the source task relation with the acquired labels in the first step. For a simpler understanding, it can be seen as a two step process, where first the source task is achieved through self-learning, marking the source domain labels in the process. This establishes a feature data labeling schema in relation to the corresponding inferences made toward the source task. This knowledge and relational mapping obtained through the iterations for source task then shall be extended to the target task operations, improving its performances. Such implementations often see simultaneous executions of source and target tasks, leading to a more dynamic approach toward knowledge transfer as compared to the first case of inductive transfer mechanism.

13.6   Unsupervised Transfer Learning

The unsupervised transfer learning closely follows up and is very similar in procedural details to the inductive transfer learning model. The functionality of this scheme is similar to the unlabeled source domain case of the inductive transfer of neural knowledge.

The variation in such a scenario from the typical unlabeled source domain case of inductive learning arises with the difference in the target domain of feature space of the two learning paradigms, with the unsupervised knowledge transfer operations using an unlabeled target domain in contrast to a well-labeled target domain of inductive learning scenario [6]. This variation changes the dynamic of the application of unsupervised transfer learning from the regression performance improvement of the target task by emulation of functionality of the source task mechanism to operations pertaining to feature selection and isolation and associating of source feature set with the task domain.

Given the change in the application of transfer learning in this scenario, the perception of transfer of knowledge from the source to the target changes in respect of what needs to be transferred. Given that neither the source nor the target domain is labeled, the transfer of knowledge of task perception or input to output mapping and inference is not practical. Rather than this, just as in inductive transfer with unlabeled source domain, functionality toward the accomplishment of the source task is emulated by the target operative, using the knowledge of features in the domain that weigh more than the others toward accomplishment of a given task [7]. This is achieved by completing the source task through unsupervised learning methods. The features involved in achieving the task and the labeling procedure undergone by them is then emulated by the target operative for induction of processing capabilities borrowed from the source so as to carry out the target task.

The above is implemented as a two step process. Firstly, through unsupervised learning scheme, the learning task for the source operative is undergone, where it uses the features to carry out the assigned task without usage of data labels. Such an optimization problem solving is based on intuition-based cluster generation and testing, following which the assignment of labels to the said cluster members is given. This forms the basis of solution of the source optimization problem.

Following this, once features for source operative are labeled and mapped, the target feature domain learns from the source feature space, using a vector basis as an emulation standard, so as to transfer the source domain knowledge that is beneficial for the source task.

Finally, discriminatory paradigms are applied on the obtained domain knowledge basis, finding corresponding feature space in target domain, which shall use such discriminatory paradigms for training assistance, forging the classification or regression model that the target operative task demands for solution to the optimization assignment that pertains to the said task.

13.7 Transductive Transfer Learning

We have earlier discussed the importance of finding the similarity in the setting that the two operatives (the one from which knowledge is transferred and the other which receives and applies it) function in for the establishment of a relationship between the two operations, and hence confirming the knowledge that needs to be transferred and the way in which it needs to be transferred.

Such a similarity shall be found either in the task assigned to the source and target operatives respectively or the operation domain that the operatives shall apply for toward the solution of the said assigned tasks.

So far, we have seen the similarity in the domains and background of the assigned problems in form of supervised and unsupervised transfer learning paradigms. In such cases, a common (or similar) domain space is shared between the target and the source operatives; however, their application is performed on a varied set of tasks [8]. The transductive transfer learning introduces the scenario where a similarity between the source and domain tasks is established. Though the task is similar in nature, the respective domain data that is operated upon to reach the solution to the assigned task differ. In the transductive transfer learning, the general case that is dealt with is that where a well-labeled source domain setting is emulated for the target task by the target domain space, which is either largely unlabeled or is completely untrained.

The transfer of learning paradigm from one operative to another, that operate on different domains space space, however, they function to perform a similar task, differing in the inference of their respective domain data, with contrasting functionality and perspective of problem solving for achievement of the goal pertaining to the task assigned, is known as transductive transfer of knowledge.

As can be intuitively inferred, the transductive transfer of knowledge focuses on the emulation of the source domain feature space variability and the probabilistic distribution of data across different domain groups for the target domain categorization and assistance in task functionality to an unlabeled target domain. Hence, this makes the marginal probability distribution and feature space important factors in the scheme. The different situations that arise from the variations pertaining to the above two factors, the categorization of transductive transfer learning can be done into two classes of operative settings, elucidated as follows [9]:

- In the first case, we observe a difference in source and target domains in terms of *feature spaces pertaining to the two domains being unrelated* in absolute sense. Such a situation requires domain basis sampling for risk minimization to find the common transfer basis.
- In the second case, a common feature space between the source and target domain is shared; however, the difference in domains is incurred due to the *difference in marginal probability distribution*. Such a setting demands a domain adaptation through distribution normalization, with a similar assumption basis.

13.8   Categories in Transfer Learning

With the understanding of the three methodologies of transfer learning as discussed above, we shall now expand this knowledge to study in detail the approaches to transfer learning under these categories. The above-mentioned settings bring about four possible cases based on "What to transfer" which are briefly discussed in Table 13.1 [10].

As we have seen the relationship between the four approaches of transfer learning and what to transfer, we'll now be explaining the concept behind these approaches in this section.

Table 13.1 Approaches to transfer learning.

Transfer learning approaches	Description
Instance transfer	Re-weighting some labelled instances in a source domain to use in the target domain
Feature-representation transfer	Finding an alternate feature space to bring down the error rate and reduce differences between a source and a target domain
Parameter transfer	Identify shared parameters or priors (hyperparameters) of models between a source and a target domain
Relational-knowledge transfer	Discovering relationship between a source domain data and a target domain data

13.9   Instance Transfer

In an ideal case, transfer learning aims at reusing knowledge from pre-trained models of a source domain for the tasks of a target domain. However, it is not always possible to make use of the data of the source domain directly. Rather, those particular instances of the data in the source domain which are observed to be similar to the target domain, as shown in Figure 13.4, can be reused for learning by re-weighting. These instances, when used along with a few labeled target data, improvise the results in target domain and hence provide better accuracy. An approach working on such a principle is referred to as instance-based transfer learning.

The given approach tries to improve the marginal distribution differences by reweighting the instances in the source domain itself. It then uses these reweighted instances directly in the target domain for training purposes. This enables the target learner to use only relevant information among domain source samples. The approach is most suitable for the cases where both the domains (source and target) have the same conditional distribution.

Instance transfer approach comprises of two major techniques: *instance reweighting* and *importance sampling* [11]. There are various weighting strategies supported by the instance-based transfer approach. One method is to differentiate source domain instances from target domain instances by training a binary classifier and then using it to assess the weights of the source instances. This particular method prioritizes those instances of the source domain which are similar to the target domain and hence give them higher weight. Another simple yet effective instance-based approach to reweight the source instances is to look for the weight that equals the mean of the source and target domains. This approach of instance-transfer is implemented in inductive transfer learning and transductive transfer learning settings.

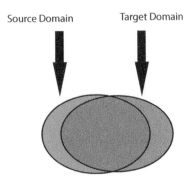

Figure 13.4 Source domain and target domain have a lot in common.

13.10   Feature Representation Transfer

The approach of feature-representation transfer of machine learning focuses on bringing down the error estimates by finding an alternate feature space which could be employed in the target domain for learning purposes while the source domain is protruded in the new space. The basic concept behind this approach is to learn or identify a good feature representation for the target domain. Here, the knowledge is encoded into the learned representation, which is then transferred from the source domain to the target domain. The new feature representation results in the minimization of domain disparity and the improvised performance of the target task.

Feature-representation transfer approach incorporates certain operations like feature subset selection and feature space transformation. The given approach can be applied in supervised or unsupervised methods, as per the availability of labeled data. In case of the large availability of the labeled data in the source domain, a feature representation is constructed by employing the supervised methods of machine learning. On the other hand, unsupervised learning methods are used when there is an absence of the labeled data. Identifying invariant features between the two datasets is crucial in this case. Once identified, the source and target domain are brought down to the same distribution, thereby making it possible to apply the supervised methods of learning [12].

In the inductive transfer learning setting, supervised feature construction is based on the idea of learning the low-dimensional representation which is transferred across similar tasks, whereas unsupervised feature construction involves the learning of higher level features for transfer learning. Unsupervised transfer learning, on the other hand, employs self-taught clustering and transferred discriminative analysis algorithm in order to construct a feature representation.

13.11   Parameter Transfer

The underlying hypothesis for this approach is that the models for similar tasks have some parameters or prior distribution of hyperparameters in common. The knowledge to be transferred is encoded into the shared parameters or priors. Thus, identification of the shared parameters or priors conditions the transfer of knowledge from the source to the target task [13] This has been depicted in Figure 13.5.

As discussed above, parameter transfer approach works on the utilization of certain model components like parameters and hyperparameters

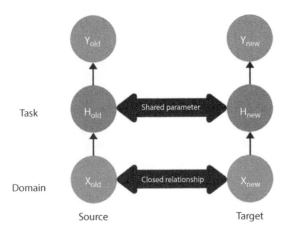

Task

Domain

Source   Target

Figure 13.5 Parameter transfer in transfer learning.

to prevail the learning or training of the target task. The approach involves operations like parameter-space partitioning and superimposing shape constraints. This approach requires substantially large number of samples so as to learn a suitable parameter accurately, thereby employing unsupervised methods for the learning purpose. For these reasons, it is preferable to use unlabeled samples in the source domain.

This approach of sharing weights or parameters finds a major use in deep learning models. Broadly speaking, deep learning models allow the sharing of weights in two ways: *soft weight sharing*, and *hard weight sharing* [14]. In soft weight sharing, the weights are supposed to have similar values. In hard weight sharing, there is a constraint of equal weights to be shared across different models.

13.12   Relational Knowledge Transfer

Unlike the previously discussed approaches, the approach of relational knowledge transfer tries to work with the data which is not independent and identically distributed (non-IID data). The approach thus handles relational domains in the process of transfer learning. This approach works on the assumption that there exist some relationships among the source domain data and the target domain data. Consequently, the knowledge from the source domain is transferred to the target domain via the relationship among the data. The approach majorly uses statistical relational learning techniques to deal with such cases.

Table 13.2 Transfer learning strategies and types of transferable components.

	Inductive transfer learning	Transducive transfer learning	Unsupervised transfer learning
Instance transfer	Yes	Yes	No
Feature representation transfer	Yes	Yes	Yes
Parameter transfer	Yes	No	No
Relational knowlege transfer	Yes	No	No

This approach can only be used in inductive learning setting of machine learning. One way to implement relational knowledge transfer in inductive learning setting is to use an algorithm called TAMAR. The algorithm uses Markov Logic Networks (MLNs) to transfer relational knowledge across relational domains. Table 13.2 gives the relationship between different transfer learning strategies and transferable components. This shall help us in understanding how transfer learning is applied in the context of deep learning.

13.13   Relationship With Deep Learning

13.13.1   Transfer Learning in Deep Learning

Deep learning can be defined as a category of machine learning algorithms that shall work on the principle of functionality of the human brain in while obtaining a set of skills and knowledge. Deep learning can be thought of as the procedural automation of predictive analysis. It follows a hierarchical stack of algorithms sorted in the order of increasing ramification and abstraction.

The working of deep learning is similar to child exploring a new concept. The input is crunched through set of algorithms, applied in a hierarchically defined order, with each applying a non-linear transformation on the said input, using its knowledge gained in the process to conceive a statistical model as an output. A threshold level of accuracy must be reached, until which the above procedure shall be iterated through repeatedly.

Deep learning functions on a relational assumption basis, with the assumption faction being known as inductive bias. These assumptions are based on and are influenced by the distribution of training data. In turn, these biases tend to guide the hypothesis space toward model generation.

This scheme is simplified by the introduction of transfer learning paradigm to deep learning settings. The proposition of borrowing knowledge from a pre-trained model with a similar domain or task instead of training the deep learning operative is a beneficial implementation.

In such a proposition, the deep learning network, instead of being trained from the bottom-up, adapts itself according to a pre-trained network that has been trained on a different domain or for a variant task. Such an adaption shall then help mould the network for shaping up its own domain as well as performing and optimizing the target task. As it has previously been seen, the two networks, one which is being emulated and the one borrowing the adaptations, are tied together either by a similar domain while performing varying tasks or by a similar task assigned while operating on different domains.

The transfer processes described above often utilize inductive biases as an instrument of transfer of characteristics between models. The inductive biases of the source operative are utilized for the assistance of the target task. This is implementable in the following ways [15]:

- Limit the model feature space by adjustments to the target task's inductive bias using source bias expanse
- Limit the defined hypothesis space by emulation of source hypothesis
- Augment the search process by the utilization of acquired knowledge from the source task

13.13.2   Types of Deep Transfer Learning

The objective of using transfer learning paradigms is reaching a solution to the target task's raised problems and challenges through the usage of knowledge gained through a different operative over a common input or output space that of the presently operated task and that of emulated operative. With advancements being made in transfer learning, many variants of its applications with deep learning paradigms have cropped up. Subsequent sections shall be briefing about the same.

13.13.3   Adaptation of Domain

The domain is defined by two components, feature space and marginal probability, as is discussed before. A set of scenarios may arise where a differing range value for marginal probabilities for the source and target domain spaces respectively. Such a scenario with different source and target domain marginal probabilities is referred to as *domain adaptation*. This is named so due to the difference in marginal probabilities leading to data distribution of the source and target domains respectively experiencing a shift with respect to each other. For the transfer of knowledge to take place, alterations to the respective source and target domains need to be made to adjust the drift in data distribution experienced in the situation [16].

As an example to the scenario, we shall consider a product review application scenario. Such an application might use a classifier with a yes or no based product satisfaction ratio. Another classifier can be used to get the customer sentiment to get a non-discrete type distribution. So as to use the latter classifier as a guideline for the former's task objective achievement, we shall need to make the necessary changes in the latter's domain. Such a scenario shall utilize domain adaptation techniques for successful transfer of knowledge from one operative to another.

13.13.4   Domain Confusion

Deep learning techniques employ a multilayer neural network for its functionality. In such a network, different network layers of the deep learning paradigm are used in an iterative manner to infer the feature space in a distributed way and not as a collective. Given this property of differentiating between features by processing them through different layers, with each layer processing only a specific family of features. This sieve technique of processing allows easy categorization and mapping of features with respective outcomes [17].

The above property of deep learning neural networks is exploited by the transfer learning paradigms toward the improvement of the transferability of knowledge across the feature domains. The transfer of feature representation can be utilized to use the deep learning topology structure for transfer. Given the ease in categorization of features and their relation with the respective output space in a deep learning network, domain constant features can be learnt by the target operative and transfer of feature representations between source and target domains can be done. Such a perspective transfer of representation shall allow the target model to forgo the learning process from scratch. The requirement for this, as mentioned before, is similarity in domains, that shall be achieved by moulding the source representation to be similar to the target domain representation for easier emulation. This is achieved in application through a sequence of pre processing steps that shall be implemented over the domain representations themselves.

The above described scheme associates additional attributes to the source model, influencing the similarity observed between the domains by confusing them, therefore naming it as *domain confusion*.

13.13.5   Multitask Learning

Given the complexity of the neural network that is employed in a deep learning scheme, employment of a multiple perception scheme is a feasible step for such a system, given the multiple abstracted processing layers involved. This property of deep learning network is exploited by the multitask learning.

A common operable domain space can be used to achieve multiple tasks. This shall be done by difference in inference of the feature space and functionality over the domain data. Such a multiple perception scheme that is operable over a common domain, but serves multiple target tasks is known as *multitask learning* [18].

In this scheme of transfer, a common domain is used for learning of several tasks, hence training for different tasks using a common domain space. No differentiation is done on the basis of task specific feature space during the learning of the said model. During the application of such a model, all the trained knowledge acquired is then used and implemented smartly using multi-perception processing of hidden layers of deep learning network.

In contrast to the traditional transfer schemes, where the target task is often not known to the learner, in the multitask learning paradigm, the inference perceptron learns all the tasks irrespective of them being source or target ones and then applies the acquired knowledge from all the learnt tasks as a collective information for achieving the target task with higher efficiency.

13.13.6   One-Shot Learning

The deep learning paradigm requires a large number of examples for training of the operative model. This need for a large training dataset toward building up the model and setting its parameters and defining its weights generates a drawback for the deep learning scheme, creating a trade-off between the high accuracy that the deep learning paradigm provides and the amount of background information about the task and example data pertaining to it that is required for the fulfillment of the given task.

Such a drawback puts the idea for genesis of neural network to a hold, namely, to make machines as intelligent as humans, by closely imitating the human brain functionality. Given the ability of humans to learn even complex task with few examples is a remarkable task that the deep learning paradigm falls behind in, despite closely matching the power perception and accuracy in its functionality to the human brain.

Propositions of processing methods that employ deep learning networks in combination with transfer learning approach have been made that shall be able to make inferences and gain the required knowledge in a few number of training examples. After the research work that introduced this idea, it is known as *one-shot learning* [19].

This paradigm uses labeled data obtained across different tasks that have been learnt to be used for current target task, employed with the help of feature selection from source domain for common feature space between the source and target operatives.

13.13.7 Zero-Shot Learning

As is common knowledge, deep learning employs supervised learning paradigms for obtaining knowledge pertaining to the task at hand. However, given the accuracy that is experienced in the deep learning paradigms, extending the application of deep neural networks to tasks where labeling is absent is an enviable idea that is made viable through transfer learning.

Zero-shot learning paradigm, also known as *zero-data learning* paradigm, is a variant of deep transfer learning scheme that does not engage any labeled examples toward the perception and inference of a task during the training of the perception model.

The working of zero-shot learning depends upon the collection and exploitation of additional information for the inference of new data. The additional data collected pertaining to the standard input is used in conjunction with the knowledge of input-output mapping from a source operative, so as to perceive the conditional probability distribution for the corresponding feature space [20].

13.14 Applications: Allied Classical Problems

The model development approach deals with the case where both the source and the target operatives have not been pre-trained or tested. In such a case, the transfer of knowledge takes place from the learning experience of one model to the task assumption of the other.

Here, we shall have a well-defined input and output data, with a known relationship and an abundance of data at both ends of the model network.

The source task shall be performed, with the source operative model using the input-output relationship as defined in its domain for output perception. Feature-based learning is performed during the process of source task achievement. The source task model is used as the basis for the target model training. The target model hence uses the source model components and parameters for emulating its own domain space, moulding the input-output mapping according to the target domain distribution. This emulated target domain labeling shall be further used toward achieving the target task.

The pre-trained model approach, as its name suggests, deals with the case where a pre-trained source model, with a labeled domain is available, which is then borrowed as the basis of the target task. In such a case, the transfer of knowledge takes place from the defined input and output mapping of one model to the parameter designation for the other model [25].

In the scenario of pre-trained model approach, the choice of the source model is important from the set of available pre-trained models. The chosen source model shall be as similar to the target as possible. The pre-trained model is then set as a starting benchmark for the target model. The target model adapts the model parameters according to the emulated pre-trained target model, depending on the technique used for modeling. The target model shall then be tuned and refined for the increased accuracy toward the target task.

13.14.1   Transfer Learning for Natural Language Processing

One of the challenging problems in the field of machine learning–based applications is textual data analysis. Here, the vectorization of the data points takes place using different techniques [21]. This vectorized field of features shall then use transfer learning paradigms to emulate feature space and distribution so as to reach its own task goals.

13.14.2   Transfer learning for Computer Vision

Deep learning has found various applications in the domain of computer vision. Some of the regular tasks performed using different deep neural network structures is object recognition and identification, which is performed with exceeding precision by the deep neural perception, albeit, with a humongous training data and time for processing [22]. As we have seen in the previous sections, the deep transfer paradigms bring down the amount of data required for the perception and hence find various traditional applications in the computer vision fields.

13.14.3 Transfer Learning for Audio and Speech

Deep learning has successfully found its use as an efficient agent for processing in the domains of natural language processing, with the help of audio data perception [23]. Given the similarity of the tasks, the field of automatic speech recognition and verification of the same finds a humongous application potential in deep neural networks. However, given the latency and the amount of data, deep learning networks needs for processing might not be ideal for a real-time application like speech verification. Given the similarity in domains and tasks in natural language processing and automatic speech recognition, it is only logical to assume the possibility of transfer learning working as a bridge between the two, considerably bringing down the processing time delay incurred. Transferability of knowledge between different language-based training is also possible in such domains [24].

13.15 Further Advancements and Conclusion

Transfer learning has become a prominent subfield in machine learning. Transfer learning helps speed up the time it takes to train and develop a model by reusing modules of already developed models, thus accelerating results. Transfer learning finds use in a variety of applications as seen in the previous section. Moreover, it unfolds various research domains and possible models which could require the ability of transferring knowledge to new tasks and could be accustomed to new domains. With the extension and growth of machine learning in numerous fields, the ability of using already existing knowledge can be used in a range of applications to address new problems. It is also possible that these already existing models start training themselves in future in order to achieve higher efficiency and produce magnificent results.

With a vast scope of its use in future applications, transfer learning also encounters certain challenges which are needed to be pondered over. The two major challenges include the automation of task mapping and the prevention of negative transfer. As we have seen, transfer learning works on the concept of finding similarity between the source and target tasks when they are assumed to be similar or identical. In some cases, there is no direct representation of similarity between the two tasks. In such conditions, a mapping needs to be done from the source to the target task for representation between them. Most of the prevalent transfer approaches require a human to provide such representations. Achieving automation in task mapping in future could make the work easier by a hundred folds. Some of the techniques used for the same include mapping by analogy, multiple mapping, equalizing task representations, etc. The other challenge of avoiding negative transfer is necessary to be addressed in cases where the source domain is not sufficiently related to the target domain and might degrade the performance instead of improving it. Thus, it is required to prevent transfer from negatively affecting performance. One way to implement this scheme is to reject bad information or transfer of harmful knowledge while learning the target task. Another approach is to choose from a pool of source tasks to transfer knowledge rather than having only one source task. Using multiple source tasks instead of choosing one is yet another approach to avoid negative transfer of knowledge.

Addressal of the above discussed challenges is bound to give a boost to transfer learning. Transfer learning is surely going to be one of the key drivers for machine learning and deep learning success. As computing power increases and application of machine learning is extended to more complex problems, knowledge transfer can only become more desirable.

References

1. Pan, S. and Yang, Q., A Survey on Transfer Learning. *IEEE Trans. Knowl. Data Eng.*, 22, 10, 1345–1359, 2010.
2. Torrey, L. and Shavlik, J., Transfer Learning. Handbook of Research on Machine Learning Applications and Trends: Algorithms, Methods, and Techniques. *IGI Global*, 4112, 242–264, 2010.
3. Dai, W., Yang, Q., Xue, G., Yu, Y., Boosting for transfer learning. *Proceedings Of The 24Th International Conference On Machine Learning - ICML '07*, 2007.
4. Raina, R., Battle, A., Lee, H., Packer, B., Ng, A., Self-taught learning. *Proceedings Of The 24Th International Conference On Machine Learning - ICML '07*, 2007.
5. Bengio, Y., Deep learning of representations for unsupervised and transfer learning, in: *Proceedings of ICML workshop on unsupervised and transfer learning*, pp. 17–36, 2012, June.
6. Weiss, K. and Khoshgoftaar, T., An Investigation of Transfer Learning and Traditional Machine Learning Algorithms. *2016 IEEE 28Th International Conference On Tools With Artificial Intelligence (ICTAI)*, 2016.
7. Eaton, E., desJardins, M., Lane, T., Modeling Transfer Relationships Between Learning Tasks for Improved Inductive Transfer. *Mach. Learn. Knowl. Discover Databases*, 5211, 317–332, 2008.
8. Croonenborghs, T., Driessens, K., Bruynooghe, M., Learning Relational Options for Inductive Transfer in Relational Reinforcement Learning. *Inductive Logic Program*, 4894, 88–97, 2008.

9. Du, B., Zhang, L., Tao, D., Zhang, D., Unsupervised transfer learning for target detection from hyperspectral images. *Neurocomputing*, 120, 72–82, 2013,.

10. Quanz, B. and Huan, J., Large margin transductive transfer learning. *Proceeding Of The 18Th ACM Conference On Information And Knowledge Management - CIKM '09*, 2009.

11. Zhang, D. and Si, L., Multiple Instance Transfer Learning. *2009 IEEE International Conference On Data Mining Workshops*, 2009.

12. Meng, J., Lin, H., Li, Y., Knowledge transfer based on feature representation mapping for text classification. *Expert Syst. Appl.*, 38, 8, 10562–10567, 2011.

13. Whitacre, C. and Shea, C., The Role of Parameter Variability on Retention, Parameter Transfer, and Effector Transfer. *Res. Q. Exercise Sport*, 73, 1, 47–57, 2002.

14. Mesquita, L., Anand, J., Brush, T., Comparing the resource-based and relational views: Knowledge transfer and spillover in vertical alliances. *Strategic Manage. J.*, 29, 9, 913–941, 2008.

15. Gopalakrishnan, K., Khaitan, S., Choudhary, A., Agrawal, A., Deep Convolutional Neural Networks with transfer learning for computer vision-based data-driven pavement distress detection. *Constr. Build. Mater.*, 157, 322–330, 2017.

16. Huang, J., Li, J., Yu, D., Deng, L., Gong, Y., Cross-language knowledge transfer using multilingual deep neural network with shared hidden layers. *2013 IEEE International Conference On Acoustics, Speech And Signal Processing*, 2013.

17. Collobert, R. and Weston, J., A unified architecture for natural language processing. *Proceedings Of The 25Th International Conference On Machine Learning - ICML '08*, 2008.

18. Ahmed, A., Yu, K., Xu, W., Gong, Y., Xing, E., Training Hierarchical Feed-Forward Visual Recognition Models Using Transfer Learning from Pseudo-Tasks. *Lecture Notes Comput. Sci.*, 5304, 69–82, 2008.

19. Lu, J., Behbood, V., Hao, P., Zuo, H., Xue, S., Zhang, G., Transfer learning using computational intelligence: A survey. *Knowledge-Based Systems*, 80, 14–23, 2015.

20. Wang, D. and Zheng, T., Transfer learning for speech and language processing. *2015 Asia-Pacific Signal And Information Processing Association Annual Summit And Conference (APSIPA)*, 2015.

21. Austin, K., Multimedia learning: Cognitive individual differences and display design techniques predict transfer learning with multimedia learning modules. *Comput. Educ.*, 53, 4, 1339–1354, 2009.

22. Lobato, J., Alternative Perspectives on the Transfer of Learning: History, Issues, and Challenges for Future Research. *J. Learn. Sci.*, 15, 4, 431–449, 2006.

23. Goodfellow, I. *et al.*, Challenges in Representation Learning: A Report on Three Machine Learning Contests. *Neural Inf. Process.*, 8228 117–124, 2013.

24. Easterby-Smith, M., Lyles, M., Tsang, E., Inter-Organizational Knowledge Transfer: Current Themes and Future Prospects. *J. Manage. Stud.*, 45, 4, 677–690, 2008.

25. Egan, T., Yang, B., Bartlett, K., The effects of organizational learning culture and job satisfaction on motivation to transfer learning and turnover intention. *Hum. Resour. Dev. Q.*, 15, 3, 279–301, 2004,

Section 5

HANDS-ON AND CASE STUDY

14

Hands on MAHOUT—Machine Learning Tool

Uma N. Dulhare[1] and Sheikh Gouse[2*]

[1]Computer Science and Engineering Department, Muffakham Jah
College of Engineering and Technology, Hyderabad, Telangana
[2]Computer Science and Engineering Department, Osmania University, Hyderabad,
Telangana, India

Abstract

Apache Mahout is an open source framework of the distributed linear algebra and Apache Software Foundation (ASF). It is a package of powerful scalable open source libraries of Machine Learning (ML) Algorithms that provided on the above of MapReduce. It holds the fundamental algorithms of clustering, classification, and recommendation system to analyze faster and efficiently. Artificial Intelligent (AI) enables machines to analyze barring being explicitly programmed and it is often used to improve future overall performance primarily based on preceding outcomes. In this work, we have implemented the hands-on installation and running of Mahout on different environments for the classification, clustering, and recommendation algorithms.

Keywords: Machine learning, hadoop, map reduce, HDFS, scalability

14.1 Introduction to Mahout

In the future, big data and machine learning (ML) with artificial intelligence will rule the world. Apache Hadoop is a distributed file system and free software framework. Hadoop Distributed File System (HDFS) is implemented on commodity hardware [1]. Apache Mahout also an open source framework that implements the ML algorithms on the top

Corresponding author: Sheikh.gouse@gmail.com

Uma N. Dulhare, Khaleel Ahmad and Khairol Amali Bin Ahmad (eds.) Machine Learning and
Big Data: Concepts, Algorithms, Tools and Applications, (363–422) © 2020 Scrivener Publishing LLC

of Hadoop MapReduce (MR) [2]. Mahout provides the ML library to perform the faster clustering, classification, and recommendation algorithms compare to traditional tool like Weka of data mining [3]. Mahout applications analyze the data much quicker, less complicated, and effectively on big data and its architecture in Figure 14.1 [4].

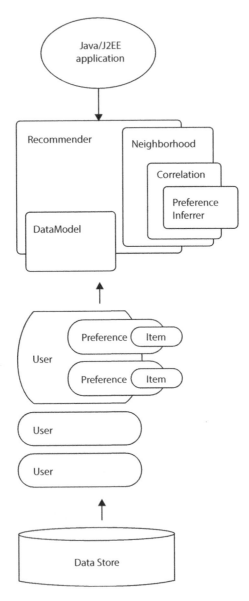

Figure 14.1 Architecture of Mahout.

Hadoop framework components are:

1. HDFS: It is a virtual file system. It consists of NameNode (NN) and DataNode(DN). It mainly provides hear beat, replication, and balancing factor.
2. MapReduce (MR): Its program runs on Java. It is batch query processor. It main task is to process the file and start the job. Its main operations are map, shuffle, and reduce for each input file [5].

Mahout scalability:

1. Scalable Architecture: Storing and processing the data more efficiently [6].
2. Scalable Libraries: High scalable ML tools and algorithms [7].
3. Hadoop Community: It is built on top of Hadoop [8, 9].

Mahout algorithms

1. Clustering [10–15]
2. Classification [16–23]
3. MapReduce [24]
4. Recommenders [25–28]
5. Distributed Linear Algebra [29]
6. Preprocessor [29]
7. Regression [29]

Prerequisites

1. Hardware Requirements
    1. Processor: i2 64 bit Processor
    2. Hard Disk: 1–4TB
    3. RAM: 8–512 GB
    4. Ethernet: 10 Gb

2. Software Requirements
    1. Java and Eclipse IDE
    2. Hadoop
    3. Mahout
    4. Maven
    5. Ubuntu or Windows operating system
    6. VMware player

14.1.1 Features

1. Framework: It's a simple coding platform for algorithms and tight coupled.
2. Scalable: It is scalable to build different algorithms [1, 2].
3. Effectively: Different applications can be easily and speedily can analyze compare traditional tool like Weka [8, 9].
4. Cluster implementation algorithms with MapReduce [10–15, 24].
5. Classification implementation algorithms [16–23].
6. Collaborative filtering
7. Samara for spark

14.1.2 Advantages

- Apache Hadoop library to empower Mahout to scale adequately in the cloud [1].
- Apache Mahout support scalable ML [2].
- It supports strong recommendation [25–27].
- Distributed linear algebra framework running on Spark, Flink, and H2O.
- Mathematically expressive Scala DSL.
- Pluggable compute back-end (Spark recommended, Flink supported) [32].
- Modular native solvers for CPU/GPU/CUDA acceleration.
- Designed for fast experimentation with clean, math-like syntax [29].
- Prototype to production with the same code.

14.1.3 Disadvantages

- It is slower than Spark [42].
- It works mainly on MapReduce [43].
- It focuses on fewer algorithms compare to Spark and R.
- No GUI.
- Less visualization and libraries.

14.1.4 Application

1. Business: The Clustering algorithms for predicting the stock markets [10–15].

2. Healthcare: The Classification algorithms for detection of cancer [16–23].

3. Social websites: The pattern mining and interest of people by Adobe, Facebook, LinkedIn, Foursquare, Twitter, and Yahoo [16, 17, 19–22].

4. Basic Needs: The Recommender algorithms used for entertainment and restaurant areas by FourSquare [25–28].

5. Collaborative filtering: It mines user behavior and makes product recommendations. Example: Amazon recommendations Vision processing, Language processing, Forecasting, Pattern recognition, Games, Data mining, Expert systems, Robotics [25–28].

14.2   Installation Steps of Apache Mahout Using Cloudera

14.2.1   Installation of VMware Workstation

Step 1: Download and install VMware Workstation/Player
Path setting to install VMware in Figure 14.2 and Figure 14.3.
Selecting the user experience settings of VMware.
Selecting the upgrade button of VMware.

Figure 14.2 Downloading VMware player.

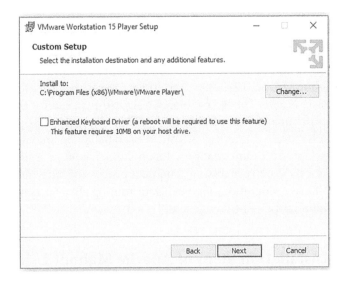

Figure 14.3 Path setting to install VMware.

14.2.2   Installation of Cloudera

Step 1: Downloading the Cloudera CDH3 [30, 31, 32, 33].

Step 2: Extract the Cloudera downloaded into a folder.

Step 3: Opening the Cloudera using VMWare Player.

Selecting the Cloudera file which is of 3 KB size in Figure 14.4.

Figure 14.4 Opening the Cloudera using VMWare Player.

Step 4: Play virtual machine.

Step 5: Select the Cloudera.

Step 6: Select the User Cloudera and give the Password – cloudera in Figure 14.5.

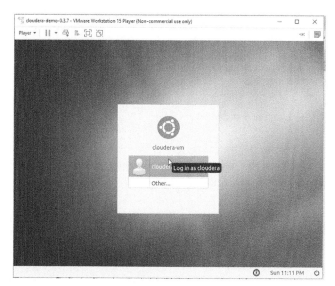

Figure 14.5 Select the user and password.

Step 7: Cloudera homepage open

Step 8: Open a terminal to update apt-get in Figure 14.6.

Command: sudo apt-get update

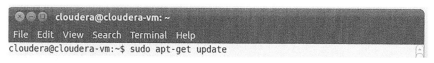

Figure 14.6 Updating the software.

Step 9: Updating the Java in Figure 14.7.

Command: sudo apt-get install default-jdk

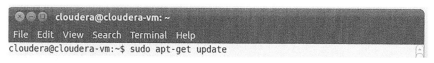

Figure 14.7 Installing the default Java.

Step 10: Checking the Java version in Figure 14.8.
Command: Java-version

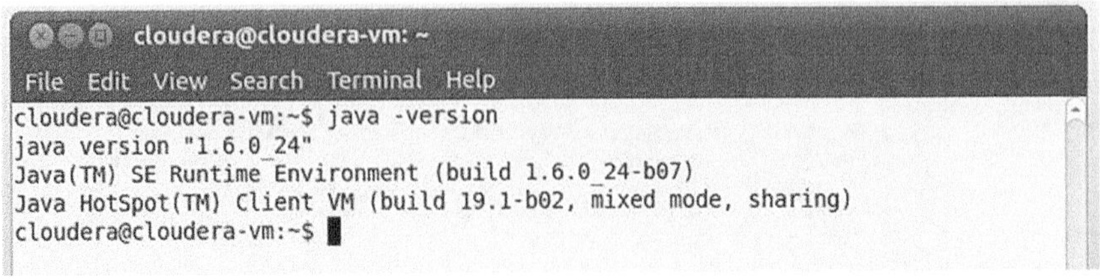

Figure 14.8 Checking the installed Java version.

Step 11: Creating the hadoop group in Figure 14.9.
Command: sudo addgroup hadoopg

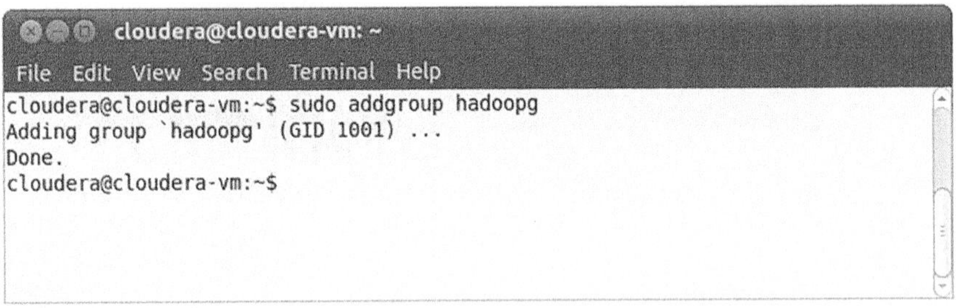

Figure 14.9 Creating a Hadoop system user.

Step 12: Creating user in hadoop group in Figure 14.10.
Command: sudo adduser - - ingroup hadoog hdgouse

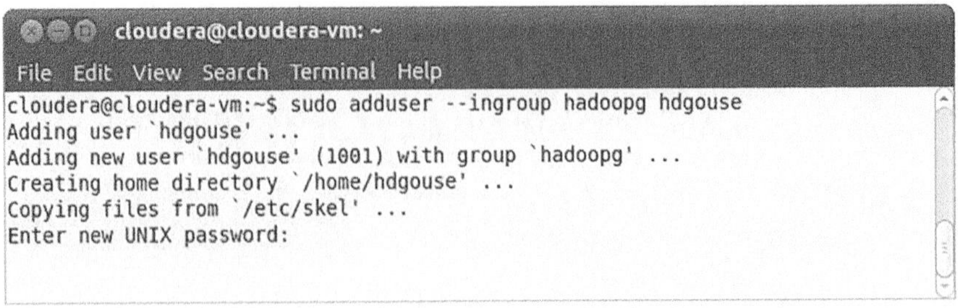

Figure 14.10 Adding a directory Hadoop user into Hadoop system.

Step 13: User details added into the group in Figure 14.11.
Command: sudo adduser - - ingroup hadoog hdgouse

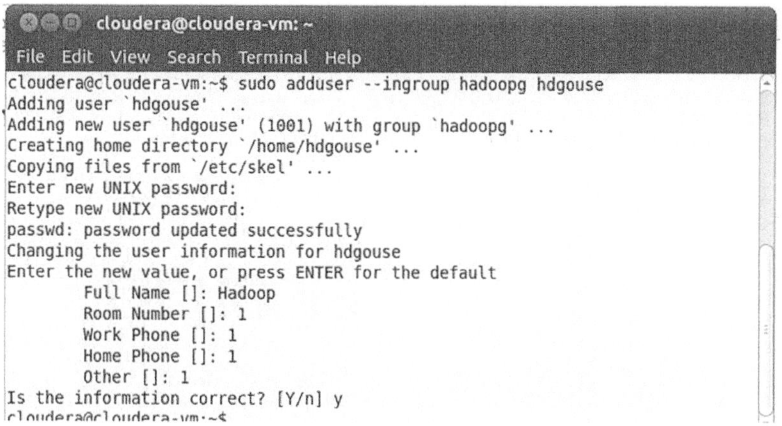

```
cloudera@cloudera-vm: ~
File  Edit  View  Search  Terminal  Help
cloudera@cloudera-vm:~$ sudo adduser --ingroup hadoopg hdgouse
Adding user `hdgouse' ...
Adding new user `hdgouse' (1001) with group `hadoopg' ...
Creating home directory `/home/hdgouse' ...
Copying files from `/etc/skel' ...
Enter new UNIX password:
Retype new UNIX password:
passwd: password updated successfully
Changing the user information for hdgouse
Enter the new value, or press ENTER for the default
        Full Name []: Hadoop
        Room Number []: 1
        Work Phone []: 1
        Home Phone []: 1
        Other []: 1
Is the information correct? [Y/n] y
cloudera@cloudera-vm:~$
```

Figure 14.11 Adding username, password, and other user details.

Step 14: Adding user to super user in Figure 14.12.
Command: sudo adduser hdgouse sudo

```
cloudera@cloudera-vm: ~
File  Edit  View  Search  Terminal  Help
cloudera@cloudera-vm:~$ sudo adduser hdgouse sudo
Adding user `hdgouse' to group `sudo' ...
Adding user hdgouse to group sudo
Done.
cloudera@cloudera-vm:~$ ▮
```

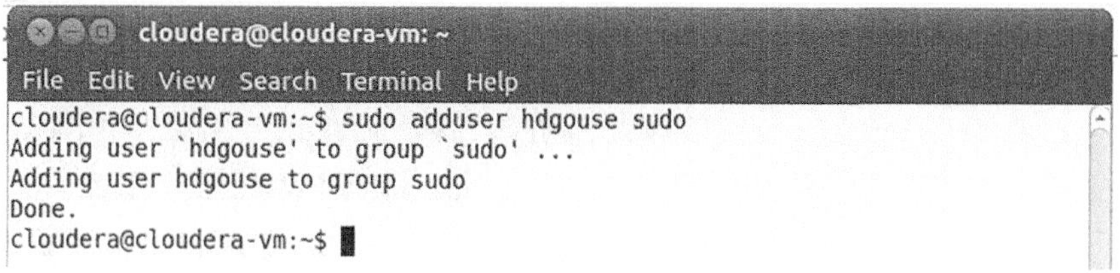

Figure 14.12 Adding user "hdgouse" as super user.

Step 15: Logging as new haoop user 'hdgouse' in Figure 14.13.
Command: su hdgouse

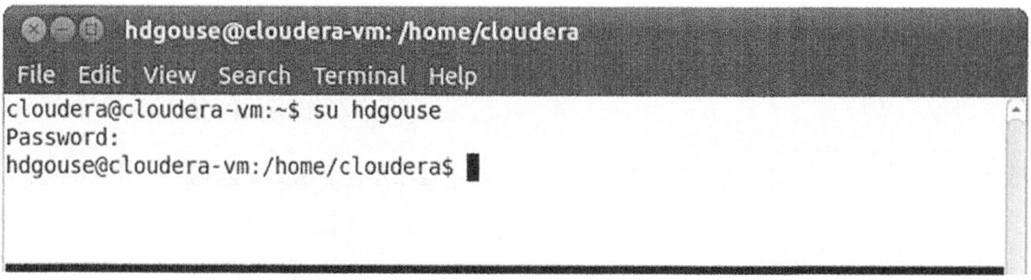

```
hdgouse@cloudera-vm: /home/cloudera
File  Edit  View  Search  Terminal  Help
cloudera@cloudera-vm:~$ su hdgouse
Password:
hdgouse@cloudera-vm:/home/cloudera$ ▮
```

Figure 14.13 Logging to the new hadoop user.

Step 16: Installing SSH and SSH switching the user in Figure 14.14.
Command: su - hdgouse

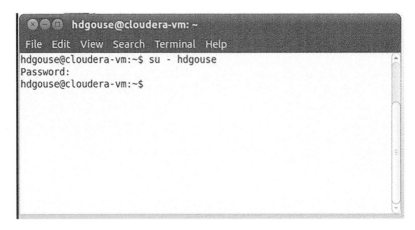

Figure 14.14 Configuration of SSH switching the user.

Step 17: SSH Key new created in Figure 14.15.

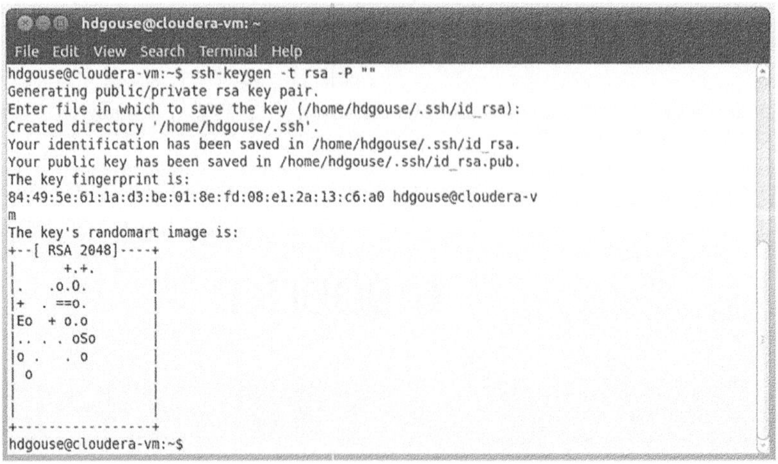

Figure 14.15 Creating a new SSH key.

Step 18: Adding ssh key to authorized_keys in Figure 14.16.

Figure 14.16 Enabling SSH with key access to authorized_keys.

Step 19: Checking SSH to connect to hadoop user as hdgouse in Figure 14.17.
Command: ssh localhost

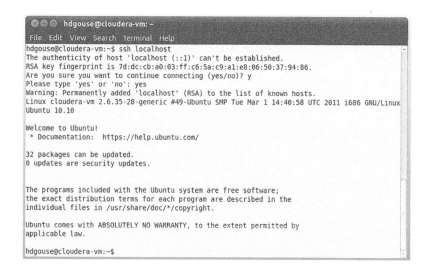

Figure 14.17 Checking SSH to connect to Hadoop user as hdgouse.

Step 20: If error to above step.19 then SSH Localhost then purge SSH and updating in Figure 14.18.
Command: sudo apt-get purge openssh-server
Command: : sudo apt-get update openssh-server

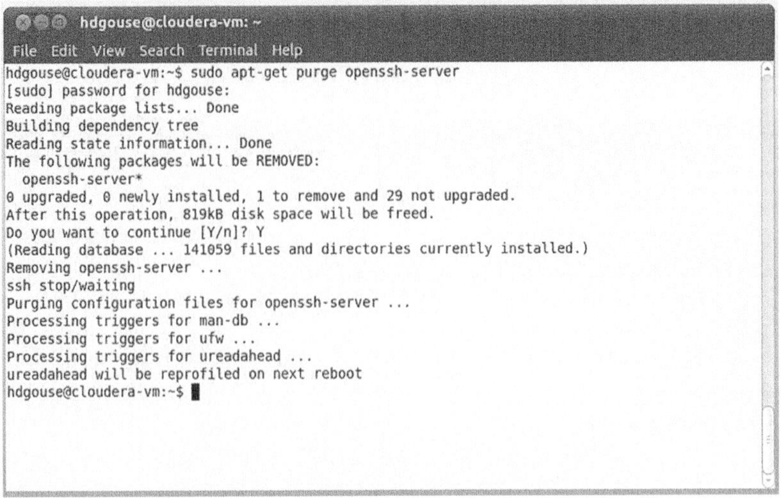

Figure 14.18 If error to SSH Localhost, then purge SSH.

Step 21: If error to above step.19 then SSH Localhost then purge SSH in Figure 14.19.

Command: sudo apt-get purge openssh-server

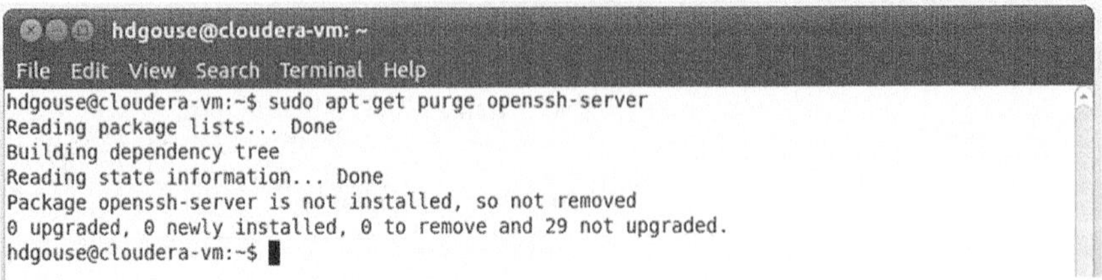

Figure 14.19 Updating the SSH.

Step 22: Installing the Hadoop in Figure 14.20.

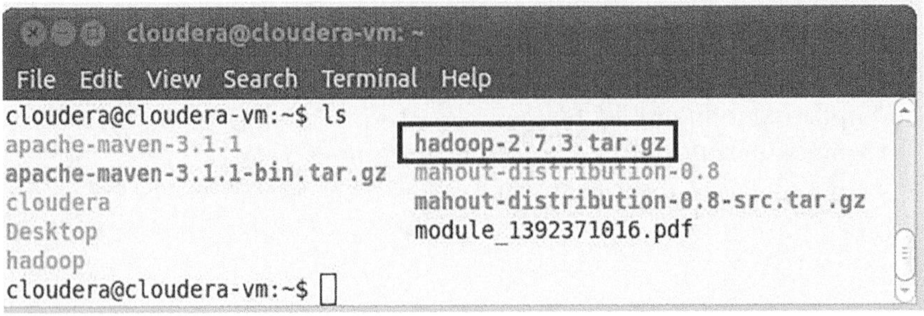

Figure 14.20 Checking the after downloading the Hadoop, Mahout, and Maven.

Downloading the following software: http://apache.spinellicreations. com/

1. Hadoop
2. Mahout
3. Maven

Command: sudo wget http://apache.spinellicreations.com/hadoop/ common/stable/hadoop-3.2.1.tar.gz

Step 23: Checking after downloading softwares in Figure 14.21.
Command: ls

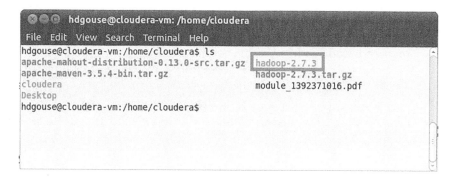

Figure 14.21 Checking the file after extracting hadoop-2.7.3.

Step 24: Moving the extracted hadoop-2.7.3 file to hadoop in Figure 14.22.
Command: sudo mv hadoop-2.7.3 hadoop

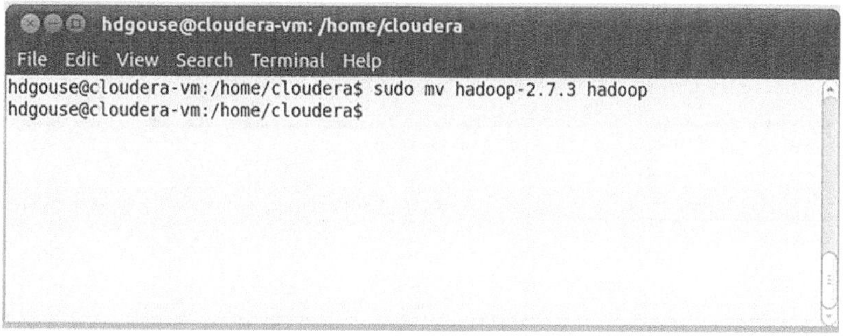

Figure 14.22 Moving the extracted hadoop-2.7.3 file to Hadoop.

Step 25: Changing the owner permission of hadoop in Figure 14.23.
Command: sudo chown –R hdgouse:hadoopg hadoop

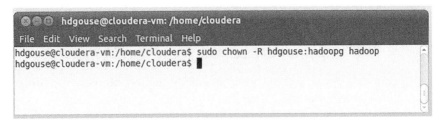

Figure 14.23 Changing the owner permission of hadoop.

Step 26: Hadoop Configuration modifying the source.bashrc (~/.bashrc)
file in Figure 14.24.
Command: sudo gedit ~/.bashrc

Figure 14.24 Modifying the source.bashrc file.

Step 27: Adding the JAVA_HOME, HADOOP_HOME and PATH in
Figure 14.25.

Figure 14.25 Editing the JAVA_HOME and HADOOP_HOME.

Step 28: Hadoop Files to be configured in Figure 14.26.
Command: /home/cloudera/hadoop/etc/hadoop/ls

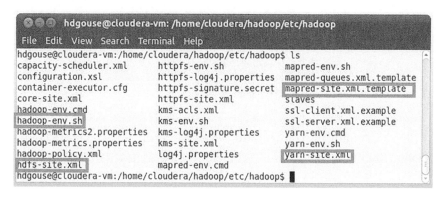

Figure 14.26 Listing of files to configured.

Step 29: Modifying the hadoop- env. sh in Figure 14.27.

```
hdgouse@cloudera-vm: /home/cloudera/hadoop/etc/hadoop
File  Edit  View  Search  Terminal  Help

hdgouse@cloudera-vm:/home/cloudera/hadoop/etc/hadoop$ sudo gedit hadoop-env.sh
```

Figure 14.27 Command for modifying the hadoop-env.sh.

Step 30: Adding the JAVA_HOME path in Figure 14.28.

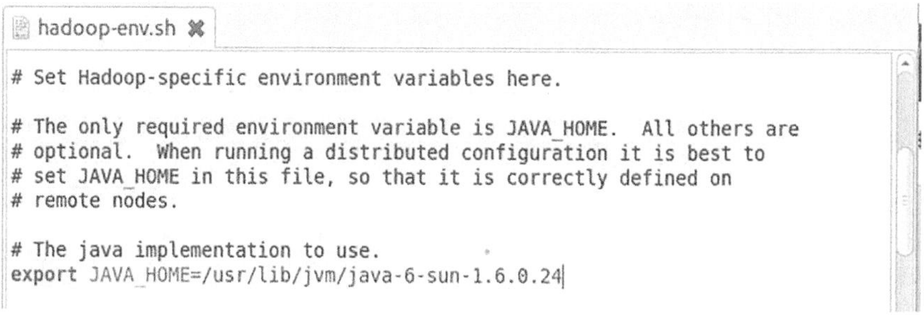

```
hadoop-env.sh ✖

# Set Hadoop-specific environment variables here.

# The only required environment variable is JAVA_HOME.  All others are
# optional.  When running a distributed configuration it is best to
# set JAVA_HOME in this file, so that it is correctly defined on
# remote nodes.

# The java implementation to use.
export JAVA_HOME=/usr/lib/jvm/java-6-sun-1.6.0.24
```

Figure 14.28 Adding the JAVA_HOME path.

Step 31: Modifying the core-site.xml in Figure 14.29.

```
⊗ ⊖ ⊙   hdgouse@cloudera-vm: /home/cloudera/hadoop/etc/hadoop
File  Edit  View  Search  Terminal  Help
hdgouse@cloudera-vm:/home/cloudera/hadoop/etc/hadoop$ sudo gedit core-site.xml
```

Figure 14.29 Command for modifying the core-site.xml.

Step 32: Adding the configuration property of core-site.xml file in Figure 14.30.

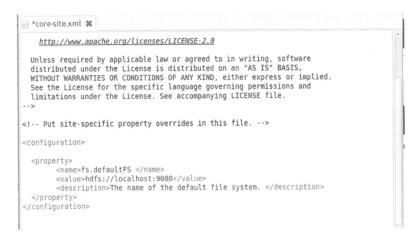

```
✓ *core-site.xml ✖

    http://www.apache.org/licenses/LICENSE-2.0

    Unless required by applicable law or agreed to in writing, software
    distributed under the License is distributed on an "AS IS" BASIS,
    WITHOUT WARRANTIES OR CONDITIONS OF ANY KIND, either express or implied.
    See the License for the specific language governing permissions and
    limitations under the License. See accompanying LICENSE file.
-->

<!-- Put site-specific property overrides in this file. -->

<configuration>

    <property>
        <name>fs.defaultFS </name>
        <value>hdfs://localhost:9000</value>
        <description>The name of the default file system. </description>
    </property>
</configuration>
```

Figure 14.30 Adding the configuration property of core-site.xml file.

Step 33: Copying the content of mapred-site.xml.template to mapred-site.xml in Figure 14.31.

```
⊗ ⊖ ⊙   hdgouse@cloudera-vm: /home/cloudera/hadoop/etc/hadoop
File  Edit  View  Search  Terminal  Help
hdgouse@cloudera-vm:/home/cloudera/hadoop/etc/hadoop$ sudo cp mapred-site.xml.template
mapred-site.xml
```

Figure 14.31 Command for copying mapred site.

Step 34: Modifying the mapred-site.xml in Figure 14.32.

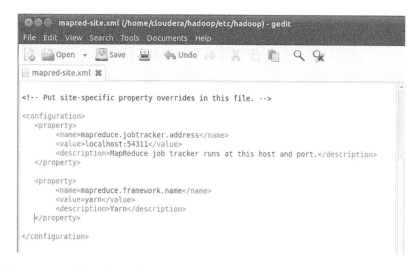

Figure 14.32 Command for modifying the mapred-site.xml.

Step 35: Adding the configuration properties of mapred-site.xml in Figure 14.33.

Figure 14.33 Adding the configuration properties of mapred-site.xml.

Step 36: Modifying the hdfs-site.xml in Figure 14.34.

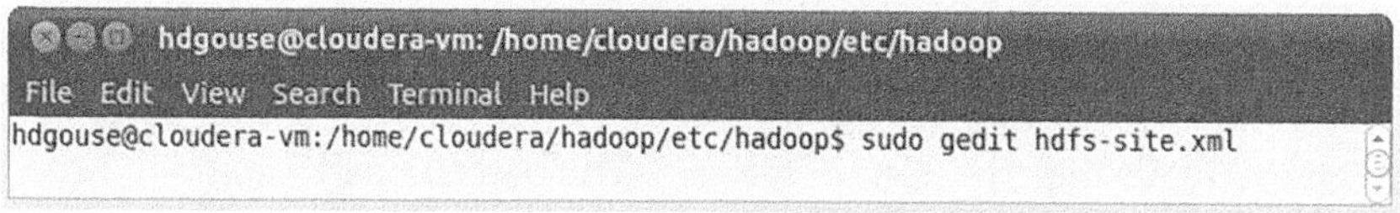

Figure 14.34 Command for modifying the hdfs-site.xml.

Step 37: Adding the configuration properties to hdf-site.xml in Figure 14.35.

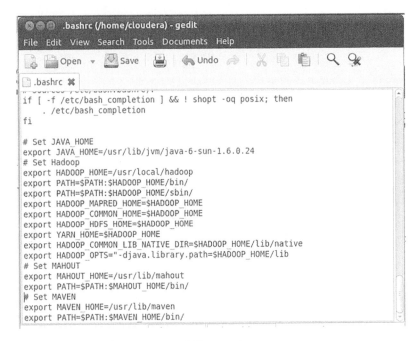

```
if [ -f /etc/bash_completion ] && ! shopt -oq posix; then
    . /etc/bash_completion
fi

# Set JAVA_HOME
export JAVA_HOME=/usr/lib/jvm/java-6-sun-1.6.0.24
# Set Hadoop
export HADOOP_HOME=/usr/local/hadoop
export PATH=$PATH:$HADOOP_HOME/bin/
export PATH=$PATH:$HADOOP_HOME/sbin/
export HADOOP_MAPRED_HOME=$HADOOP_HOME
export HADOOP_COMMON_HOME=$HADOOP_HOME
export HADOOP_HDFS_HOME=$HADOOP_HOME
export YARN_HOME=$HADOOP_HOME
export HADOOP_COMMON_LIB_NATIVE_DIR=$HADOOP_HOME/lib/native
export HADOOP_OPTS="-djava.library.path=$HADOOP_HOME/lib
# Set MAHOUT
export MAHOUT_HOME=/usr/lib/mahout
export PATH=$PATH:$MAHOUT_HOME/bin/
# Set MAVEN
export MAVEN_HOME=/usr/lib/maven
export PATH=$PATH:$MAVEN_HOME/bin/
```

Figure 14.35 Adding the properties to hdf-site.xml.

Step 38: Modifying the hadoop.sh in Figure 14.36.
Command: su gedit /etc/profile.d/hadoop.sh

Figure 14.36 Command for modifying the hadoop.sh.

Step 39: Adding the HADOOP_HOME path to hadoop.sh in Figure 14.37.

Figure 14.37 Adding the HADOOP_HOME path.

Step 40: Adding the configuration properties of yarn-site.xml in Figure 14.38.

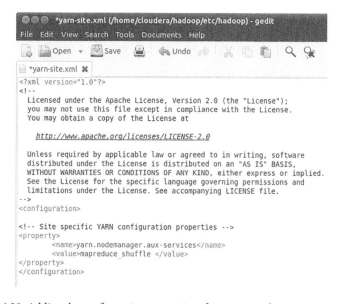

Figure 14.38 Adding the configuration properties of yarn-site.xml.

Step 41: Adding the datanode and namenode in hdfs in Figure 14.39.

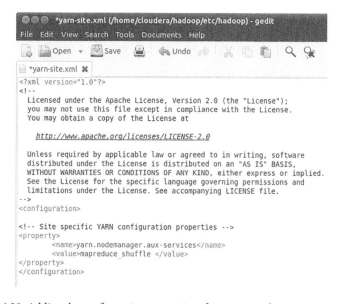

Figure 14.39 Adding the datanode and namenode in hdfs.

Step 42: Changing the owner permission of hdfs in Figure 14.40.

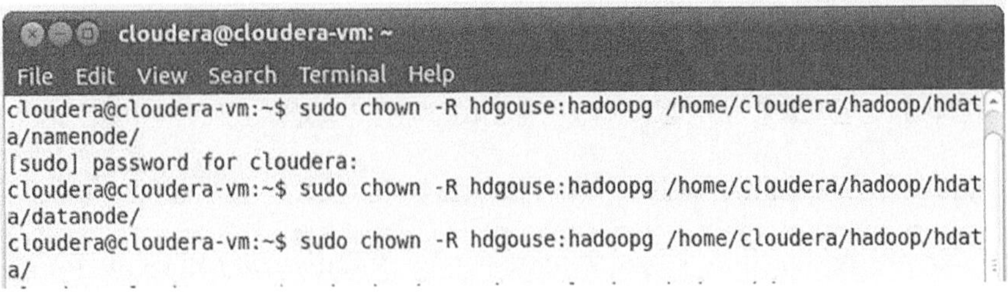

```
cloudera@cloudera-vm: ~
File  Edit  View  Search  Terminal  Help
cloudera@cloudera-vm:~$ sudo chown -R hdgouse:hadoopg /home/cloudera/hadoop/hdat
a/namenode/
[sudo] password for cloudera:
cloudera@cloudera-vm:~$ sudo chown -R hdgouse:hadoopg /home/cloudera/hadoop/hdat
a/datanode/
cloudera@cloudera-vm:~$ sudo chown -R hdgouse:hadoopg /home/cloudera/hadoop/hdat
a/
```

Figure 14.40 Changing the owner permission of hdfs.

Step 43: Changing the modes of the hdfs file in Figure 14.41.

```
cloudera@cloudera-vm: ~
File  Edit  View  Search  Terminal  Help
cloudera@cloudera-vm:~$ sudo chmod 750 /home/cloudera/hadoop/hdata/
```

Figure 14.41 Changing the modes of the hdfs file.

Step 44: Formatting the namenode in Figure 14.42.
Command: hadoop namenode –format

```
cloudera@cloudera-vm: ~
File  Edit  View  Search  Terminal  Help
cloudera@cloudera-vm:~$ sudo gedit .bashrc
[sudo] password for cloudera:
cloudera@cloudera-vm:~$ sudo gedit .bashrc
[sudo] password for cloudera:
cloudera@cloudera-vm:~$ hadoop namenode -format
19/10/18 00:49:35 INFO namenode.NameNode: STARTUP_MSG:
/************************************************************
STARTUP_MSG: Starting NameNode
STARTUP_MSG:   host = cloudera-vm/127.0.1.1
STARTUP_MSG:   args = [-format]
STARTUP_MSG:   version = 0.20.2-cdh3u0
STARTUP_MSG:   build =  -r 81256ad0f2e4ab2bd34b04f53d25a6c23686dd14; compiled by
 'root' on Sat Mar 26 00:14:04 UTC 2011
************************************************************/
Re-format filesystem in /var/lib/hadoop-0.20/cache/hadoop/dfs/name ? (Y or N) █
```

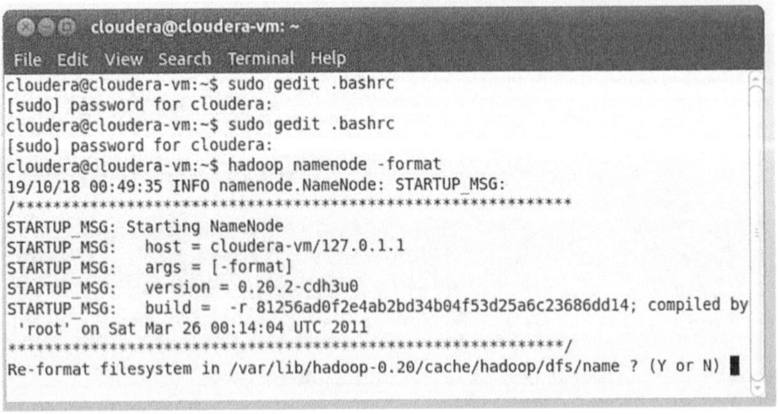

Figure 14.42 Formatting the namenode.

14.2.3   Installation of Mahout

Step 1: Downloading the Mahout Distribution file in Figure 14.43.

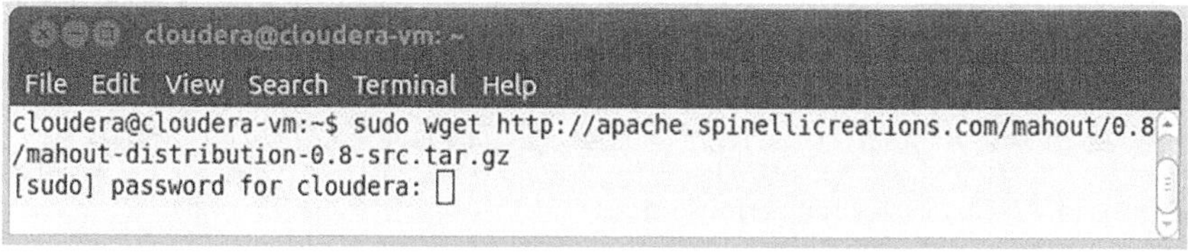

```
cloudera@cloudera-vm: ~
File  Edit  View  Search  Terminal  Help
cloudera@cloudera-vm:~$ sudo wget http://apache.spinellicreations.com/mahout/0.8
/mahout-distribution-0.8-src.tar.gz
[sudo] password for cloudera: []
```

Figure 14.43   Downloading the Mahout.

Step 2: Extracting the downloaded jar file in Figure 14.44.

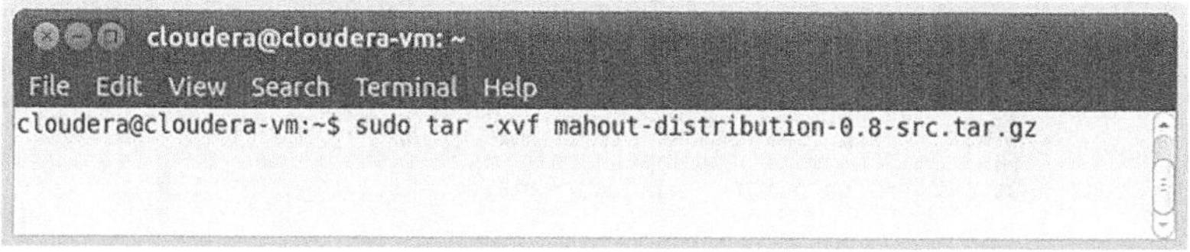

```
cloudera@cloudera-vm: ~
File  Edit  View  Search  Terminal  Help
cloudera@cloudera-vm:~$ sudo tar -xvf mahout-distribution-0.8-src.tar.gz
```

Figure 14.44   Extracting the Mahout file.

Step 3: Make directory for Mahout in Figure 14.45.

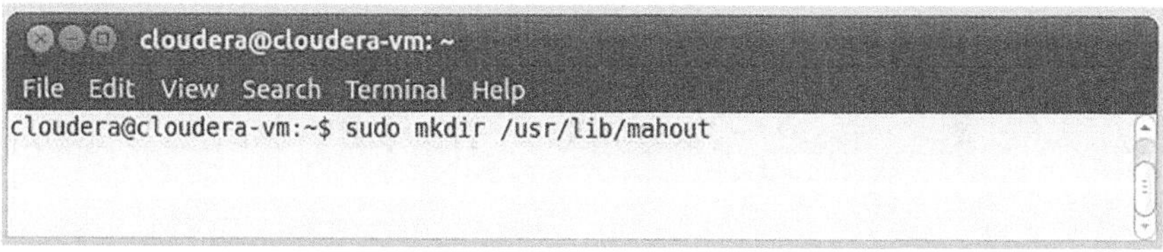

```
cloudera@cloudera-vm: ~
File  Edit  View  Search  Terminal  Help
cloudera@cloudera-vm:~$ sudo mkdir /usr/lib/mahout
```

Figure 14.45   Creating a Mahout Directory.

Step 4: Extracted jar file to moved to created directory in Figure 14.46.

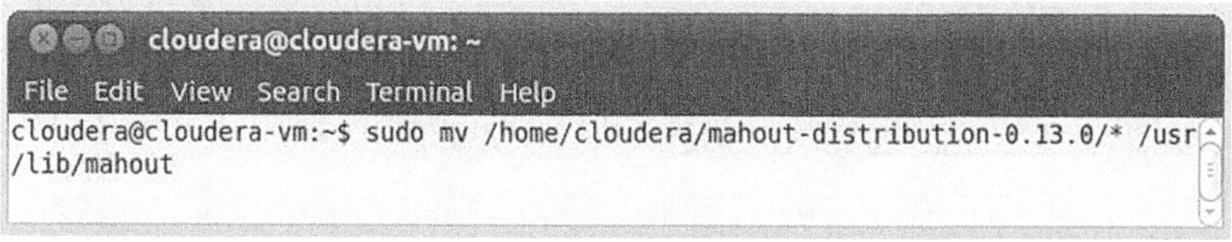

```
cloudera@cloudera-vm: ~
File  Edit  View  Search  Terminal  Help
cloudera@cloudera-vm:~$ sudo mv /home/cloudera/mahout-distribution-0.13.0/* /usr
/lib/mahout
```

Figure 14.46   Moving the extracted file into Mahout directory.

Step 5: Mahout bin folder change the permission to rwxin Figure 14.47.

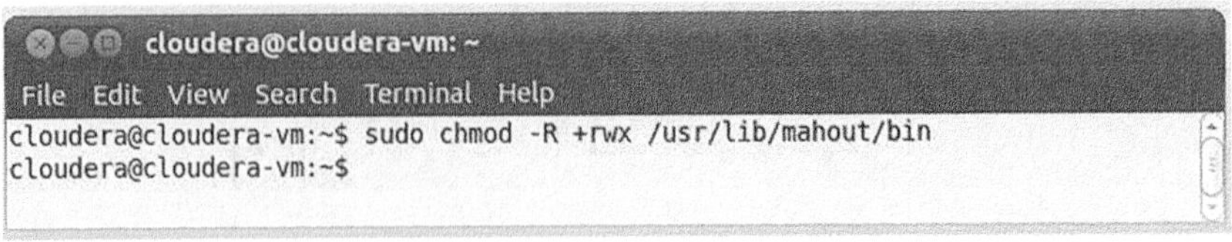

Figure 14.47 Change the bin permission.

14.2.4 Installation of Maven

Step 1: Download apache Maven 3.1.1 tar file
Step 2: Extract downloaded maven in Figure 14.48.

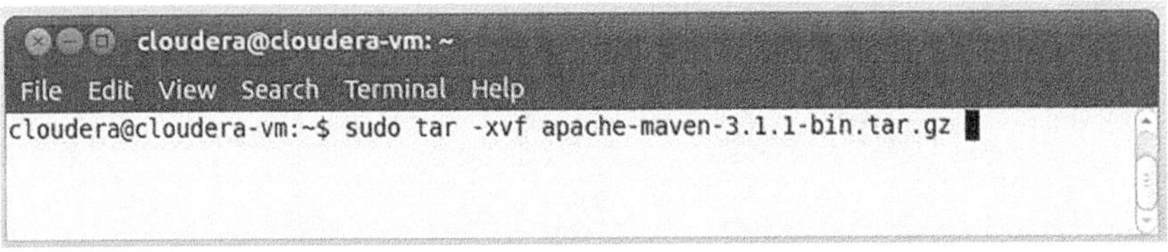

Figure 14.48 Extracting the maven tar file.

Step 3: Make a directory for Maven under usr lib in Figure 14.49.

Figure 14.49 Creating a maven directory under usr/lib.

Step 4: Extracted maven moved to the created maven
Moving the extracted maven file to created maven floder under usr/lib
Step 5: Setting the environment variables in bashrc file in Figure 14.50.

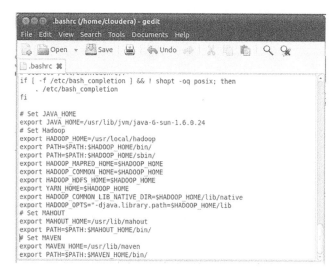

Figure 14.50 Setting the Maven path.

Step 6: Change the directory in Figure 14.51.

Figure 14.51 Adding environmental variables in bashrc.

Step 7: Load the changes made.

```
cloudera@cloudera-vm: /usr/lib/mahout
File  Edit  View  Search  Terminal  Help
[INFO] ------------------------------------------------------------------------
[INFO] Reactor Summary:
[INFO]
[INFO] Mahout Build Tools ............................... SUCCESS [1:52.309s]
[INFO] Apache Mahout .................................... SUCCESS [13.630s]
[INFO] Mahout Math ...................................... SUCCESS [1:15.689s]
[INFO] Mahout Core ...................................... SUCCESS [1:17.406s]
[INFO] Mahout Integration ............................... SUCCESS [2:09.654s]
[INFO] Mahout Examples .................................. SUCCESS [14.851s]
[INFO] Mahout Release Package ........................... SUCCESS [0.005s]
[INFO] ------------------------------------------------------------------------
[INFO] BUILD SUCCESS
[INFO] ------------------------------------------------------------------------
[INFO] Total time: 7:05.195s
[INFO] Finished at: Fri Oct 18 21:03:13 PDT 2019
[INFO] Final Memory: 33M/138M
[INFO] ------------------------------------------------------------------------
cloudera@cloudera-vm:/usr/lib/mahout$
```

Figure 14.52 Checking Mahout working or not.

Source.bashrc
Step 8: Checks the Mahout is working or not in Figure 14.52.

14.2.5   Testing Mahout

1. Start Hadoop
2. Download some data to foldername/test_data,
3. Copy the data to HDFS in Figure 14.53(a).

```
|hadoop fs -mkdir testdata
 hadoop fs -put synthetic_control.data testdata
```

Figure 14.53 (a) i. Copying the data command.

4. Perform clustering in Figure 14.53(b).

```
$MAHOUT_HOME/bin/mahout  org.apache.mahout.clustering.syntheticcontrol.kmeans.Job

$MAHOUT_HOME/bin/mahout  clusterdump --input output/clusters-10-final --pointsDir
output/clusteredPoints --output clusteranalyze.txt
```

Figure 14.53 (b) ii. Performing k-mean analysis command.

5. Sending data to local file system
```
hadoop fs -get output ~/Ghouse/mahout.results|
```

iii. Copying the data to local system command

6. Test visualization
```
org.apache.mahout.clustering.display
```

Above command for Visualization the output command

7. Final output: display
```
$MAHOUT_HOME/bin/mahout  org.apache.mahout.clustering.display|
```

14.3   Installation Steps of Apache Mahout Using Windows 10

14.3.1   Installation of Java

Step 1: Check the java available: Open the command prompt

Step 2: Checking java version

Step 3: If Java not installed then download the JDK1.8 64 bit and installed into C drive i.e, C:\Java

14.3.2 Installation of Hadoop

Step 1: Download link: Hadoop cluster in Figure 14.54.

Step 2: Unzip the file

Step 3: Past into C Drive i.e, C:\hadoop-2.8.0

https://archive.apache.org/dist/hadoop/core//hadoop-2.8.0/hadoop-2.8.0.tar.gz

hadoop-2.8.0.tar	7/18/2019 9:28 PM	WinRAR archive	419,853 KB

Figure 14.54 Hadoop tar file.

14.3.3 Installation of Mahout

Step 1: Download Link: Mahout in Figure 14.55.

Step 2: Unzip the file

Step 3: Past into C Drive i.e, C:\mahout

http://www.apache.org/dist/mahout/0.12.2/apache-mahout-distribution-0.12.2.tar.gz

apache-mahout-distribution-0.13.0.tar	7/18/2019 10:28 PM	WinRAR archive	222,735 KB

Figure 14.55 Downloaded Mahout distribution tar file.

14.3.4 Installation of Maven

Step 1: Download Maven Link:

https://maven.apache.org/download.cgi/apache-maven-3.6.1-bin

apache-maven-3.6.1-bin	7/26/2019 7:00 PM	WinRAR ZIP archive	8,967 KB

Figure 14.56 Downloaded Maven file.

Step 2: Unzip the file in Figure 14.56.

Step 3: Past into C Drive i.e, C:\apache-maven-3.6.1-bin

Step 4: Path location of Hadoop, Mahout and Maven in C drive in Figure 14.57.

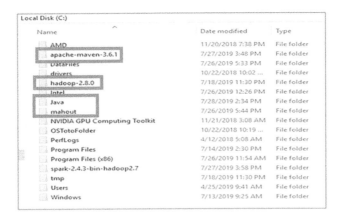

Figure 14.57 Copying of Hadoop, Mahout, and Maven in C drive.

14.3.5   Path Setting

a)   Java Path Setting
Step 1: Setting environment variable of Java Creating New variable name and value for Java home

b)   Hadoop path setting
Step 2: Adding Hadoop Variable name and variable value in Figure 14.58.

Figure 14.58 Creating New variable name and value for Hadoop home.

c) Mahout path setting

Step 3: Adding Mahout Variable name and variable value in Figure 14.59.

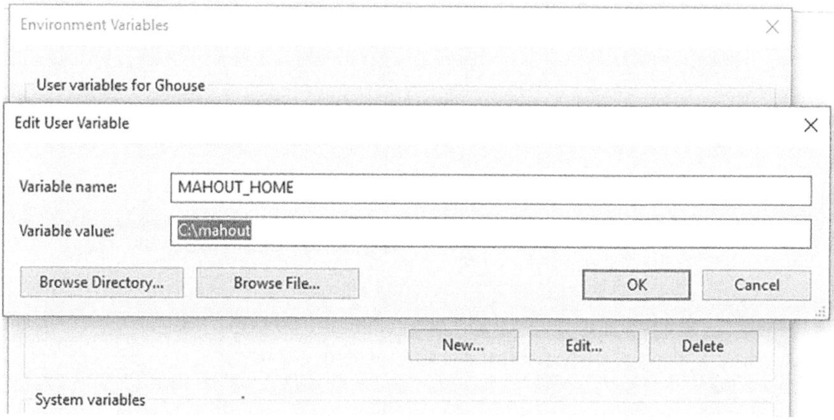

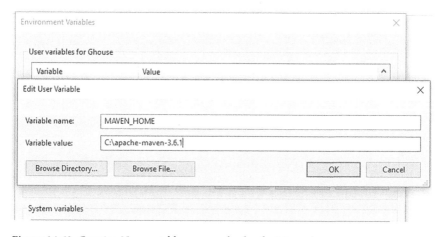

Figure 14.59 Creating New variable name and value for Mahout home.

d) Maven path setting

Step 4: Adding Maven Variable name and variable value in Figure 14.60.

Figure 14.60 Creating New variable name and value for Maven home.

Step 5: Adding Maven M2_Home Variable name and variable value in Figure 14.61.

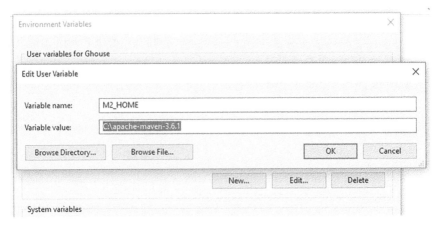

Figure 14.61 Creating New variable name and value for M2 home.

Step 6: Checking all the Java, Hadoop, Mahout, and Maven path setting in Figure 14.62.

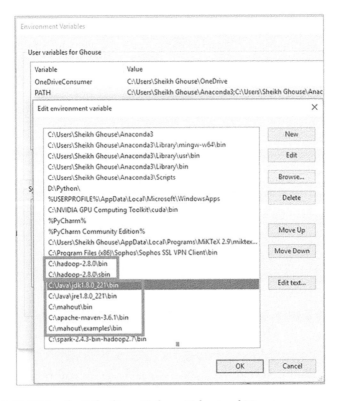

Figure 14.62 Editing the Path of Java, Hadoop, Mahout and Maven.

14.3.6   Hadoop Configuration

a) Create the namenode and datanode in data directory of hadoop-2.8.0 in Figure 14.63.

Figure 14.63 Creating two new folders datanode and namenode under data of hadoop.

b) Hadoop list of configuration files core-site.xml, hdfs-site.xml, mapred.xml and yarn.xml in Figure 14.64 to Figure 14.68.
Path: C:\hadoop-2.8.0\etc\hadoop

Local Disk (C:) > hadoop-2.8.0 > etc > hadoop

capacity-scheduler	configuration	container-executor.cfg
core-site 1	hadoop-env 5	hadoop-env
hadoop-metrics.properties	hadoop-metrics2.properties	hadoop-policy
hdfs-site 3	httpfs-env	httpfs-log4j.properties
httpfs-signature.secret	httpfs-site	kms-acls
kms-env	kms-log4j.properties	kms-site
log4j.properties	mapred-env	mapred-env
mapred-queues.xml	mapred-site 2	mapred-site.xml.template
slaves	ssl-client.xml.example	ssl-server.xml.example
yarn-env	yarn-env	yarn-site 4

Figure 14.64 Listing of file to edited in hadoop folder.

c) Editing the core-site xml file

```
<!-- core-site.xml-->
<configuration>
        <property>
                <name>fs.defaultFS</name>
                <value>hdfs://localhost:9000</value>
        </property>
</configuration>
```

Figure 14.65 Adding property fields.

d) Editing the mapred-site.xml

```
<!-- mapred-site.xml -->

<configuration>
 <property>
   <name>mapreduce.framework.name</name>
   <value>yarn</value>
 </property>

</configuration>
```

Figure 14.66 Adding property fields.

e) Editing the hdfs-site.xml

```
<configuration>|
        <property>
                    <name>dfs.replication</name>
                    <value>1</value>
        </property>
        <property>
                    <name>dfs.namenode.name.dir</name>
                    <value>hadoop-2.8.0/data/namenode</value>
        </property>
        <property>
                    <name>dfs.datanode.data.dir</name>
                    <value>hadoop-2.8.0/data/datanode</value>
        </property>
</configuration>
```

Figure 14.67 Adding property fields.

f) Editing the yarn-site.xml

```
<!-- yarn-site.xml -->|
</configuration>
 <property>
   <name>yarn.nodemanager.aux-services</name>
   <value>mapreduce_shuffle</value>
  </property>

  <property>
    <name>yarn.nodemanager.aux-services.mapreduce.shuffle.class</name>
    <value>org.apache.hadoop.mapred.ShuffleHandler</value>
   </property>
</configuration>
```

Figure 14.68 Adding property fields.

g) Editing the hadoop-env.cmd

@rem The java implememtation to use. Required. set JAVA_HOME= C:\Java\jdk1.8.0_221

h) Configure the Hadoop

1. Download the Hadoop configuration zip file
2. Delete bin flooder from hadoop-2.8.0. C:\ hadoop-2.8.0\bin

a) Hadoop Formatting the name node hdfs namenode - format. Formatting the name node in Figure 14.69 to Figure 14.75.

```
19/07/29 00:48:26 INFO util.GSet: Computing capacity for map cachedBlocks
19/07/29 00:48:26 INFO util.GSet: VM type       = 64-bit
19/07/29 00:48:26 INFO util.GSet: 0.25% max memory 889 MB = 2.2 MB
19/07/29 00:48:26 INFO util.GSet: capacity      = 2^18 = 262144 entries
19/07/29 00:48:26 INFO namenode.FSNamesystem: dfs.namenode.safemode.threshold-pct = 0.9990000128746033
19/07/29 00:48:26 INFO namenode.FSNamesystem: dfs.namenode.safemode.min.datanodes = 0
19/07/29 00:48:26 INFO namenode.FSNamesystem: dfs.namenode.safemode.extension     = 30000
19/07/29 00:48:26 INFO metrics.TopMetrics: NNTop conf: dfs.namenode.top.window.num.buckets = 10
19/07/29 00:48:26 INFO metrics.TopMetrics: NNTop conf: dfs.namenode.top.num.users = 10
19/07/29 00:48:26 INFO metrics.TopMetrics: NNTop conf: dfs.namenode.top.windows.minutes = 1,5,25
19/07/29 00:48:26 INFO namenode.FSNamesystem: Retry cache on namenode is enabled
19/07/29 00:48:26 INFO namenode.FSNamesystem: Retry cache will use 0.03 of total heap and retry cache entry expiry time
is 600000 millis
19/07/29 00:48:26 INFO util.GSet: Computing capacity for map NameNodeRetryCache
19/07/29 00:48:26 INFO util.GSet: VM type       = 64-bit
19/07/29 00:48:26 INFO util.GSet: 0.029999999329447746% max memory 889 MB = 273.1 KB
19/07/29 00:48:26 INFO util.GSet: capacity      = 2^15 = 32768 entries
19/07/29 00:48:31 INFO namenode.FSImage: Allocated new BlockPoolId: BP-1559929442-192.168.224.1-1564341511542
19/07/29 00:48:31 INFO common.Storage: Storage directory C:\Users\Sheikh Ghouse\hadoop-2.8.0\data\namenode has been succ
essfully formatted.
19/07/29 00:48:31 INFO namenode.FSImageFormatProtobuf: Saving image file C:\Users\Sheikh Ghouse\hadoop-2.8.0\data\nameno
de\current\fsimage.ckpt_0000000000000000000 using no compression
19/07/29 00:48:31 INFO namenode.FSImageFormatProtobuf: Image file C:\Users\Sheikh Ghouse\hadoop-2.8.0\data\namenode\curr
ent\fsimage.ckpt_0000000000000000000 of size 323 bytes saved in 0 seconds.
19/07/29 00:48:31 INFO namenode.NNStorageRetentionManager: Going to retain 1 images with txid >= 0
19/07/29 00:48:31 INFO namenode.FSImage: Exiting with status 0
19/07/29 00:48:31 INFO namenode.NameNode: SHUTDOWN_MSG:
/************************************************************
SHUTDOWN_MSG: Shutting down NameNode at Ghouse/192.168.224.1
************************************************************/

C:\Users\Sheikh Ghouse>
```

Figure 14.69 Namenode formatting success.

```
C:\WINDOWS\system32>start-all.cmd
This script is Deprecated. Instead use start-dfs.cmd and start-yarn.cmd
starting yarn daemons
```

Figure 14.70 Command for starting of namenode, datanode, resource manager and node manager.

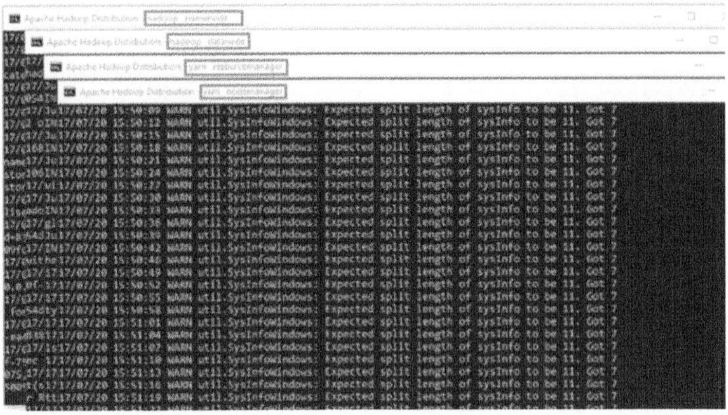

Figure 14.71 Starting of namenode, datanode, resource manager and node manager.

(a)　　　　　　　　　　　　　(b)

Figure 14.72 Name node information overview (a) and summary (b).

(a)　　　　　　　　　　　　　(b)

Figure 14.73 Name node status (a) and Datanode information (b).

a. Testing Mahout with a sample

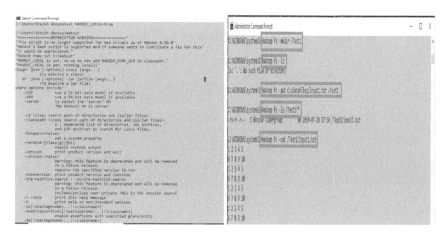

Figure 14.74 Creating a directory Test1, Copying input file to cluster and displaying.

Figure 14.75 Checking Test1 directory from browser and Checking input file directory from Test1 directory browser.

14.4   Installation Steps of Apache Mahout Using Eclipse

14.4.1   Eclipse Installation

Eclipse IDE latest version: https://www.eclipse.org/downloads/ with 64-bit in Figure 14.76 to Figure 14.80.

Select the workspace either creating own or default then launch
Loading the workbench of eclipse

14.4.2   Installation of Maven Through Eclipse

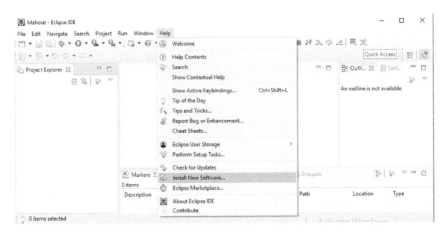

Figure 14.76 Select the Install New Software from Help tab.

Figure 14.77 Work with url paste the maven link https://download.eclipse.org/
technology/m2e/releases/.

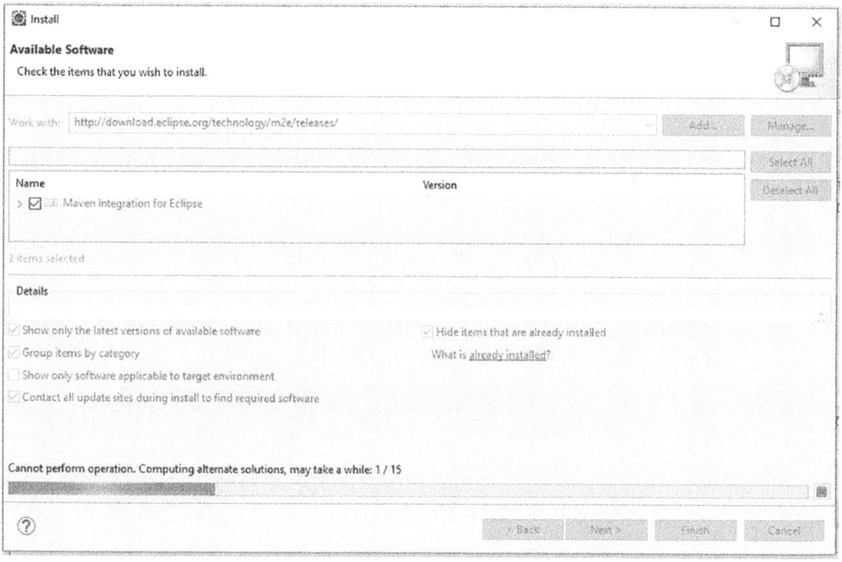

Figure 14.78 Select the Maven Integration for Eclipse.

Figure 14.79 Install the Remediation page.

Figure 14.80 Installing the Maven.

Accept the license agreement and select finish button

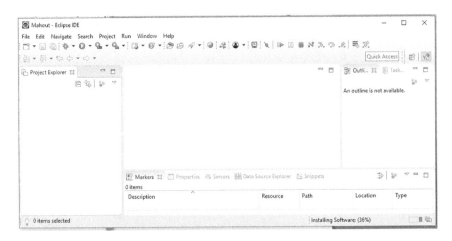

Figure 14.81 Maven installed.

14.4.3   Maven Setup for Mahout Configuration

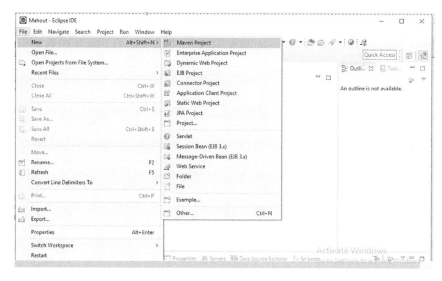

Figure 14.82 Select File tab → New → Maven Project.

Figure 14.83 Creating New Maven Project. Select Next tab.

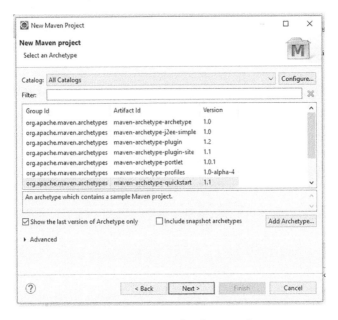

Figure 14.84 Select the show the last version of Archetype only.

Figure 14.85 Enter a group id for the artifact details.

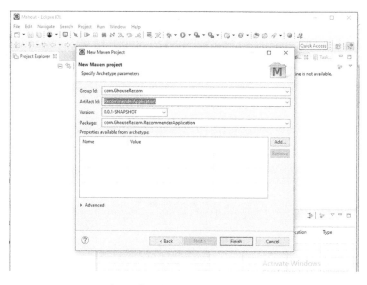

Figure 14.86 Create GroupId, ArtifactId, Version, and Package.

GroupId: com.GhouseRecom
ArtifactId: RecommenderApplication
Version: 0.0.1 SNAPSHOT
Package: com.GhouseRecom.RecommenderApplication
Then, select Finish in Figure 14.81 to Figure 14.87.

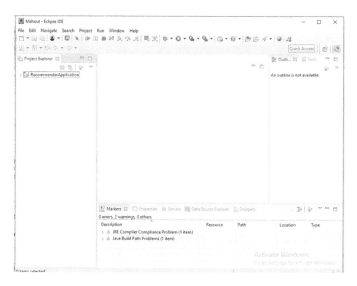

Figure 14.87 Artifact created.

14.4.4 Building the Path-

Select file->properties in Figure 14.88 to Figure 14.90.

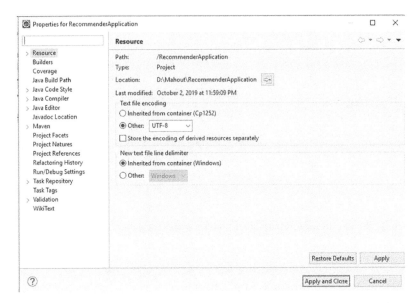

Figure 14.88 Select Properties for Recommender Application.

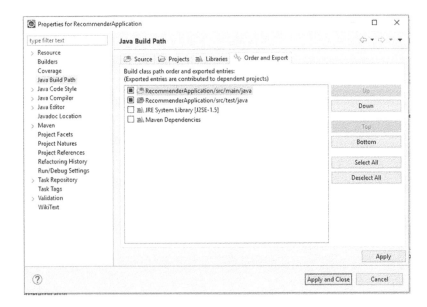

Figure 14.89 Select JavaBuildPath → Order and Exports.

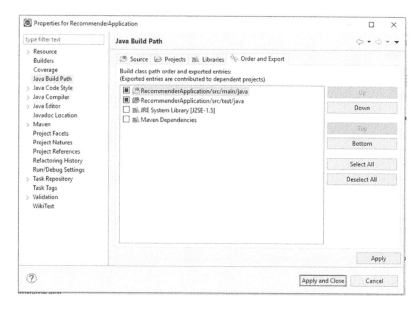

Figure 14.90 Select the Build class path order. It creates main and test folders under Artificate Id.

RecommenderApllication/src/main/java and RecommenderApplication/src/test/java in Figure 14.91.

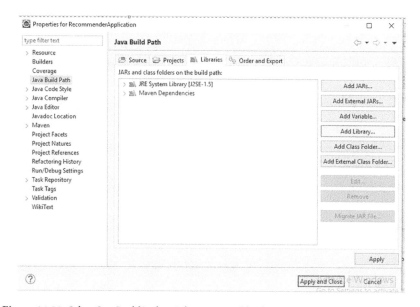

Figure 14.91 Select JavaBuildPath → Libraries → Add Library.

Select JRE System Library and Next in Figures 14.92 to Figure 14.97.

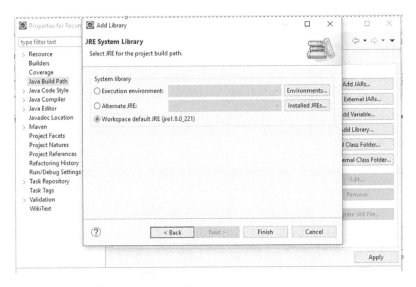

Figure 14.92 Select Workspace default JRE.

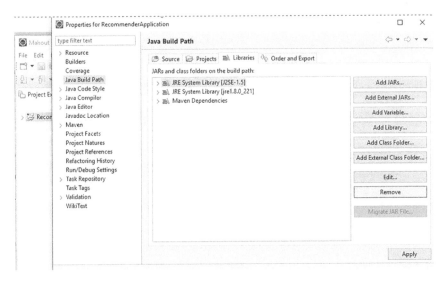

Figure 14.93 Remove the JRE System Library [J2SE-1.5].

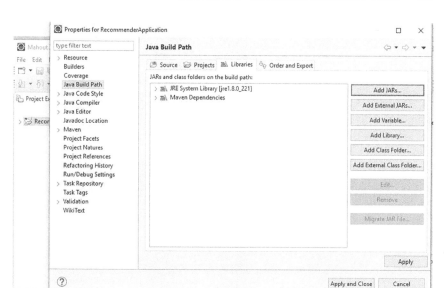

Figure 14.94 Apply and Close.

14.4.5   Modifying the pom.xml File

Figure 14.95 pom.xml file.

Figure 14.96 pom.xml file create dependency.

Figure 14.97 pom.xml file change the version tag.

14.4.6   Creating the Data File

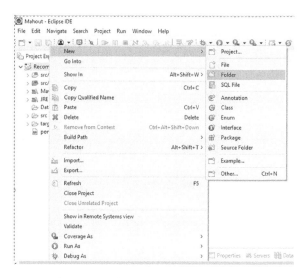

Figure 14.98 Creating the new data file:

Select the ProjectFile → Rightclick →select New → Select Folder → write Folder Name in Figure 14.98 to Figure 14.107.

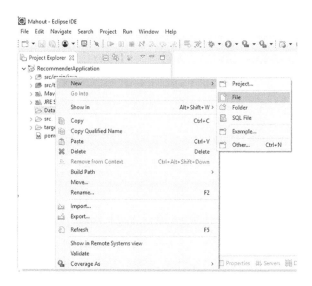

Figure 14.99 Creating the new data file: Select the ProjectFile →Rightclick →select New→Select File → write File Name.

Figure 14.100 Creating the new data file: Select the ProjectFile → Rightclick →select New → Select Folder → write FileName.csv →Finish.

14.4.7   Adding External Jar Files

Figure 14.101 Creating the new data file: Select the Project File →Right click → select Build Path →select Configure Build Path.

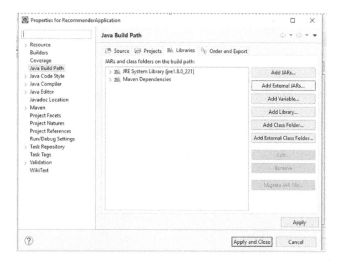

Figure 14.102 Select→ Libraries →Add External JARs.

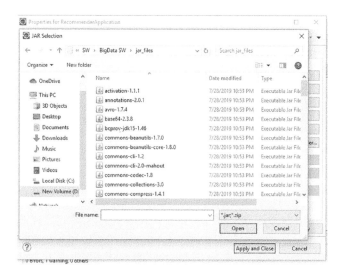

Figure 14.103 Select→ All jar files which downloaded → Open → Apply and Close.

14.4.8   Creating the New Package and Classes

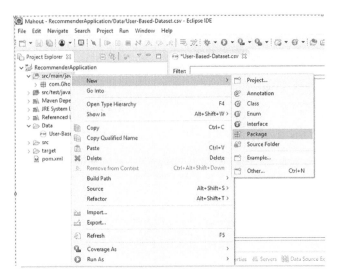

Figure 14.104 Create a new package. Right Click → src/main/java → New → Package.

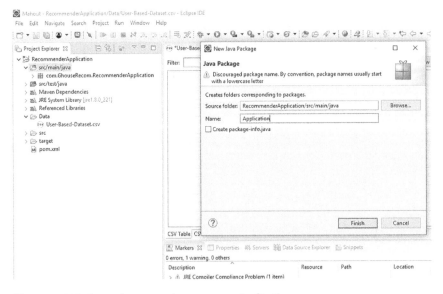

Figure 14.105 Create the new package name as Application.

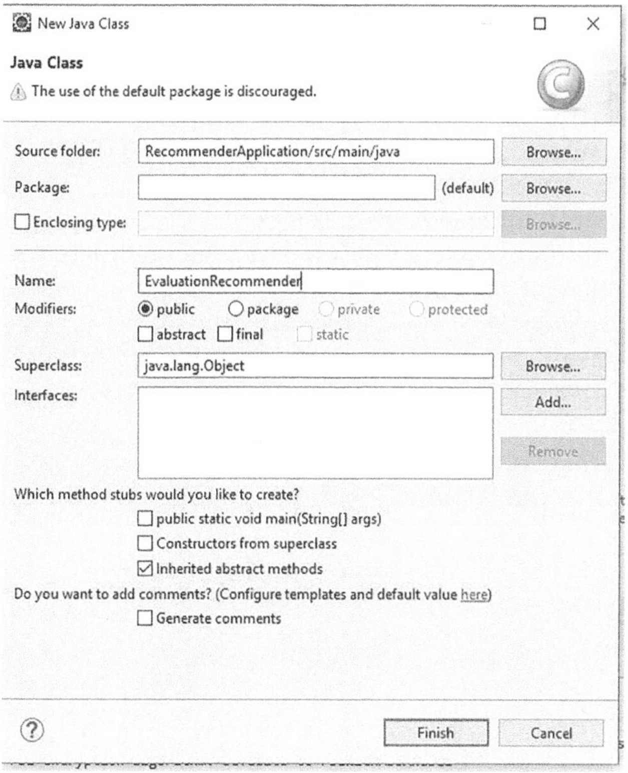

Figure 14.106 Create new class Evaluation Recommender under src/main/java.

14.4.9   Result

Figure 14.107 Run and the Result of the EvaluationRecommender class.

14.5   Mahout Algorithms

14.5.1   Classification

Classification Algorithm: NAIVE BAYES [35, 36, 37]

1. Dataset: 20News-All
2. Download: 20news-bydate.tar.gz.
3. Two files: Extract the two files 20news-bydate-test and 20news-bydate-train
4. Copy to HDFS: Two files copied to hdfs
5. Make directory MahoutTest and copy two filesin Figure 14.108 and Figure 14.109.

```
C:\WINDOWS\system32 hadoop fs -mkdir /MahoutTest
```

```
C:\WINDOWS\system3 >hadoop fs -put D:/Data20News/20news-bydate-test/* /MahoutTest

C:\WINDOWS\system32>
C:\WINDOWS\system32>hadoop fs -ls /MahoutTest/*
Found 319 items
-rw-r--r--   1 Ghouse supergroup        950 2019-07-26 18:17 /MahoutTest/alt.atheism/53068
-rw-r--r--   1 Ghouse supergroup       3995 2019-07-26 18:17 /MahoutTest/alt.atheism/53257
-rw-r--r--   1 Ghouse supergroup       2215 2019-07-26 18:17 /MahoutTest/alt.atheism/53260
-rw-r--r--   1 Ghouse supergroup       1321 2019-07-26 18:17 /MahoutTest/alt.atheism/53261
-rw-r--r--   1 Ghouse supergroup       7264 2019-07-26 18:17 /MahoutTest/alt.atheism/53262
-rw-r--r--   1 Ghouse supergroup       1994 2019-07-26 18:17 /MahoutTest/alt.atheism/53265
-rw-r--r--   1 Ghouse supergroup       2419 2019-07-26 18:18 /MahoutTest/alt.atheism/53272
-rw-r--r--   1 Ghouse supergroup        696 2019-07-26 18:18 /MahoutTest/alt.atheism/53276
-rw-r--r--   1 Ghouse supergroup        639 2019-07-26 18:18 /MahoutTest/alt.atheism/53277
-rw-r--r--   1 Ghouse supergroup        765 2019-07-26 18:18 /MahoutTest/alt.atheism/53278
```

Figure 14.108 Copying the 20news data into MahoutTest.

Local Disk (C:) > mahout > examples > bin		
Name	Date modified	Type
resources	7/26/2019 5:44 PM	File folder
classify-20newsgroups	4/15/2017 10:40 AM	SH File
classify-wikipedia	4/15/2017 10:40 AM	SH File
cluster-reuters	4/15/2017 10:40 AM	SH File
cluster-syntheticcontrol	4/15/2017 10:40 AM	SH File
factorize-movielens-1M	4/15/2017 10:40 AM	SH File
factorize-netflix	4/15/2017 10:40 AM	SH File
get-all-examples	4/15/2017 10:40 AM	SH File
lda.algorithm	4/15/2017 10:40 AM	ALGORITHM File
README	4/15/2017 10:40 AM	Text Document
run-item-sim	4/15/2017 10:40 AM	SH File
set-dfs-commands	4/15/2017 10:40 AM	SH File
spark-document-classifier.mscala	4/15/2017 10:40 AM	MSCALA File
SparseSparseDrmTimer.mscala	4/15/2017 10:40 AM	MSCALA File

Figure 14.109 Running the classify-20newsgroups.sh from bin folder of mahout.

Run:

C:\mahout\bin\mahout classify-20newsgroups.sh in Figure 14.110.

output:

```
=========================================================
Confusion Matrix
---------------------------------------------------------
   a   b   c   d   e   f   g   h   i   j   k   l   m   n   o   p   q   r   s   t   u   <--Classified as
 381   0   0   0   0   9   1   0   0   1   0   0   2   0   1   0   0   3   0   0   |  398  a  = rec.motorcycles
   1 284   0   0   0   0   1   0   6   3  11   0  66   3   0   1   6   0   4   9   0   |  395  b  = comp.windows.x
   2   0 339   2   0   3   5   1   0   0   0   1   1  12   1   7   0   2   0   0   |  376  c  = talk.politics.mideast
   4   0   1 327   0   2   2   0   0   2   1   1   0   5   1   4  12   0   2   0   0   |  364  d  = talk.politics.guns
   7   0   4  32  27   7   7   2   0  12   0   0   6   0 100   9   7  31   0   0   0   |  251  e  = talk.religion.misc
  10   0   0   0   0 359   2   2   0   1   3   0   1   6   0   1   0   0  11   0   0   |  396  f  = rec.autos
   0   0   0   0   1 383   9   1   0   0   0   0   0   0   0   0   0   3   0   0   |  397  g  = rec.sport.baseball
   1   0   0   0   0   0   9 382   0   0   0   0   1   1   0   2   0   2   0   0   |  399  h  = rec.sport.hockey
   2   0   0   0   0   4   3   0 330   4   4   0   5  12   0   0   2   0  12   7   0   |  385  i  = comp.sys.mac.hardware
   0   3   0   0   0   0   1   0   0 368   0   0  10   4   1   3   2   0   2   0   0   |  394  j  = sci.space
   0   0   0   0   0   3   1   0  27   2 291   0  11  25   0   0   1   0  13  18   0   |  392  k  = comp.sys.ibm.pc.hardware
   8   0   1 109   0   6  11   4   1  18   0  98   1   3  11  10  27   1   1   0   0   |  310  l  = talk.politics.misc
   0  11   0   0   0   3   6   0  10   6  11   0 299  13   0   2  13   0   7   8   0   |  389  m  = comp.graphics
   6   0   1   0   0   4   2   0   5   2  12   0   8 321   0   4  14   0   8   6   0   |  393  n  = sci.electronics
   2   0   0   0   0   0   4   1   0   3   1   0   3   1 372   6   0   2   1   2   0   |  398  o  = soc.religion.christian
   4   0   0   1   0   2   3   3   0   4   2   0   7  12   6 342   1   0   9   0   0   |  396  p  = sci.med
   0   1   0   1   0   1   4   0   3   0   1   0   8   4   0   2 369   0   1   1   0   |  396  q  = sci.crypt
  10   0   4  10   1   5   6   2   2   6   2   0   2   1  86  15  14 152   0   1   0   |  319  r  = alt.atheism
   4   0   0   0   0   9   1   1   8   1  12   0   3   6   0   2   0   0 341   2   0   |  390  s  = misc.forsale
   8   5   0   0   0   1   6   0   8   5  50   0  40   2   1   0   9   0   3 256   0   |  394  t  = comp.os.ms-windows.misc
   0   0   0   0   0   0   0   0   0   0   0   0   0   0   0   0   0   0   0   0   0   |    0  u  = unknown
```

Figure 14.110 Output of 20 dataset.

14.5.2   Clustering [36, 38, 39]

Procedure:

1. START SERVER
2. MAKE A 3 DIR (INPUT,OUTPUT,SEQU)
3. COPY INPUT FILE TO HDFS in Figure 14.111.
4. MAKE SEQU FILE in Figure 14.112(a).
5. RUN CLUSTER ALGORITHM in Figure 14.112(b).
6. DISPLAY DATA

Dataset: Synthentic_control.data of 1999

Description: 600 examples of control charts of 6 fields (N, C, I, D, U, D)

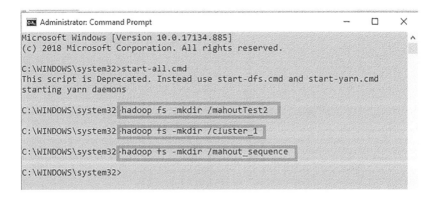

```
Command Prompt                                                                    —   □   ×

C:\Users\Sheikh Ghouse>hadoop fs -mkdir /Test2

C:\Users\Sheikh Ghouse>hadoop fs -put C:/DataFiles/synthetic_control.data /Test1

C:\Users\Sheikh Ghouse>hadoop fs -cat /Test1/synthetic_control.data
28.7812 34.4632 31.3381 31.2834 28.9207 33.7596 25.3969 27.7849 35.2479 27.1159 32.8717 29.2171 36.0253 32.337  34.5249
32.8717 34.1173 26.5235 27.6623 26.3693 25.7744 29.27   30.7326 29.5054 33.0292 25.04   28.9167 24.3437 26.1203 34.9424
25.0293 26.6311 35.6541 28.4353 29.1495 28.1584 26.1927 33.3182 30.9772 27.0443 35.5344 26.2353 28.9964 32.0036 31.0558
34.2553 28.0721 28.9402 35.4973 29.747  31.4333 24.5556 33.7431 25.0466 34.9318 34.9879 32.4721 33.3759 25.4652 25.8717
24.8923 25.741  27.5532 32.8217 27.8789 31.5926 31.4861 35.5469 27.9516 31.6595 27.5415 31.1887 27.4867 31.391  27.811
24.488  27.5918 35.6273 35.4102 31.4167 30.7447 24.1311 35.1422 30.4719 31.9874 33.6615 25.5511 30.4686 33.6472 25.0701
34.0765 32.5981 28.3038 26.1471 26.9414 31.5203 33.1089 24.1491 28.5167 25.7906 35.9519 26.5301 24.8578 25.9562 32.8357
28.5322 26.3458 30.6213 28.9861 29.4047 32.5577 31.0205 26.6418 28.4331 33.6564 26.4244 28.4661 34.2484 32.1005 26.691
31.3987 30.6316 26.3983 24.2905 27.8613 28.5491 24.9717 32.4358 25.2239 27.3068 31.8387 27.2587 28.2572 26.5819 24.0455
35.0625 31.5717 32.5614 31.0308 34.1202 26.9337 31.4781 35.0173 32.3851 24.3323 30.2001 31.2452 26.6814 31.5137 28.8778
27.3086 24.246  26.9631 25.2919 31.6114 24.7131 27.4809 24.2075 26.8059 35.1253 32.6293 31.0561 26.3583 28.0861 31.4391
27.3057 29.6082 35.9725 34.1444 27.1717 33.6318 26.5966 25.5387 32.5434 25.5772 29.9897 31.351  33.9002 29.5446 29.343
25.774  30.5262 35.4209 25.6033 27.97   25.2702 28.132  29.4268 31.4549 27.32   28.9564 28.9916 29.9578 30.2773 30.4447
24.3037 24.314  35.0966 25.3679 32.0968 33.3303 25.0102 35.3155 31.6264 29.2806 34.2021 26.5077 32.2279 25.5265 24.824
27.5587 28.3714 32.3667 26.9752 35.9346 35.1146 24.3749 27.6083 27.8433 29.8557 32.4185 26.8908 31.3209 29.3849 34.3336
24.7381 35.769  31.8725 34.2054 31.156  34.6292 28.7261 28.2979 31.5787 34.6156 32.5492 30.9827 24.8938 27.3659 25.3069
27.1798 29.2498 33.6928 25.6264 24.6555 28.9446 35.798  34.9446 24.5596 34.2386 27.9634 25.3216 35.4154 34.862  25.1472
29.4686 33.1739 31.1274 31.3701 26.5173 28.6486 31.6565 35.9497 33.0321 24.6001 31.2025 27.4335 32.6355 35.8773 28.0295
33.1247 33.4129 26.9245 30.2123 29.6526 30.8644 24.5119 33.9931 33.3094 33.204  31.2651 27.9072 35.111  35.0757 33.833
25.9481 29.1348 24.2875 32.3223 34.9244 27.7218 27.9601 35.7198 27.576  35.3375 29.9993 34.2149 33.1276 31.1057 31.0179
25.5067 29.7929 28.0765 34.4812 33.8    27.6671 30.6122 25.6393 30.1171 26.5188 30.1524 27.8514 29.5582 32.3601 29.2064
26.1001 33.4677 33.901  29.2674 34.8311 31.9815 26.496  32.6645 27.7188 35.7385 32.8380 30.1509 30.5593 27.3321 27.4559
24.2361 34.7268 29.9207 27.273  35.9963 32.3917 27.139  26.4589 25.0466 35.5002 27.9961 25.8897 31.3951 30.7583 34.9652
28.0919 35.6706 33.4401 28.458  31.1795 26.9458 35.8381 26.7134 25.1641 27.341  25.2093 33.4669 24.1094 33.1669 35.4907
28.6989 29.2101 30.9291 34.6229 31.4138 28.4636 35.9115 32.9058 28.7669 24.2868 34.8983 33.7291 29.1154 26.2804 34.4559
31.6103 33.3061 24.553  29.1587 27.8378 25.3525 25.2126 26.9565 27.9928 29.5057 31.0723 26.3605 27.7434 34.0438 25.1053
24.4462 35.4191 33.3472 32.2356 34.5244 29.4635 24.6889 28.1962 34.2994 31.6316 30.8005 35.7727 31.3444 25.5691 32.7839
32.7707 24.1047 34.006  28.8249 24.0499 29.8274 24.0323 31.0756 34.5358 25.893  35.6732 25.1869 29.6669 26.4637
30.9493 34.317  35.5674 34.8829 30.6691 35.2667 35.895  25.9022 28.8917 32.2092 28.9898 26.0572 31.7516 32.294  31.0631
24.1612 26.6554 25.2452 30.5956 31.391  32.1604 33.7765 31.1336 32.626  28.8616 27.6223 33.9381 33.9836 34.8895 29.4617
34.5734 32.4431 30.0745 25.0495 29.2942 28.2689 28.4819 29.8917 33.1162 26.4574 27.4442 33.0784 33.2286 27.5837 24.4895
26.2151 24.0331 26.4765 34.8568 30.5934 35.4341 31.1248 24.2424 29.7172 35.9365 36.0107 26.3866 33.1042 31.3025 34.523
35.2538 34.6402 35.7584 28.551  25.6518 29.6442 31.94   35.9086 28.9622 24.6224 29.7635 29.5098 28.2109 34.2855 27.5473
25.4274 32.3429 34.79   33.7012 25.3495 33.7603 26.4442 24.5097 30.4135 28.4948 28.8433 32.4284 24.5071 31.7032 29.8722
35.852  35.7172 27.1922 24.3206 25.2698 29.6203 24.3243 31.1824 25.0701 31.8824 28.6468 32.857  24.7469 29.3045 27.3994
```

Figure 14.111 Clustering synthetic data copied into cluster.

```
Administrator: Command Prompt                                                    —   □   ×
Microsoft Windows [Version 10.0.17134.885]
(c) 2018 Microsoft Corporation. All rights reserved.

C:\WINDOWS\system32>start-all.cmd
This script is Deprecated. Instead use start-dfs.cmd and start-yarn.cmd
starting yarn daemons

C:\WINDOWS\system32>hadoop fs -mkdir /mahoutTest2

C:\WINDOWS\system32>hadoop fs -mkdir /cluster_1

C:\WINDOWS\system32>hadoop fs -mkdir /mahout_sequence

C:\WINDOWS\system32>
```

Figure 14.112 (a) commands for creating directory for Synthetic data.

Commands for Running: $MAHOUT_HOME/bin/

1. Canopy:

$MAHOUT_HOME/bin/mahout org.apache.mahout.clustering.syntheticcontrol.canopy.Job

2. KMean:

$MAHOUT_HOME/bin/mahout org.apache.mahout.clustering.syntheticcontrol.kmeans.Job

3. FuzzyKmeans:

$MAHOUT_HOME/bin/mahout org.apache.mahout.clustering.syntheticcontrol.fuzzykmeans. Job

4. Dirichlet:

$MAHOUT_HOME/bin/mahout org.apache.mahout.clustering.syntheticcontrol.dirichlet.Job

5. MeanShift:

$MAHOUT_HOME/bin/mahout org.apache.mahout.clustering.syntheticcontrol.meanshift.Job

Figure 14.112 (b) Commands for running clustering algorithms.

14.5.3   Recommendation

In 2013, recommendation known for Multimodal that is data in all forms [40, 41]. Eclipse IDE execution steps in the Figure 14.113 (a), (b), (c), (d), (e), (f).

It architecture consists of the following:

1. Application
2. Search Engine
3. Database User Interaction
4. Mahouts spark item simulation

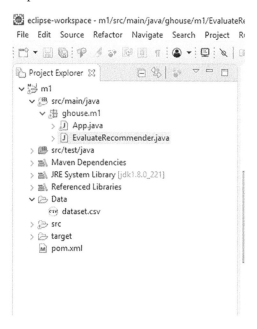

Figure 14.113 (a) Eclipse path for Recommender.

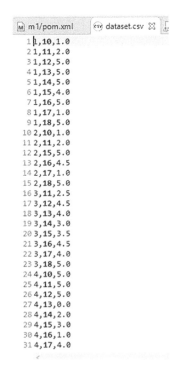

```
m1/pom.xml ⌧   ᴄˢᵛ dataset.csv     ᴊ App.java     ᴊ EvaluateRecommender.java
1⊖ <project xmlns="http://maven.apache.org/POM/4.0.0" xmlns:xsi="http://www.w3.org/2001/XMLSch
2     xsi:schemaLocation="http://maven.apache.org/POM/4.0.0 http://maven.apache.org/xsd/maven-4
3     <modelVersion>4.0.0</modelVersion>
4
5     <groupId>ghouse</groupId>
6     <artifactId>m1</artifactId>
7     <version>0.0.1-SNAPSHOT</version>
8     <packaging>jar</packaging>
9
10    <name>m1</name>
11    <url>http://maven.apache.org</url>
12
13⊖   <properties>
14       <project.build.sourceEncoding>UTF-8</project.build.sourceEncoding>
15    </properties>
16
17⊖   <dependencies>
18⊖     <dependency>
19        <groupId>org.apache.mahout</groupId>
20        <artifactId>mahout-math</artifactId>
21        <version>0.13.0</version>
22     </dependency>
23
24⊖     <dependency>
25        <groupId>junit</groupId>
26        <artifactId>junit</artifactId>
27        <version>3.8.1</version>
28        <scope>test</scope>
29     </dependency>
30    </dependencies>
31 </project>
```

Figure 14.113 (b) pom.xml.

```
m1/pom.xml     ᴄˢᵛ dataset.csv ⌧  [
1 1,10,1.0
2 1,11,2.0
3 1,12,5.0
4 1,13,5.0
5 1,14,5.0
6 1,15,4.0
7 1,16,5.0
8 1,17,1.0
9 1,18,5.0
10 2,10,1.0
11 2,11,2.0
12 2,15,5.0
13 2,16,4.5
14 2,17,1.0
15 2,18,5.0
16 3,11,2.5
17 3,12,4.5
18 3,13,4.0
19 3,14,3.0
20 3,15,3.5
21 3,16,4.5
22 3,17,4.0
23 3,18,5.0
24 4,10,5.0
25 4,11,5.0
26 4,12,5.0
27 4,13,0.0
28 4,14,2.0
29 4,15,3.0
30 4,16,1.0
31 4,17,4.0
```

Figure 14.113 (c) Recommender Dataset.

```
M m1/pom.xml    csv dataset.csv    J *App.java ⋈    J EvaluateRecommender.java
 1  package ghouse.m1;
 2
 3  import java.io.File;
 4  import java.io.IOException;
 5  import java.util.List;
 6  import org.apache.log4j.PropertyConfigurator;
 7  import org.apache.mahout.cf.taste.impl.model.file.FileDataModel;
 8  import org.apache.mahout.cf.taste.impl.neighborhood.ThresholdUserNeighborhood;
 9  import org.apache.mahout.cf.taste.impl.recommender.GenericUserBasedRecommender;
10  import org.apache.mahout.cf.taste.impl.similarity.PearsonCorrelationSimilarity;
11  import org.apache.mahout.cf.taste.model.DataModel;
12  import org.apache.mahout.cf.taste.neighborhood.UserNeighborhood;
13  import org.apache.mahout.cf.taste.recommender.RecommendedItem;
14  import org.apache.mahout.cf.taste.recommender.UserBasedRecommender;
15  import org.apache.mahout.cf.taste.similarity.UserSimilarity;
16
17  public class App
18  {
19      public static void main( String[] args ) throws Exception
20      {
21        String log4jConfPath = "LOG4J/log4j.properties";
22        PropertyConfigurator.configure(log4jConfPath);
23
24        DataModel model = new FileDataModel(new File("data/dataset.csv"));
25        UserSimilarity similarity = new PearsonCorrelationSimilarity(model);
26        UserNeighborhood neighborhood = new ThresholdUserNeighborhood(0.1, similarity, model);
27        UserBasedRecommender recommender = new GenericUserBasedRecommender(model, neighborhood
28
29        List<RecommendedItem> recommendations = recommender.recommend(2, 3);
30        for (RecommendedItem recommendation : recommendations) {
31          System.out.println(recommendation);
32        }
```

Figure 14.113 (d) App.java.

```
M m1/pom.xml    csv dataset.csv    J *App.java    J EvaluateRecommender.java ⋈
11  import org.apache.mahout.cf.taste.impl.recommender.GenericUserBasedRecommender;
12  import org.apache.mahout.cf.taste.impl.similarity.PearsonCorrelationSimilarity;
13  import org.apache.mahout.cf.taste.model.DataModel;
14  import org.apache.mahout.cf.taste.neighborhood.UserNeighborhood;
15  import org.apache.mahout.cf.taste.recommender.Recommender;
16  import org.apache.mahout.cf.taste.similarity.UserSimilarity;
17
18  public class EvaluateRecommender {
19
20      public static void main(String[] args) throws Exception {
21        |
22        DataModel model = new FileDataModel(new File("data/dataset.csv"));
23        RecommenderEvaluator evaluator = new AverageAbsoluteDifferenceRecommenderEvaluator();
24        RecommenderBuilder builder = new MyRecommenderBuilder();
25        double result = evaluator.evaluate(builder, null, model, 0.9, 1.0);
26        System.out.println(result);
27
28      }
29
30  }
31
32  class MyRecommenderBuilder implements RecommenderBuilder {
33
34      public Recommender buildRecommender(DataModel dataModel) throws TasteException{
35        UserSimilarity similarity = new PearsonCorrelationSimilarity(dataModel);
36        UserNeighborhood neighborhood = new ThresholdUserNeighborhood(0.1, similarity, dataModel)
37        return new GenericUserBasedRecommender(dataModel, neighborhood, similarity);
38
39      }
40
41  }
42
43
```

Figure 14.113 (e) EvaluatorRecommender.java file.

```
Markers   Properties   Servers   Data Source Explorer   Snippets   Console ⊠                  ⬛ ✖ ✖

<terminated> EvaluateRecommender [Java Application] C:\Java\jdk1.8.0_221\bin\javaw.exe (Jul 29, 2019, 2:48:31 AM)
0.25000011920928955
|
```

Figure 14.113 (f) Result of Recommender.

14.6   Conclusion

Apache Mahout is a package of powerful scalable open source libraries of ML algorithms of clustering, classification, and recommendation system to analyze faster and efficiently. It is placed on the top MapReduce. It provides libraries for mathematics, statistics, and linear algebra. Mahout applications analyze the data much quicker, less complicated, and effectively on big data. It is mainly designed for data scientists to generate new algorithms using Scala and Flink.

References

1. Owen, S., Anil, R., Dunning, T., Friedman, E., *Mahout In Action*, Manning Publications Co., NY, USA, 2012.
2. Solanki, R., Ravilla, S.H., Bein, D., Study of Distributed Framework Hadoop and Overview of Machine Learning using Apache Mahout. *2019 IEEE 9th Annual Computing and Communication Workshop and Conference (CCWC)*, Las Vegas, NV, USA, 0252–0257, 2019.
3. Srinivasulu, Subbarao, C.D.V., Y, J.K., High dimensional datasets using hadoop mahout machine learning algorithms. *International Conference on Computing and Communication Technologies, Hyderabad*, 1–1, 2014.
4. Zhou, L., Pan, S., Wang, J., Vasilakos, A.V., Machine learning on big data: Opportunities and challenges. *Neurocomputing*, 237, 350–361, 2017.
5. Oussous, A., Benjelloun, F.Z., Lahcen, A.A., Belfkih, S., Big Data technologies: A survey. *J. King Saud Univ. Comput. Inf. Sci.*, 30, 4, 431–448, 2018.
6. Elshawi, R., Sakr, S., Talia, D., Trunfio, P., Big Data Systems Meet Machine Learning Challenges: Towards Big Data Science as a Service. *Big Data Res.*, 14, 1–11, 2018.
7. Shadroo, S. and Rahmani, A.M., Systematic survey of big data and data mining in internet of things. *Comput. Netw.*, 139, 19–47, 2018.
8. Eluri, V.R., Ramesh, M., Al-Jabri, A.S.M., Jane, M., A comparative study of various clustering techniques on big data sets using Apache Mahout. *2016 3rd MEC International Conference on Big Data and Smart City (ICBDSC)*, Muscat, 1–4, 2016.

9. Ghani, N.A., Hamid, S., Abaker T Hashem, I., Ahmed, E., Social media big data analytics: A survey. *Comput. Hum. Behav.*, 101, 417–418, 2019.

10. Jain, E. and Jain, S.K., Using Mahout for clustering similar Twitter users: Performance evaluation of k-means and its comparison with fuzzy k-means. *2014 International Conference on Computer and Communication Technology (ICCCT)*, Allahabad, 29–33, 2014.

11. Langcai, Zhihui, L., Yuanfang, L., Research of text clustering based on improved VSM by TF under the framework of Mahout. *2017 29th Chinese Control And Decision Conference (CCDC)*, Chongqing, 6597–6600, 2017.

12. Esteves, R.M., Pais, R., Rong, C., K-means Clustering in the Cloud – A Mahout Test. *2011 IEEE Workshops of International Conference on Advanced Information Networking and Applications*, Singapore, 514–519, 2011.

13. Esteves, R.M. and Rong, C., Using Mahout for Clustering Wikipedia's Latest Articles: A Comparison between K-means and Fuzzy C-means in the Cloud. *2011 IEEE Third International Conference on Cloud Computing Technology and Science*, Athens, 565–569, 2011.

14. Xhafa, F., Bogza, A., Caballé, S., Barolli, L., Apache Mahout's k-Means vs Fuzzy k-Means Performance Evaluation. *2016 International Conference on Intelligent Networking and Collaborative Systems (INCoS)*, Ostrawva, 110–116, 2016.

15. Sahu, L. and Mohan, B.R., An improved K-means algorithm using modified cosine distance measure for document clustering using Mahout with Hadoop. *2014 9th International Conference on Industrial and Information Systems (ICIIS)*, Gwalior, 1–5, 2014.

16. Wang, J. and Zeng, Y., The Optimization of Parallel Frequent Pattern Growth Algorithm Based on Mahout in Cloud Manufacturing Environment. *2014 Seventh International Symposium on Computational Intelligence and Design*, Hangzhou, 420–423, 2014.

17. Dhumal, P. and Deshmukh, S.S., Retrieval and extraction of unique patterns from compressed text data using the SVD technique on Hadoop Apache MAHOUT framework. *2016 International Conference on Computing Communication Control and automation (ICCUBEA)*, Pune, 1–5, 2016.

18. Salur, M.U., Tokat, S., Aydilek, İ.B., Text classification on mahout with Naïve-Bayes machine learning algorithm. *2017 International Artificial Intelligence and Data Processing Symposium (IDAP)*, Malatya, 1–5, 2017.

19. Xhafa, F., Bogza, A., Caballé, S., Performance Evaluation of Mahout Clustering Algorithms Using a Twitter Streaming Dataset. *2017 IEEE 31st International Conference on Advanced Information Networking and Applications (AINA)*, Taipei, 1019–1026, 2017.

20. He, J., Xue, Z., Gao, M., Wu, H., A mahout based image classification framework for very large dataset. *Proceedings of 2014 International Conference on Cloud Computing and Internet of Things*, Changchun, 119–122, 2014.

21. Jain, E. and Jain, S.K., Categorizing Twitter users on the basis of their interests using Hadoop/Mahout platform. *2014 9th International Conference on Industrial and Information Systems (ICIIS)*, Gwalior, 1–5, 2014.
22. Cunha, J., Silva, C., Antunes, M., Health Twitter Big Bata Management with Hadoop Framework. *Procedia Comput. Sci.*, 64, 425–431, 2015.
23. Demirbaga, U. and Jha, D.N., Social Media Data Analysis Using MapReduce Programming Model and Training a Tweet Classifier Using Apache Mahout. *2018 IEEE 8th International Symposium on Cloud and Service Computing (SC2)*, Paris, 116–121, 2018.
24. Bora, D.J., Chapter 3 - Big Data Analytics in Healthcare: A Critical Analysis, in: *Advances in ubiquitous sensing applications for healthcare, Big Data Analytics for Intelligent Healthcare Management*, N. Dey, H. Das, B. Naik, H.S. Behera (eds.), pp. 43–57, Academic Press, 2019.
25. Wang, Y. and Zhu, L., Research on Collaborative Filtering Recommendation Algorithm Based on Mahout. *2016 4th Intl Conf on Applied Computing and Information Technology/3rd Intl Conf on Computational Science/Intelligence and Applied Informatics/1st Intl Conf on Big Data, Cloud Computing, Data Science & Engineering (ACIT-CSII-BCD)*, Las Vegas, NV, 400–405, 2016.
26. Jabakji, and Dag, H., Improving item-based recommendation accuracy with user's preferences on Apache Mahout. *2016 IEEE International Conference on Big Data (Big Data)*, Washington, DC, 1742–1749, 2016.
27. Farooque, U., Implementing user based collaborative filtering to build a generic product recommender using Apache mahout. *2016 3rd International Conference on Computing for Sustainable Global Development (INDIACom)*, New Delhi, 984–987, 2016.
28. Bagchi, S., Performance and Quality Assessment of Similarity Measures in Collaborative Filtering Using Mahout. *Procedia Comput. Sci.*, 50, 229–234, 2015.
29. https://mahout.apache.org/docs/latest/algorithms/linear-algebra/
30. https://hadoop.apache.org/docs/stable/hadoop-project-dist/hadoop-common/SingleCluster.html
31. http://hadooptutorial.weebly.com/single-node-install.html
32. http://hadooptutorial.weebly.com/install-apache-mahout.html
33. https://www.edureka.co/blog/install-hadoop-single-node-hadoop-cluster
34. https://www.datasciencecentral.com/profiles/blogs/how-to-install-and-run-hadoop-on-windows-for-beginners
35. https://mahout.apache.org/general/downloads
36. https://mahout.apache.org/docs/latest/algorithms/clustering/
37. http://people.csail.mit.edu/jrennie/20Newsgroups/20news-bydate.tar.gz
38. http://mahout.apache.org/users/clustering/clustering-of-synthetic-control-data.html
39. https://kdd.ics.uci.edu/databases/synthetic_control/synthetic_control.data.html
40. https://mahout.apache.org/docs/latest/algorithms/recommenders/

41. https://mahout.apache.org/users/recommender/userbased-5-minutes.html
42. Pradeep Kumar, J., Gouse., S, Amarendra Reddy, P., Migration of Big Data Analysis from Hadoop's MapReduce to Spark, in: *First International Conference on Artificial Intelligence and Cognitive Computing. Advances in Intelligent Systems and Computing*, Bapi R., Rao K., Prasad M. (eds), vol. 815, Singapore, Springer, 2019.
43. Amarendra Reddy, P., Gouse, S., Bhaskara Reddy, P., Security and Privacy Mechanisms of Big Data. *Int. J. Eng. Technol.*, 7, 4.39, 730–733, 2018.

15

Hands-On H2O Machine Learning Tool

Uma N. Dulhare[1], Azmath Mubeen[2*] and Khaleel Ahmad[3]

*[1]Department of Computer Science, Muffakham Jah College of
Engineering & Technology, Hyderabad, India
[2]Department of Computer Science, University College for Women, OU,
Hyderabad, India
[3]Department of Computer Science and Information Technology,
Maulana Azad National Urdu University, Hyderabad, India*

Abstract

In the recent era, we have seen a huge increase in AI and machine learning adoption, there has been a major growth in the numerous software tools available for developers to make use of H2O that is a free source software tool which can be easily downloaded from the web. H2O has been implanted within the machine learning area for corporate organizations and designers. H2O was developed by the corporation H2O.ai and is developed in the object oriented languages Java, Python, and R. H2O is developed with the programming languages designers that are acquainted with in order to build it comfortable for them to use the machine learning tools and predictive analytics. H2O can all be utilized to evaluate and analyze datasets which is available in the cloud and Apache Hadoop file systems. H2O aids the broadly utilized arithmetic and knowledge engineering algorithms comprising gradient boosting algorithms, comprehensive multivariate regression models, deep machine learning, and beyond. H2O platform is utilized by more than 18,000 organizations worldwide and has been widely accepted in both the object oriented languages R and Python. It can be used on any of the operating systems like Linux, MacOS, and Microsoft Windows. In this chapter, we are applying H2O tool for predicting diabetes.

Keywords: H2O, machine learning, Python, diabetes prediction, model training, deep learning

*Corresponding author: azmathmubeen2012@gmail.com

Uma N. Dulhare, Khaleel Ahmad and Khairol Amali Bin Ahmad (eds.) Machine Learning and
Big Data: Concepts, Algorithms, Tools and Applications, (423–454) © 2020 Scrivener Publishing LLC

15.1 Introduction

Machine learning is the scientific discipline dealing with the approaches in which machines learn from experience. For many of the scientists, the term "machine learning" is similar to the term "artificial intelligence", given that the probability of learning is the main trait of an object called intelligent in the comprehensive sense. The main aim of expert systems is the evolution of computer systems which familiarize and discover from their experience. H2O is software which is developed for machine learning, data prediction, and analysis. H2O is a free of cost software accessible as an open source and it is a distributed in-memory machine learning platform with linearly scalable. Darren Cook in his book "Practical Machine Learning with H2O" writes that he was impressed with the capabilities of H2O which are

- Free and open source (the liberal Apache license) available on web
- Ease of use
- It has Scalability with big data
- Well-documented and business oriented
- H2O is in its third version (i.e., a mature architecture)
- It has wide support with a range of OS/language support.

While machine learning has come a long way, H2O appears to be not only a cost-effective family car for it, but also it is a large load delivery truck for it. Extending the vehicle correlation little more, this book will not only display what the dashboard controls do, but also the best methods to use them to move from A to B. This will be as useful as probable, with only the bare least description of the mathematics or theory behind the learning algorithms [4]. H2O also has a business controlling autoML application that spontaneously runs through all the algorithms and their hyper parameters to generate a leaderboard of the top models. H2O aids the very broadly used statistical and machine learning algorithms comprising gradient boosted machines, comprehensive linear models, deep learning and many more. H2O also has an industry prominent AutoML application that automatically functions with all the algorithms and their hyper parameters to create a leaderboard of the top prototypes. The algorithms created from the base for computing in distributed systems and for both supervised and unsupervised methods comprising Random Forest, Generalized Linear Model (GLM), Gradient Boosting framework, XGBoost, Generalized Low

Rank Models (GLRM), Word2Vec, and various others. We can apply any language to program with which we are already acquainted with like R, Python, and many other languages to create prototypes in H2O, or we can make use of H2O flow, an interactive user interface, which is a graphical notebook and it does not require any programming constructs. To automate the machine learning system, we can make use of H2O's AutoML that comprises programmed instruction and altering of different prototypes and models in a specified time constraint. Unstructured combinations will thus be significantly trained on sets of distinct models to generate exceptionally analytical collective prototypes that, in general, will be the top working models in the AutoML leader board. When dealing with memory processing, it works with fast serialization between nodes and clusters to support huge datasets. Big data provides dispersed, shared, or distributed processing. So, distributed processing over big data provides huge speeds up to 100× with excellent fine-grainy parallelism, supporting optimized competence without putting forward the deterioration in establishing the calculation exactness. It is very simple to implement POJOs and MOJOs to use models for fast and precise scoring in any settings, comprising very large models.

15.2   Installation

15.2.1   The Process of Installation

It starts by downloading the zip file from H2O.ai.

Step 1
Download a release from the official website http://h2o.ai/download. The downloaded container will comprise the H2O jar file.

Pip is an abbreviation which stands for pip installs packages.

PIP is a container controlling system used to install packages from the repository. We can use pip to install numerous software packages offered by http://pypi.python.org/pypi.

If we already have Python loaded in our system. Then, simply we can run the command prompt change the directory to Scripts directory of Python 2.7 the prompt changes to C:\Python2.7\Scripts>

At the above prompt type Pip install h2o.

Figure 15.1 shows the output of the command Pip install h2o. The output screen shows that h2o3.24.8 has been successfully installed.

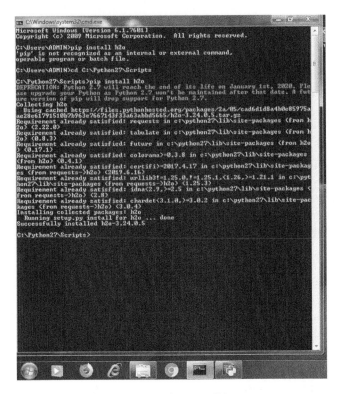

Figure 15.1 Output screen for the command Pip install h2o.

Step 2:

After h2o is successfully installed, give the following commands one after the other as shown in Figure 15.2. Pip install requests and then Pip install tabulation the output is as follows.

Figure 15.2 shows the output of the commands where we are installing the requests package and tabulate package. The requests command installs latest requests from the python\lib\site-packages. If it is already available, then it gives requirement already satisfied; otherwise, it will install the requests.

Pip install tabulate is given to

- print small tables without any difficulty, we can just give the command and the layout and structuring is directed with the facts themselves.
- formulating flat documents for using trivial plain-text markup and manifold output designs appropriate to support extra checkover or conversion.

Figure 15.2 Output screen of commands pip install requests and pip install tabulate.

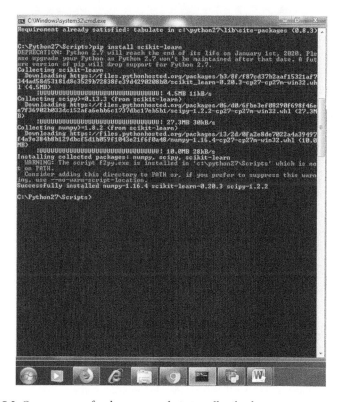

Figure 15.3 Output screen for the command pip install scikit-learn.

- legible appearance of combined text and numeral data and elegant column orientation, and also for conFigureuring, number formatting, and position in a decimal point.

Step 3:

After successfully installing the requests and tabulate packages, we have to install the scikit-learn package. Pip install scikit-learn. The output of the command is shown in Figure 15.3.

Figure 15.3 shows that when the command pip install scikit-learn is given, it installs the collected packages numpy, scipy, and scikit-learn.

Step 4:

Next step is to install colorama. The output is shown in Figure 15.4.

Figure 15.4 shows that the requirement is already satisfied because the package has already been installed. If it is not installed already, it will install

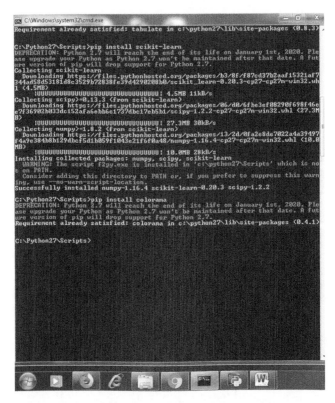

Figure 15.4 Output screen for the command pip install colorama.

and give the message successfully installed. The command Pip install colorama is used to provide a straightforward application which can be used on multiple operating systems and Application Programming Interface to produce hued display text from Python applications. The escape character combinations of ANSI or series occur generally applied to create colored textual display on Unix. Colorama also offers a few quick and easy to generate ANSI sequences but works well in combination with any other ANSI sequence generation library, like the revered Termcolor.

Step 5:
Next step in the installation process is to install the future package. The output of the pip install future command is shown in Figure 15.4.

The pip install future command gives the screen as shown in Figure 15.5. If it is already installed, otherwise it will give successfully installed. The future of the package is that the package will be missing compatibility tier linking between Python's version 2 and Python's version 3. This will allow the user to utilize for a single use, clean Python 3.x-consistent codebase to maintain both, Python 2 and Python 3 with nominal transparency.

Step 6:
Next step is to instal the latest version of h2o python module, which is shown in Figure 15.6.

The command given in Figure 15.6 installs the latest version of h2o python module. If it is not installed already it will install and the output shows successfully installed. If the python module is already installed the output is as shown in Figure 15.6 which shows that the requirement is already satisfied which means the module has already been installed.

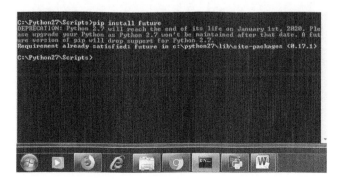

Figure 15.5 Output screen of Pip install future.

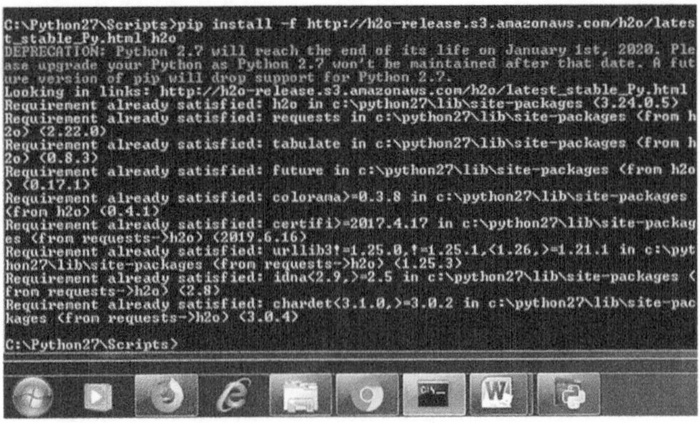

Figure 15.6 Output screen of pip install -f http://h2o-release.s3.amazonaws.com/h2o/latest_stable_Py.html h2o.

Step 7:
At the python prompt, type the following command:

> Import h2o
> Then type
> h2o.init() the output window is shown in Figure 15.7.

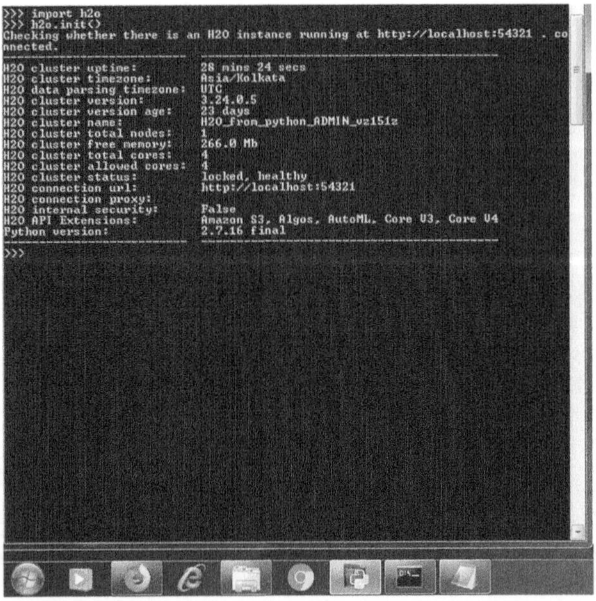

Figure 15.7 Output screen of pip install -f http://h2o-release.s3.amazonaws.com/h2o/latest_stable_Py.html h2o.

The output screen shows that the command in Figure 15.7 checks if available an instance functioning at http://localhost:54321. The screen in Figure 15.7 shows that it has connected.

Now, we can start working with h2o.

To check whether h2o is working or not we will check by giving the following command to check with demo in Figure 15.8.

H2o.demo("glm")
Then, give the command h2o.init()

Figures 15.8 to 15.11 show the resultant output of H2o.demo("glm") and h2o.init().

15.3   Interfaces

H2O works with familiar user interface like programming languages "R", "Python", "Scala", "Java", "JSON", and the "Flow notebook" which is an interface to the web and operates effortlessly upon big data tools like "Hadoop" and "Spark". H2O can simply and rapidly develop perceptions from the datasets

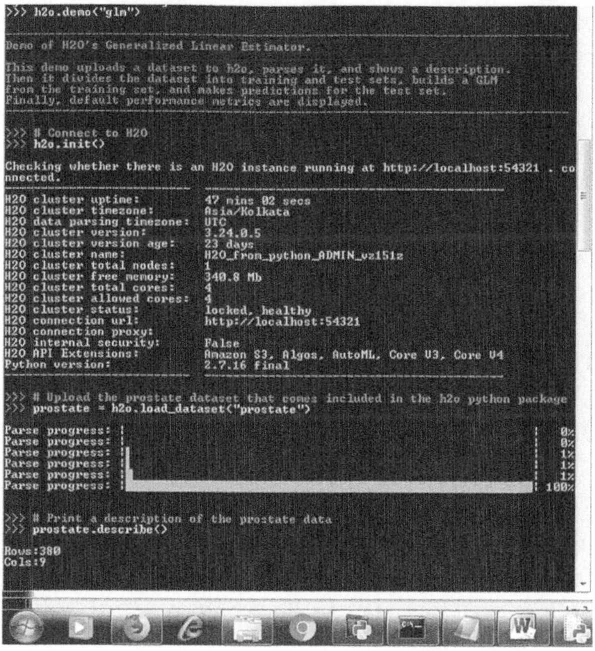

Figure 15.8 Output screen of H2o.demo ("glm") and h2o.init ().

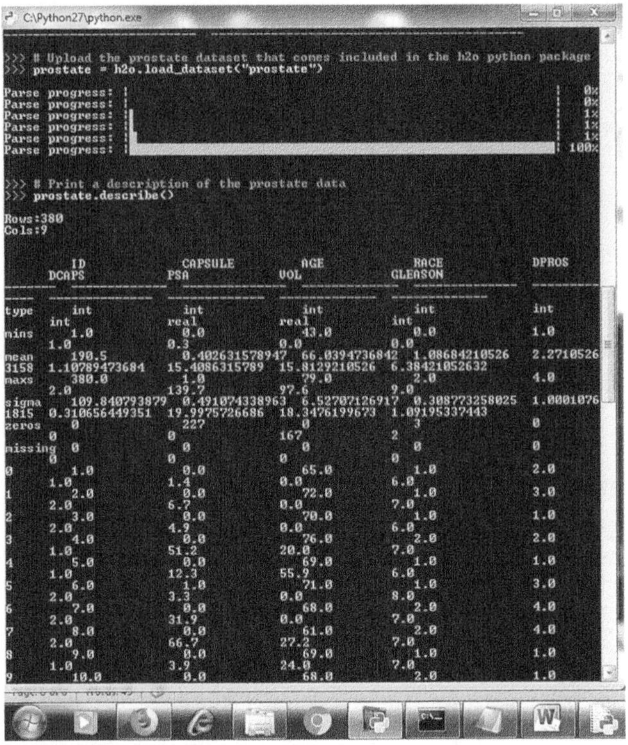

Figure 15.9 Output screen of H2o.demo ("glm") and h2o.init ().

in an effective, efficient faster and better analytical and predictive modeling. H2O handles to import data directly from multiple sources and has a rapid, scalable, and distributed computable engine written in Java. Here, the authors represent a high-level summary of the H2O scaffold. Once H2O is up and running, all you need to do is point your browser to http://localhost:54321.

15.4 Programming Fundamentals

15.4.1 Data Manipulation

15.4.1.1 Data Types

H2O can support the following data types:

- any floating type data can be represented using float (any IEEE double) data type.
- any integer type data can be declared with integer (up to 64 bit).

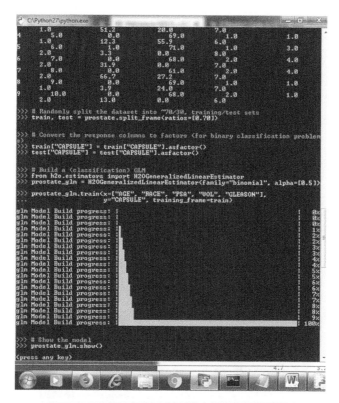

Figure 15.10 Output screen of H2o.demo ("glm") and h2o.init ().

- factor is equivalent to integer; however, it has a sequence aligning which is frequently managed differently with different methods.
- epoch or time is similar to 64-bit integer, except with a time-since-Unix-epoch elucidation.
- The Universal Unique Identifier (UUID) is a 128-bit number, it is used for identification of information; however, mathematics is not permitted.
- Any series data is given with String data type.

The requirement is that the data should be conFigured as an organized listing of distinctive numbers, the rank keys should be >= 1 and the columns have to be in increasing order.

The Sparse data is inherently maintained by getting a sparse matrix from a Support Vector Machine (SVM) Light file. Additionally, H2O comprises a precise translation of a sparse array into a H2O Frame in Python2.7

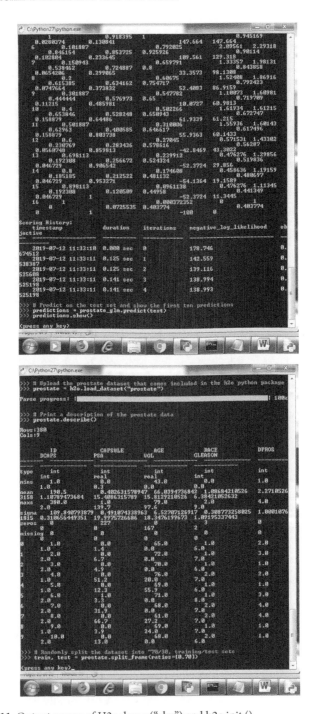

Figure 15.11 Output screen of H2o.demo ("glm") and h2o.init ().

through the functionh2o.H2OFrame (). For the sparse file, H2O creates a sparse array to SVM Light design and then backs up using Python's h2o. import_file.

If we are using Python, the representation of sparse array is done using scipy.parse. For example:

```
Import scipy.sparse as sp1
Ap = sp1.csr_matrix([[1, 2, 0, 5.5], [0, 0, 3, 6.7], [4, 0, 5, 0]])
frd = h2o.H2OFrame(A)
Ap = sp1.lili_matrix((1000, 1000))
Ap.setdiag(10)
for k in range(999):
Ap[k, i + 1] = -3
Ap[k + 1, i] = -2
frd = h2o.H2OFrame(Ap)
```

15.4.1.2   Data Import

Consider a given illustration where we can get a dataset and train a model thereon. flightTrainingData<- h2o.importFile("https://s3.amazonaws.com/h2o-airlines-unpacked/allyears2k.csv") H2O consequentially will copy data file to analyze it [7]. Hence, we try to predict the data type of each field. H2O accomplishes an immense role at data type classification; though, every conclusion will be capable of overruling by the user manually, when needed. The data file which is imported will be given a name using the parameter destination_frame. Consider the illustration where we are importing the.csv file.

h2o.importFile("https://s3.amazonaws.com/h2o-airlines-unpacked/allyears2k.csv", destination_frame='flightTraining_train') gets actual dataset file with flight waits which can additionally be adopted with label "flightTraining_train", yet from additional user interfaces for Python, a new R console, directly from Application Programming Interface (API) calls, Java, Flow, Java, or. In case we do not provide name, H2O will create as imulated name, in simple terms, an imported data file is known as Frame in H2O. We will be able present a list of frames by calling function h2o.ls(). An illustration for calling the output for h2o.ls() function is represented in the example snippets given in this chapter. The first entry in the instance is an identified frame, and the alternative or the additional entry is the frame name created impulsively by H2O.

15.4.2   Models

A few popular prototypes offered by H2O are given below. To know more regarding the working, usage and executing of these models in "R" with H2O, we can check current functioning models. H2O backs the following prototype models:

- The model for Deep Learning
- The Naive Bayes Model
- The algorithm for Principal Components Analysis (PCA)
- The K-means algorithm
- Model for the Supervised collection of machine learning algorithms known as Stacked Ensemble
- The General Linear Model (GLM) algorithm
- The Gradient Boosting Machine (GBM) algorithm which in short is known as GBM.

15.4.2.1   Model Training

After importing data, a prototype can be created without any delay. Around several algorithms present in H_2O. In this chapter, a popularly known GBM method will be applied. In this chapter, we will prepare a prototype that will foresee whether the airplane lands behind time are not dependant on day or week, month, and the total area, the airplane travels prior to completing its journey and arriving at its terminus. By calling h2o.gbm(...) method, H2O will utilize and run a GBM algorithm on the specified data. Here, numerous variables are available to work with; and all data scientists can learn and use on their own easily. Superseding the default hyper parameters will only make this chapter further difficult. H_2O only requires three things:

- the fields which have to be predicted-the predictor columns,
- the reply variable column,
- the training or preparation frame—a data file to train or prepare the prototype or model on.

This can still predict or estimate the allocation of the response or output variable, although as specified earlier, the whole can be countermanded manually by the data scientist, when needed. Following training of a prototype, we can display the basic information about the model by entering the label of the field aiming to the prototype model which is trained, here, the gbmModel.

>gbmModel<- h2o.gbm(v=cal("Month", "DayOfWeek", "Distance"), w="Is-ArrDelayed", training_frame = flightTrainingData)

If we want to store or transfer a file to a directory which is native to our H2O cluster, we can utilize h2o.importFile (), that is concurrent or dispersed state of data file. It needs records accessible to all the points of H2o in a multinodus collection. The method h2o.uploadFile () will upload the data file native of our H2o collection or clutch and also it can upload data native to our "R" term. The data file barely must be present with the user system, and the transfer is specifically distinctly specified in a given path of execution of process. In addition, we state the instance of H2o in language "R" and the full standardized data file location of the data file.

An illustration in "R"

```
irisUrl = system.file("extdata", "iris.csv", package="h2o")
iris.hex = h2o.uploadFile(path = irisUrl, destination_frame =
    "iris.hex")
```

15.4.3   Discovering Aspects

In order to find whether any field includes categorized data file, we can make use of h2o.anyFactor(), with the reference object of R.

An illustration in R is given below

```
irisUrl = system.file("extdata", "iris_wheader.
    csv",package="h2o")
iris.hex = h2o.importFile(path = irisUrl)
h2o.anyFactor(iris.hex)
```

15.4.3.1   *Converting Data Frames*

If we have to transform H2o analyzed data file instance to a "R" data-frame which will be controlled using "R" language instructions, we can utilize the command as.data.frame() using identifier of the "R" pointer instance passed as a parameter.

Note: Although it would be very useful, we have to be very careful at the time of the usage of the instruction to change H2o analyzed data file instances. H2o is able to simply manage data files that are frequently very huge to be controlled consistently fair in "R".

An model in "R"

```
1# Builds an instance which describes the trail.
2 prsPth<- system.file("extdata", "pro.csv",package="h2o")
3. pros.hex = h2o.import File(path = prsPth,destination_
   frame="pro.hex")
5# Transforms the given data-frame to an "R" data frame
6. pros.R<- as.data.frame(pro.hex)
7# Shows the gist of data-frame in which the abstract was
   carried out in "R"
9 summary(pros.R)
```

15.4.4 H2O Cluster Actions

15.4.4.1 H2O Key Value Retrieval

H2O can perform the following key value access commands.

h2o.assign: This command assigns H2O hex.keys for various instances within the "R" setting.

h2o.getFrame: This command will fetch a pointer to a current H2O dataset.

h2o.getModel: This will find a pointer to a current H2O model.

h2o.ls: It can show a record of object instance keys in currently executing object of H2O.

h2o.rm: To eliminate the instances of H2O created in the server where the H2O object is currently executing although it will not delete it from the R setting.

h2o.loadModel: The H2OModel instance can be loaded from the disk.

h2o.saveModel: We use it to store an H2O Model instance to the disk and again to load back into H2O we use h2o.loadModel.

15.4.4.2 H2O Cluster Connection

To establish connection, the cluster connection, we use the following:

h2o.init (nthreads = -1): To make a connection with an executing H2O object utilizing every processor on the system and examine that the native H2o "R" package is the appropriate edition.

.h2o.shutdown: While closing a connection, we need to close specific H2O object. So, the records on the server will be exhausted.

15.4.5   Commands

To divide a given dataset into a number of partitions or chunks, we can make use of the following:

h2o.rebalance: For balancing load across distributed nodes, we can make use of rebalance (repartition) on a current H2O dataset to partition it into a number of pieces.

15.4.5.1   Cluster Information

To get the complete information about the cluster, we use the following:

- url: This is given to retrieve the complete URL of the server to which are going to connect. This can be given as an alternative to ip + port + https.)
- ip: To retrieve the location or the host label from the remote host system on which H2O instance is executing.
- port: To know the port number to which the H2O facility is attending.
- https: This option is set to True to link up via secure http //, i.e., https in place of simple http://.
- insecure: Letting the value to TRUE will inactivate Secure Socket Layer certificates verification when using https.
- username: While using basic authentication, it is the username to be logged on with.
- password: While using basic authentication, the password is given to log on.
- cookies: To add to each request, we can make use of Cookie.
- proxy: We can use it to retrieve the proxy server address.
- start_h2o: If this is set to False, we cannot try to open an H2O server once a link to an existing server has crashed.
- nthreads: While launching a new H2O server, "Number of threads" option is given.

- ice_root: When we start a new H2O server, then this will be the folder for provisional files for the fresh server.
- log_dir: While we start a new instance directory for H2O logs and to store the logs we use log-dir. This can be ignored if we are connecting to an already existing node.
- log_level: When we are starting a new instance and to know the logger level for H2O, we can make use of log_level. It is one of TRACE, DEBUG, INFO, WARN, ERRR, FATA. The default value is INFO. This can be overlooked if linking to an already accessible node.
- enable_assertions: For a new H2O server, if we want to enable assertions in Java.
- max_mem_size: It gives the maximum memory which can be used for the new H2O remote server. Numeric data will be calculated as gigabytes. Other measurements can be stated by passing in a string (e.g., "160M" for 160 megabytes).
- min_mem_size: It gives the lowest memory which can be utilized by the new H2O server. Numeric data will be calculated as gigabytes. Additional units may be stated by accepting within a string for example "180M" for 180 Megabytes.
- strict_version_check: If it is set to TRUE, an inaccuracy will be created if the user and server adaptations do not complement.
- ignore_conFigure: When we are handling .h2oconFigure file this indicates whether a processing must be controlled otherwise uncontrolled. In general, it evaluates to False.
- extra_classpath: This gives listing of routes for the library files that must be contained on the class path of Java when initiating H2O from Python.
- kwargs: this comprises all remaining disapproved attributes.
- jvm_custom_args: This option can initiate user-defined parameter for the JVM where H2O is started. This can be overlooked if there is an object of H2O currently executing and the user process connects to it.
- bind_to_localhost: This is a flag specifying if an entry to the H2O object should be constrained to the native computer or if it can be extended from different nodes or computers on the network.

15.4.5.2   General Data Operations

Subscripting example to pull pieces from data object.

```
1   x[j]   ## note: chooses column J, not row J
2   x[i, j]
3   x[[i]]
4   x$name
5   x[i] <- value
6   x[i, j, ...] <- value
7   x[[i]] <- value
8   x$i <- value
```

15.4.5.2.1   Subsetting
To find an initial or final part of an object, we can make use of the following:

head: This returns the first part of an object
tail: This will retrieve last part of an object

15.4.5.2.2   Concatenation
There are basically two types of commands that can be used in H2O for combining. They are given below:

c: If we want to combine values into a Vector or List we can make use of c.
h2o.cbind: To combine H2O datasets by column, we can make use of h2o.cbind.

15.4.5.2.3   Data Attributes
The following data attributes can be used with H2O data objects:

colnames: For a given parsed H2O data object this will return the column names.
colnames<-: To get or set the names of an array object.
names: To retrieve the identification of an instance.
.names<-: To fix the identification of an instance.
dim: We can use this to know the aspects(length, breadth, and height) of an instance.
length: To know the dimension of paths and features.
nrow: To know the calculate the total rows in an H2O analyzed data instance.

ncol: To calculate the total columns in an H2O analyzed data instance.

h2o.anyFactor: To find whether an H2O analyzed data file instance will have any divisional or definite data fields.

is.factor: To find whether in a given column, there exists any categorical data.

15.4.5.2.4   Data Type Coercion

as.factor: To change a field from integer to feature.

as.Date: This transforms a field from feature to day of the week.

15.4.5.3   *String Manipulation Commands*

h2o.gsub: For all the occurrences the string is globally substituted.

h2o.strsplit: To split the string we use h2o.strsplit.

h2o.sub: The first occurrence of the string is substituted.

h2o.tolower: To change string to lower type.

h2o.toupper: To change string to upper type.

h2o.trim: To truncate extra gaps we can use h2o.trim.

15.5   Machine Learning in H2O

15.5.1   Supervised Learning

General Linear Model: The GLM offers an adaptable simplification of common linear regression of output features containing any fault dispersal prototypes in addition to Gaussian distribution. The GLM combines several additional numerical or analytical models, comprising Poisson, linear, and logistic regression models.

Distributed Random Forest: The distributed random forest will find average of multiple decision trees, of which each one is created on distinct arbitrary examples of rows and columns. This ensues simple for implementing, random, and offers response for significance of every analyst in the prototype, making it among the very strong and robust algorithms for erroneous and noisy files.

Gradient Boosting Machine: The GBM algorithm creates estimated and analytical prototype as a set of uncertain analytical prototypes. It constructs the prototype in a step by manner and is simplified by permitting a random differentiable loss function. It is one of the strong existing procedures.

Deep Learning: The deep learning algorithm creates models of sophisticated generalizations in data with the help of non-linear transformations using layering. Deep learning is an illustration of supervised learning that uses unnamed which is not done by other algorithms.

Naive Bayes: The Naïve Bayes classifier is used to generate probability–based classification that presumes the estimate of a specific characteristic is distinct to the occurrence or inexistence of any other characteristic where the class variable is specified. It is mostly implemented for text classification.

Stacked Ensembles: When we want to use multiple prototypes created from various algorithms, Stacked Ensembles unearths the top viablegroup of predictionalgorithms using a method called "stacking."

XGBoost: An improved gradient boost library called the XGBoost employs expert systems within the GBM structure. XGBoost is among the most GBM structures used for several problems. In many other cases, the H2O GBM algorithm becomes the top priority.

15.5.2   Unsupervised Learning

K-Means: The K-Means algorithm discloses collections or clusters of data positions for splitting. The studies are clustered grouped and made of k-number of positions with the closest mean.

Principal Component Analysis (PCA): The PCA algorithm is applied on a group of probably collinear characteristics and accomplishes analteration to yield a different collection of non-correlated characteristics.

Generalized Low Rank Model (GLRM): This approach rebuilds missing values and detects significant characteristics in diversified datasets. Moreover, this approach recognizes numerous readings of small level features that permit clustering of examples or of qualities.

Anomaly Detection: Anomaly detection is used to identify the deviation in the data with the deep-learning auto encoder, a strong sample detection paradigm.

15.6   Applications of H2O

15.6.1   Deep Learning

Deep Machine Learning is an area of expert systems which is stimulated with operational humanoid intelligence and sense organs. The stored data file is clinched to the input level of the neural network. The neural network utilizes grading of concealed layers which continuously create compressed and high intensity generalizations of the stored data file. This therefore generates simulated stored characteristics. Semantic network with three tiers or above are studied. "Deep".H2o can be applied for various datasets. In this chapter, an implementation of h2o on diabetes dataset is illustrated which is collected from different hospitals of Hyderabad. Application of Deep Learning Estimator is shown below which is implemented in Python [8].

```
import h2o
h2o.init()
datasets = "C://Python27/datasets/"
data = h2o.import_file(datasets + "diabet.csv")
w = "age" [4]
v= data.names
```

Figure 15.12 Output screen of deep learning algorithm applied on diabetes dataset. The Deep Learning algorithm is applied to the data set of diabetes patients which is manually collected from 3 Diabetic Care centers of Hyderabad. The Figure 15.12 shows the progress of the Deep Learning model.

```
v.remove(y)
train, test = data.split_frame([0.8])
o=h2o.estimators.deeplearning.H2ODeepLearningEstimator()
o.train(x, y, train)
q = m.predict(test)[4]
```

The output of the above implementation is shown below.

Implementation of H2o on diabetes dataset for prediction and parsing uses various factors like age, gender, weight, height, stress of work and sleeping hours. The below code in Python displays the parsing and builds a model for the diabetes data set. The training and testing data is split in 60:40 percent. The output is shown in Figure 15.13.

```
import h2o
h2o.init()
diabe=h2o.import_file("c://python27/datasets/diabet.csv")
```

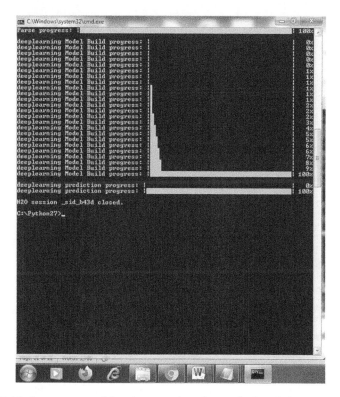

Figure 15.13 Output screen of deep learning algorithm applied on diabetes dataset.

```
diabe["name"]=diabe["name"].asfactor()
diabe["gender"]=diabe["gender"].asfactor()
diabe["age"]=diabe["age"].asfactor()
diabe["weight"]=diabe["weight"].asfactor()
diabe["height"]=diabe["height"].asfactor()
diabe["stressed_work"]=diabe["stressed_work"].asfactor()
diabe["body_mass_index"]=diabe["body_mass_index"].asfactor()
diabe["sleeping_hours"]=diabe["sleeping_hours"].asfactor()
diabe["detect_diabetes"]=diabe["detect_diabetes"].asfactor()
diabe["blood_relatives_diagnosed_diabetes"]=diabe["blood_
    relatives_diagnosed_diabetes"].asfactor()
diabe["medicines_diabetes"]=diabe["medicines_diabetes"].
    asfactor()
diabe["insulin"]=diabe["insulin"].asfactor()
```

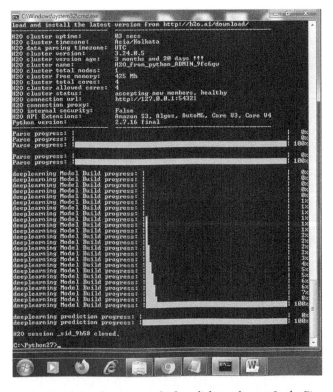

Figure 15.14 Output Screen of parsing applied on diabetes dataset. In the Figure 15.14 we can observe the Deep Learning Model Prediction progress which is applied on the diabetes data set which has been collected from 3 Diabetes Care Centers.

```
datasets = "C://python27/datasets/"
data = h2o.import_file(datasets + "diabet.csv")
w = "age"
v = data.names [4]
v.remove(y)
train, test = data.split_frame([0.6])
o=h2o.estimators.deeplearning.H2ODeepLearningEstimator()
o.train(x, y, train)
q = m.predict(test)[4]
```

Implementing classification based on two different diabetes datasets is given below. The output for the following code is given in Figure 15.15.

```
import h2o
h2o.init()
train = h2o.import_file("c://Python27/datasets/diabet.csv")
test = h2o.import_file("c://Python27/datasets/diabetes.csv")
train.describe()
test.describe()
```

Figures 15.16 and 15.17 show the classification of two different datasets of diabetes.

Figure 15.15 Output screen of classification applied on diabetes dataset.

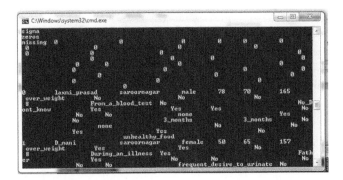

Figure 15.16 Output screen of classification applied on diabetes dataset.

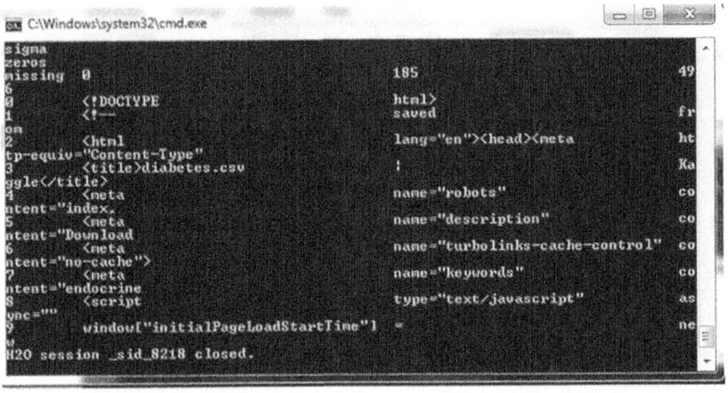

Figure 15.17 Output screen of classification applied on diabetes dataset.

15.6.2　K-Fold Cross-Authentication or Validation

The K-Fold Cross-Train authentication is performed on drill dataset and in case the value stated for n folds is a positive number in which cross-validation values calculated moreover saved as pattern output. If storing the estimated values generated through cross-validation, put hold cross-validation estimates to true. This prepares computation of routine cross-validated implementation of implementation values for the R or Python model [2]. High-level managers will be able to stipulate a fold field or column which states the suspended fold is related with every record. In general, the suspended fold job is arbitrary; however, more methods like round-robin task implementing the modulus operator is backed [2]. In illustrative code given below, we are using a five-fold cross-validation on diabetes data.

　# Perform 5-fold cross-validation on training_frame

```
import h2o      [2]
h2o.init()
```

```
from h2o.estimators.deeplearning import
    H2ODeepLearningEstimator
train = h2o.import_file("c://Python27/datasets/diabet.csv")
test = h2o.import_file("c://Python27/datasets/diabetes.csv")
datasets = "C://Python27/datasets/"
data = h2o.import_file(datasets + "diabet.csv")
# Specify the response and predictor columns
w = data.names
v= "age"
z=train.namesparameter[0:20]
model_cv = H2ODeepLearningEstimator (distribution="mul-
    tinomial",activation="RectifierWithDropout",
hidden=[32,32,32],input_dropout_
    ratio=0.2,sparse=True,l1=1e-5,epochs=10,nfolds=5)
model_cv.train(w=w,v=v,training_frame=train)    [2]
```

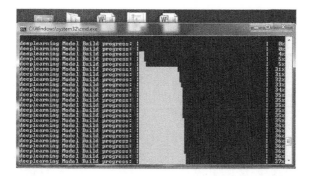

Figure 15.18 Output Screen of five-fold cross-validation on diabetes dataset.

Figure 15.19 Output Screen of five-fold cross-validation on diabetes dataset. Five fold cross validation was performed on the diabetes data set collected from 3 Diabetes Care Centers, the progress of the Deep Learning Model is shown in the figures Figure 15.18 and Figure 15.19.

15.6.3   Stacked Ensemble and Random Forest Estimator

Stacked Ensemble creates aassembled cooperative group (alias a "super learner") expert system technique which implements two or above H2o learning procedures to improvise analytical and projecting performance. This is a loss-based supervised learning activity which can detect the ideal permutation in a group of analytical procedures. In the approach, it aids regressive analysis and dual or binary categorization or classification [3]. A random forest classification algorithm is a meta quantifier which suits numerous decision-tree-classifier in several sub-sampled data of the data files and moreover utilizes average for improvising the predictive accurateness and regulate over-fitting [4].

The example code given below illustrates the Stacked Ensemble and Random Forest Estimator implemented on diabetes data set. The code below is taken from h2o.docs.

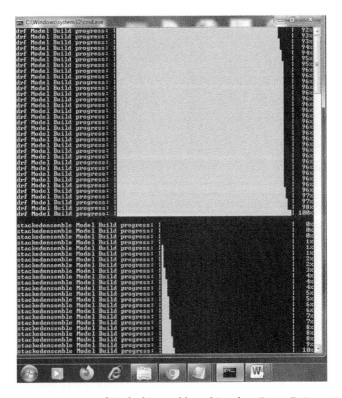

Figure 15.20 Output screen of Stacked Ensemble and Random Forest Estimator implemented on diabetes data set.

```
import h2o[3]
h2o.init()
from h2o.estimators.random_forest import
    H2ORandomForestEstimator
from h2o.estimators.gbm import
    H2OGradientBoostingEstimator
from h2o.estimators.stackedensemble import
    H2OStackedEnsembleEstimator
data = h2o.import_file("C://python27/datasets/diabet.csv")
train, test = data.split_frame(ratios=[.8], seed=1)
v = ["name","local_address","gender","age","-
    weight","height","body_mass_index"]
w = "age"
nfolds = 5
```

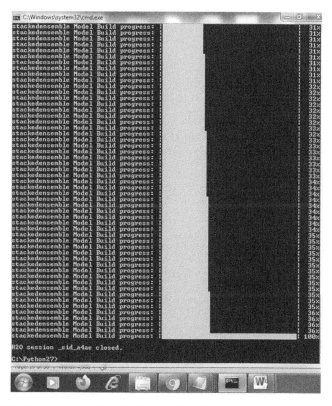

Figure 15.21 Output screen of Stacked Ensemble and Random Forest Estimator implemented on diabetes data set.

```
miy_gbm = H2OGradientBoostingEstimator(nfolds=nfolds,
    fold_assignment="Modulo",
    keep_cross_validation_predictions=True)
miy_gbm.train(v=v, w=w, training_frame=train)
miy_rf = H2ORandomForestEstimator(nfolds=nfolds,
    fold_assignment="Modulo",
    keep_cross_validation_predictions=True)
miy_rf.train(v=v, w=w, training_frame=train)
stack = H2OStackedEnsembleEstimator(model_id="my_
    ensemble", training_frame=train, validation_frame=test,
    base_models=[miy_gbm.model_id, miy_rf.model_id])
stack.train(v=v, w=w, training_frame=train,
    validation_frame=test)
stack.model_performance()[3]
```

The output of the above code is shown Figures 15.20 and 15.21.

15.7 Conclusion

H2O is a robust tool, and given its capabilities, it can really change the data science process for good. The competencies and benefits of AI should be made accessible to everybody and not a select few. The real essence of democratization and democratizing data science should be essentially implemented for resolving real problems threatening our planet. Although H2O is easy for non-experts to study machine learning, there is yet an adequate evidence of knowledge and background in data science that is needed to construct high-performing machine learning models. Deep neural networks in precise are extremely strenuous for a non-expert to tune properly. For machine learning software to be truly open to non-experts, an easy-to-use interface is shown in this chapter which systematizes the method of preparing a huge range of entrant prototypes. H2O's AutoML can also useful tool for the inventive user, by proposing a simple binding function that accomplishes a huge amount of modeling-associated accountabilities which would usually need several lines of instructions. H2O is not so perfect, as there are a few concerns like there is no GPU support and no SVM algorithm. To conclude, it tries to help many platforms; henceforth, each one has some unsymmetrical controls, and extension is sometimes diminished by attempting to keep them all in sync.

References

1. H2O, https://www.kdnuggets.com/2018/01/deep-learning-h2o-using-r.html
2. H2O, http://docs.h2o.ai/h2o/latest-stable/h2o-docs/data-science/deep-learning. html
3. H2O, http://docs.h2o.ai/h2o/latest-stable/h2o-docs/booklets/DeepLearning Booklet.pdf
4. H2O, https://scikit-learn.org/stable/modules/generated/sklearn.ensemble. RandomForestClassifier.html
5. Cook, D., *Practical Machine Learning with H2O*, O'Reilly Media, December 2016, H2O O'Reilly Media, Inc.USA.
6. H2O, https://builders.intel.com/docs/aibuilders/accelerate-ai-development-with-h2o-ai-on-intel-architecture brief.pdf
7. H2O, https://dzone.com/articles/machine-learning-with-h2o-hands-on-guide-for-data
8. H2O, http://www.safaribooksonline.com

Case Study: Intrusion Detection System Using Machine Learning

Syeda Hajra Mahin[1]*, Fahmina Taranum[1] and Reshma Nikhat[2]

[1]Department of Computer Science and Engineering, M.J.C.E.T, Hyderabad, Telangana, India
[2]Department of Management Studies, M.A.N.U.U, Hyderabad, Telangana, India

Abstract

Machine learning has played a crucial role lately in the progress made in the field of technology, thereby providing a wide range of applications. This chapter reflects the developments made in pattern recognition and machine learning technologies targeting at its applications in the field of mobile networks. Since mobile networks specifically MANETs are prone to numerous kinds of intrusions and attacks, designing a defense system oriented on the notion of pattern recognition is hardly concentrated by the researches. Pattern recognition is widely used to study the patterns in the data through the applications and implementation of extensive algorithms which are either classification based or clustering based. With the aim to provide a better understanding of how the pattern recognition can be applicable as an IDS to an unrelated area like networks, a case study is done for detecting anomalies by deploying the black hole attack in the network using QualNet simulator. The prime idea of this chapter is to comprehend the practical applications of machine learning accompanied with pattern recognition through the medium of MATLAB software to formulate an IDS countering the black hole attack.

Keywords: Pattern recognition, classification, MANET, IDS, black hole attack, QualNet

*Corresponding author: hajraziaulhussain@gmail.com

Uma N. Dulhare, Khaleel Ahmad and Khairol Amali Bin Ahmad (eds.) Machine Learning and Big Data: Concepts, Algorithms, Tools and Applications, (455–486) © 2020 Scrivener Publishing LLC

16.1   Introduction

The proposal is to detect and prevent a network from malicious nodes. The scenario consists of modules like Deployment, Detection, and Avoidance, which are designed using QualNet simulator and for justification of correctness of result MATLAB classifiers are used. The type of attack demonstrated is Black Hole and performance metrics used are based on amount of data lost, data delivered, and average delay occurred for transmitting the data packets. The aim is to curb the network attacks and analyze the post effects using the notion of intrusions working with two classes: anomalous and non-anomalous by formulating the IDS based on inspection of anomalies.

The objective is to improvise the security issues in MANETs with respect to intrusion detection and prevention using series of operations for obtaining a better performance. The chief objective of this work includes the following:

- To propose a novel intrusion tolerant system for wireless *ad hoc* network by deploying, diagnosing, and deterring the effects of the black hole in the network and its justification using an anomaly-based IDS with detailed analysis using different classifiers to opt for the finest of them.
- To assess the network conduct during the black hole attack against varying metrics like PDR, throughput, packet drop, and average transmission delay.

16.1.1   Components Used to Design the Scenario Include

16.1.1.1   Black Hole

The intrusions in the network occur by the demonstration of a pseudo path to the destination node. As soon as the anomalous node gains a path requesting control packet, it forwards the packet to the source which manifests a shorter pathway to the destination. After the reception of this erroneous information, this anomalous node starts acquiring the data packets for further communication to the destination. These kinds of nodes perform activities like dropping the to-be transmitted data packets or holding up the further conveyance of it [12].

One scenario of a black hole node is depicted in Figure 16.1. For carrying out the case study, the network communications are examined prior to the deployment of the erroneous nodes in the network. Lately, the network

Network Diagram with Black Hole Node

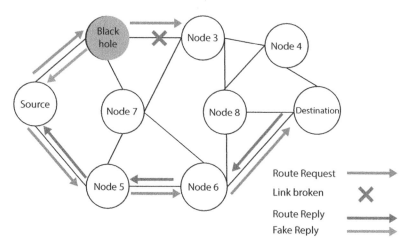

Figure 16.1 Architecture of a black hole node.

is incorporated with anomalous nodes by boosting their network participation capabilities layer wise. Post which an IDS is proposed to deter this attack.

16.1.1.2   *Intrusion Detection System*

An IDS is a mechanism for tracking any infringements in a network during the course of data transmission. An IDS is used to detect suspicious activity by monitoring network traffic and altering the components of the network in case of any misbehavior.

Network intrusion detection systems (NIDSs) are widely used for ensuring security to the networks. These scrutinize the congestion in a network to check for any violations. Other IDS widely accepted is the host-based intrusion detection systems (HIDSs) which checks for any discrepancies by examining the OS files. Based upon the scheme for detection these can be grouped as the following.

- Signature-oriented
- Anomaly-oriented
- Reputation-oriented

In the anomaly-oriented system, machine learning is adapted to build a model of reliable activities against the newly discovered patterns. This mode-based IDS is an upper hand of the signature-based IDS because this model can be skilled as over the configurations and requirements. Though this model works well in identifying new patterns, it is subjected to high FP rates and is applied in the proposal.

16.1.1.3   Components Used From MATLAB Simulator

16.1.1.3.1   Learning in Pattern Recognition

Making a system understand the patterns becomes a tedious and difficult task mainly because programming a system to work with patterns requires a lot of processing as these patterns hold vast information containing multidimensional perspective. An IDS is principled to recognize any intrusions by scrutinizing the overall network execution. The aim is to find similarities between these and integrate them. In the put forward chapter, the pattern recognition framework is adopted for fabricating the detection system in order to deter the black hole attack in the designed network and upgrade the network performance.

The decision to take the percentage of data towards training and testing also plays a major role. Learning enables the pattern recognition model to skill and adapt to the given outcome by analyzing and training against the input data set accurately. The learning of the model depends upon the learning algorithm implemented. Using the training data set, the classifier is trained to correctly categorize the test data set records into respective classes. The learning algorithm can be supervised, semi-supervised, or unsupervised. The process of learning involves working with two data sets namely, training data set and testing data set, as manifested in the Figure 16.2.

Training set: The first set of data is the training set which works by generating the pattern recognition model. This data set includes those patterns

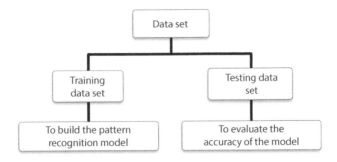

Figure 16.2 Types of data sets.

or features against which the recognition model is trained and learnt. Alongside this, the learning algorithm implemented by the model provides details of how the input needs to be processed to gain accurate outcomes.

Testing set: The second set of data is the testing set which functions by evaluating the validity of the pattern recognition model. The motive of considering this data set is to validate the results obtained by the trained model against the actual values. The rightness of the pattern recognition model is assessed against the accuracy rates and misclassification rates.

In this work, we have used 60% of the records for training, 15% for validation, and 25% for testing.

16.1.1.3.2   Approaches for Pattern Recognition

The key idea for designing this proposal is to incorporate the interpretation of the larger data records with the aid of pattern-based identification to diagnose the network intrusions and safeguard against them. This system recognizes the participating nodes either as normal or intruding based on their network involvement. The framework is first designed and experimented with generated data set to impose a pre-classification process for identifying a normal and abnormal node. The selected data is trained to measure its accuracy and reach final error free conclusions. The patterns discovered are contingent to the nature or characteristics of the data records. Occasionally, the patterns might also be oriented on the structural and analytical characteristics of the data, and occasionally, it might not. In any of the two cases, the pattern recognition model has to be trained and formulated to make sure that it functions accurately and respond error freely. The neural network recognition system is inspired by the processing and storing of the human nervous system data. This network comprises of a directed graph comprising of artificial neurons and their associations. The neural networks work effectively even in the presence of complex input-output linkage by making adjustments to the network periodically. Different types of classification techniques available are depicted in Figure 16.3.

16.1.1.3.3   Classifier

Pre classification of the data records is a prerequisite for the accumulating of the CBR and VBR generated data records. The constant bit rate (CBR) and variable bit rate (VBR) are traffic generators used while formulating the network topology. For the proper functioning of the pattern-based IDS, the training of the classifiers is necessary. This training data set includes the recognized classes, in this case they are normal and anomalous. The labeling of the records in the training set is the deciding factor for the working

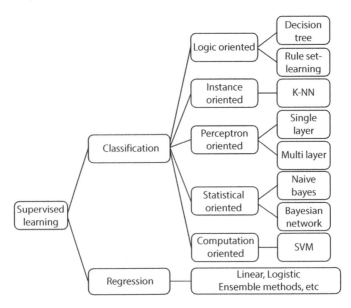

Figure 16.3 Types of classification techniques.

of the designed intrusion system. This detection system is based on the machine learning classifiers. These classifiers work to ensure that the data records are classified in the right category based on their exhibited network patterns. The learning techniques adapted by the pattern recognition model can be categorized as either supervised or unsupervised version of learning [8].

In the supervised genre of learning, the objective is to discover the association between the input and the target variables often referred to as independent and dependent attributes. Whilst in the unsupervised genre of learning, the model predominantly infers the output by scrutinizing the input attributes in the absence of their target classes from the data sets. Furthermore, the supervised learning can be breached into two classes, namely, classification and regression, as shown in the Figure 16.4. In the designed scenario, supervised learning is used.

16.1.1.3.4   Selecting the Classifiers of MATLAB

Classification learner is used to train a selection of different classification models on the data set collected from QualNet to check the validity of the results or the conclusion made by running the scenarios. By using the predefined training model, the selection is made for percentage of records to be applied for testing, training, and validation, in order to authenticate

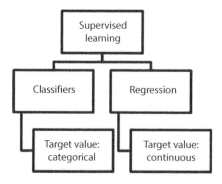

Figure 16.4 Categories of supervised learning.

the system. Different classifiers are applied and its accuracy is tested and compared, the best among all the classifier is selected to validate the system. Where, classification is the process of anticipating the target labels for a given set of input data. Classification plays a very crucial role for designing systems based on knowledge discovery. A classifier classifies the data points only after the association between the input data points and the target labels from the training data set is learnt by it.

The key differences between the classification and clustering techniques are demonstrated in the Table 16.1. Table 16.2 provides a brief description of the features and issues with different classifiers.

Table 16.1 Comparisons of classification and clustering approaches.

Classification	Clustering
The learning approach is supervised.	The learning approach is unsupervised.
Functions using labeled data items.	Functions with unlabeled data items.
Definable no. of classes.	Definable no. of clusters.
Has a training phase.	Does not have a training phase.
Classifies the testing data set.	Traverses through the data.
Output classes are pre-determined.	Output clusters are not pre-determined.

Table 16.2 Description of the classification techniques.

Classification technique	Classification algorithm	Features	Issues
Logical oriented	Decision tree	• No prior knowledge is required. • Can handle high dimensional data. • Uncomplicated interpretation.	• Works with categorical targets. • Cannot operate accurately for smaller training set. • Searching time is high.
Instance oriented	K-NN	• It is not limited to linearly separable data. • Uses the principle of feature similarity. • Involves trouble free implementation. • Parameters to be tuned are limited (only distance metric and K).	• Sensitized to noisy data. • Larger time and storage requirements.
Perceptron oriented	Artificial neural network (ANN)	• Can work with noisy data. • Association between input and target attributes is discovered easily.	• Requires more time for processing. • Troublesome interpretation. • Over-fitting • Over training is unavoidable.
Statistical oriented	Naïve Bayes	• Works well for classification and prediction problems. • Easier to implement.	• The accuracy and correctness of the classifier depends on the amount of records in the set. • Susceptible to bias.
Computation oriented	SVM	• Works for both linearly separable and inseparable data. • Low misclassification rates compared to other classifiers. • Can handle over-fitting.	• Costly implementation • Requires more memory and storage space. • Deciding for the appropriate kernel function can be difficult.

16.1.1.3.5   Evaluating a Classifier

The accuracy and precision of the classifier is dependent on the training undergone by it. The data set used for this purpose is the training set. After training the classifier, the next task is to evaluate the extent of its correctness and aptness for solving the classification problem. The conduct and relevance of the classifier is examined by using any of the following methods.

- Hold out validation
- Cross validation
- Boot strap

Hold out validation: This is a commonly used validation scheme where the entire data set is segregated into two individual sets, namely, training and testing set. Usually, the data sets are partitioned in the ratio of 8:2, where 80% of it is considered for training and 20% is considered for testing. The classifier is trained with 80% of the records and is tested against the 20% records to assess the conduct and accuracy of the specified classifier.

Cross validation: also referred to as K- fold validation is a validation scheme where the entire data set is fragmented into "k" sets. Any one of the set is taken up for testing and the other "k−1" sets are taken for training the model. This procedure is carried out several times until each of the set has been used as the testing data set. This validation scheme takes more time compared to the hold out validation. The problem of over-fitting is also avoided in this scheme by taking unshared and unique data sets.

Boot strap validation: This is another validation technique where the data records are cleft and training set is formulated with substitution. In simpler words, the probability of reselecting the same data record which has already been used for the training is high in the boot strap validation. This validation method is noted to be more optimal and efficient for smaller data sets. Among many boot strapping techniques, the 0.632 boot strap validation is extensively used.

The conduct of the classifier can be evaluated from receiver operating characteristic curve (ROC) and confusion matrix also explained in Figure 16.5.

Packet loss and average delay in conveying the data packets are picked as the features for the IDS. The training data set pertaining to these two features are used to train the machine learning classifier models. The decision tree (DT), support vector machine (SVM), neural network (NN), and K-nearest neighbor (KNN) classifiers are incorporated for implementing the detection system. The classification learner is a toolbox of the MATLAB

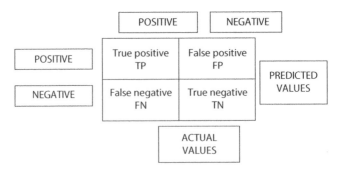

Figure 16.5 Confusion matrix.

which provides all of these data mining classifiers. The evaluation metrics which are to be considered are accuracy rates, misclassification rates, sensitivity, fall out, specificity, miss rate, etc.

$$PDR = \frac{NO.\ of\ collected\ packets}{No.\ of\ dispatched\ packets} * 100 \qquad (16.1)$$

$$Delay = D = \sum_{i=1}^{m} \frac{y^i}{m} \qquad (16.2)$$

Accuracy rate: $\dfrac{(TP + TN)}{Total}$ \qquad (16.3)

Misclassification rate: $\dfrac{(FP + FN)}{Total}$ \qquad (16.4)

Sensitivity/Recall/True positive rate (TPR): TP/Actual YES \qquad (16.5)

Fall out/False positive rate (FPR): FP/Actual NO \qquad (16.6)

Specificity/Selectivity/True negative rate (TNR): TN/Actual NO \qquad (16.7)

Miss rate/False negative rate (FNR): FN/Actual YES \qquad (16.8)

Training and testing the pattern recognition model using pertinent and meaningful features aid in predicting the patterns accurately.

16.2   System Design

The configuration file is created in QualNet with 50 nodes, two of them act as malicious, and the traffic is attracted toward these nodes because of the extra privileges assigned to them. The attacker is of type I in which the data is transmitted without modification. The intension of the attacker is to keep destination node deprived of traffic. The terrain size is the area of the network. The mode of traffic is constant bit rate with the size of the packet taken to be 100 bytes and the speed of node traversal is 10 m/s. The routing protocol used is Dynamic Manet on demand protocol (DYMO). Unlike Secure protocols, DYMO lacks the security related features like authentication, integrity, and confidentiality. DYMO has certain vulnerabilities which makes security a major concern here. The parameters are listed in Table 16.3.

16.2.1   Three Sub-Network Architecture

Node 3 and node 8 are taken as dual IP nodes using QualNet simulator. One thousand data packets each holding dimensions of 100 bytes is conveyed between the source and target nodes 1 and 14 using a CBR generator. The overall duration of execution of the network activities is fixed for 1,000 s. Tunnels are also incorporated by the dual IP nodes in the network with the aim to convey the packets to the nodes working in heterogeneous environment. The red color nodes are the black hole nodes, which are taken in to loop for deactivation using Human-In-The-Loop commands (HITL). The HITL instructions permit the users to convey instructions to the QualNet during the execution. The involvement of the nodes in the network activities can be controlled by activating or deactivating them as per the need. This feature provided by the QualNet enables us to deactivate the intruders as soon as they are detected. The mesh in circular shape shows the region of reach-ability. The three sub-network architecture configured with varied versions of Internet protocols (IPv6-IPv4-IPv6) is shown in Figure 16.6. The HITL file encompasses the HITL commands together with the time as when the command needs to be delivered to the simulator as depicted in Table 16.4. The syntax of this is as follows: <Time><command>

16.2.2   Using Classifiers of MATLAB

The practical analysis of pattern recognition-based IDS is carried out considering supervised learning algorithms like KNN, SVM, Decision tree, Naïve Bayes, and Neural network. The simulations are carried out using

Table 16.3 Scenario parameters of QualNet.

Network variables	Value
Simulation tool used	QualNet 7.4
Routing protocol	DYMO
Aggregate nodes	16
Anomalous nodes	2
Mobility Speed	10 ms
Pause time	30 s
Dimensions of terrain	X-1500, Y-1500
Network protocol	IPv4, IPv6
Seed	1
Network topology	File
Mobility model	Random way point
Total channels	3
MAC protocol	802.11
PHY radio type	802.11b
Network traffic gen.	CBR
Aggregate packets forwarded	1,000
Item size	100 bytes
Duration of simulation	1,000 s
Frequency	2.4 GHz

QualNet network simulator and the IDS are designed on MATLAB to execute the proposal. To formulate the IDS based on classifiers, the data set of 150 records is considered. Five-fold cross-validation scheme is implemented to model and evaluate the classifier. The two features selected as input/independent variables are average transmission delay and packet drop rate. The output class/target class labels are 0 and 1, where 0 corresponds to non-malicious node and 1 corresponds to malicious node class.

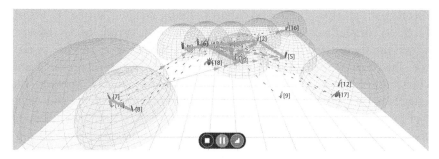

Figure 16.6 Scenario in QualNet.

Table 16.4 Commands to implement HITL.

Commands	Description
D <node ID>	This specific node is deactivated and stopped from further participation in the network transmissions. Ex: D 5 (This deactivates the node 5)
A <node ID>	This specific node is activated and allowed to further participate in the network transmissions again. Ex: A 5 (This activates the node 5.)
P <priority>	The CBR sessions are prioritized by this command. Only integer values can be used to provide priorities.
T <interval>	The inter packet arrival time can be modified using this command to alter the sessions of CBR traffic in the experiment. The unit of time is milliseconds and only integer or real numbers can be taken up.
L <rate-factor>	This works by altering the CBR rates for all the ongoing sessions by modifying the inter packet arrival times. The product of present inter packet interval and rate factor is taken up for deciding the new interval. Ex: If the present interval is 0.5 and L 0.1 is the command then the new calculated interval becomes 0.05.

16.3   Existing Proposals

The classification techniques can furthermore be categorized into different kinds which include logic oriented, instance oriented, perceptron oriented, statistical oriented, and computation oriented [3]. Clustering mechanism groups object into clusters relying on their similarity values [4, 5]. In simpler words, a cluster can be defined as a group of data objects which are contrasted based on either the similarity or dissimilarity factor. The clusters are formulated in a manner that the objects in the same cluster have the minimum distance keeping the distance between the objects belonging to two different clusters maximum. Since a clustering algorithm is designed in such a way that it uses the similarity index to form clusters, opting for the best feasible distance metric becomes a requisite. This concept is extended to *ad hoc* network architecture in our proposal as the configuration of the nodes taken is from the standard IEEE 802.11. The degree of similarity between different data points in a multi-dimensional space can be assessed using distance criteria. Different distance functions yield different values, hence deciding on the apt distance function for designing the clustering algorithm is important [4]. To find the minimum distance between the nodes, Euclidean distance algorithm is applied in DYMO routing protocol, while executing the configuration files. There are numerous algorithms designed for resolving the clustering problem [7]. The permissible type of patterns that can be applied to the proposed analysis includes recurring and recognizable, i.e., a means of recurring the attack and a way to recognize them. Pattern recognition enables the system to perceive the environment, acquire knowledge of the patterns, and make conclusions about the classes of patterns. Systems that are configured to recognize patterns assist in detecting any anomalies prevailing in the system. The easiest techniques based on attack are the way to detect an attack. Pattern recognition is an area of machine learning which deals with analysis and classification of patterns into varied classes based on the features exhibited by them using computer algorithms [9, 11]. Pattern recognition is majorly used to study the patterns in the data through the implementation of extensive algorithms which are either classification based or clustering based. The data sets are required to be effective enough to encapsulate and demonstrate all the possible nodal patterns during a network simulation. In this designed IDS, there are only two major categories of nodal patterns observed. Here in the proposal, machine learning concepts are used to detect and justify the approach. These clustering algorithms are based on some model and are observed to follow certain framework to give optimal results. K-Means clustering follows this approach, where the value of "K" has to be pre specified [10]. For designing a pattern recognition system, a major task is to examine the data set and settle on to features which aid in differentiating varied patterns observed in the data [11]. This task of deciding on the features that are most relevant to the model is referred to as feature selection. It is a phase where the inputs for the training model are determined. Selection of features and their extraction from the data sets can be done by implementing various techniques involving statistical tools, extraction algorithms, etc. The measure of extracting features has a direct impact on the amount of preprocessing required. On that account, there are various techniques that can be adapted to make the pattern recognition process logical and hassle free [11]. Some of these techniques are:

1. Template matching
2. Statistical classification
3. Syntactic matching
4. Neural networks

The template matching is the most commonly used recognition technique which stores templates or prototypes of the patterns with the aim to juxtapose it with the unrecognized patterns. This type of recognition scheme is computationally expensive [11].

The statistical recognition scheme considers a dimensional space where the patterns are plotted as data points. To differentiate between the classes, decision boundaries are administered in the multi-dimensional space.

The syntactic or structural classification technique works by computing a feature vector which comprises of a set of relevant features [11]. A range of classified patterns is taken up for training the recognition model.

16.4   Approaches Used in Designing the Scenario

16.4.1   Algorithm Used in QualNet

Algorithm used to detect and prevent a black hole node is shown in Figure 16.7. The aggregate duration of time needed by the data to get to the destination is taken up as the sole principle behind the recognition of the attacking nodes. In order to keep track of this duration, a value is prespecified and used as a threshold for examination. Those of the member nodes that pass this value are regarded as the anomalies. For the deterrence of such identified nodes, the HITL file is implemented to avoid the further participation of them in the data relaying. The enhancement would be to consider the power consumption issue.

Exploring the area of networks using the notion of machine learning is a new concept. Existing research in this domain proves that a lot more can be done to secure the networks from the intrusions.

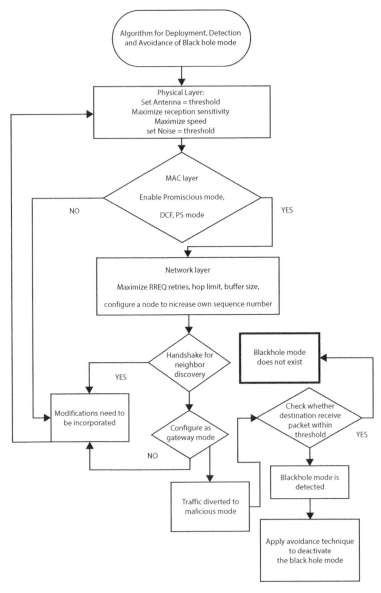

Figure 16.7 Algorithm for detection and prevention of black hole node.

As the main principle behind any of these pattern recognition algorithms is to trace the patterns or regularities in the data, designing an intrusion detection system (IDS) plus implementing these algorithms will serve best to detect any intrusions or anomalies in the considered network [2, 6].

One of the predominantly occurring threat in MANETs is a black hole attack, where a spiteful node performs malicious activities like packet delay and packet drop to degrade the overall network conduct [2]. To detect a malicious activity the amount of data lost and average delay for relaying the data are taken into account. If the value of these performance metrics is beyond the defined threshold, then the node is detected as malicious; the process of avoiding data transmission to this node is taken in to consideration.

16.4.2   Algorithm Applied in MATLAB

Algorithm for designing an IDS

> Step 1: Extraction of the features and data sets for training and testing the classifiers.
> Step 2: Training and testing the NN, DT, KNN, and SVM classifiers using the data sets.
> Step 3: Computing the TPR, TNR, FPR and FNR of each of the classifier
> Step 4: Computing the misclassification rate of the classifiers.
> Step 5: Computing the accuracy rates for the classifiers.
> Step 6: Selecting a classifier with high accuracy, TPR, and TNR.
> Step 7: Analyzing the thresholds for the selected features based on the selected classifier.
> Step 8: Inspecting nodes against these threshold values to detect anomalies.
> Step 9: Post detection of black hole attack, apply prevention strategy.

The performance analysis is done for all the above classifiers and on the basis of their accuracy value and misclassification rate the best of them is aimed to be selected.

16.5   Result Analysis

16.5.1   Results From QualNet

16.5.1.1   Deployment

The results generated from the QualNet consist of deployment, detection, and the avoidance. Figure 16.8 is a snapshot of the network topology after detecting

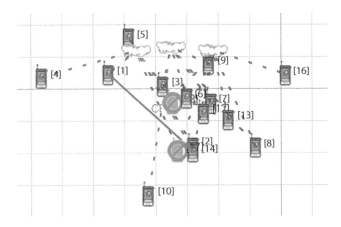

Figure 16.8 Network topology.

two black hole nodes represented by a red cross on them indicating their deactivation., i.e., module I. The black hole is administered in the scenario by the nodes labeled as node 17 and node 18. Here, node 1 is sender and node 14 is the receiver of data connected by using constant bit rate traffic option. The cloud shape component shown in Figure 16.8 is internet via which the default devices are connected. The nodes are mobile and are *ad hoc* in nature. The blue dotted line shows the connection of the default nodes to the internode. Each square grid in the figure shows the area of 100 meter * 100 meter referred as terrain size.

16.5.1.2   Detection

To detect the black hole node, the performance metric selected is packet drop rate. The analysis of the same is shown in Figure 16.9. The black hole

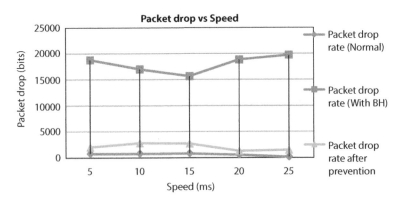

Figure 16.9 Packet drop versus speed for two black hole nodes.

node drops the packets captured from the network; hence, the maximum packet drop is found at the malicious node.

16.5.1.3   Avoidance

To avoid the malicious activity, the analysis is made for packet drop rate for different simulation time as shown in Figure 16.10. Then, time of deactivation is selected as 25 s as the least drop rate is at 25 s; the malicious node is taken into loop from 25 s after the start of the simulation time to the end of the simulation.

16.5.1.4   Validation of Conclusion

After applying the avoiding strategy, the threshold is fixed for the metrics and an analysis is performed to justify the conclusion. Further, the comparison is made in Figure 16.11 after applying the threshold and avoiding the black hole. It may be noted that the performance upgrades on applying the avoidance technique.

16.5.2   Applying Results to MATLAB

The values obtained from the .stat files of the QualNet are taken up as the training set for training the data mining-based classifiers.

The data set generated as a result of the proposal in QualNet is shown in Figure 16.12.

The data set in the excel format is imported to the MATLAB for analysis as shown in Figure 16.13.

Figure 16.14 shows the parameters selected and its classification results.

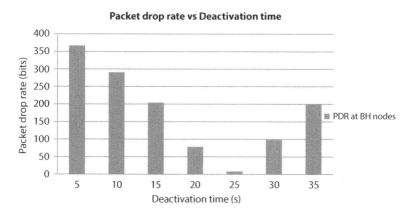

Figure 16.10 Selection of deactivation time for avoidance.

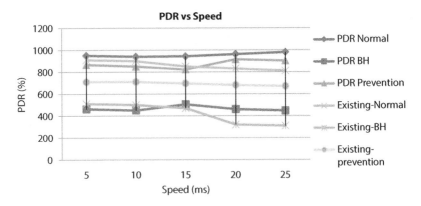

Figure 16.11 Packet delivery ratio.

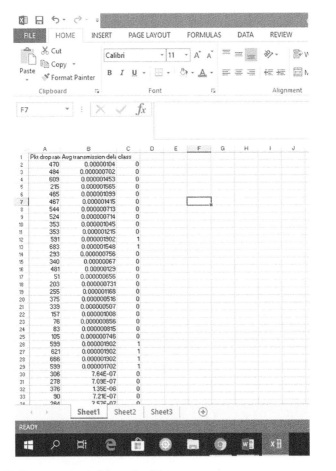

Figure 16.12 Dataset generated from QualNet.

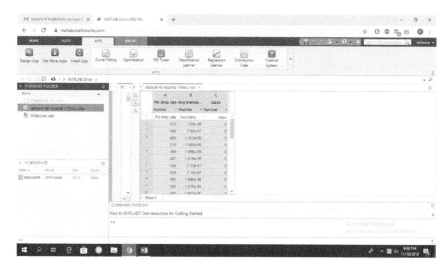

Figure 16.13 Dataset imported from QualNet to MATLAB.

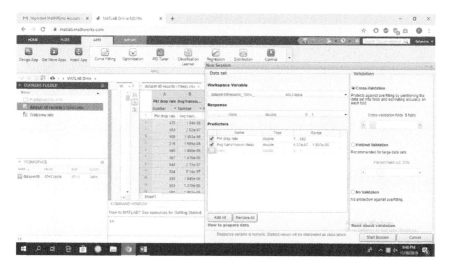

Figure 16.14 Dataset imported to MATLAB on classification.

16.5.2.1 K-Nearest Neighbor

K-nearest neighbor is another classification algorithm implemented in this project where the predictions are done based upon the training set. From Figure 16.15, it can be interpreted that the KNN-based IDS delivers a TPR-58%, TNR-96%, FNR-42%, and FPR-4%. The KNN-based IDS proves to be 93.3% accurate.

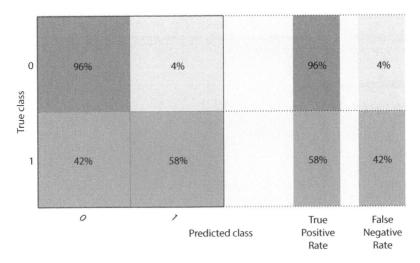

Figure 16.15 Confusion matrix for KNN.

Area under the curve (AUC) is computed for the values of X and Y parameters to return a result as a scalar value or a 3-by-1 vector. The AUC obtained for the KNN classifier is 0.77 as can be seen from Figure 16.16 for the proposed statistical analysis.

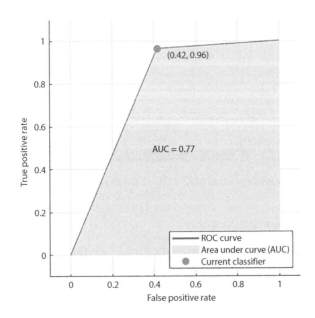

Figure 16.16 ROC for KNN.

The conduct of the classifiers is assessed by the use of confusion matrix. The confusion matrix aids the task of analysis as it provides clear and accurate values of the model performance. It helps to visualize the performance of the defined algorithm.

16.5.2.2   SVM

The SVM models the data records in the form of support vectors on the hyper plane to distinguish the patterns in the data. The IDS formulated from the SVM-based classifier showcases the TPR-58%, TNR-99%, FNR-42%, and FPR-1% as shown in Figure 16.17 for the data set generated using QualNet. The SVM classifier for this designed scenario is 96% accurate. The classifiers are trained for a data set covering 200 records.

The AUC is depicted in Figure 16.18 with a value of 0.94.

16.5.2.3   Decision Tree

The IDS designed with the decision tree-based classifier exhibits a TPR of 67%, FNR of 33%, TNR of 97%, and FPR of 3% as illustrated in Figure 16.19. The assessed accuracy rate for the decision tree-based IDS is noted to be 94.7%.

AUC = 0.81, which is depicted in the graph as shown in Figure 16.20. It is used to define the after effects of the attack.

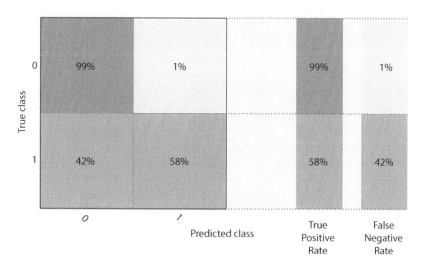

Figure 16.17 Confusion matrix for SVM.

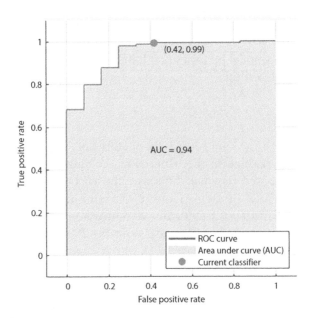

Figure 16.18 ROC for SVM.

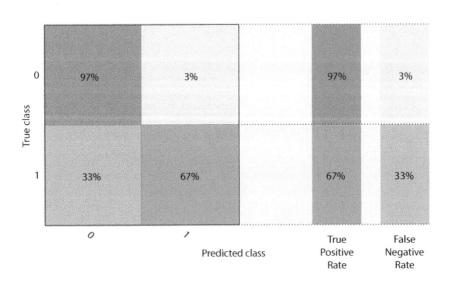

Figure 16.19 Confusion matrix for decision tree.

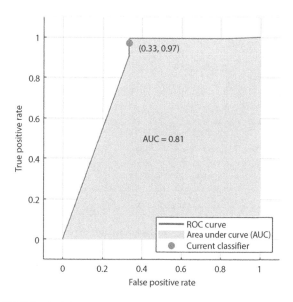

Figure 16.20 ROC for decision tree.

16.5.2.4   Naïve Bayes

With the Naïve Bayes algorithm, the IDS exhibit an accuracy rate of 94.7%. Figure 16.21 summarizes the TPR-50%, TNR-99%, FNR-50%, and FPR-1%.

The naïve Bayes classifier demonstrates AUC = 0.92 as depicted from Figure 16.22.

16.5.2.5   Neural Network

A neural network oriented IDS is designed for detecting the black hole attack. For the NN-based classifier, the data set has to be segregated into three sets, *viz.*, training set, validation set, and testing set. Here, 60% of the data records are used for training (89 samples), 5% of the data records are used for validation (8 samples), and 35% of the data records are used for testing (53 samples). Figure 16.23 displays the confusion matrix for all the three sets. The accuracy and the misclassification rate of the neural network are perceived to be 90.7% and 9.3% from the analysis.

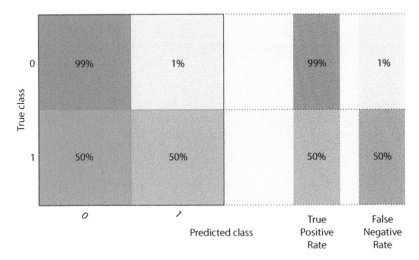

Figure 16.21 Confusion matrix for naïve Bayes.

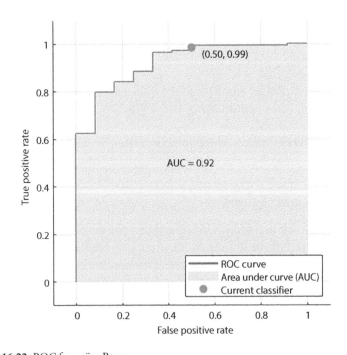

Figure 16.22 ROC for naïve Bayes.

Figure 16.23 Confusion matrix for neural network,

The ROC curve for all the three data sets, i.e., training, testing, and validation, is showcased in Figure 16.24.

ANNs, Naïve Bayes, and DT are few of the instances of the eager learner–based classification algorithms.

Figure 16.25 summarizes the performance of KNN-based classifier. It is noted that the KNN-based IDS gives high TPR and FNR rates.

The KNN-based IDS has positive predictive value of 85% and a false discovery rate of 15%, which can be seen from Figure 16.26.

The graph from Figure 16.27 demonstrates the accuracy rates of the five classifiers considered. On carefully examining the graph, it can be perceived that the SVM classifier has optimal accuracy rates compared to the rest of

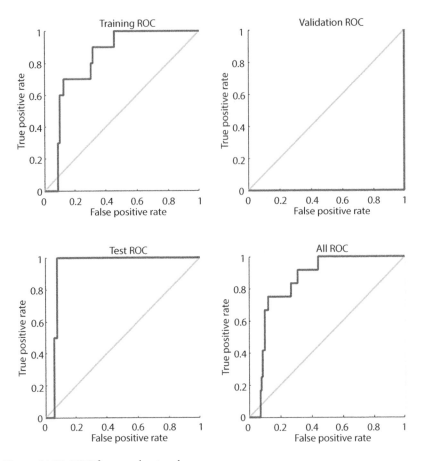

Figure 16.24 ROC for neural network.

the considered classifiers. By using an SVM-based IDS, the network performance can be improved as it proves to be efficient in detecting any anomalies and intrusions prevailing in the network. The X-axis represents the classifiers and Y axis represents the percentage of accuracy.

For performing detailed analysis of the classifier-based models, their accuracy parameter is assessed. Figure 16.27 visualizes the assessment values obtained for the differing classifiers.

SVM gives the accuracy of 96% and hence is selected as the best classifier for the designed scenario.

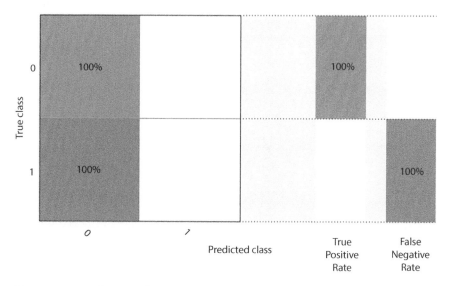

Figure 16.25 Performance for KNN using TPR and FNR.

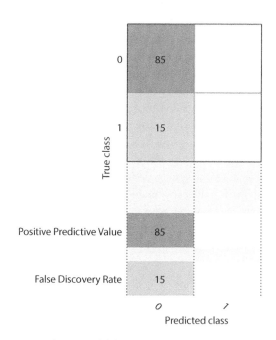

Figure 16.26 Positive predictive and false discovery rates for KNN.

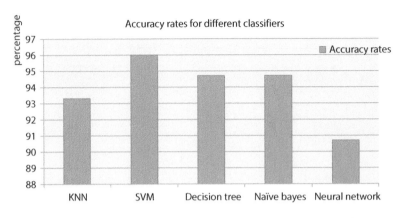

Figure 16.27 Accuracy rates for different classifiers.

16.6   Conclusion

After employing the designed IDS in the network, the proposed system is noted to be efficient enough to diagnose the anomalous nodes of the network based on the threshold values of the features selected (average delay in relaying packets and packet drop rate). The SVM classifier after training is noted to take 1.5×10^{-6} and 600 as thresholds for average delay in relaying packets and packet drop rate. Any node possessing its values higher than these is declared as a black hole node. After applying these approaches, we end up concluding that the SVM tool gives the highest accuracy; hence, it is taken as an appropriate tool for the proposed strategy.

In the experimentation using QualNet, the average packet drop rate is 591 for malicious nodes, whereas the calculated value with SVM is 600; therefore, the accuracy of SVM is 96%. The system designed for IDS shows an accuracy for the analysis generated from QualNet by tracing the .stat and .trace files. Hence, we conclude that these extracted features are applied to MATLAB for further processing to justify the anomaly detection process with 96% success rate.

References

1. Taranum, F., Mahin, S.H. *et al.*, Detection and Interception of Black Hole Attack with Justification using Anomaly based Intrusion Detection System in MANETs. *Int. J. Recent Technol. Eng. (IJRTE)*, 8, 2S11, 2392–2398, 2019.

2. Mahin, S.H., Fatima, L.N., Taranum, F. *et al.*, Proposals on the Mitigation Approaches for Network Layer Attacks on MANET. *Int. J. Recent Technol. Eng. (IJRTE)*, 7, 6S, 16–21, 2019.

3. Soofi, A.A. and Awan, A., Classification Techniques in Machine Learning: Applications and Issues. *J. Basic Appl. Sci.*, 13, 459–465, 2017.

4. Irani, J., Pise, N., Phatak, M., Clustering Techniques and the Similarity Measures used in Clustering: A Survey. *Int. J. Comput. Appl.*, 134, 7, 9–14, 2016. (0975–8887).

5. Xu, D. and Tian, Y., A Comprehensive Survey of Clustering Algorithms. *Data. Science*, 2, 165, 2015.

6. Pavani, K. and Damodaram, Dr. A, Anomaly detection system for Routing Attacks in Mobile Ad Hoc Networks. *Int. J. Network Secur.*, 6, 13–24, 2014.

7. Patel, D., Modi, R., Sarvakar, K., A Comparative Study of Clustering Data Mining: Techniques and Research Challenges. *IJLTEMAS*, 3, IX, 2014.

8. Sathya, R. and Abraham, A, Comparison of Supervised and Unsupervised Learning Algorithms for Pattern Classification. *Int. J. Adv. Res. Artif. Intell.*, 2, 2, 34–38, 2013.

9. Asht, S. and Dass, R., Pattern Recognition Techniques: A Review. *Int. J. Comput. Sci. Telecommun.*, 3, 8, 25–29, 2012.

10. Kanungo, T., Mount, D.M., Netanyahu, N.S., Piatko, C.D., Silverman, R., Wu, A.Y., An efficient k-means Clustering Algorithm: Analysis and implementation. *IEEE Trans Pattern Anal. Mach. Intell.*, 24, 7, 881–892, 2002.

11. Jain, A.K., Duin, R.P.W., Mao, J., Statistical pattern recognition: A review. *IEEE Trans Pattern Anal. Mach. Intell.*, 22, 4–37, 2000.

12. Nitnaware, D. and Thakur, A., Black Hole Attack Detection and Prevention Strategy in DYMO for MANET. *3rd International Conference on Signal Processing and Integrated Networks (SPIN)*, 279–284, DOI: 10.1109/SPIN.2016.7566704, 2016.

13. Arif, F. and Dulhare, U.N., A Machine learning based approach for Opinion Mining on Social Network Data, in: *Computer Communication, Networking and Internet Security*, 135–147, Springer, Singapore publisher, 2017.

14. Geetha S., Dulhare U.N., Sivatha Sindhu S.S., Intrusion Detection using NBHoeffeding rule based decision tree for wireless sensor networks. *IEEE ICAECC-2018, Second International Conference on Advances in Electronics, Computers and Communications (ICAECC)*, 1–5, Publication date 2018/2/9.

## 17

Inclusion of Security Features for Implications of Electronic Governance Activities

Prabal Pratap[1*] and Nripendra Dwivedi[2]

[1]*Ministry of Defence, IMS Ghaziabad, Ghaziabad, India*
[2]*Computer Science, IMS Ghaziabad, NCR, Delhi, India*

Abstract

E-governance uses technology to achieve the enhancement of transparency, reducing remoteness and empowering people to contribute in the political processes that shape their lives. For easy access of government information, E-governance can be encouraged. Information should be sent to people in the local language content by electronic media.

Creating the E government extensive as a mode of Digital INDIA, it involves providing the internet of good speed at rural areas. The full implementation of E-Goverence is difficult for developing countries. But, it is very useful. We can achieve our goal as implementation of ecommerce by putting our best efforts. It is very challenging task to store and cater all the information because the data is increasing at an exponential rate every year. This huge data comes in the class of Big Data. Govt. of India has done great effort for finding a realistic approach to capture information about data of citizens. Advance Data Analytics is needed to handle huge valuable information.

Keywords: Big data, e-governance, data analytics, internet, ecommerce

17.1 Introduction

E-governance is a part of government which uses latest technologies (information technology) to improve a package of efficiency, effective planning,

---
Corresponding author: prabalpr@gmail.com

Uma N. Dulhare, Khaleel Ahmad and Khairol Amali Bin Ahmad (eds.) Machine Learning and Big Data: Concepts, Algorithms, Tools and Applications, (487–504) © 2020 Scrivener Publishing LLC

execution and monitoring, and cost effectiveness to provide a user-friendly government services to its citizen.

E-governance = Precision + responsibility + efficiency + monitoring

E-governance is beyond the computerization of all government work not at risk of government security and maintaining its confidentiality. It helps in improvement and implementation of effectual management information system and performance measurement methods for prevention of crimes also by facilitating police and judiciary and collectorate. E-governance strengthens and makes existing process more efficient. It does not change the hierarchy structure of an organization; however, e-governance improves the communication system of one government organization to other government organization and in same government organization. In simple words, the use of information technology in the functioning of governance is termed as e-governance. Its main purpose is to make all types of information accessible to the public easily.

Phase of the scheme:
This plan may be completed in four phases:

a) Computerization: Installing the IT equipments in all government offices and gathering related information.
b) Networking: Connecting various government organizations to each other.
c) Online presence: All organizations have to make their website by mentioning about the goal of the organization, what effort have been made by organization to achieve the objective, preparation of the report, and what is the purpose of the generation of this report, etc.
d) Online contact: With the help of this parameter, all departments may contact among themselves. Government may contact to different departments and the general public would be able to get information about all government schemes.

It is very challenging task to store and cater all the information because the data is increasing at a doubling rate every year. This huge data falls in category of big data. Government of India had done great effort lot with findings a realistic approach to capture information about data of citizens. But when it appears in form of data, it shows a lot of complexity. Some data are new, some are in structured and unstructured form, and some already stored in database. Data generated by biometric machines, sensors, and video are unstructured. Management of such type of data is defined in three characteristics:

1. Huge volume of data
2. Broad variety of data
3. High velocity of data

All this convert normal data in "big data". As we know, the basic definition of system, it gives the desired output in form of information which was acquired in past for use in present.

It becomes necessary for government agencies to simplify the big data into three categories: volume, variety, and velocity. It becomes important to build a successful big data management architecture which capture, organize, integrate, analyze, and act. The cycle of management of big data is shown in Figure 17.1.

So, segregation of "Identity" of individual as a data and its analysis results in future prediction of e-governance in administration. For analysis of such type of big data, proper analytics solution should be developed under big data management architecture. Figure 17.2 shows the typical scheme of big data analytics used for e-governance.

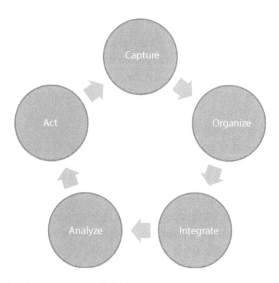

Figure 17.1 Cycle of management of big data.

Figure 17.2 Analytics solution.

E-governance Services:
Different type of government services are as follows:

G2C (Government-to-Citizen):
The G2C shows the government facilities that are used by the citizen of the country. It supports the normal persons to decrease the expenses and competition time to execute a transaction. People can avail the facilities anytime from anywhere. Different facilities, *viz.*, taxpaying and renewal of license, are very important in G2C. The services of G2C help the normal people to complete the task in minimum possible time. It also removes the geographic ground constraints.

G2G (Government-to-Government):
The G2G shows to the communication among different government unit, institutes, and organizations. It boosts the competence of government functionality. By this system, government organizations can use the same database system with the help of online communication. The government units can work simultaneously. This facility can enhance international mediation and associations.

Hence, G2G facilities can be at the local level and global level. G2G can correspond with local government and global government. Thus, it facilitates safe and sound inter-relationship between foreign and domestic government. G2G organizes a worldwide database system for all members to enhance facilities.

G2B (Government-to-Business):
The G2B is the swap of facilities between G2B groups. G2B is proficient for both business organizations and government. It facilitates access to related forms desired to obey. The G2B also consists of many facilities swapped between government and business group.

Moreover, the G2B facilitates to find appropriate information based on business. A business organization has simple and suitable online access relevant to government sectors. It acts a vital role in business expansion. G2B increases the effectiveness and excellence of communication for transparency among the government projects.

G2E (Government-to-Employee):
The G2E is the inner component of G2G segment. The objective of G2E is to bring employees jointly and manage information sharing.

Hence, G2E facilitates online services to the staff. It includes online management of leave, salary payment, and holidays. The G2E system facilitates human resource education and progress. Thus, G2E is the correlation among employees, government institutions, and their management.

17.2   Objective of E-Governance

E-Government uses technology to achieve the enhancement of transparency, reducing remoteness and empowering people to contribute in the political processes that shape their lives.

Nurturing the Effectiveness of E-Governance:
For nurturing the effectiveness of e-governance, following points play a vital role.

Leadership:
For enhancement of e-governance, effective leaders at all layers of government should be identified who understand the goals of E-governance and technology of e-governance.

Strong leader can initiate the eE-governance functionality at different level of multiple sectors and unify them to achieve the required goal.

Expand Access to Government Information:
In developing countries, government should publish all information online with effective manner. e-government is the way to publish government-related information electronically.

For fast access of government information without traveling to different offices, standing in long lines or pay bribes or involvement of bureaucrats in corruption can be avoided with the help of e-government. Using easy access of government information, e-governance can be promoted.

We can move forward to expand access of government information based on following points:

- There should be proper strategy to get online information.
- Information should be posted to people in the local language content.

- Content should be focused to cover all major areas, *viz.*, education, health sector, economic growth, foreign investment, anticorruption, etc.
- Fix up achievable outcome using accessible resources.
- Information should be with in-depth coverage, ideation, and clarity.

Providing Online Available Government Services:
For e-governance, we should provide easily accessible online government services to all people of country. Users should be habitual to access online service very frequently. There should be integration of all services for easy accession.

With the help of integration of all online services, we can effectively implement the e-commerce to provide the benefit to users.

Government may create the number websites and mobile applications for successful execution of online transaction. Manual functioning of all activities is more time consuming and it is in efficient. Direct web link of services can make the facility round the clock.

Valuable Recommendations for Strategic Investment:
Rising nations must prefer projects cautiously, indirection to maximize their throughput with appropriate dealing of time and assets. Projects should be focusing to enhance lucidity, civilian involvement in the governance activities, cutting bureaucratic dominance, and reducing expenses.

Valuable Recommendations for Strategic Investment:

- Catalog available assets, ranging from funding to persons.
- Define clear objective.
- Make different effective term plans with anticipated outcomes by reduction of expenses.
- Construct a coordinating body that will manage planning and budget.
- Adopt multi-technology strategies. Motivate people to invest budget based on multi-technological environment. For broadcasting the information, television can also be used.
- Technology should be used to facilitate users by seeing the area-wise effectiveness in coordination with local communities.

17.3   Role of Identity in E-Governance

17.3.1   Identity

Identity is very important term. Every individual has its traditional identity; this traditional identity should be mapped with digital identity. That identity should be based on authenticated by any Trusted Third Party. It is necessary to keep track of a single user's identity throughout an engagement with a system or set of systems. We can assume identity of any individual or entity is in form of unstructured data. If we use basic big data system based on Lambda Architecture having series of layers like speed layer, serving layer, and batch layer. In this system, all the data is in form of captured identity run to get the batch view that contains all data which stores the master copy of data set. The batch layer emits batch views as the result of its functions. Now, all views should be loaded so that they can be queried. This query process is done in serving layer. Serving layer updates time to time. When batch layer ultimately overrides speed layer. It compensate for high latency of updates to serving layer. It is very important to store and retrieve captured data. For this, conception of "cloud" may be used. Data as a Service (DaaS) is a platform independent service that would let us connect to cloud. Apart from DaaS, there are number of cloud delivery models also exist.

Verification of identity of any individual or entity must be verified by any cryptographic mechanism like PKI [1, 2]. Anyone can verify the identity by its digital certificate which was digitally signed and approved Trusted Third Party (sub CA). Identity is associated with concept Digital Identity like Digital Signature, User name, Passwords, PINs, Tokens, and Biometric Identities. Digital signature is a certificate analogous to "notarizing" the identity in physical world. For digital signing, generate a key pair (public and private) and get registered his/her public key by ant trusted agency.

Digital signature is an electronic identification of a person or entity created by using a public key algorithm; it is intended to verify to a recipient the integrity of data and identity of the sender of the data. It also provides non-repudiation, which means that it prevents the sender from claiming that he or she did not actually send the information. It is advanced to a handwritten signature in that it is nearly impracticable to counterfeit, plus it attests to the contents of the information as well as to the identity of the signer.

The purpose of the digital signature on a certificate is to state that a Third Party has attested to the certificate information as shown in Figure 17.3. Digital certificates are used to prevent attempts to substitute one person's key for another.

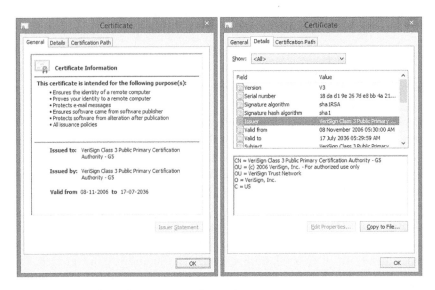

Figure 17.3 Digital certificate to prove identity for e-governance.

17.3.2   Identity Management and its Buoyancy Against Identity Theft in E-Governance

Identity management and its buoyancy against Identity theft in e-governance environment is very important and critical issue for personal and entity. Identity based on cards, for example, credit card, allows attacker to attack through PIN phishing and causes unauthorized transaction by *stealing the Identity*.

Identity can be saved by applying Public Key operation mechanism in card; this will provide secure access with authentication also. Secure card Tokens based on X.509 format of PKI are the solution for prevention of identity. This PKI card will behave as trusted component and perform operation of challenge-response signature.

Basic identification of human being is "Fingerprint". Because it is unique and do not change. Data base of this identity is used for investigation and authentication purpose for police and investigating agencies also. Initially, Kingston [11] suggested a semi-automated classification scheme. The principle behind is that the identification of any fingerprint is to be identified and its features are extracted by system and then features are matched against the features of stored fingerprint. The basic model is shown in Figure 17.4.

Some other advance methods are also available for establishment of identity in e-governance environment are of non-digital nature [3] based on only acceptance and rejection modes shown in Table 17.1.

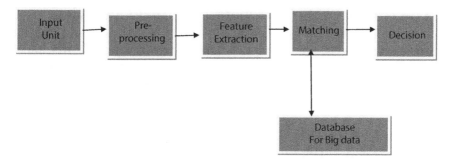

Figure 17.4 Basic model for storage of identity: fingerprint.

Table 17.1 Advance methods for establishment of IDENTITY in e-governance.

Biological feature based (behavior, handwriting)	DNA Signature Voice recognition
Artificial feature based	RFID tags Unremovable bands
Physical feature based	Fingerprint Face recognition Iris recognition Heart beat

Implication of digital identity in E-Government can reduce fraud. This digital identity becomes critical when used on online services; this will be termed as transactional identity and will be treated as transactional data of digital and paperless identity system. This results in "behavioral big data". Best example is Aadhar as shown in Figure 17.5.

Figure 17.5 Aadhar as a digital identity.

17.4 Status of E-Governance in Other Countries

Improvement is required in internal organizational process of government functioning and improving the credibility and accountability which is assisted by e-governance. There is impact on application of e-governance on administration policies are as follows:

- It restructures the old-age, out-of-date, and majestic procedure of government. It eliminates existing dysfunctional system of governance.
- It can improve the efficiency, time boundedness, and cost efficiency.
- It brings in a swift change in management pattern, such as collapse of hierarchy in administration and increase in synchronization activity.
- It helps in quick and better clearance of grievance of citizen and comments.
- It modernizes the vigilance and monitoring.

17.4.1 E-Governance Services in Other Countries Like Australia and South Africa

As per several analysis by Steman, Canadian Library Association, Muir and Oppenheim, Australia is one of the most developed countries in terms of e-government, in developed countries, the information and communication technologies perspective had been developed and taking shape. Australian government and New South Wales government strongly focus on electronic service deliverance for proper application on E-Governance in their countries [4–7].

As per the survey and analysis in South Africa, South African government have pierced a number of e-government programmes, like Batho Pele portal, SARS e-filing, electronic processing of grant applications from remote sites and huge quantity of departmental information website [8].

17.4.2 Adaptation of Processes and Methodology for Developing Countries

Government of developing countries use information technology to streamline government work culture and procedure. Purpose of government should be to collect and summarize the all the associated information which can provide the assistance to government officials. Basic elements are required for successful e-government transformations are as follows:

I.   Process reorganization
II. Leadership
III. Public engagement
IV. Alliance

Some of the challenges faced in design and implementation of e-governance by developing countries is as follows:

I.   Security: Some cyber frauds breach our security system, which are mentioned below:
     a. Cracking of Password: Intruder breaks a system's protection and captures the legitimate passwords. With the help of this password, intruder gains access to system valuable resources [8].
     b. Data Diddling: Altering the data before/during/after in to the system is referred as data diddling.
     c. Denial-of-Service Attack (DOS): It is a destructive activity that disallows the authorized access to avail the facility related to Information system by its authorized users.
        DOS hampers the proper functionality of system. Therefore, it results delay of critical operation.
     d. Piggybacking: It is another way of breaching the security. Tapping of data of telephone line is known as piggybacking. This is unauthorized network access.
     e. Round Down: IT system round downs the fractional part of all calculations related to interest up to two decimal places. All remaining fraction is placed in to account of IT system executer.
     f. Monetary cyber frauds: It is a cyber fraud which includes non-delivery of remunerated items purchased in the course of sale of online transaction, etc.
     g. Phishing: It refers to the action to get unauthorized information, *viz.*, credit/debit card detail, user ID, authorization passwords, etc., by masking as authorized user in IT services

h. Spam: It is an act of sending electronic mail with same content to everyone in one or more groups is known as Spam. Spam can be used to spread computer viruses.

i. Network Scanning: Network Scanning is a procedure to spot lively group of an active organization, for the intention of finding detail about network information like IP(Internet protocol) addresses, etc.

j. Malicious Code/Virus: According to cyber Law IT (Information Technology) Act, 2000, Section 43 "Virus" of Computer is described as any computer system instruction, data, information, or program that damages, destroy, or harmfully deteriorate the functionality of a IT resource or enclosed itself to another IT resource and control when a instruction/program/data is executed or some other activity take place in that IT resource.

k. Malware Propagation/Website Compromise: It covers website defacements. It is used for negative intention hosting malware on websites in an illegal manner.

l. Eavesdropping: It is an act to the listen of the confidential data/voice communications, frequently listening (tapping) typically over a phone line like surveillance.

m. Email Threats: communicating a threatening note to attempt and find receiver to act some negative activity that would make it achievable to defraud him is known as threatening of E-mail.

n. Scavenging: It refers to find access about private details by retrieving the company data.

o. Hacking: It is an act of illegal access of IT systems, normally by means of computer system and network communication channel. Ethical hackers not to cause any damage.

p. Data Leakage: It shows the illegal replication of company information such as computer files.

q. Internet Terrorism: It is an act of disturbing e-commerce with the help of Internet and to demolish corporate and personal communication.

r. Impersonation or Masquerading: It refers that executor finds access to the organization by making believe to be an illegal client.

    s. Social Engineering Techniques: It refers that performer tricks the member of staff into providing out the information required to enter in the organization.

    t. Supar Zapping: This is an act of illegal use of particular IT system modules to avoid standard IT system controls and executes unlawful activities.

    u. Trap Door: As per this procedure, performer go into in the IT system using a rear gate that not follow usual system controls and commit unlawful activity.

II.   Infrastructure Development

III.   Trust

IV.   Privacy

V.   Convenience

VI.   Edification and Marketing

VII. PPP (Public Private Partnership) Collaboration

17.4.3   Different Programs Related to E-Governance

a) SWAN (State Wide Area Network):
It provides connectivity to connect and facilitate central projects. It helps in connecting the central projects to the state level projects. In the following diagram, different levels of the offices are shown in the form of structure [9–11].

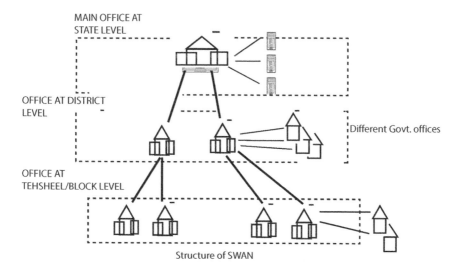

MAIN OFFICE AT STATE LEVEL

OFFICE AT DISTRICT LEVEL

Different Govt. offices

OFFICE AT TEHSHEEL/BLOCK LEVEL

Structure of SWAN

b) SDC (State Data Center):

If central government wants to see the data of any state government, then state data center program helps in this action. Functioning of data center is shown with the help of following diagram using core, spine, and leaf.

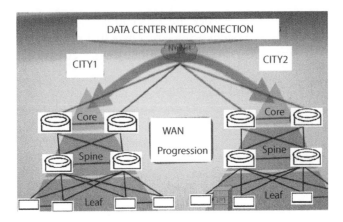

c) NKN (National Knowledge Network):

It is used to provide data very fast at the national level. In other words, it is the big network of information like a spider's web. Knowledge network is shown with the help of interconnection among network of different domain [13, 14].

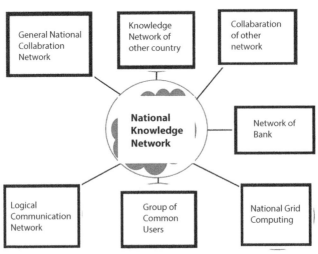

National Knowledge Network: (NLN) Structure

d) KCC (Kisan Call Center):
   It is helpful in solving all the problems related to farmers. Relevant information is communicated in a very efficient manner.

Kisan Call Center

17.5 Pros and Cons of E-Governance

Advantages: The e-government is beneficial in terms of saving money and time.

The smaller business finds opportunity to compete with government and larger business in context of betterment of system. Business and society can obtain information at a more rapid speed and it is accessible at any time of the day.

Switching from a traditional system (heavily paper based system) to a paperless electronic system will decrease the requirement of employees. Hence, this technique supports the practice to be handled by lesser man power [12]. Therefore, it reduces operational expenditure. The capability of an e-government facility to be accessible to people irrespective of locality of the entire world brings the next and potentially largest advantage of an electronic-government facility. The statistical information is posted online with the help of electronic media; it supports the concept of an "opened up" the system like government strategy, information, etc.

Disadvantages: There are certain disadvantages of e-governance. The major drawback of an electronic government is shifting the government services toward electronic-based system. This system loses the dealings among persons which is very much important by a majority of people.

The e-governance is totally depending on technology; it is very simple to compose excuses like server is down; services are hampered due to technological problem, etc. Lack of literacy of the users about the functioning of computer is also a major problem. Citizens who do not familiar how to read or write on computer would require support. Senior citizens face such type of problem.

17.6   Challenges of E-Governance in Machine Learning

Machine learning scientist and academician countenance different type of challenge compare to other professional. Companies have their anticipation that machine learning algorithms work very swiftly and accomplish very fast and deliver defined predictions to all complex queries. The typical algorithm of machine learning is artificial neural network that has millions of parameters and training set. One of challenge in artificial neural network is quality of data that goes in conciliation, if aspect of data is reduced to such an extent. An additional difficulty which is stumble upon in machine learning artificial neural networks is internal covariate shift. The statistical distribution of the input keeps changing as training proceeds. This can cause a significant change in the domain and hence, reduce training efficiency. Challenge in genetic algorithm is difficult to obey equality constraints because genetic algorithm is based in stochastic component not depend on deterministic approach. One more challenge in genetic algorithm is that it does not work for large dimensions, i.e., for large number of genes on chromosomes. Genetic algorithm has genetic operators like crossover and mutation; particles update themselves with the internal velocity. Some algorithms based on machine learning are accuracy of information retrieval and identification of relationship is poor. It is difficult to solve the problem based on structural complication; mathematical methods are not capable of solving them. For machine learning implementation, normally, we face different challenges based on following main parameters:

1) High-Priced Computational Requirements: For huge data processing, we need a lot of graphical processing units (GPUs) to synchronize the demand and supply issues based on fulfilment of required output.

2) The Skilled Manpower Need: For implementation of machine learning concept with proper understanding, there are requirements of skilled people with appropriate technical ability. If we are not having people with technical

proficiency, then we cannot realize and visualize the concept of machine learning.

3) Requirement of Labeled Data: For the completion of projects based on machine learning, there is a challenge of availability of labeled data. With the help of labeled data, analysis can be done very efficiently.

4) Huge Storage: Arrangement of large working memory is also a major challenge for storage of huge data for realization of machine learning concept.

17.7 Conclusion

It becomes very difficult for any developing country to fully implement the E-Governance in its administration. The chapter has conflict that E-Governance is of concern to information delivery services for the exclusive reason that E-Government is about information. Divide was discussed in this chapter; these divide are best felt in comparison of delivery of E-Governance services in rural and urban areas. The potential of E-Governance is up till now to be required to improve. Institutional capacity is required to build for governance restructuring. Creating the E-Governance extensive as a mode of Digital INDIA, it involves providing the internet of good speed at rural areas. Developing countries enable the adding of shared services on to the core services and when required, a special common services of the gateway without affecting the core functionality of the gateway. In future, if concept of big data analytics can help to guide leadership to create well-versed decision, appropriate economic planning and policy formulation can solve the major issues of all developing countries like weak economy, unemployment, corruption, and many more [15].

In the prospect of new 5G technology [16–18], more intelligence, fast speed, and security are required in prevention of Digital Identity like individual medical records, social relationship, etc. Advance Data Analytics is needed to handle such information.

References

1. LoPucki, L.M., Human Identification Theory and the Identity Theft Problem. *Texas Law Rev.*, 80, 89–134, 2001. http://ssrn.com/abstract=263213.
2. Grassfield, and Grassfield, L., Biometrics: Securing electronic commerce, 2000. http://www.tinucci.com/Papers/Grassfield - Biometrics.html.

3. Wilson, S., Moustafa, N., Sitnikova, E., A digital identity stack to improve privacy in the IoT. *IEEE 4th world Forum on Internet of Things (WF-IoT)*, p. 25–29, 2018.

4. Berryman, J., E-government: Issues and implications for public. *Aust. Libr. J.*, 53, 4, 349–359, Nov 2003.

5. Stedman, D., *Transformation not automation: The e-government challenge*, p. 103.aspx, Demos, London, January 2004, Available at www.demos.co.uk/catalogue/transformation.

6. Harfouche, A., The Same wine but in new bottles. Public E-Services divide and low citizens' Satisfaction: An Example from Lebanon. *Int. J. Electron. Gov. Res.*, 6, 3, 73–105, 2010. Available at: http://www.irmainternational.org/viewtitle/45742/.

7. Mutula, S.M., Challenges and opportunities of e-government in South Africa. *Electron. Libr.*, 28, 1, 38–53, 2010.

8. Moyo, A., Depoliticise e-govt agenda, SA told, 2011. Available at: http://www.itweb.co.za/index.php?option=com_content&view=article&id=48292:de-politicise-egovt-agenda-sa-told&catid=69.

9. FCC Workshop Reveals Secrets of 5G, Hogan Lovells, March 15th, 2016.

11. Finger, M. and Pecoud, G., From e-Government to e-Governance? Towards a Model of e-Governance. *3rd European Conference on e-Government Switzerland*.

12. Neil Y. Yen , Qun Jin, Ching-Hsien Hsu, Qiangfu Zhao, M., Special Section: Hybrid Intelligence for Growing Internet and its Applications, Science Direct, Vol. 37, pp. 1–534, 2014.

13. Picciano, A.G., The Evolution of Big Data and Learning Analytics in American Higher Education. *J. Asynchronous Learn Netw.*, 16, 9–20, 2012.

14. Dobre, C. and Xhafa, F., Intelligent services for big data science. *Future Gener. Comput. Syst.*, 37, 267–281, 2013. Elsevier.

15. Philip Chen, C.L. and Zhang, C.Y., Data-intensive applications, challenges, techniques and technologies: A survey on big data. *Inf. Sci.*, 314–347, 2014. Published in Elsevier.

16. Raghupathi, W. and Raghupathi, V., Big data analytics in healthcare: Promise and Potential. *Health Inf. Sci. Syst.*, 2014.

17. Miller, K., Big Data Analytics in Biomedical Research. *Biomed. Comput. Rev.*, 14–21, 2011/2012.

18. KOICA, Nigerian e-government master plan, 2014.

Index